The HOME EXPERT
Dr. D.G. Hessayon

1st Impression   400,000

Other Books in the EXPERT Series:
THE GARDEN EXPERT
THE FLOWER EXPERT
THE TREE & SHRUB EXPERT
THE HOUSE PLANT EXPERT
THE ROSE EXPERT
THE LAWN EXPERT
THE VEGETABLE EXPERT
THE INDOOR PLANT SPOTTER

pbi PUBLICATIONS · BRITANNICA HOUSE · WALTHAM CROSS · HERTS · ENGLAND

Contents

Printed and bound in Great Britain by Jarrold & Sons Ltd, Norwich

ISBN 0 903505 24 X   © D. G. HESSAYON 1987

CHAPTER 1

INTRODUCTION

The purpose of this book is quite simple. It sets out in non-technical language to explain the basic structure of your home plus the various services, techniques, materials and pieces of equipment which make it run smoothly. Sometimes it doesn't run smoothly, so some of the pages are devoted to the problems which crop up from time to time.

The book's purpose may be simple, but between the covers there is a vast range of subjects. This range is restricted neither to DIY nor to home maintenance. The correct choice of pots and pans is described as well as the way to paint an outside wall — credit cards and the proper way to wrap a parcel are discussed as well as nails, screws and plywood. The basics of home decorating are here and so is the way to carry out simple repairs, but you will have to look elsewhere if you want guidance on installing a central heating system or building a sink unit. There are a number of excellent DIY manuals available but a word of caution. Major constructional work often calls for experience and not just clear diagrams.

Your home is a complex place. The flood of new products, equipment and ideas continues unabated, so it is easy to be baffled. In these 160 crowded pages you will find both background information and instruction.

No excuse is made for the mixture of metric and imperial units which appears in the various sections. The reason is that we continue to use a mixture of measurements in our everyday lives. A pint of beer is bought at the pub on the way to the supermarket — to buy 70 cl of wine, 375 g of cornflakes and 5 lb of potatoes!

So get to know something about the mysteries of your home with the help of this book. Find out the basics of the water supply, electrics etc and prepare for emergencies. Carry out simple maintenance work as necessary — a message running throughout the pages is that if you do the right thing, and you do it at the right time, then caring for your home becomes much less of a problem. Maybe this book will not make you an expert, but at least it will enable you to understand the experts when they talk to you.

Making ends meet

There is no 'right' way to start a book on the home. The obvious beginning would be the joy (and pitfalls) of buying a new house, but only a small proportion of the population change homes each year. Another way would be to talk about the basics of DIY, but many householders run a perfectly good home without ever lifting a saw or bending a pipe.

The starting point should be a subject which concerns everyone, and that subject is money. Apart from a fortunate few the problem of making ends meet involves us all. The basic requirement for efficient money management is a **budget** — a plan based on the money you expect to come in and the money you will have to spend during a fixed period in the future. Most wives know about the weekly housekeeping budget, but relatively few people prepare an annual overall budget. It really is a good idea to prepare one, especially if things are tight or if there has been a significant change in circumstances — a better job, the arrival of a baby etc.

Write down the inputs — for most people this is straightforward as their wages or salary is the mainstay. Put down the minimum you expect, and don't include possible gifts, legacies or other windfalls which are not certain.

Then write down the outgoings — begin with the routine daily and weekly expenditure followed by the monthly, quarterly and yearly bills you expect to receive, and finally the one-offs such as a car which you plan to buy or a room you plan to decorate during the period.

The inputs total should be larger than the sum of the outgoings — you need a comfortable buffer for the unexpected. If inputs are smaller than the outgoings you are in trouble. You must increase your inputs and/or decrease your outgoings — the next 3 pages should help.

INPUTS
The money you receive

Examples: Wages (for manual work) • Salary (for non-manual work) • Bonuses • Pensions • Dividends & Interest • Gifts • Gambling wins • Loans • Government grants & benefits

OUTGOINGS
The money you spend

Examples: Mortgage & Loan repayments • Housekeeping • Insurance & Pensions • Income Tax & VAT • Services (Gas, Water etc) • Clothes • Car expenses • Alcohol & Cigarettes • Holidays • DIY • Gifts

SAVINGS
The money you have left after the outgoings

Examples: Money in your pocket or cheque-book account • Assurance policies • Building Society shares • National Savings • Christmas clubs • Local Government bonds • Bank deposit accounts • Shares, Bonds & Unit Trusts

INCREASING INPUTS with the home in mind

For most of us the only satisfactory way of significantly increasing our inputs is to get a better job. This may mean acquiring fresh skills, seeking promotion, working harder if there is a bonus or seeking employment elsewhere. This subject is outside the scope of this book, but there are several other ways of increasing inputs which can be considered here.

- **OBTAIN BETTER RETURNS FROM SAVINGS**
Money kept in your wallet, purse or current account at the bank earns nothing for you. See page 6 for the basic rules of investment.

- **BORROW MONEY**
The instant method of increasing inputs — one moment you are short of money and in the next instant you have the money you require. But beware — see page 5.

- **OBTAIN ALL THE ALLOWANCES TO WHICH YOU ARE ENTITLED**

Not all allowances are claimed. Many people, especially the older generation who now need help, still remember the days when allowances and benefits really were a matter of charity.

Another reason for failing to claim is the incredibly complex nature of the social security and council benefit systems. There are scores of different schemes, and eligibility varies greatly from one scheme to another. If you think you might qualify for a State benefit or allowance, go to your local **Health & Social Security Office**. If you like to read and study information, ask for the *Which Benefit?* leaflet (a general guide) and pick up any appropriate leaflets. If you would rather talk than read, discuss the situation with one of the staff. If you feel that you may be eligible for a local authority benefit or allowance, go to the **Council Offices** for leaflets and advice. If you are still in doubt or if you are bothered by large offices, seek advice from your local **Citizen's Advice Bureau**.

UNEMPLOYMENT BENEFIT Amount depends upon your N.I. contributions. There can be problems if you resigned. Lasts for 1 year.

RETIREMENT PENSION Amount depends upon your N.I. contributions. Starting date 65 (men), 60 (women). Up to 70 (men), 65 (women) the pension is reduced if you continue to work and earn more than a certain amount.

SUPPLEMENTARY BENEFIT (SB) Amount depends upon your circumstances — N.I. contributions are not involved. Payment is made to adults who are not in full-time employment and who have neither the savings nor earnings to make ends meet. There is a means test — if SB is granted, you receive a weekly allowance plus low income benefits (see page 5). You may be entitled to a heating allowance. SB can be paid in addition to other benefits or allowances.

CHILD ALLOWANCES There are a number of allowances, including the contributory Maternity Allowance and a Social Fund Maternity Payment for those on Supplementary Benefit. In addition there are the standard Child Benefit paid weekly (irrespective of earnings) and the Family Income Supplement (FIS) for the low paid with young children.

SICKNESS ALLOWANCES There are a number of allowances, including the short-term Sick Pay and the long-term Invalidity Benefit. In addition there are the Attendance Allowance for the chronically sick and the Mobility Allowance for the handicapped.

SINGLE PAYMENT SCHEMES If you are a pensioner or if you receive Supplementary Benefit you can apply for an allowance if you are moving house. An allowance to replace worn-out furniture and to buy clothing is available to the sick and long-term SB recipients.

OTHER ALLOWANCES There are many, including allowances for guardians, one-parent families, bereaved families, widows, divorcees with children, etc.

- **OBTAIN ALL THE HOME IMPROVEMENT GRANTS TO WHICH YOU ARE ENTITLED**

There are several schemes operated by your local authority which will pay part of the cost of home improvement. Obtain the appropriate application form from the Grants Office. The following details relate to the most important grants available in England and Wales — Scotland has its own schemes. The amount paid is part or all of the cost up to a specified maximum — the proportion paid depends on the grant involved and the strength of your case. Do not assume that these grants are only for the low paid — the Intermediate Grant depends solely on the state of your house and not on your income.

GRANT	PURPOSE	DISCRETIONARY OR MANDATORY	EXAMPLES	LIMITATIONS
IMPROVEMENT GRANT	To pay part of the cost of a major improvement or conversion so that the dwelling will be brought to a satisfactory standard. Repair work as well as structural work can be included	Discretionary. Local authority decides on whether to give a grant. If awarded, amount depends on need. Range about 50 – 75% of cost	Rewiring electrical circuits · Replacing rotten timber · Extending a kitchen · Putting in a damp-proof course	Not available if the house is already in a satisfactory state or if the rateable value is above the specified limit
REPAIR GRANT	To pay part of the cost of major structural repairs to a pre-1919 dwelling so that it will be brought to a satisfactory standard	Discretionary. Local authority decides on whether to give a grant. If awarded, amount depends on need — up to 75% of cost	Re-roofing · Replacing rotten joists and floorboards · Repairing cracked foundations	Not available if the house is already in a satisfactory state or if the rateable value is above the specified limit
INTERMEDIATE GRANT	To pay part or all of the cost of installing an amenity which is absent and is considered essential. Repair work associated with the installation can be included	Mandatory. Local authority must pay the grant if the amenity is absent	Bath · Inside WC · Hot and cold water system · Basin or sink	Not available if the amenity is already present — it is not a grant for improving the amenity
HOMES INSULATION GRANT	To pay part of the cost of insulating the loft and lagging pipes, cistern and hot water cylinder	Discretionary. Local authority decides whether you are eligible. If awarded, amount is 66% of cost	Loft · Pipes · Cisterns · Hot water cylinder	Not available if existing insulation is more than 30 mm thick or if the house was built after 1975
DHSS REPAIR GRANT	To pay for necessary home repairs required by people receiving Supplementary Benefit	Discretionary. DHSS decides whether you are eligible	Repairs necessary to maintain the health of the occupants and/or the fabric of the house	Not available to people who do not receive Supplementary Benefit

DECREASING OUTGOINGS with the home in mind

There is far more scope to reduce your expenditure than to increase your earnings. You can cut down on smoking, drinking, holidays, gifts and so on — but the essential payments have to be made. Fall behind in mortgage payments and you can face eviction — fall behind in payment for services and you can have the supply disconnected. If you get into financial trouble seek help and advice — never, never ignore the bills.

● REDUCE YOUR BORROWING

There are times when you have to borrow money — house purchase is the classic example. A major repair to the house, a new car or a not-to-be-missed bargain at the sales can all call for seeking credit on the item or seeking a loan to pay for it.

The problem is that borrowing has become very easy, and all sorts of shops and organisations sell on a buy now – pay later basis. Leading this movement are the bank credit cards — more than a third of shop sales involve plastic cards. These cards have several virtues — interest-free credit for several weeks if you settle in full at the proper time, entitlement to compensation if the purchased goods are faulty, etc. They can, however, be a menace if you use one to buy things you don't really need and which you can't really afford. All too often credit is taken to the limit of the card, and although small amounts are paid off each month there is an annual interest charge of over 25 per cent on the debt if you use a bank credit card. Interest charges are usually even higher if you use a store card — 22-37 per cent.

With easy credit the average family debt has reached record heights and each year about 500,000 families now have to seek help from a Money Advice Centre.

The golden rule is not to borrow unless it is essential to do so. If you must borrow then seek the route which charges the least interest. Every lender must declare the APR — Annual Percentage Rate of Charge. Go for the lowest APR over the period in which the debt is to be settled. Never look at the weekly or monthly payments alone — work out the *total* repayment in order to see just how much the loan will cost you.

Finally, there are rules to follow if you do have to buy now and pay later. If you can raise the money in a few weeks after purchase, use a bank credit card and that means no interest need be paid. Alternatively, take advantage of interest-free credit terms offered by the supplier — as long as no extra charge has been built into the price. If you can repay in a matter of months, seek an overdraft from the bank. If on the other hand you need longer to pay then seek a bank personal loan, a loan on an insurance policy (lowest APR available) or a loan from a finance company (watch the APR). Do not use a bank credit card if you cannot repay the debt in a few months.

Money required for home improvement is a special case. Seek an additional mortgage as this will be stretched over a long period and may be eligible for tax relief.

● OBTAIN ALL THE BENEFITS TO WHICH YOU ARE ENTITLED

A range of allowances (sometimes described as benefits) available from the State and your local authority are listed on page 4. These grant one-off payments or regular payments every week. Closely related to these allowances are a series of benefits which provide goods or services without cost or at a reduced price. For more information follow the action set out on page 4.

RETIREMENT BENEFITS Starting date 65 (men), 60 (women). Your local authority will provide a number of benefits — free travel, home help, meals on wheels etc. Some (but not all) depend on your circumstances. Ask for details at the Council Offices.

LOW INCOME BENEFITS A wide range of benefits are available to people receiving Supplementary Benefit and also to those who don't qualify but are still judged to be in need. Items include free prescriptions and dental treatment, free spectacles, free school meals for children, etc. Ask for details at the Health & Social Security Office.

CERTIFICATED HOUSING BENEFIT (CHB) People receiving Supplementary Benefit automatically have their rates paid in full. If you rent a council house you will also have the rent paid. If you rent from someone else, you will receive a rent allowance to cover the cost. There is no need to apply for CHB.

MORTGAGE INTEREST PAYMENT Another benefit for people on Supplementary Benefit, but you will have to apply to the DHSS for it. Mortgage or loan interest is paid for you, but there is no repayment of capital.

STANDARD HOUSING BENEFIT (SHB) This benefit is a reduction of the rates bill. This rebate is in the hands of the local authority, not the DHSS. Its award depends on your circumstances and the formula is complex. People with above-average incomes may qualify if both the family and rateable value are large enough. A Housing Benefit Supplement plus Low Income Benefits may be awarded if you are not in full-time employment and both your earnings and savings are low.

● SHOP WISELY

The obvious ways of reducing the price you pay for goods do not need underlining — compare prices from different outlets before buying a costly item and try to purchase during a sale. Seek discounts wherever you can and balance the convenience of the corner shop against the lower prices of the supermarket. When pennies count, collect and use the many money-off coupons now available.

A not-so-obvious way of cutting the food bill (20 per cent of total household expenditure) is to buy in bulk — provided that the larger units are easily transported and the amount purchased can be used in a reasonable time. Consider milk as an example — a 4 pint container costs 20 per cent less than four 1 pint cartons or bottles.

● BANK WISELY

Banks set a minimum level for the amount which must stay in the account if you are to enjoy free banking services. If you fall below this level there may be hefty bank charges, so try to keep above the limit.

● CONSIDER A BANK BUDGET ACCOUNT

Many people can balance their budget on an annual basis but cannot cope with the peaks and troughs of bill settlement dates. They have regular incomes which do not go up and down to match the demands.

You can open a budget account with one of the High St. banks to overcome this problem. Add all the bills you expect to receive during the coming year and divide by 12 — the bank will take this amount out of your current account each month and put it into the newly-created budget account. In this way you can pay your bills as they come in. A good idea, but don't use this service unless you have to. There is a charge, and that will add to your outgoings.

● DON'T GAMBLE BEYOND THE PLEASURE LEVEL

Treat the cost of gambling as any other entertainment — drinking at the pub, going to the theatre, etc. In other words, do not expect a return and never rely on one. If you are gambling more than you can afford, cut back to a level where the money spent does not hurt. If you *must* aim for that £100,000 nest egg, buy Premium Bonds where you do not lose your stake money.

DECREASING OUTGOINGS continued

● SEEK A LOWER RATING VALUATION

The environment around your home may have changed since you moved in. It may be noisier, more difficult to get to or more unsightly. If you think the environment has changed for the worse, you can apply for a reduction in valuation which will in turn lower your rates bill. Apply to the local Valuation Office of the Inland Revenue.

● REDUCE YOUR TAX BILL

If your affairs are complicated then you will need an accountant to make sure that your tax bill is no higher than necessary. People on PAYE often think that such things need not concern them, but it is not uncommon to find that salaried people with uncomplicated lives are still paying too much tax. Discuss it with your bank manager or Citizen's Advice Bureau. You can discuss it with the local Income Tax Office — they do regard it as part of their job to make sure that you pay the right amount of tax.

● REDUCE YOUR EXPENDITURE ON SERVICES

About 7 per cent of the average net income goes on services such as gas, electricity, telephone and postage (see page 7). All sorts of ways of decreasing the cost of services are described in this book. Some of the important ways are:

★ Close windows and outside doors in winter.

★ Turn down the thermostat on the central heating system until you feel chilly — then turn it up in stages until you are comfortable. Lowering the temperature by just 3°F can cut 10 per cent off your fuel bill.

★ Switch off lights when a room is not in use.

★ Telephone at off-peak times.

★ Insulate the loft and draught-proof windows and doors.

★ Instal an Economy 7 meter if this cheaper electricity fits in with the way you live.

★ Take advantage of off-season low prices for oil and coal.

● INSURE WISELY

With insurance you pay money now so that if a misfortune or loss occurs in the future you will be financially protected. You get nothing back unless the misfortune or loss actually occurs — assurance is a type of insurance where you are guaranteed some return.

Only car insurance is compulsory by law, although a mortgage company will insist on house and perhaps life insurance as a condition of the loan. In all other cases you must decide whether you want to stand the risk. In some cases (e.g luggage insurance) it is a matter of opinion — with house insurance it would be a matter of madness to take the risk yourself. The outgoings involved in case of fire, burglary, storm damage etc could be ruinous.

The rule is that you must not only insure the house and contents — you must insure them fully. Most policies say that the *full* rebuilding cost must be covered — if you under-insure then you will be paid only a proportion of the rebuilding cost. The difference can be enormous. The same thing applies to contents — undervalue them and the assessor will not allow your full claim in case of loss. Your Insurance Company or the Association of British Insurers will supply you with an up-to-date guide to the cost of rebuilding and a guide to the way to insure the contents — follow these instructions. There are special rules for valuable items.

The next rule is to study the policy carefully. Make sure that all likely risks are covered — flooding? subsidence? rented television? injury to visitors? Check the type of insurance cover for contents — is it full replacement or is it the lower-priced present value replacement which takes account of wear and tear? Above all, don't be misled by the phrase 'all risks'. No policy will cover *all* risks.

Keep the policy up to date. Make sure it is index-linked so that the premium rises automatically with building costs, and tell the Insurer about any major changes to the structure of the house, its use or its contents.

Take the correct action if you have to make a claim. There may be things to do before ringing the Insurer for a claim form — tell the police about a robbery and in case of house damage make emergency repairs and keep the bills. However, never delay sending in your claim form for longer than necessary.

SAVINGS

Keep some money in your purse, wallet or cheque-book account for immediate needs — the rest should be invested. The average family puts about 4% of its income into savings, and these savings are spread over a large number of investments and saving schemes. Choosing the right ones for you is not easy — consider the 3 factors below before making your decision.

Choosing the right investment

TAX RATE

Most investments pay interest or dividends from which the standard rate of Income Tax has been deducted. If you pay a high rate, investments which yield tax-free interest (e.g National Savings Certificates) are attractive. People who do not pay tax (the unemployed, children etc) should choose an investment which is paid without deduction of tax (e.g National Savings Bank Investment Account).

RISK

With a no-risk investment the amount invested is completely secure. The interest received may go up or down periodically (e.g Building Society Accounts, Bank Deposit Accounts and Index-linked National Savings Certificates) or the rate may be fixed from the start (e.g National Savings Certificates and Yearly Plan). Premium Bonds distribute the interest as prizes in a weekly and monthly draw.

Some investments do involve risk. Shares are the classic example — if the amount is relatively small it is better to buy Unit Trusts.

High risk investments include shares in the Business Expansion Schemes and commodity trading (e.g coffee, cocoa). Take care.

AVAILABILITY

The Building Society Account is the most popular form of saving in Britain, and an Ordinary Account gives you immediate access through a local branch. Even quicker access for paying bills is the Cheque Deposit Account run by financial institutions.

Many investments can be cashed in a matter of days or weeks — Bank Deposits, National Savings Bank Ordinary Account, Shares, Unit Trusts etc. As a general rule, however, Shares and Unit Trusts are best regarded as longer-term investments.

Some investments either provide much reduced interest or impose penalties if there is early withdrawal — National Savings Certificates, National Savings Income Bonds, Yearly Plan etc are examples. These investments should be kept for years. The main method of long-term saving (10 years or more) is Life Assurance. Effective, but early withdrawal carries heavy penalties.

CHAPTER 2

THE SERVICES

Two basic services are on tap in virtually every home in Britain. There is water for drinking, washing and the removal of sewage, and for our comfort there is electricity to provide light and perhaps heat.

It is these two fundamental inputs which support modern domestic life. Of course, there are other important services which add greatly to our material comfort and well-being — there is a universal postal service delivering letters each day and both TV and radio waves serve the whole country. The removal of the domestic rubbish which collects during the week is carried out by the local council, but the list of universal services ends there.

Gas has long been a major source of fuel energy for the home. Most central heating boilers are gas-fired — the fuel requires no storage, it fares very well in price comparison tables and has lost its poisonous stigma with the advent of North Sea gas. But it is not universal — gas is available in 85 per cent of British homes.

Mains drainage is taken for granted by the urban dweller — each year about 10,000 gallons of washing water and foul waste per person are transported to the public sewerage system without us having to give it a thought. But in some rural areas it is different — rainwater is led to a soakaway and the waste water plus foul waste go to either a cesspool (an underground storage tank which must be emptied frequently) or a septic tank (a miniature sewage works which requires emptying much less frequently).

Thus, both gas and mains drainage are not for everyone but they do play a vital role in most homes. Coal and coal-based fuels, however, have slipped from being the age-old mainstay of home heating to a minor source of domestic energy.

All fuels have their advantages and disadvantages, as shown below. Price is an important consideration, and for many years gas has held the crown as the cheapest fuel. But marked changes in the cost of oil in the mid 1980s rendered many price comparison charts out of date — get a current comparison if you want to compare heating costs.

The trade associations and suppliers of the major fuels produce excellent booklets and operate efficient advisory services. Ask for help — it won't cost you anything. There is one piece of advice that all of these people will give you — make sure your equipment is installed properly and ensure that it is serviced regularly.

Picking the right fuel

FUEL	PAGE NUMBER	ADVANTAGES	DISADVANTAGES
ELECTRICITY	15	Available everywhere • Clean • Multipurpose — used for lighting, heating, cooking • No storage problems — always on tap • No flue needed • Minimal servicing	Only one supplier — power cuts stop the supply • Standard rate is expensive — storage heaters using Economy 7 off-peak electricity are economical, but control can be difficult
GAS	20	Clean • Dual purpose — used for heating and cooking • 'Real' log-fire effect now available • Inexpensive, but only if used for heating as well as cooking	Not available everywhere • A flue is required • Only one supplier • Boilers need regular servicing — faulty equipment and blocked chimneys can be dangerous
OIL	14	Available everywhere • As with gas the control of the central heating system can be fully automatic • The price has fallen since the Oil Crisis days	A flue is required • Boilers need regular servicing • Can be smelly • Popular use limited to central heating • Storage tank required • More expensive than gas
COAL & COAL PRODUCTS	22	Available everywhere • Many suppliers — you can shop around for discounts • Dual purpose — used for heating and cooking • For many nothing beats a real fire	A flue is required • Boilers need regular servicing • Regular refuelling and ash removal are necessary • Dirty • More expensive than gas • Covered storage required
WOOD	22	Available free of charge in some localities • Dual purpose — used for heating and cooking • For many nothing beats a real fire	A flue is required – regular sweeping is essential • Equipment needs regular servicing • Regular refuelling and ash removal are necessary • Cannot be used in a Smokeless Zone
BOTTLED GAS (LPG)	23	Available everywhere — the standard alternative where piped natural gas is not laid on • Dual purpose — used for heating and cooking • Portable models available	More expensive than mains gas • Supplies have to be ordered regularly — you are dependent on deliveries • Cylinders can be heavy — central heating needs a storage tank
PARAFFIN	23	Available everywhere • Modern heaters have built-in safety devices • Flue not necessary • Useful portable standby in case of a power cut	Needs good ventilation — can cause condensation • Smelly • Regular refuelling is necessary • Supplies have to be ordered regularly • collection may be necessary
SOLAR ENERGY	—	Solar panels mounted on the roof provide energy free of charge • Unaffected by power cuts or delivery hold-ups • Keeps you ahead of the neighbours	Heats the domestic hot water supply only — not the central heating • Extra heat source needed in dull weather • Cost of installation (approx £1,500) takes many years to recover

Services Water

The average householder regards the provision of hot and cold water on tap as one of the blessings of modern life, and also as one of its mysteries. Changes and repairs to the plumbing system are left to the professional, despite the introduction of push-fit plastic pipes and scores of well-illustrated DIY manuals.

For most people this is a wise decision — fixing new pipes and changing a cistern or boiler need the right tools and experience. Make sure that you choose a competent plumber — contact the Institute of Plumbing, 64 Station Road, Hornchurch, Essex if you don't know one. Remember that the local Water Authority will require at least 7 days' notice before you can start a major alteration or adding a new fixture such as an extra bath or lavatory.

You can't leave *everything* to the plumber. Frozen pipes or a burst main call for immediate action by you, so you should get to know how your system works, where the various valves are, what to do in case of an emergency, and how to carry out a few simple repairs.

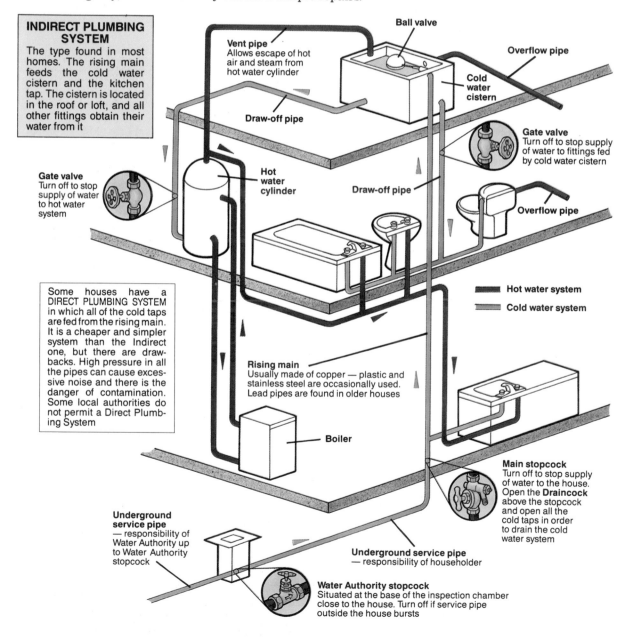

INDIRECT PLUMBING SYSTEM
The type found in most homes. The rising main feeds the cold water cistern and the kitchen tap. The cistern is located in the roof or loft, and all other fittings obtain their water from it

Vent pipe
Allows escape of hot air and steam from hot water cylinder

Ball valve

Overflow pipe

Cold water cistern

Draw-off pipe

Gate valve
Turn off to stop supply of water to fittings fed by cold water cistern

Gate valve
Turn off to stop supply of water to hot water system

Hot water cylinder

Draw-off pipe

Overflow pipe

Some houses have a DIRECT PLUMBING SYSTEM in which all of the cold taps are fed from the rising main. It is a cheaper and simpler system than the Indirect one, but there are drawbacks. High pressure in all the pipes can cause excessive noise and there is the danger of contamination. Some local authorities do not permit a Direct Plumbing System

▬▬ Hot water system
═══ Cold water system

Rising main
Usually made of copper — plastic and stainless steel are occasionally used. Lead pipes are found in older houses

Boiler

Main stopcock
Turn off to stop supply of water to the house. Open the **Draincock** above the stopcock and open all the cold taps in order to drain the cold water system

Underground service pipe
— responsibility of Water Authority up to Water Authority stopcock

Underground service pipe
— responsibility of householder

Water Authority stopcock
Situated at the base of the inspection chamber close to the house. Turn off if service pipe outside the house bursts

HOT WATER SYSTEMS

INDIRECT SYSTEM

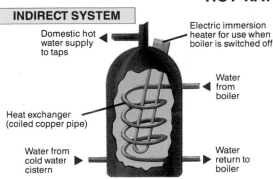

Domestic hot water supply to taps

Electric immersion heater for use when boiler is switched off

Heat exchanger (coiled copper pipe)

Water from boiler

Water from cold water cistern

Water return to boiler

This system is used where the boiler is required to heat both the domestic water supply and the central heating system. The primary circuit from the boiler heats the coiled pipe in the cylinder and also the radiators which make up the central heating system. This primary circuit has a feed-and-expansion cistern. The secondary circuit, fed by the cold water cistern, supplies the hot water taps around the house.

DIRECT SYSTEM

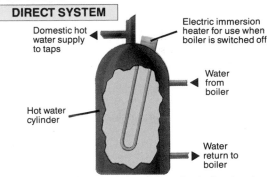

Domestic hot water supply to taps

Electric immersion heater for use when boiler is switched off

Hot water cylinder

Water from boiler

Water return to boiler

Less expensive and easier to instal than the Indirect system, but not suitable for hard water areas nor for linking with a central heating system.

INSTANTANEOUS SYSTEM

The Ascot style of water heater can be attached directly to the rising main. The gas jets or electric elements are activated by the water flow when the unit is switched on. There is no storage capacity, but Instantaneous heaters are economical and can be installed in situations where a water storage system would not be possible nor practical.

Hard Water

Most of the water in S and E England is hard. The cause is the presence of dissolved salts of calcium and magnesium — in the presence of soap a curd or scum is formed. Bathroom fixtures are stained, washed woollens are matted and soap does not lather properly.

The serious problem starts when the water is heated above 140°F. Kettles develop fur and hot water pipes develop scale. This scaling increases the cost of running the system and can cause damage to the boiler and immersion heater.

Proprietary descalers are available for kettles and the hot water system can be descaled by putting chemicals into the cold water cistern. It is much better, however, to avoid scaling rather than trying to cure it. Instal an Indirect cylinder (see above) to replace a Direct one, and avoid water temperatures appreciably above 140°F.

A number of chemical water softeners such as Calgon are available, but the most satisfactory solution is to fit a water softener. This works on the ion exchange principle, sodium being added to the water in exchange for calcium and magnesium. It must occasionally be regenerated by adding salt. The unit should be fitted to the rising main *above* the cold water tap in the kitchen.

TAPS & VALVES

Taps and valves control the flow of water

A **valve** is located in the middle of a pipe

A **tap** is located at the end of a pipe

VALVES

STOPCOCK (stop valve)
Used when water is at mains pressure. Most have a single bar handle

GATE VALVE
Used when water is at less than mains pressure (e.g water supply from cistern). Most have a wheel handle

DRAINCOCK (drain valve)
Unlike others, it is usually kept closed. Used to drain water away. Most have a square nut instead of a handle

BALL VALVE
Technically a 'tap', not a valve. Used in a cistern or tank to prevent water rising above a pre-set level

TAPS

BIB TAP
Water enters horizontally. Handle is usually a crutch (single bar) or a capstan (cross bars). Securing screw is visible

PILLAR TAP
Water enters vertically. Handle is usually a shrouded head, made of metal or plastic. Securing screw is under the plate at the top

SUPATAP
Water enters vertically. A variation of the pillar tap — washer can be changed without having to turn off the water supply

MIXER TAP
Water enters horizonally or vertically — supplies are mixed together. Kitchen types have a movable spout — bathroom types may have a shower attachment

AVOIDING WATER PROBLEMS

- **LOCATE AND TEST THE VALVES**
  Look for the various valves in your water system — don't wait for an emergency. Label if necessary. Turn the handles off and on once a year to make sure that they are working properly.

- **KEEP A ROLL OF WATERPROOF MASTIC TAPE**
  This material can be used to make a temporary repair to a leaking joint or a burst pipe.

- **CHECK THE COLD WATER CISTERN OCCASIONALLY**
  Make sure the lid fits properly — it should keep out light, flies and spiders but it should not be airtight. Look for corrosion both inside and outside the tank — consult a plumber if there are brown patches on the outside of a metal cistern.

- **CHECK THE WASHING MACHINE PIPES OCCASIONALLY**
  The hoses on washing machines occasionally work loose and split. Examine them carefully every few months — refit or replace if necessary.

- **USE THE COLD TAP IN THE KITCHEN FOR DRINKING WATER**
  The water reaching the rising main in your house will have been tested by the Water Authority. Some districts add fluoride to reduce the incidence of tooth decay in children. The purest water will be obtained from the cold tap in the kitchen. If lead piping is present in your home and you live in a soft water area, run the water for about ½ minute before use in the morning or after a holiday.
  Water drawn from the cold water cistern is best avoided for drinking purposes unless you know that the tank is clean and free from corrosion. *Never* use water from the hot water system for filling the kettle.

- **TAKE PRECAUTIONS BEFORE A WINTER HOLIDAY**
  There is a high risk of water freezing in the pipes if a house is left unoccupied and unheated for 2 or 3 weeks in winter. To avoid problems, leave the central heating on at a low level and open internal doors. If this seems costly or there is no central heating, drain both the cold and hot water systems. On your return, remember to refill the system before turning on the heat.

- **LAG THE TANKS AND PIPES**
  The purpose of lagging the hot water system is to keep the heat *in*, thereby reducing the fuel bill. The role of lagging the cold water system is to keep the cold *out* in winter, which reduces the risk of freezing. Loft insulation to keep the house warmer has become popular in recent years, but it can spell danger. The cistern and associated pipes above the insulation will be colder than before and so some protection is necessary. Do not cover the area below the cistern when insulating the loft, and lag both the cistern and pipes. Remember to lag the overflow pipe as well as those carrying water.

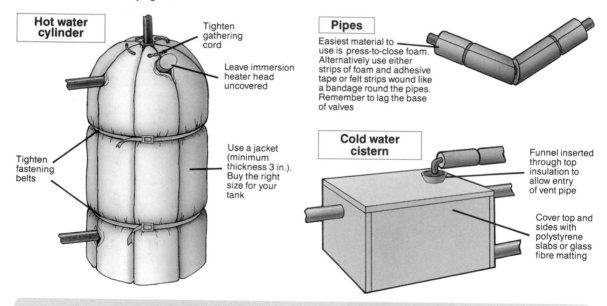

Hot water cylinder

Tighten gathering cord

Leave immersion heater head uncovered

Tighten fastening belts

Use a jacket (minimum thickness 3 in.). Buy the right size for your tank

Pipes

Easiest material to use is press-to-close foam. Alternatively use either strips of foam and adhesive tape or felt strips wound like a bandage round the pipes. Remember to lag the base of valves

Cold water cistern

Funnel inserted through top insulation to allow entry of vent pipe

Cover top and sides with polystyrene slabs or glass fibre matting

Draining the system

There are times when it is necessary to drain all or part of the system. A pipe may have burst, a washer may have to be fitted or a new piece of equipment installed.
Collect some water in the bath for flushing the toilet and in pans for drinking purposes. Then turn off the central heating — damp down the solid fuel boiler if one is present. Turn off the appropriate stopcock or gate valve if the problem area can be isolated — otherwise turn off the main stopcock to close down the whole system.

Open all the cold water taps to drain the pipes and cistern as quickly as possible. If the problem is an upstairs leak and water is coming through the ceiling, switch off the lights and work with a torch. Make holes with a large nail where the water is dripping.
Drain the hot water system by opening the hot water taps and the draincock situated close to the cylinder. The central heating system is drained by opening the valve which is situated at the lowest point of the system.

DEALING WITH WATER PROBLEMS

● **DRIPPING TAP**
A tap which drips when closed needs a new washer. Drain the system and leave the tap open. With a capstan head tap (see page 9) unscrew the shield below the handle. It is a little trickier with a modern shrouded head tap — you will need to prise up the cover to find a small retaining screw which must be released. Pull off the head.

Use a spanner to undo the hexagonal nut which is revealed — lift out the top half of the tap. At the base of this assembly you will find a washer secured with a small nut. Remove this nut and fit a replacement rubber or nylon washer of the same diameter (½ in. for standard taps). Reassemble the tap and then restore the water supply.

If the tap continues to leak after fitting a new washer, the tap seating requires refacing. Consult a plumber.

● **SEEPING TAP**
If water seeps out round the spindle, there is a fault in the gland unit. Buy a repair kit from your local DIY shop or consult a plumber.

● **LITTLE OR NO WATER WHEN THE TAP IS OPEN**
If the mains water is running and the cold water cistern is full, the cause in the cold water system is a frozen pipe — see FROZEN PIPES. In the hot water system the cause is an airlock — the symptoms are a spluttering noise and little or no water from the tap.

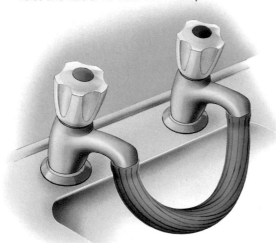

Attach a piece of hose between the hot and cold tap in the kitchen. Open the hot taps in the bathroom and then open the kitchen taps. The pressure of the mains water should drive out the air bubble — consult a plumber if the airlock is not removed as there may be a fault in the system.

● **NOISY PIPES**
It is normal for pipes carrying hot water to creak or knock occasionally as they expand. Insert plastic foam below the problem area if you are able to locate it. The presence of scale in the pipes is a common cause of noisy pipes in hard water areas.

A loud banging and vibration in the pipes is a water hammer, caused by the flow of water being shut off too quickly. The culprit is a worn washer or a faulty gland unit in a tap or an unsuitable ball valve in the cistern.

● **LEAKING PIPES**
There are several possible causes — a hole caused by a nail being driven into the pipe or a fracture due to corrosion or freezing. Immediate action is necessary to prevent damage to carpets, wall coverings etc. Drain the system and dry the affected pipe area. For a small hole, drive in the point of a pencil and then break it off. Tightly bind the area with waterproof tape. If the trouble is a split rather than a hole, bind the fracture with waterproof tape. If the split is large, spread an epoxy glue over and around the fracture before binding with tape. After carrying out the temporary repair, restore the water supply and call a plumber to replace the pipe section.

● **FROZEN PIPES**
Inspect the pipes — if there is a fracture turn off the main stopcock and drain the system. Apply a temporary repair (see above) and then partly open the stopcock. To thaw a pipe, open the tap and apply heat, moving from the tap gradually backwards along the pipe. Never use a naked flame — employ a hair dryer or a hot-air paint stripper.

● **LEAKING JOINTS**
Where nuts are present (compression joint) tighten by a series of quarter turns. If this does not stop the leak or if the joint is a soldered one (capillary joint), treat as for a leaking pipe, using waterproof tape or an epoxy glue plus tape.

● **DRIPPING OVERFLOW PIPE**
Carefully bend the lever arm of the ball valve downwards slightly to ensure cut off before the overflow level is reached.

● **POURING OVERFLOW PIPE**
There are several possible causes. Raise the ball float gently and see if the water flow ceases. If it does, the ball is faulty and needs replacing. To change a ball float, close the valve by tying the lever arm to a piece of wood across the top of the cistern. Empty the tank and unscrew the ball. Buy a plastic replacement and attach to the lever arm.

If the water continues to flow when the ball is raised, the cause is a defective valve which will need to be replaced.

● **NOISY CISTERN**
A problem with old-fashioned cisterns. Replace the present ball valve with a modern one.

● **DIRTY WATER**
The usual cause is an inadequate cover on the cold water cistern. Drain the system, bale out remaining water in the cistern and clean the tank thoroughly. Restore water supply and fit a satisfactory cover.

● **RUSTY WATER**
If the cold water system is affected, then corrosion has occurred in the cistern. Rusty water is much more usual from the hot tap after a large volume of water has been drawn off. This indicates that the boiler has corroded — consult a plumber who will probably advise the installation of an Indirect hot water system (page 9).

Services Drainage

Three distinct types of drainage water have to be carried away from the house. There is the soapy *waste water* from sinks, basins and bath plus the foul *soil water* from the WC. In addition there is *rainwater* collected by the gutters on the roof.

Until quite recently it was thought that it was essential to keep waste water and soil water apart, which meant that different pipes were installed within the house — the standard Two Pipe System. In modern houses, however, there is a single main stack into which the water from the upstairs WC, bath and basins flows — the One Pipe System.

Before making any changes to your drainage system you will need to obtain permission from your Borough or District Council. Permission is also required if you plan to erect an extension, garage or shed over a manhole cover.

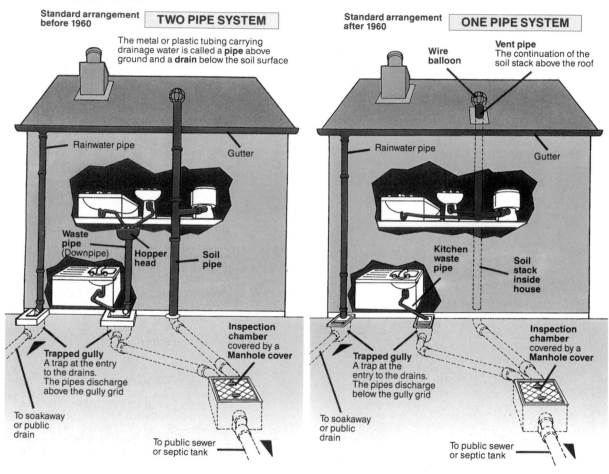

Standard arrangement before 1960 TWO PIPE SYSTEM

The metal or plastic tubing carrying drainage water is called a **pipe** above ground and a **drain** below the soil surface

Rainwater pipe

Gutter

Waste pipe (Downpipe)

Hopper head

Soil pipe

Trapped gully A trap at the entry to the drains. The pipes discharge above the gully grid

Inspection chamber covered by a **Manhole cover**

To soakaway or public drain

To public sewer or septic tank

Standard arrangement after 1960 ONE PIPE SYSTEM

Wire balloon

Vent pipe The continuation of the soil stack above the roof

Rainwater pipe

Gutter

Kitchen waste pipe

Soil stack inside house

Trapped gully A trap at the entry to the drains. The pipes discharge below the gully grid

Inspection chamber covered by a **Manhole cover**

To soakaway or public drain

To public sewer or septic tank

TRAPS

A trap is a water-filled pipe or device which prevents foul air entering the house from the drains. It is generally attached to the outlet pipe, but with a WC it is part of the fitting

U TRAP
The old-fashioned trap you will find on metal pipes. The trap is emptied by unscrewing the access plug at the base

BOTTLE TRAP
A modern, chromium-plated trap — popular where pipework is exposed. Main drawback is that it can slow down the flow rate

P TRAP
A modern plastic trap which can be unscrewed for clearing. The type to choose for a horizontal exit pipe

S TRAP
A modern plastic trap which can be unscrewed for clearing. The type to choose for a vertical exit pipe

AVOIDING DRAINAGE PROBLEMS

● **CLEAN OUT GUTTERS**

A cake of fallen leaves, bird droppings and other debris collects in gutters. The space for water is reduced and this can cause overflowing during heavy rain.

Once a year remove this rubbish with a trowel — put it into a bucket and not down the pipe. Cover the mouth of this pipe with a ball of wire netting.

● **KEEP WASTE PIPES CLEAR**

The kitchen waste pipe is most at risk — do not put peelings, tea leaves, melted fat etc into the sink. You must instal a waste disposal unit (see page 28) if you wish to enjoy the luxury of washing away kitchen waste.

Washing soda in hot water will remove grease from the pipework. If blockage has been a problem, use a plunger about once a year to prevent further trouble.

DEALING WITH DRAINAGE PROBLEMS

● **BLOCKED SINK, BASIN OR BATH**

First of all, check that only one sink, basin or other fitting is affected. If more than one is blocked, your problem is in the soil pipe or a drain — see BLOCKED DRAINS.

A frozen trap in winter will prevent water from draining away. Thaw gently with a hair dryer or use rags soaked in hot water. If ice is not the problem, suspect a trap blocked with kitchen waste, hair or other household debris. The first step is to use a plunger. Press it down firmly and pump up and down rapidly about a dozen times. Pull off to break the seal and then repeat the pumping action until the sink empties.

Plug overflow hole with wet cloth

Bale out water until 3-4 in. remain

Coat bottom edge with petroleum jelly

If using the plunger fails to unblock the sink or basin, remove the trap or open the access plug. Make sure a large bucket is in place under the outlet pipe before opening the trap, and use a piece of wire or cane to clear the pipes on either side of the trap. Thoroughly wash the pipe trap or bottle trap and then replace.

Run the taps. If water does not drain away then the blockage must be beyond the trap. Use a flexible metal 'snake' or clearing rods hired from your local shop. In most cases, however, it is advisable to call a specialist drain-cleaning company at this stage.

You can buy drain-clearing chemicals based on caustic soda. These materials are useful in improving the flow through sluggish pipes, but should not be used if there is a complete blockage.

● **BLOCKED DRAINS**

There are several symptoms of this distressing and often difficult problem. Several fittings may refuse to drain or one fitting may fill up when another is emptied. There may be an unpleasant smell or a gully may overflow.

Put on old clothes and an overall before working on faulty drains. Wear gloves. Call a plumber if the problem is not a simple one. When the trouble is a blocked gully, remove any rubbish which may be covering the grid before removing this protective cover. Use a stick to break up compacted debris — flush with a hosepipe when water starts to run away freely.

The problem may be in the soil stack or pipe.

Many DIY books describe in detail the way in which to unblock a soil pipe. First, locate the clearing eye (illustrated above) and undo the retaining screw, standing to one side as you open up the inspection hole. Clearing rods or a flexible auger are used to clear the blockage, after which the taps are turned on and the WC flushed several times to wash the inside of the pipe.

Do not open that clearing eye, however, unless you are prepared for an unpleasant job. Cover the area with rags and have buckets handy for the flooding — better still, call in a specialist company if you can possibly afford it.

● **BLOCKED WC**

The most likely cause is a blocked trap. Buy or hire a special WC plunger — this is larger than the standard sink model and has a metal disc around the base of the suction cap. Alternatively, use a mop with a polythene bag tied over the head. Bale out some of the water so that the bowl is only about half full. Move the plunger or mop up and down rapidly about a dozen times. A gurgling sound will tell you that the trap is cleared — flush the cistern several times.

Services **Oil**

Until 1970 oil reigned supreme as the main fuel for central heating. In the years which followed, the central heating boom took place and oil lost its lead and gas took over as the major fuel for domestic boilers. The reason for this shift was twofold. The price of oil had spiralled upwards so making it uncompetitive with natural gas, and there were also physical disadvantages. These disadvantages include the need for outside storage — a 600 gallon tank measuring 6 ft × 4 ft × 4 ft is hard to conceal in a small garden. There is also the need to arrange for supplies each time the oil level is low, and an oil-fired boiler is often noisier, smellier and larger than a gas-fired one.

This does not mean that oil has had its day. Oil prices have tumbled and so this fuel is an excellent choice where piped supplies of natural gas are not available. There has also been a marked improvement in boiler design during the past few years, and oil-fired cookers are available.

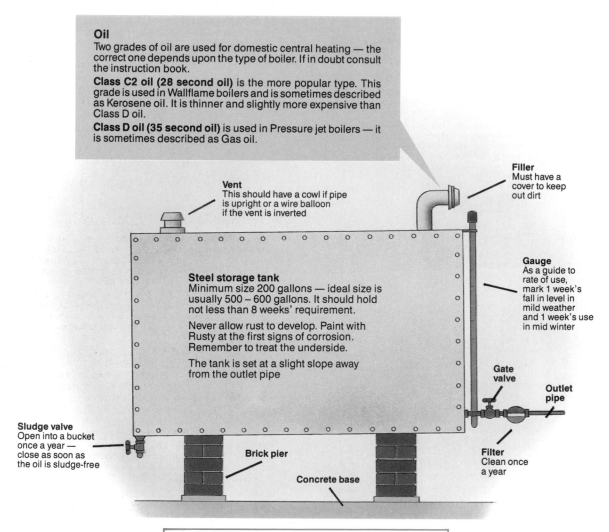

Oil
Two grades of oil are used for domestic central heating — the correct one depends upon the type of boiler. If in doubt consult the instruction book.
Class C2 oil (28 second oil) is the more popular type. This grade is used in Wallflame boilers and is sometimes described as Kerosene oil. It is thinner and slightly more expensive than Class D oil.
Class D oil (35 second oil) is used in Pressure jet boilers — it is sometimes described as Gas oil.

Vent
This should have a cowl if pipe is upright or a wire balloon if the vent is inverted

Filler
Must have a cover to keep out dirt

Gauge
As a guide to rate of use, mark 1 week's fall in level in mild weather and 1 week's use in mid winter

Steel storage tank
Minimum size 200 gallons — ideal size is usually 500 – 600 gallons. It should hold not less than 8 weeks' requirement.

Never allow rust to develop. Paint with Rusty at the first signs of corrosion. Remember to treat the underside.

The tank is set at a slight slope away from the outlet pipe

Gate valve

Outlet pipe

Sludge valve
Open into a bucket once a year — close as soon as the oil is sludge-free

Brick pier

Filter
Clean once a year

Concrete base

AVOIDING OIL PROBLEMS

● **DO NOT LEAVE ORDERING TO THE LAST MINUTE**
During the warm months you can order supplies when it is most convenient — keep watch for money-saving discounts from your supplier in the off-season. During winter you will find that oil consumption increases rapidly in bitterly cold weather — make sure that you order when you still have about 2 weeks' supply. Snow, ice and heavy demand can result in tanker delays.

● **HAVE YOUR INSTALLATION SERVICED REGULARLY**
Never let a year go by without having your oil central heating system serviced. No matter how well it is running, it will be necessary to clean the burner, flue and the combustion chamber. Do not attempt to do this task yourself — have a service contract with a qualified heating engineer who will check that the installation is running at maximum efficiency.

Services Electricity

A power cut in the middle of winter serves as a reminder that the modern home cannot function without electricity. No light, no heat, no facility for cooking and the steady deterioration of food in the refrigerator and freezer.

Fortunately power cuts rarely last for more than a few hours but they do increase our respect for electricity. The basic principles are not difficult to understand and every householder should get to know them. The reason for this knowledge is not to turn you into an amateur electrician — the main purpose is to avoid the misuse due to ignorance which leads to so many tragic fires each year. Learn to spot the danger signs.

Of course, there is no reason why you shouldn't tackle DIY electrical jobs — fitting plugs, replacing sockets and mending fuses are tasks which anyone can perform. You can be more ambitious and lay new cables — there are no regulations to prevent you carrying out alterations, nor are there any authorities to be informed. However, you should never attempt a major job unless you are absolutely confident that you know what you are doing. Consult a comprehensive DIY manual and look at the Institution of Electrical Engineers Wiring Regulations in your local library.

If you have recently moved house or if you have not had the system looked at for many years, ask your local Electricity Board to send round one of their experts to give you a report. The cost will be small but the saving may be your home, possessions and even your life.

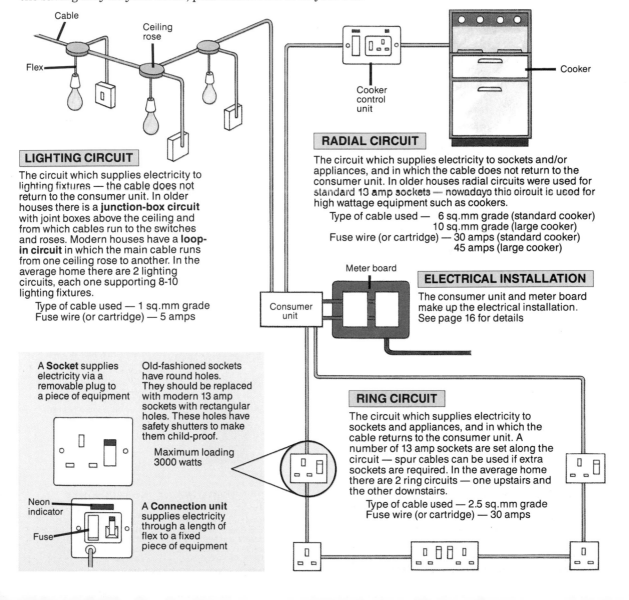

LIGHTING CIRCUIT

The circuit which supplies electricity to lighting fixtures — the cable does not return to the consumer unit. In older houses there is a **junction-box circuit** with joint boxes above the ceiling and from which cables run to the switches and roses. Modern houses have a **loop-in circuit** in which the main cable runs from one ceiling rose to another. In the average home there are 2 lighting circuits, each one supporting 8-10 lighting fixtures.

Type of cable used — 1 sq.mm grade
Fuse wire (or cartridge) — 5 amps

RADIAL CIRCUIT

The circuit which supplies electricity to sockets and/or appliances, and in which the cable does not return to the consumer unit. In older houses radial circuits were used for standard 13 amp sockets — nowadays this circuit is used for high wattage equipment such as cookers.

Type of cable used —   6 sq.mm grade (standard cooker)
10 sq.mm grade (large cooker)
Fuse wire (or cartridge) — 30 amps (standard cooker)
45 amps (large cooker)

ELECTRICAL INSTALLATION

The consumer unit and meter board make up the electrical installation. See page 16 for details

A **Socket** supplies electricity via a removable plug to a piece of equipment

Old-fashioned sockets have round holes. They should be replaced with modern 13 amp sockets with rectangular holes. These holes have safety shutters to make them child-proof.

Maximum loading 3000 watts

A **Connection unit** supplies electricity through a length of flex to a fixed piece of equipment

RING CIRCUIT

The circuit which supplies electricity to sockets and appliances, and in which the cable returns to the consumer unit. A number of 13 amp sockets are set along the circuit — spur cables can be used if extra sockets are required. In the average home there are 2 ring circuits — one upstairs and the other downstairs.

Type of cable used — 2.5 sq.mm grade
Fuse wire (or cartridge) — 30 amps

THE ELECTRICAL INSTALLATION IN YOUR HOME

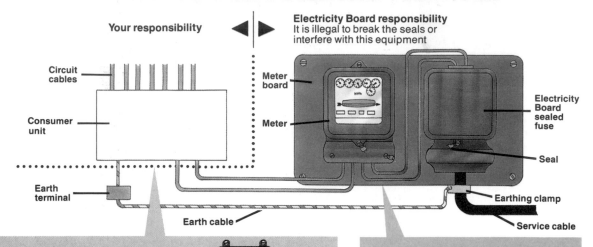

Your responsibility

Electricity Board responsibility
It is illegal to break the seals or interfere with this equipment

Circuit cables

Consumer unit

Meter board

Meter

Electricity Board sealed fuse

Seal

Earth terminal

Earthing clamp

Earth cable

Service cable

OLD-FASHIONED 'CONSUMER UNIT'
Before 1950 there were no true consumer units — each circuit had its own fuse box and mains switch

STANDARD CONSUMER UNIT
Each circuit has its own fuse, which is of the rewirable or cartridge type. The mains switch is used to cut off or restore the electricity supply to the house

MODERN CONSUMER UNIT
There are no fuses — there are instead **miniature circuit breakers** (MCBs) which switch off if there is a fault or if the circuit is overloaded. To reset, merely correct the fault and press the button or flick the switch on the MCB.
There is a **residual circuit current breaker** (RCCB) instead of the mains switch. This provides protection against shocks — very useful if you use electricity outdoors

Standard meters have a series of clock-like dials. To read the meter, ignore the red dial and read the remainder from left to right. If the pointer is between 2 numbers, take the lower one. A modern meter has a digital counter which gives a read-out in numbers, just like a pocket calculator. The meter measures the number of units used, and your electricity bill will be based on a standing charge and a set amount for each unit, irrespective of when it was used. You can change to Economy 7 tariff — you will pay a slightly higher standing charge and perhaps a slightly higher day-time unit rate, but the cost of night-time electricity will be much lower. Your electrical installation will have to be changed. There will be a dual-rate (white) meter to replace your present meter, and a time switch which at night allows electricity to pass to the storage heater or other equipment

---

Wiring a plug

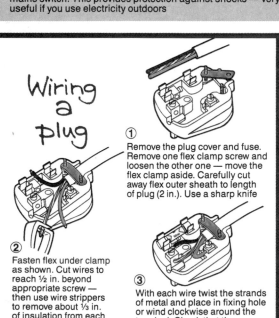

① Remove the plug cover and fuse. Remove one flex clamp screw and loosen the other one — move the flex clamp aside. Carefully cut away flex outer sheath to length of plug (2 in.). Use a sharp knife

② Fasten flex under clamp as shown. Cut wires to reach ½ in. beyond appropriate screw — then use wire strippers to remove about ⅓ in. of insulation from each wire. Make sure the wires are directed to the correct terminals

③ With each wire twist the strands of metal and place in fixing hole or wind clockwise around the terminal. Check that there are no loose strands. Tighten the screws, and fit correct fuse in holder. Replace the plug cover

---

The meaning of electrical symbols

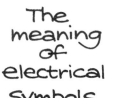

BEAB SYMBOL
This label on a piece of equipment indicates that it has been approved by the British Electrotechnical Approvals Board as a result of testing a sample of the product to the safety requirements of the British Standards Institution

NICEIC
The National Inspection Council for Electrical Installation Contracting is an independent organisation which has a code of practice to safeguard customers against defective workmanship. All Electricity Boards and most members of the Electrical Contractors' Association are on its list. Your Electricity Showroom will have a list of local Approved Contractors

DOUBLE INSULATION MARK
This label on a piece of equipment indicates that it is double insulated and therefore does not need earthing. The appliance can be safely used with 2-core flex

WHAT THE WORDS MEAN

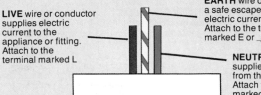

LIVE wire or conductor supplies electric current to the appliance or fitting. Attach to the terminal marked L

EARTH wire or conductor provides a safe escape to earth for the electric current if a fault develops. Attach to the terminal marked E or ⏚

NEUTRAL wire or conductor supplies electric current away from the appliance or fitting. Attach to the terminal marked N or P

The *Pressure* which drives the current through the wire is measured in **VOLTS** (V). The pressure in the U.K. is 240 V. This pressure occasionally falls in winter if there is a sudden surge in demand — if this drop in voltage is large enough you will find that the TV picture shrinks and fluorescent lighting may not switch on.

The *Power* required by an appliance is measured in **WATTS** (W). This is what you pay for — the more watts used, the higher your bill will be. Some appliances require little electric power, such as a radio or refrigerator, but others have a high power requirement — a large cooker requires 3000-4000 watts.

1000 watts = 1 kW (1 kilowatt)

The *Amount* of current flowing through the circuit is measured in **AMPS** (A). As the power requirement is increased (watts), so is the amount of current flowing through the circuit (amps). Fuse wire is measured in amps.

Watts ÷ Volts = Amps

Your electricity bill will tell you the price of 1 unit. A **UNIT** is the amount of electricity used by a 1000 watt (1 kW) appliance in an hour.

Appliance	Watts	Time you get for 1 Unit
BLANKET	100	10 hours
CLOCK	1	1000 hours
FAN HEATER	3000-1000	20 minutes-1 hour
FOOD MIXER	200	5 hours
FREEZER	80	12 hours
HOT PLATE	4000-3000	15-20 minutes
IMMERSION HEATER	3000	20 minutes
IRON	500	2 hours
KETTLE	2000	30 minutes
LIGHT BULB	150-40	7-25 hours
OVEN	4000-3000	15-20 minutes
POWER DRILL	250	4 hours
RADIANT HEATER	3000-1000	20 minutes-1 hour
RADIO	30	35 hours
REFRIGERATOR	100	10 hours
SPIN DRIER	500	2 hours
TOWEL RAIL	250	4 hours
TUMBLE DRIER	2000	30 minutes
TV — Black & White	150	7 hours
TV — Colour	350	3 hours
VACUUM CLEANER	250	4 hours
WASHING MACHINE	3000	20 minutes

CABLE & FLEX

CABLE

Carries electricity from the consumer unit to sockets, switches and ceiling roses

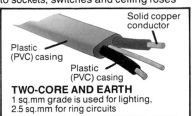

Plastic (PVC) casing

Solid copper conductor

Plastic (PVC) casing

TWO-CORE AND EARTH
1 sq.mm grade is used for lighting, 2.5 sq.mm for ring circuits

FLEX (Flexible cord)

Carries electricity from a socket to an appliance and from a ceiling rose to light fitting

Plastic (PVC) casing

Core of copper threads

Plastic (PVC) casing

THREE-CORE SHEATHED
Standard flex for most purposes. Various grades (0.5-4 sq.mm) — the higher the wattage, the higher the grade number

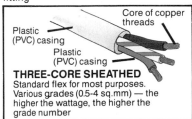

THREE-CORE BRAIDED
Cotton braid surrounds wires covered by synthetic rubber. Good insulation — used for kettles and irons

TWO-CORE SHEATHED
Used for plastic lampholders and double-insulated appliances

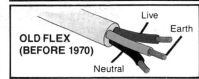

Live

Earth

OLD FLEX (BEFORE 1970)

Neutral

FUSES

A fuse is a weak point which is deliberately inserted in the circuit. The fuse 'blows' by melting if there is an overload.

PLUG FUSES

3A

Use for equipment rated at less than 750 W. Never use a 3 A fuse for heating or cooking appliances

13A

Use for equipment rated at more than 750 W

MAINS FUSES

The fuses in the consumer unit protect the lighting circuits, and also act as back-up protection for the other circuits. These supply electricity through sockets and fuse-protected plugs.

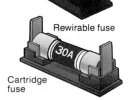

Rewirable fuse

Cartridge fuse

In most cases the consumer unit contains a row of **Rewirable fuses** — a length of fuse wire is held between 2 brass screws. **Cartridge fuses** are easier to change — simply remove the blown cartridge and slip in the replacement

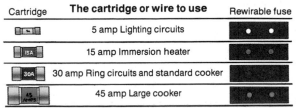

Cartridge	The cartridge or wire to use	Rewirable fuse
	5 amp Lighting circuits	
	15 amp Immersion heater	
	30 amp Ring circuits and standard cooker	
	45 amp Large cooker	

AVOIDING ELECTRICAL PROBLEMS

● **KEEP AN ELECTRICITY TOOL KIT HANDY**
Few special tools are needed for electrical repairs. However, trouble can strike quickly and without warning, so it is wise to have the essential equipment together in a box — this will save having to hunt for tools in the dark.

The essential kit:

Torch
A free-standing one will leave your hands free

Electrician's pliers
Insulated handles; jaws for shaping and cutting wire

Wire strippers
Used to cut through insulation without cutting through the wire

Knife
Used to cut through PVC sheathing

Fuse wire or cartridges
The type of consumer unit determines whether wire or cartridges will be required

Plug fuses
Both 3 A and 13 A fuses should be kept

Electrician's screwdriver
Insulated handle; parallel-sided tip

Optional extras: Mains tester (a screwdriver with a neon bulb which lights when the blade touches a live connection). Connector strips for joining flex. Multimeter for testing circuits and batteries. Long-nosed pliers. Diagonal cutters for cutting cables. Cable clips for attaching cables to supports.

● **LABEL FUSES IN THE CONSUMER UNIT**
Make a list of the role of the fuses in the consumer unit. This list is usually written on the inside of the fuse unit cover, but it can be placed alongside or on adhesive strips stuck on the face of the consumer unit. Such a list will enable you to pull out the right fuse when one has blown — hunting for the correct fuse is a frustrating job when all the lights are off.

● **CONSIDER REPLACING THE WIRING**
If your house was built before the mid 1950s, the electric cables will be sheathed in rubber. This will have started to deteriorate, and there is a chance that wires may be exposed. If you overload such a system there is the possibility of the copper conductors becoming hot and a fire may result. Look for the danger signs — round-pin plugs, old-fashioned switches, fuses blowing frequently, a smell of burning or sparks from sockets. Call in the Electricity Board and ask for an inspection.

● **DON'T OVERLOAD THE CIRCUIT**
It is a great temptation these days to overload the circuit. There are so many new pieces of equipment — computers, food mixers, microwave ovens, lawn aerators etc . . . but the capacity of the domestic installation has not increased.

The maximum loading for a ring circuit is about 7 kW (7000 watts). At 10 kW the cartridge fuse in the mains will blow — if the fuse system uses wire it will not blow until 14 kW is being used. If blown fuses due to overloading are a recurring problem, cut down the load or have an additional ring circuit installed.

The standard 13 A plug has a maximum loading of 3 kW. You can put in an adaptor to run 2 appliances instead of one from the socket, but it is better to have twin sockets as a permanent home for the 2 plugs. At all costs avoid a 'Christmas tree' arrangement of plugs and adaptors. It is also unwise to plug equipment into a lampholder.

● **FOLLOW THE SAFETY RULES WHEN DEALING WITH APPLIANCES**
It is essential that you should use the appropriate plug, fuse and flex size when installing a piece of equipment. Use a 3-pin plug if an earth run is present. Buy an unbreakable plug if it is to be regularly pushed in and pulled out of sockets. Do not pull out a plug by tugging the flex, and keep the flex well away from a source of heat.

Do not touch metal appliances with wet hands and do not immerse kitchen implements such as food mixers, electrical carving knives, etc in water. Never stand a vase of cut flowers on the TV. Whenever practical switch off equipment at the socket and remove the plug. Once a year check the flex and plug for wear and tear, and have large items such as washing machines, dishwashers and microwave ovens serviced regularly. The time interval between services will depend on the appliance — use the supplier or instruction book for guidance.

● **FOLLOW THE SAFETY RULES WHEN DEALING WITH CABLES AND FLEX**
Unless there is an emergency, plan to work in daylight. Before you start, switch off the supply at the mains and remove the appropriate fuse. Put it in your pocket and do not replace it until the task is finished.

Never use ordinary staples to attach cables or flex to joists or skirting boards. Use insulated cable clips. Do not try to mend damaged flex with insulation tape — replace it with new flex of the correct type.

The length between the plug and the appliance should be kept as short as possible. Trailing flexes are a hazard, and flexes placed under a carpet can lead to a fire.

Above all, never attempt to tackle a major task unless you know what you are doing, and never attempt to take short cuts with electricity.

● **FOLLOW THE SAFETY RULES IN THE BATHROOM**
Electricity and water are a hazardous mixture, so there are special rules for bathrooms. With the exception of a shaver point, you should not fix a socket in a bathroom. Furthermore you should make sure that all switches within the bathroom are of the cord-operated type.

Do not bring in portable equipment such as a hairdryer and make sure that all lampholders are out of reach of anyone standing in the bath or shower. A wall-mounted heater must also be placed out of reach.

● **FIX AN RCCB IF USING ELECTRICAL EQUIPMENT OUTDOORS**
An RCCB (residual circuit current breaker — see page 16) instead of a mains switch is a good idea if you are using an electrical hedgetrimmer or lawnmower in the garden or a power drill around the house. If the consumer unit does not have an RCCB, you can buy a plug fitted with one and so you can protect yourself against shocks from a single socket.

● **EMPLOY A PROFESSIONAL ELECTRICIAN FOR OUTDOOR WIRING**
Although approval is not required for house wiring, the situation is different for wiring to provide lighting around the garden or to operate a pump in the pond. Here a contractor on the roll of the NICEIC (page 16) should be employed. A Board Test Certificate must be submitted to the Electricity Board before they will test and then connect the circuit.

● **INSTAL SUITABLE EQUIPMENT**
The standard voltage in the U.K. is 240 V — equipment is generally marked 200 – 250 V AC (alternating current) or 200 – 250 V AC/DC. Equipment which is marked only DC (direct current) is not suitable.

When buying plugs, equipment and accessories always look for the BEAB symbol (page 16) or the BSI kitemark.

DEALING WITH ELECTRICAL PROBLEMS

● APPLIANCE FAILURE

If an appliance fails to work when switched on, check that other equipment on the circuit is working. If so, the most likely cause is a blown fuse in the plug.

Switch off and remove the plug. Check the wire connections — if all is in order remove the fuse. Test the fuse with a multimeter or an ordinary metal torch — see below.

Screw off the base of a metal torch. Hold the metal part of the fuse against the torch casing and the other end of the fuse on the base of the battery. Switch on. If the torch lights the fuse is sound.

Replace the fuse if necessary and refit plug cover. If the appliance still fails to work and if the flex is sound, the fault is in the equipment and should be repaired by an electrician.

● CIRCUIT FAILURE

If all the lights or sockets on a circuit are dead, then the most likely problem is a blown fuse in the consumer unit. You may have overloaded the circuit, or there may be a fault at one of the outlet points. If the circuit wasn't overloaded, you should switch off all the appliances or lights and then repair the fuse or reset the MCB (see page 16). Now switch on the lights or appliances one by one — if the fuse blows again you will have isolated the trouble spot. Check for loose connections — if you can't find the cause of the problem you should call in an electrician.

● HOUSE SYSTEM FAILURE

If the whole electricity system fails, check with your neighbours. When you find that the district and not just your house is affected there is a power cut and there is nothing you can do about it. If your neighbours are not affected, you have house system failure. Check the fuses in the consumer unit — if they have not blown then you will most probably have a fault in the Electricity Board sealed fuse unit. Call the Electricity Board immediately.

● POWER CUT

Power cuts can occur for several reasons — storm damage to power lines, mechanical faults or industrial action. They *do* happen, although they are rare, so you should keep a survival kit handy — a torch, candles and a small paraffin or butane stove.

When you are first plunged into darkness, switch off appliances and most lights. Pull out the TV plug but do not switch off the refrigerator or the freezer. The freezer can be a problem, although the food will remain frozen for up to 12 hours during a power cut. Do not open the refrigerator or freezer doors until power is restored. When the power cut is over, reset all clocks and timers.

● FLEX EXTENSION

It is sometimes necessary to extend a length of flex when an appliance is moved to a new position. You should never wind the wire ends together and bind the join with insulation tape — such a join is a source of danger.

You can use an extension lead, but it is better to join an extra length of flex to the appliance wiring by means of a connector. Several types are available — the most straightforward is the one-part connector shown below.

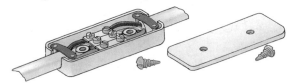

● LIGHT BULB FAILURE

If an ordinary tungsten filament bulb fails to light when switched on, check other lights on the circuit. If the problem is an isolated one, the most likely cause is a dead light bulb. You will need a new bulb — do not use one with a higher wattage than is recommended for the lamp or shade. If in doubt, do not exceed 60 watts.

Switch off, remove the bulb and replace. Remember to push the bulb firmly into the lampholder before twisting anti-clockwise to remove. If the bulb is broken in the socket, switch off at the mains and then push a cork into the broken base of the lamp bulb. Press and twist.

If the new bulb fails to light when switched on, the lampholder may be at fault. One of the metal plungers may have stuck or the holder may need rewiring.

Failure of a fluorescent tube to light may indicate a blown tube, but there are also several other possible causes — a defective starter switch, poor contact between the tube pins and the lampholder, a drop in voltage, a defective ballast, or a marked change in temperature. For more details about fluorescent lighting, see page 36.

● UNPLEASANT SMELL

A fishy smell is disagreeable but is not a danger signal. A type of plastic which was once used in the manufacture of light fittings emits this odour when hot. Fortunately these fittings are no longer made and the only answer to the problem is to replace the fluorescent unit or lampholder.

An acrid smell of burning rubber or wood is much more worrying. Check equipment quickly — if an appliance is causing the problem you must switch off and unplug it. Inspect sockets and plugs — if one is hot then take out the appropriate fuse and call an electrician immediately. If you cannot trace the fault then seek expert advice as soon as you can.

● BLOWN FUSE

When a fault develops in a piece of equipment, it is the plug fuse which generally blows. If there is a fault in the flex or cable, or if the ring circuit has been overloaded, the fuse in the consumer unit blows. In a lighting circuit the cause of a blown fuse lies in either the bulb or the wiring.

If the fuse has blown because of overloading, the answer is simple. Repair the fuse and cut down the loading on that circuit. If, however, the fuse keeps blowing even when the circuit is not heavily loaded, you should call an electrician. What you must never do is to fit heavier wire in an attempt to resist blowing — a fuse is a safety valve which melts before the wiring overheats. Stop it blowing when there is a problem and you can have burnt-out wiring (or worse) on your hands.

To repair a rewirable fuse, turn off the main switch and remove the fuse carrier. You will find that the wire is broken and there may be scorch marks — loosen the 2 screws and remove all of the old wire. Wind a length of new wire of the correct rating (see page 17) round one screw and pass enough wire through the fuse to enable you to wind the end around the second terminal. Tighten the screws, cut off the excess wire, replace the fuse and switch on the current.

With a cartridge fuse insert a new cartridge between the 2 metal holders on the fuse carrier. With an MCB flick the switch or press the button to reset.

● OVERHEATED PLUG OR SOCKET

If a plug feels warm, remove the top and see if a connection is loose or broken. Repair the fault and replace the plug cover.

If a socket is warm or sparking, seek professional advice.

Services Gas

Although electricity has a virtual monopoly in the lighting of homes, gas still remains the main source of domestic energy. The type of gas has changed — the poisonous town gas obtained from coal has been replaced by the non-toxic natural gas extracted from the bed below the North Sea and elsewhere.

Gone is the murder by an unlit gas fire so beloved in detective stories, but natural gas should still not be regarded as risk-free. The chance of an explosion remains if this fuel is carelessly handled and danger signs ignored, and if incorrectly burnt the by-product (carbon monoxide) *is* poisonous.

There are laws to protect you and your neighbours — ignore them and you could be fined up to £2,000. It is illegal to either instal or service a piece of gas equipment unless you are competent, and that means either calling in British Gas or a CORGI registered installer (see below). Gas installation is not for the DIY enthusiast, unless he or she has been properly trained.

There are other points of law — you must not use any equipment which you think may be faulty and you must take action if you believe that there is a gas leak. This calls for turning off the main gas tap, informing your local gas service centre and leaving the supply turned off until the fault has been repaired.

Gas is an excellent source of energy — inexpensive for central heating, easily controllable for cooking and highly versatile for heating. You must, however, treat it with respect and have equipment serviced regularly. As a general rule don't buy a second-hand appliance unless you can be sure of its safety — according to British Gas second-hand appliances are involved in most faulty equipment accidents.

Help for elderly and handicapped people

British Gas have an excellent arrangement for people who could be at risk because of age or infirmity. If you live alone and are over 65 or if you are a registered disabled person, you can ask a representative to call and give you a full safety check and advice free of charge. There are a number of attachments and adaptors available to make life easier, such as extended handles for meters and cookers, and Braille controls for central heating control units.

Lighting the gas

In the old days a match was the only way to light gas appliances, and many an eyebrow was singed. Battery-operated spark guns were introduced to keep fingers away, and the pilot light was a great step forward. This small flame, however, has to be relit each time the appliance is switched off at the main tap and then switched on again. It can also go out in some appliances when the pressure drops, and so modern gas appliances have piezo ignition. This provides an instant spark when the control knob is turned or the ignition button is pressed.

The Balanced Flue

The exhaust fumes from a gas appliance must be allowed to escape — an old chimney must be carefully checked and cleaned before a gas appliance is attached to it. If there is no chimney a Balanced Flue system can be installed. This is attached to an outside wall and both the fresh air intake and flue outlet are sealed from the room.

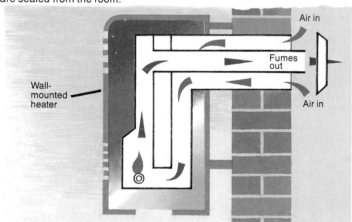

The Balanced Flue system is ideal for both wall-mounted room heaters and boilers and Ascot-type water heaters, but access to an outside wall is necessary. An alternative is the Instaduct system in which a flue duct is taken above the roof and is hidden within the house by a prefabricated chimney breast.

The meaning of gas symbols

BSI SAFETY MARK
This label on an appliance indicates that it meets the requirements of the Quality Assurance Council of the British Standards Institution

BSI KITEMARK
This ticket issued by the Society of British Gas Industries assures that the product conforms with all requirements laid down by the British Standards Institution for safety, quality and performance in a domestic gas appliance

CORGI
A CORGI Registered Installer has been approved by the Confederation for the Registration of Gas Installers. The work is periodically checked by CORGI Inspectors to ensure safety standards are being met

AVOIDING GAS PROBLEMS

● **LOCATE & TEST THE MAIN GAS TAP**
Look for the main gas tap — it is generally located close to the meter. Test the handle — if it is stiff, call the gas service centre. They will fix it free of charge. Never try to force the handle or fix it yourself.

● **SWEEP THE CHIMNEY BEFORE FITTING AN APPLIANCE**
A blocked chimney will not allow fumes to escape — the air in the room will be polluted. It is therefore essential to have the chimney swept before fitting a fire or other fixed appliance.

● **DO NOT BLOCK A VENTILATOR**
Ventilators provide a constant stream of fresh air, and this allows natural gas to burn efficiently. Blocking a ventilator to cut down draughts or for some other reason can have harmful or even fatal results.

● **HAVE APPLIANCES SERVICED REGULARLY**
Central heating and fires should be serviced annually — other appliances every 1–2 years. Do not attempt to service or repair equipment or appliances — call your local Gas Service Centre or a CORGI Registered Installer. It is a good idea to have a regular servicing contract.

● **CONSIDER SWITCHING OFF THE SUPPLY IF YOU ARE GOING AWAY**
Before leaving on holiday you should switch off the main gas tap — check that there is no food in a gas-operated refrigerator or freezer. The situation is different if you are going away for a week or two in winter and your home is heated by gas central heating or if you have a gas water heater. Leave the gas on to avoid burst pipes, but turn the thermostat down.

Switching off the main gas tap

OFF   ON

Turn off *all* appliance taps and pilot lights before turning the handle of the main gas tap to the OFF position. To restore the supply, move the handle to the ON position and relight the pilot lights immediately.

DEALING WITH GAS PROBLEMS

● **A SMELL OF GAS**
Act immediately:

1. Put out all naked flames. Do not smoke.

2. Do not operate any electrical switches or bell pushes.

3. Open doors and windows to allow the gas to escape. Do not close them until the problem has been solved.

4. The most likely cause of a gas escape is a pilot light which has gone out or a tap which has been turned on but not lit. Relight, allow the smell to disappear and then close the doors and windows.

5. If you cannot locate and remove the cause of the problem, turn off the main gas tap — see the illustration above.

6. Call the Gas Escapes number listed under Gas in the telephone directory. A fitter will call to inspect the installation — the check, first 30 minutes of work and any small parts which may be required are provided free. Of course, if the fault is on the street side of the meter then no charge whatever is made for its repair.

If the smell of gas is only slight and localised near a pipe joint, you can test for a leak by brushing soapy water over the area. The appearance of bubbles tells you that gas is escaping — turn off the main gas tap and call British Gas.

If you smell gas outside the house or when walking along the street, call British Gas at once.

● **BROWN MARKS AROUND APPLIANCES**
If brown or sooty marks appear above a gas fire or around the top of a water heater, the fumes are not escaping properly and you must have the installation inspected immediately.

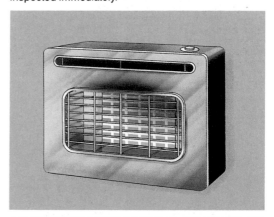

A blocked chimney is the usual cause of the trouble, and staining is only one of the by-products of faulty fume escape. The flame is usually yellow rather than blue, and carbon monoxide may build up in the room. This gas is poisonous — the main symptoms are headaches, drowsiness and weakness.

Services Solid fuel

Wood and then coal were once our most widely used fuels, but not any more. The magic of gas and then electricity made the use of solid fuels seem so time-consuming. Storage had to be provided and the fire required to be fed every few hours. There were ashes to remove, sparks to guard against and automatic heat control was not always possible.

Despite these drawbacks, solid fuel has staged a comeback. For many people the satisfaction of an open fire in winter is worth all the trouble, and for some housewives the slow cooking action of a solid fuel cooker makes it preferable to all other fuels. Above all, there has been a revolution in appliance design — you can buy multi-fuel heaters which will burn wood as well as coal, and some appliances can use ordinary coal in Smokeless Zones. There are types with trays which hold a week's ash and others with hoppers which feed the fire with fuel. Forget your old ideas and pick up a Solid Fuel Advisory Service leaflet. Coal is sold under all sorts of names. There is house coal — cheap but not smokeless and sold in various grades. Anthracite and Welsh dry steam coal are natural smokeless coals — there are in addition numerous brands of manufactured smokeless fuels.

Wood is popular in areas where it is free for the taking, but use it with care. It should have been left to dry, for a year if possible, and the chimney must be properly lined. Sweeping will be necessary once a month if you burn wood every day.

It is illegal to emit smoke from your chimney if you live in a Smoke Control Area (Smokeless Zone). This means that you must use a smokeless fuel or an exempted appliance burning coal. Not all appliances are suitable for smokeless fuels — ask your coal merchant. If you have to change, check with your local council — you may be eligible for a grant of up to 70% of the cost.

	OPEN FIRE	ROOM HEATER	BOILER	COOKER
The Solid Fuel Advisory Service is an active organisation with 60 offices throughout the country. Telephone the nearest office for information or advice.				
Heating the room	✓	✓		An advantage in winter, but can be a drawback in summer
Providing domestic hot water	✓ If a back boiler is fitted	✓ If a back boiler is fitted	✓	✓ If a boiler is fitted
Central heating (maximum capacity)	Up to 5 radiators if a high-output back boiler is fitted	Up to 10 radiators if a high-output back boiler is fitted	12 radiators or more — outputs available up to 44 kW	Up to 6 radiators if a boiler is fitted
Notes	There are the standard inset on a hearth, the free-standing fire and the 'hole-in-the-wall' fire set above floor level. Underfloor draught fires and fires with fan assistance increase the range of suitable fuels	The fire is enclosed in a firebox with a glass door or doors. This arrangement gives greater safety and much better heat control. Both radiant and convected heat is supplied — see page 29. Gravity-feed refuelling is available	Small boilers heat the domestic water supply — large ones run the central heating as well. Conventional boilers will require fuel every few hours, but the gravity-feed ones need refuelling only once a day	There are usually 2 ovens — a 'hot' one for roasting and a 'cold' one for warming dishes. Cookers are available in a range of colours and sizes — a large cooker/boiler can use up to 50 lb of fuel a day
Suitable fuels 'smokeless' in green 'non-smokeless' in red	House coal 'Royal'/'Rexco' 'Homefire' 'Coalite'	Anthracite 'Royal'/'Rexco' 'Phurnacite' 'Coalite' 'Sunbrite'	Anthracite 'Royal'/'Rexco' 'Phurnacite' 'Coalite' 'Sunbrite'	Anthracite 'Royal'/'Rexco' 'Phurnacite' 'Coalite' 'Sunbrite'

AVOIDING SOLID FUEL PROBLEMS

● **KEEP THE SYSTEM CLEAN**
Decoke the parts where soot and ash build up — do this every month or as often as the makers advise. Have the chimney swept once a year.

● **AVOID THE RISK OF FIRE**
Use a fireguard at all times when the fire is lit — it should be attached to the wall if small children are present. Do not hang clothes on a fireguard.

Never use paraffin to start the fire and never bank it up with fuel to a dangerous level. Never use a sheet of newspaper to draw a coal fire.

● **ACT QUICKLY IF SOMETHING IS WRONG**
Call the fire brigade immediately if the chimney catches fire or if the chimney breast suddenly gets too hot to touch.

The opposite may happen — the fire burns very slowly and there is a strong smell of coal fumes. Let the fire go out and thoroughly clean the appliance. Call the Solid Fuel Advisory Service if the fumes persist — do not continue to use the fire.

● **LIGHT THE FIRE PROPERLY**
You can use the traditional newspaper and firewood if you do not live in a Smoke Control Area — if you do then you will have to use white firelighters or an electric firelighter.

Services Other fuels

Paraffin and bottled gas share a number of features, but there are also important differences. Both are stored as liquids — paraffin in ordinary cans and bottled gas in special steel canisters. Bottled gas is a gaseous fuel which has been liquefied and kept in this form by the pressure in the container. When the valve is opened it escapes as a gas into the appliance.

Neither paraffin nor bottled gas needs a flue, and this makes them suitable for portable space heaters. It is this use for which they are best known — such heaters can be moved from one spot to another and they are efficient. None of the heat is lost up the flue as with a gas fire or an oil boiler.

These paraffin and bottled gas heaters are used to provide warmth where there is neither mains electricity nor a natural gas supply — in the workshop, caravan, boat or greenhouse. They are also used to provide extra warmth in winter and standby heat in case of a power cut.

There are one or two problems. Good ventilation is essential if condensation is to be avoided. Thermostatic control is not available, although modern bottled gas heaters have 3 or 4 settings. Accidents do happen with these heaters so follow the instructions. Some models get very hot to the touch so site appliances away from the line of traffic.

Despite the similarities, there are important differences between paraffin and bottled gas. Paraffin has a limited range of uses — these days it is almost entirely restricted to space heaters. The appliance needs regular attention if smells are to be avoided. Bottled gas is quite different — the appliance is attached to a canister or storage tank from which gas passes to the burner. Here it behaves just like natural gas — it can be used for fixed fires, cookers and central heating systems.

Paraffin

BSI KITEMARK
The BSI Kitemark on a paraffin heater indicates that it meets the relevant standards set by the British Standards Institution

Paraffin is a grade of kerosene, coloured pink or blue for identification. It is generally bought in small amounts for convector and/or radiant heaters — such models are usually portable but fixed versions are available. A modern paraffin stove is a useful standby if the basic source of heat fails, but do buy an appliance with the BSI kitemark. Such heaters will have a fail-safe device which extinguishes the flame if the appliance is knocked over.

Time has passed paraffin by for general heating. Compared with electricity or gas, there is too much work involved. Cans have to be brought home, tanks have to be filled and wicks have to be trimmed. Furthermore, automatic control is not available.

Bottled gas

PROPANE

BUTANE

Bottled gas is the popular name for LPG — liquefied petroleum gas. Two types are available — the canisters of butane and propane are painted differently to avoid confusion. Do not use a butane canister for propane or vice versa — the two liquefied gases work at different pressures.

Canisters are available in various sizes. The usual one for a portable space heater is 15 kg — this weighs 30 kg when full so bottled gas is cumbersome to handle. You will have to pay a hire charge for each canister and at least 2 will be required — one in use and the other to replace it when empty. Both smaller and larger canisters can be obtained — the larger ones are used for cookers.

Bottled gas can be kept outdoors in a special storage tank. Supplies are obtained from a tanker and this is the most economical way to use bottled gas. It will fuel a central heating system just like natural gas but it will be appreciably more expensive. Unlike natural gas, bottled gas is heavier than air when it leaves the canister. Escaped gas will not disperse if you open a window — it collects at floor level. This can be a risk — follow the storage instructions listed below.

AVOIDING PROBLEMS

- **STORE THE FUEL PROPERLY**
  Paraffin should not be stored in the house. Bottled gas canisters should be stored outdoors wherever possible. If the canisters have been stored in a room or shed, make sure that the area is ventilated by opening the door before you strike a match or switch on the light. The storage area should be cool but an underground room such as a cellar should be avoided.

  Fixed storage tanks for bottled gas should be sited well away from the house.

- **HAVE EQUIPMENT SERVICED REGULARLY**
  Large pieces of equipment such as central heating and cookers using bottled gas should be serviced each year. Hoses connecting cylinders to appliances should be checked regularly for leaks. This is done by brushing soapy water over them — the appearance of bubbles indicates a leak.

- **HANDLE BOTTLED GAS CANISTERS WITH CARE**
  Extinguish all naked flames when changing canisters — follow the supplier's instructions carefully.

- **VENTILATE THE ROOM**
  Good ventilation is essential for both paraffin and bottled gas stoves. This means opening a window slightly if the doors are draught-proofed — failure to do so will result in excessive condensation. Ventilation is necessary, but direct draughts must be avoided.

- **HANDLE APPLIANCES WITH CARE**
  Never fill a paraffin heater whilst it is still lit. Try to fill it outdoors and make sure the cap is properly secured after filling. Wipe the outside of the tank. Never move a heater when it is lit. Keep it away from curtains, furniture etc and face the appliance towards the centre of the room. Keep it out of the path of children and animals.

Services TV & Radio

We have become a nation of TV addicts. The average time spent viewing is 3 to 4 hours each day — more than in any other country in Europe. More than 1 in every 4 homes has a video recorder — another record-breaking statistic.

The range of TV receivers is now enormous — from tiny models which fit into your pocket to large projector models with screens measuring several feet across. The choice of most people, however, is quite specific — a 20 in. or 22 in. colour set. The pocket-sized models have not become as popular as expected — the cost of batteries is high and picture quality is often poor. The giant sets have also failed to become established and so we remain addicted to the medium-sized set.

To rent or buy remains a vexed question. Both sides have their committed disciples, but it seems quite clear that on purely financial grounds it is better to buy unless you plan to change your set more often than every 2 or 3 years. Before buying or renting you should inspect the set in the shop. Make sure you like the overall appearance of the model you have chosen and ensure that it has the features you require — remote control, stereo, teletext etc. But do not pick a model because it has the best picture in the shop — all modern sets will give satisfactory and quite similar results when properly adjusted. It is the aerial which really decides picture quality with a new TV — an outside aerial is nearly always essential and it must be properly adjusted. Problems such as interference lines or snowy dots are sometimes an aerial and not a receiver fault.

Radio remains a popular form of home entertainment for millions and so does the record player. But there have been drastic changes over the years. Hi-fi has become a serious hobby and the compact disc has joined the cassette tape for playing recorded music.

TV

Screen Size and Shape

A TV screen is usually measured in inches — the stated size is the distance from corner to corner of the face of the glass screen. Some modern sets have screens which are measured in centimetres, and this is not a simple conversion. The centimetre size is the distance from corner to corner of the actual picture area, which is a rather smaller space than the total glass screen.

FST (Flatter, Squarer Tube) sets are now available. The front of the tube has squarer corners than the traditional type and the face is much flatter. The makers claim that the set can be viewed from a wider angle without distortion and there is less chance of room reflections spoiling the picture. On the other hand the price is higher and some people prefer the traditional tube. FST screens are always measured in centimetres.

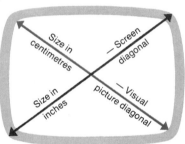

Screen size											
In inches ▷	12	14	–	16	–	20	–	22	24	26	28
In centimetres ▷	V 30	V 34	V 36	V 38	V 46	V 48	V 51	V 53	V 59	V 63	V 66

WHERE TO SIT

This recommended distance is 4 – 5 times the size of the screen

Electronic Information Services

VIDEOTEX

There are several systems, each of which offers a wide selection of pages on your TV screen. Typical subjects include news, financial information, sports results, weather forecasts and travel information. There are also subtitles of TV programmes for the deaf.

TELETEXT·

These services come to your set with the normal signal. You do not have to pay extra for the service, but a special set or adaptor is required. Pages are changed by means of a remote control unit — the number of pages is much more restricted than with Prestel.

CEEFAX

The Teletext service of BBC 1 and BBC 2.

ORACLE

The Teletext service of ITV and C 4.

VIEWDATA

These services come to your set through a cable.

PRESTEL

The Viewdata service of British Telecom. Prestel uses your telephone line and you have to pay for the service. There is a quarterly standing charge and a local call charge when in use. The call rate is increased during business hours and many pages have a viewing charge. You will need a Prestel receiver or TV adaptor. On the credit side there are hundreds of thousands of pages to choose from, and you can send messages to information providers and other users. Goods can be ordered and there are specialist services for doctors, farmers, investors etc.

Video Recorders

The video recorder (VCR) has revolutionised home entertainment. TV programmes can be recorded for later viewing, pre-recorded tapes can be hired for amusement, education or titillation and they can be used to show home-produced films.

Many models are available and you will have to choose between 2 popular systems. VHS is the standard one — Beta is less expensive but also less endowed with pre-recorded tapes. The V2000 system has never become popular, and the Video disc system failed to become a serious rival. Video 8 is a recent introduction — the tapes are about the size of an ordinary audio cassette.

Blank tapes are in various lengths, lasting for 30 minutes – 4 hours (30 minutes – 3¼ hours for Beta tapes). They can be used over and over again if the safety tab is not removed. Tapes are extremely durable but the video heads in your machine will eventually wear out. Distorted or muffled sound is the usual symptom.

Remote Control

The remote control unit is a handy gadget which allows you to change channels, increase the sound level, change the picture quality, cut off the sound ('mute') and use teletext without having to leave your armchair. Invaluable for the infirm or the idle, but it is medically unwise to sit in one position for hours on end without moving. Even if you have a remote control, stand up and stretch your legs every hour or so!

Stereo

The general introduction of stereo sets is expected to be the next step forward in television marketing, and this will mean some improvement in sound. Remember, however, that you cannot expect a true stereo effect if the speakers are set on either side of the tube. For that you would need speakers which are several feet apart.

Cable TV

Cable TV is not new — it has been used for years to distribute BBC and ITV programmes to subscribers. The recent innovation has been to extend the range of programmes to include films etc which are not available on the ordinary channels. This service is restricted to a number of urban areas.

Satellite TV

It is now possible to obtain overseas programmes via a satellite by installing a large dish aerial in the garden and by purchasing a supplementary licence. It is predicted that both dish size and cost will decrease in the next few years.

The Licence

You have to buy a TV licence each year — the fee is payable in advance and a colour licence costs about 3 times more than a black and white one. Blind people get a rebate, which is not surprising.

It is your family and not your set which is licensed. It allows your family (and its servants) to have any number of TV sets, radios and video recorders at the address on the licence or in student accommodation away from home.

It is estimated that about 1½ million households do not have a licence. Detector vans really do contain sophisticated equipment and there are more than 100,000 prosecutions each year. Evasion is, of course, nearly always a deliberate act but the complexity of the rules makes it quite easy to make an innocent mistake.

Radio

Radio Wavelengths

	Waveband	Transmission System
MHz (88, 90·2, 92·4, 94·8, 104·8)	**VHF (Very High Frequency)** Mono and stereo transmissions without interference. In some circumstances there may be a background hum on stereo — press mono button to remove it	**FM (Frequency Modulation)** The FM transmission system produces better quality music than AM, especially in the higher register. A good FM aerial is necessary
kHz (603, 630, 693, 909, 1053, 1089, 1197, 1215, 1548, 1602)	**MW (Medium Wave)** The basic waveband for most BBC and all independent stations on AM. If Radio 2 reception is poor, try the alternative wavelength	**AM (Amplitude Modulation)** The AM transmission system has the advantage of working well with a simple aerial and each station has a wide reception area. The drawbacks are interference from other stations (especially at night) and the danger of fading. There are no stereo transmissions
kHz (200)	**LW (Long Wave)** Radio 4 (LW) is a necessary alternative to Radio 4 (VHF) — it broadcasts talks/music at Schools & Open University transmission times	

Key: ☐ BBC Radio 1 ■ BBC Radio 2 ■ BBC Radio 3 ▨ BBC Radio 4 ■ BBC Local ☐ Independent Local

Hi-fi

The meaning of the word is simple — High Fidelity Sound Reproduction. A precise definition, however, is not possible. In general terms it is the reproduction of very high quality stereophonic sound by using carefully-balanced components which are more complex and powerful than those found in standard radio/cassette players.

Buying separates Hi-fi enthusiasts prefer to buy the components separately. You can then pick the most appropriate items and you are not tied to one manufacturer.

Hi-fi COMPONENTS A Hi-fi system has several components

Buying a combined unit For the non-enthusiast a Hi-fi rack or a Music Centre is a better idea — the problem of selecting compatible units is avoided.

PROGRAMME SOURCE/S

A **Radio Tuner** is required to pick up broadcast programmes. Look for an illuminated tuning aid, a mono button, LW as well as MW/VHF wavebands and pre-set tuning.

A **Record Deck** plays records. Check that the pick-up cartridge is magnetic and correct for the arm. Also look for automation (autostop and automatic arm return) and a damped cueing lever.

A **Cassette Deck** (Tape Deck) plays cassettes — look for autostop, Dolby noise reduction and a tape counter. Ordinary ferric tapes are suitable for most purposes, but for top quality sound there are chrome and the even more expensive metal tapes. Don't use these high-quality tapes unless your deck has a switch for them.

A **Compact Disc (CD) Deck** plays compact discs — the latest addition to the world of hi-fi. There are many advantages for these small shiny discs — they don't wear out, music is more life-like and playing time is for an hour or more. There is fast access to individual tracks but the discs available at the present time are limited.

AMPLIFIER

The electrical signals from the programme source are magnified for use by the loudspeakers. The difference between various brands of equal power is small — it is the power rating which is all-important. A rating of 25 watts per channel is usually quite sufficient. A graphic equaliser with all its sliders for tone adjustment looks impressive, but is not really necessary for the amateur. Combined tuner/amplifiers are available.

LOUDSPEAKERS

These are the most important components governing the quality of the sound. Do not economise here — there is a large difference between brands and you must match the power of the amplifier. Set loudspeakers at least 6 ft apart.

Services Telephone

Until quite recently the range of telephones was limited and the equipment had to be hired from the only supplier, British Telecom. Not any more. Now you can buy as well as rent, and you can choose a non-British Telecom model as long as it is approved. There are scores to choose from, ranging from round-dial traditional to electronic ultra-modern. The wiring, however, still belongs to British Telecom. There is a charge for changing the wall-mounted block terminal into a new plug-in socket for a modern phone. You can, however, buy and fit your own extension sockets.

CHOOSING A PHONE

All phones offered for sale bear a label, usually on the underside. A green circle on this label indicates that the phone has been approved by the British Approvals Board for Telecommunications. A red triangle denotes that it is prohibited. It is quite legal to sell and to buy such equipment, but British Telecom will disconnect your line if they discover that you have installed such an item.

APPROVED for use
with telecommunication systems
run by British Telecommunications
in accordance with the conditions
in the instructions for use.

PROHIBITED
from direct or indirect
connection to any telecommunication
system run by British Telecommunications. Action may be taken
against any one so connecting this
apparatus.

Phones have become very sophisticated these days. A wide selection of shapes and colours is available, and push-button dialling is now standard. There are many additional features — choose a phone which will make life easier but is no more complex than you need.

Memory store Allows you to call frequently-dialled numbers by simply pressing 1 or 2 buttons.

Last number redial Allows you to call the last number you dialled by simply pressing 1 or 2 buttons.

Volume control Allows you to increase or decrease the sound level of the ringing tone and/or the earpiece.

Visual digital display Allows you to see the time or the number you are calling. Can incorporate an alarm clock, call timer or calculator.

Big button keys Extra-large embossed keys — useful for the infirm or elderly.

One-piece unit The base unit is incorporated into the handset to produce a space-saving, all-in-one telephone.

Hands-free unit A built-in loudspeaker and microphone allows you to use your hands for note-taking etc when making phone calls.

Cordless unit The handset will make and receive calls up to 100 – 200 metres away from the base unit. Regular recharging is necessary.

Answering facility Allows you to give a pre-recorded message to callers and to record their messages to you when you are out.

Alarm facility Allows up to 4 numbers to be dialled automatically when a panic button is pressed or the infra-red sensor detects an intruder.

Mute facility Allows you to speak to others in the room without the caller hearing the conversation.

Radio facility The base unit contains a radio which is switched off when the phone is in use.

Changing your number

You can change your telephone number or you can have it deleted from directories and directory enquiries. Apply to British Telecom who will send you a form. A fee of a few pounds is payable.

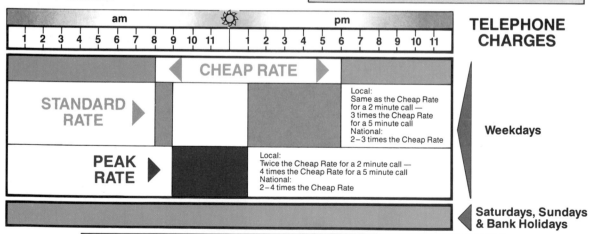

TELEPHONE CHARGES

	am		pm	
	1 2 3 4 5 6 7 8 9 10 11		1 2 3 4 5 6 7 8 9 10 11	

CHEAP RATE

STANDARD RATE ▶

Local:
Same as the Cheap Rate
for a 2 minute call —
3 times the Cheap Rate
for a 5 minute call
National:
2 – 3 times the Cheap Rate

PEAK RATE ▶

Local:
Twice the Cheap Rate for a 2 minute call —
4 times the Cheap Rate for a 5 minute call
National:
2 – 4 times the Cheap Rate

Weekdays

◀ **Saturdays, Sundays & Bank Holidays**

DEALING WITH TELEPHONE PROBLEMS

● **TELEPHONE WON'T WORK**
Dial 151 from a working phone — tell the engineer what is wrong. In most cases the fault will be repaired within 2 working days — call the Customer Service division if it is not and they will give you a line rental rebate on your next bill.

● **POOR QUALITY CALL**
You may occasionally have a crossed line, a wrong number, a noisy connection or you may be cut off for no apparent reason. Ring the operator if your call was a U.K. one — your account will be credited.

Services Post

Each working day about 40 million letters are delivered to homes and businesses throughout Britain. The standard pattern is morning and lunchtime deliveries on weekdays, single deliveries on Saturdays and no mail at all on Sundays or Bank Holidays. There are disadvantages and advantages in rural areas — here you will often find only a single delivery on a weekday but the postman may pick up letters for posting when he is making his rounds.

The vast majority of letters are sent by First Class Post when we want speedy delivery and by the cheaper Second Class Post when urgency is not a problem. But there are several other services available, and these are described below.

Occasionally something goes wrong. If a letter or parcel has been lost or damaged, obtain form P58 from the Post Office. Compensation of up to £18 may be paid if the authorities consider the claim to be a genuine one. Obviously, for valuable items this cover would be far too small and therefore such letters and small packages should be sent by Registered Post. The rules for Overseas and Parcel Post are different — see the excellent Post Office Guide (available for inspection or sale at Post Offices) for details.

POSTING A LETTER

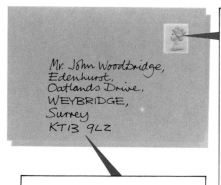

Mr. John Woodbridge,
Edenhurst,
Oatlands Drive,
WEYBRIDGE,
Surrey
KT13 9LZ

The postcode should always be the last line — do not write anything to the right or below the code. Use block capitals and leave a space between the two halves of the postcode. Do not include full stops or commas.

The purpose of the postcode is to allow mail to be electronically sorted. Unless you receive a large amount of mail the number is not exclusive to you — on average a code is shared by 15 addresses.

INLAND MAIL

First Class Post: Basic rate is for 60 gm (about 10 sheets of standard sized stationary plus envelope). No maximum weight, but packages must be less than 2 ft long. Postage can be made up of 1 or more stamps and there is no need to write 'First Class Post' on the envelope. The Post Office will give you a Certificate of Posting if requested — no charge. The aim is to deliver 90% of inland mail on the next working day after collection.

Second Class Post: Basic rate is for 60 gm. Maximum weight is 750 gm — packages must be less than 2 ft long. The Post Office will give you a Certificate of Posting if requested — no charge. The aim is to deliver 96% of inland mail by the third working day after collection.

Recorded Delivery: Extra charge on First or Second Class Post — provides proof of posting and delivery. No extra financial protection — maximum compensation for loss or damage is the same as for ordinary post. Do not use Recorded Delivery for valuables.

Registered Post: Extra charge on First Class Post — keep the Certificate in order to obtain compensation if letter or package is lost. Maximum compensation is £1,750. For an additional fee there is **Consequential Loss Insurance** — up to £10,000 for damage suffered if the letter is lost.

No Charge Post: No stamps are required for a FREEPOST address. The service is not *really* free — postage is paid by the receiver. There is also no charge for books, papers and letters posted to or by a blind person if the items are linked to the disability. A final oddity — no stamp is required to send a petition to the Queen.

Special Delivery: Extra charge on First Class Post — the fee is refunded if the letter or package is not delivered on the next working day after posting.

Datapost Sameday Delivery: Extra charge on First Class Post — the fee is refunded if the letter or package is not delivered on the same day as posting.

PACKING A PARCEL

Surround each fragile article with at least 2 in. of packing material — tissue paper, crushed newspaper or polystyrene chippings.

Seal the box along all the edges with self-adhesive tape which should be at least 1½ in. wide.

Put on the proper postage. Do not assume that Parcel Post is always cheaper than Letter Post — it costs less to send a 1 lb parcel by First Class Post than by the parcel service.

Use a stout cardboard box or a Royal Mail box which can be bought from a Post Office. For books use a padded bag. Corrugated paper, brown paper and string are acceptable for wrapping a non-fragile parcel, but a box and sealing tape are always preferable.

Address the parcel clearly. Write your own address, marked 'Sender', at right angles to the destination. Before sealing the box, include a piece of paper with your own and the destination address.

Services Refuse disposal

We collect a surprising amount of rubbish in our homes, and so regular disposal is essential. Since the War there has been a decline in the amount of ash and cinders, but the weight of refuse collected from the average household each week has risen to 30 lb.

There are several reasons for this increase. The steady rise in incomes and the much greater range of goods in the shops have meant that we buy appreciably more these days. The amount of packaging material has grown dramatically, and deposits are no longer charged on beverage bottles. In addition, one day's newspaper is often bulkier than a whole week's collection of 40 years ago.

The disposal of refuse is basically a matter of putting kitchen and other domestic waste into a suitable container for weekly collection by the local council. Many councils appeal to residents to place bottles in bottle banks (see below) and to take paper and cardboard to collection sites for recycling.

DOMESTIC WASTE

Your local council has a statutory duty to collect normal household refuse from you on a regular basis. The cleansing department may ask for your co-operation in various ways (emptying medicine bottles, excluding broken glass etc) and they have a right to impose their own set of rules.

● You must use the type of container which is specified by the council — dustbins, paper bags or polythene sacks. They also have the right to specify the number you can use — exceed the number or leave out rubbish in non-authorised containers and the council has the right to leave them or charge for their disposal. There are times when the specified number of bags or bins is not enough — you may have been spring cleaning or redecorating. Ring the cleansing department and ask them about disposal — many councils supply extra bags at no charge.

● You must leave the rubbish at the pick-up point they dictate. This may be at the back of the house or at the front of your property. It is an offence to leave it in the street.

Make sure you close the top of the container to keep out prying animals. Look in your local paper for collection arrangements close to Bank Holidays.

If you live in an isolated area your council may claim that it is not reasonable for them to have to collect your rubbish on a regular basis. The law is a little vague on the meaning of 'isolated' — appeal to the Secretary of State for the Environment.

BOTTLE BANKS

Many councils have set up bottle banks in car parks and near supermarkets. The bottle bank code includes removing tops, rinsing bottles and jars, and separating the glass into different colours. The contents of the banks are bought by glass manufacturers and so this recycling operation helps to provide funds for the council.

Public support has been good — about 100,000 tons of glass is now recycled each year. However, we lag behind several European countries — environment-conscious West Germany puts about 700,000 tons annually into its bottle banks. Switzerland tops the league — 37 lb of glass per person goes into their banks.

KITCHEN WASTE

The usual plan is to place kitchen waste (peelings, bones, scraps etc) inside a plastic liner held in a polythene bin. Moving the filled liners to the dustbin is a chore in winter and a source of flies and smells in summer. If you are remodelling your kitchen, it's a good idea to fit a waste disposal unit.

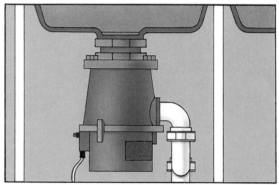

The unit fits below a sink bearing a 90 mm outlet. Waste material is ground to a slurry which is then washed down the drain. There are 2 types — the *batch feed* unit (waste has to be fed into the unit as a series of separate loads) and the more popular *continuous feed* unit (waste can be fed into the unit continually). Check that the model has reverse action and an overload cut-out.

GETTING RID OF LARGE ITEMS

Occasionally you will be faced with the problem of getting rid of a bulky item, such as an old carpet, cooker, fridge, a piece of furniture or a mattress. You must not dump it on waste land — abandoning a car carries a £100 fine. You should also refrain from burning old chairs, carpets etc — the smoke is a nuisance and some modern plastics emit poisonous fumes.

Consider whether the item would be useful to a local charity. If not, the right thing to do is either to ask the council to take the large item away for you or to transport it to the nearest household waste site. To get rid of an old car, report it to the local authority and they will send you a form to complete. Hand this over with your log book and they will take the vehicle away free of charge. Some councils will take away other large objects for nothing, but many impose a charge. Ask for a quotation before requesting the cleansing department to collect — they may not charge you if you are a senior citizen or out of work.

Your local council has a statutory duty to provide household waste sites, usually referred to as tips or dumps. Some councils impose a small fee for this use of their property, and there may be a list of items which they will not accept. Examples of restricted objects are dead animals, rubber tyres, asbestos and oil. Always break the door off a fridge or freezer before dumping.

CHAPTER 3
USING THE SERVICES

HEATING

Warmth is basic to comfort — even the most superbly furnished house is a miserable place without adequate heat in winter. This means that you are bound to have some form of basic heating, and there should be a topping-up facility for abnormally cold weather.

The vast range of heaters and heating systems is bewildering, and there is no 'right' choice for everyone. If you live in a flat and go to work all day, central heating could well be unnecessary, but for most people central heating is the correct choice. There is, of course, a high initial outlay but this is more than offset by the comfort, convenience and the opportunity to use a cheap source of fuel. So be comfortable, but not at any cost. Do read the section on Cutting Heating Bills (page 34).

Comfort levels

BATHROOM 65°F	BEDROOM 60°F For young babies it should be 70°F	BEDROOM 60°F For the elderly it *must* be above 50°F
DINING ROOM 70°F	KITCHEN 65°F	LIVING ROOM 70°F

TYPES OF HEAT

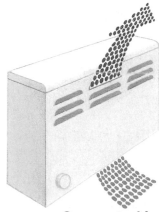

Radiant heat
Radiant heat is a form of energy which moves away (radiated) from a very hot object. The source is usually 'red' heat — glowing coals, burning wood, red-hot electric elements etc. This type of heat does not warm the air in the room — it warms objects which the rays touch. These rays move in straight lines, so the back of an object is not warmed.

There are several advantages — electric and gas radiant fires are generally less expensive than convectors and there is an instant warming effect. The fire emits a cheerful glow and you can heat just part of a room if required. But there are drawbacks — when first lit or switched on there is the well-known 'hot front, cold back' effect and there is also the hazard of a very hot heating element. This must be guarded, but even so there is a danger to furnishings and young fingers placed too close to the protective shield. In addition, effective thermostatic control is not really practical.

Despite these drawbacks the use of radiant fires remains popular. The 'hot front, cold back' effect declines or disappears after a few hours — as the objects in the room are warmed they emit convected heat and so the temperature of the air in the room rises steadily.

Convected heat
Convected heat consists of air currents which have been warmed by contact with a warm or hot object. The heated air rises upwards as it moves away from the source of heat. In convector heaters the source does not need to glow. It is generally 'black' heat — hot metal panels or tubes, hot wire filaments etc. With this type of heat it is the warm air and not direct rays which warm you.

There are several advantages — the heating elements are well guarded and the heating can be thermostatically controlled. There is all-over warmth, which means that temperature variations around the room are not large. But there are drawbacks — there is no cheerful glow and a specific area cannot be quickly warmed. In addition, the ceiling area of the room is appreciably warmer than the floor area.

The drawbacks can be overcome by using a modification of the standard convector heater. A fan-assisted convector (fan heater) will provide instant warmth as the hot air is forcibly driven into the room, and a radiant/convector heater provides visible radiant heat as well as warm air.

SOURCES OF HEAT

INDIVIDUAL ROOM HEATING: PORTABLE EQUIPMENT

A self-contained heater which warms all or part of a room and can be moved without great effort from one room to another. Portable heaters are relatively inexpensive to buy but are expensive to run, having to rely on full-rate electricity, paraffin or bottled gas. It is useful to have at least one to use when other sources of heat break down or when extra warmth is required for a short time.

INDIVIDUAL ROOM HEATING: FIXED EQUIPMENT

A self-contained heater which warms all or part of a room and is either fixed to the floor or wall, or is too cumbersome to move from room to room. Fixed heaters are generally cheaper to run than portable ones, as they can use cheaper fuels such as gas and off-peak electricity. Note carefully that some types are much more efficient than others. A back boiler can sometimes be fitted to provide hot water or partial central heating.

CENTRAL HEATING

A system which has a central heat source from which warmth is distributed to some or all of the rooms in the house. The heart of the system is generally a boiler. The source of heat in each room is a radiator or convector heater warmed by hot water or a duct emitting warm air. Gas is the most popular fuel.

FREE HEATING

A supply of heat derived from a piece of equipment which is not designed as a heater. An important factor in kitchens (cooker, refrigerator, washing machine etc) but less so in other rooms. Lights and people supply heat — up to one quarter of the total winter requirement is supplied as 'free' heat.

INDIVIDUAL ROOM HEATING: PORTABLE EQUIPMENT

ELECTRIC RADIANT FIRE

Recommended for occasional use and for heating a small area. One, 2 or 3 bars are present, each with an output of 0.6 – 1 kW. The heating effect is both visible and rapid, but thermostatic control is not possible. Heat is reduced by turning off one or more of the bars. A wire guard must be present. Even so, take care.

ELECTRIC FAN HEATER

Hot air is blown out horizontally. This is the best of the electric portables — safe, thermostatically controlled and capable of warming a large area very quickly. They are easy to carry, weighing about 6 or 7 lb, and a range of 2 kW and 3 kW models are available. Can be used without heat to cool a room in summer. Noise is the one serious drawback.

ELECTRIC CONVECTOR HEATER

Useful for providing background heat where central heating is absent or in a room where there isn't a radiator. It may take several hours for the air to warm to a satisfactory level, but there is thermostatic control, no noise and no obvious hazards. Make sure the model is not too heavy if you plan to move it from room to room.

ELECTRIC OIL-FILLED RADIATOR

Portable versions of the fixed electric radiator are available. These types are single-panelled and free-standing, and are light enough to be moved about the house. Useful for providing background heat in a normally unheated room during a cold snap. There are usually several settings plus thermostatic control.

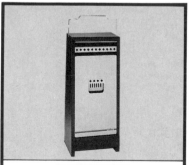

PARAFFIN STOVE

Modern versions of the old standby show several improvements, including improved efficiency and automatic cut-out if it falls over. But all the major drawbacks remain — smell, need for regular refuelling, lack of thermostatic control and troublesome condensation in the absence of adequate ventilation. Still, a life-saver during a power cut.

LPG HEATER

LPG (bottled gas) heaters produce both radiant and convected warmth — no chimney is needed and large areas can be quickly warmed. But there are drawbacks — lack of thermostatic control and troublesome condensation in the absence of adequate ventilation. Cylinders have to be replaced regularly. Still, efficiency is equal to natural gas.

INDIVIDUAL ROOM HEATING: FIXED EQUIPMENT

ELECTRIC RADIANT FIRE

There are types for mounting on the wall or standing in the fireplace. Some are quite plain, consisting of 2 or 3 heating bars like the standard portable model, but you can buy radiant/convector types which emit heated air into the room, and there are also artificial coal and artificial log models.

ELECTRIC STORAGE HEATER

The most economical electric heater. It is programmed to use cheap-rate electricity at night — the heat stored in the solid brick core is then released during the day. One of the problems has been the danger of the heat being exhausted by the end of the day — modern models have a booster control.

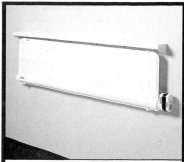

ELECTRIC OIL-FILLED RADIATOR

The large panels or tubes contain oil which is heated by the electric elements contained within. Floor-standing and wall models are available — the heating action is identical to a water-filled radiator in a central heating system. The room is warmed slowly and evenly. Expensive — full-rate electricity is used.

ELECTRIC UNDERFLOOR HEATER

The underground version of the electric storage heater. Uses cheap-rate electricity at night — the stored heat is released during the day through elements buried in the concrete floor. Obviously this form of heating can only be installed when the house is being built. Not very popular despite the even distribution of heat all round the room.

GAS RADIANT FIRE

The traditional type of gas fire bears a series of elements which glow when heated by a series of gas jets. There is rapid visible warmth, but it is better to buy a radiant/convector heater which warms the air as well as the objects in front of it. There are glass-fronted models with heating elements in the form of 'logs' or 'coals'.

GAS CONVECTOR HEATER

It is slightly more efficient to turn gas energy into convected rather than radiant heat, but a gas convector lacks a cheery glow. There are no hot elements to guard against and so the convector heater is the closest gas-fired equivalent to a standard radiator in the absence of central heating. Buy a thermostatically-controlled model.

GAS LOG-EFFECT FIRE

There are now gas fires which produce real flames above a bed of artificial logs or glowing coals — the cheeriness of a 'real' fire without the mess and trouble of coal or wood. There is a major drawback — such fires are thermally inefficient as most of the heat goes up the chimney. They are also a hazard like any other open fire.

SOLID FUEL OPEN FIRE

In the past this was the *only* type of heater, and even today it is regarded by many people as an essential domestic feature. Guard against the dangers of flying sparks and naked flames. There are several modern improvements — throat restriction, fan assistance and underfloor ventilation. The chores of refuelling and regular cleaning remain.

SOLID FUEL ROOM HEATER

An improvement on the open fire — the room heater is both safer and more efficient but partly hides the 'real' fire effect. The heat passes into the room through glass doors — buy one which needs refuelling only once a day, bears convector grilles and has a damper which automatically closes down when the burning rate is too high.

CENTRAL HEATING

Putting in central heating is not cheap — mistakes in design or installation can be frustrating and costly. DIY central heating is possible, but never undertake such a venture unless you have already tackled several large-scale plumbing jobs. For nearly everyone it is much better to employ a qualified heating engineer. It will be up to you to decide which fuel to use and the number of rooms to be heated — it will be up to him to recommend a suitable system and its components. The size of the boiler will depend on the number of radiators required, and it is most unwise to skimp at this stage. It really isn't worthwhile installing a system for just 2 or 3 radiators.

The installer will quote for a standard layout and may also recommend several optional extras such as thermostatic radiator valves, convectors and independently controlled hot water and heating systems. Make sure you understand what is being offered before saying yes or no.

WET SYSTEM
Water is heated in a boiler and then circulated through pipework to the heaters, which are radiators or convectors. Here the water loses some of its heat and returns to the boiler for reheating

DRY SYSTEM
Much less popular than the Wet system. Heated air is blown from the boiler through ducts into the rooms. This system is installed when the house is being built and has several drawbacks, such as noise and grime around the ducts

GRAVITY FLOW
Rarely used nowadays. The flow is created by the natural tendency of hot water to rise and for cold water to fall. Large bore pipes are needed

PUMPED FLOW
The standard domestic system. A pump is used to send the water around the pipework and through the radiators. Small or micro-bore pipes are used

OPEN VENTED TYPE
The standard U.K. type of Wet system. There is a feed-and-expansion cistern which keeps the water topped up if there is evaporation. It also allows steam and excess water to escape

SEALED TYPE
Popular in the U.S. and on the Continent — not often used in the U.K. A closed expansion vessel takes the place of the feed-and-expansion cistern. Not all boilers and radiators are suitable

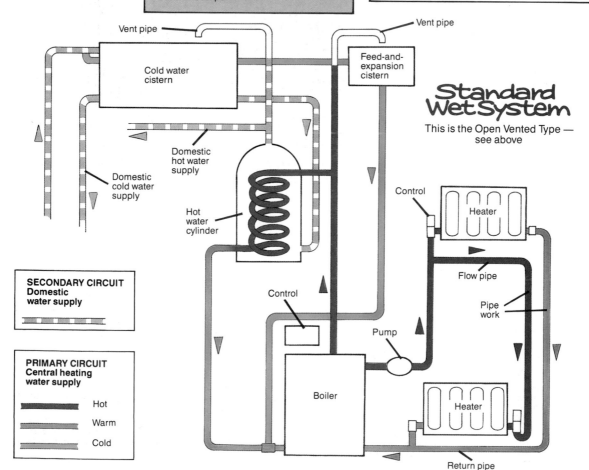

Standard Wet System

This is the Open Vented Type — see above

Vent pipe

Vent pipe

Cold water cistern

Feed-and-expansion cistern

Domestic hot water supply

Domestic cold water supply

Hot water cylinder

Control

Heater

Flow pipe

Pipe work

Control

Pump

Control

Boiler

Heater

Return pipe

SECONDARY CIRCUIT
Domestic water supply

PRIMARY CIRCUIT
Central heating water supply

Hot

Warm

Cold

BASIC COMPONENTS

BOILER   The centre of the system — it produces the heat

The boiler should be large enough to provide the desired level of warmth in the rooms to be heated when the outside temperature is 30°F. If it is too small it will not warm the rooms sufficiently in mid winter. If it is too large it will be inefficient — boilers need to run at near full capacity.

There are a number of decisions to make. First of all, the fuel to use. The usual choice is between oil and gas, and most people these days pick gas — it is cheap, clean, requires no storage and can be accurately controlled. Even within a single fuel type there may be a wide choice of models — free-standing boilers, wall-mounted boilers and back boilers for placing behind a fire or heater. Correct siting calls for a strong floor, easy access for servicing and adequate ventilation if the fuel is gas, oil or coal.

Electric Economy 7 boiler   Water is heated in a large tank during the night and pumped round the system during the following day. The drawback is the large size of the tank.

Gas boiler   Choose carefully. There are types which can be fitted to a conventional chimney and there are balanced flue models — see page 20. There are wall-mounted types in a variety of colours and there are types which can be fitted into the wall. The most efficient one is the condensing gas boiler. Bottled-gas boilers are available.

Oil boiler   There are both floor-standing and wall-mounted models. The most popular type in use remains the Wallflame in which oil is fed into a circular burner. The modern pressure jet, however, is both quieter and more compact.

Solid fuel boiler   There have been improvements — the hopper-fed boiler needs refuelling only once or twice a day and the boilers fitted with combustion air fans can give a degree of heat control which was quite impossible with simple, hand-fed boilers.

PUMP   The heart of the system — it circulates the water round the pipes

It was the development of the near-silent and highly efficient pump which allowed the change-over from the gravity system to the pump system. This meant that during the 1950s domestic central heating using small bore pipes became a truly practical proposition.

At first the pump was connected only to the primary circuit which supplied the radiators — the domestic hot water system (secondary circuit) relied on gravity. Nowadays the pump usually moves the water in both circuits.

HEATERS   The purpose of the system — they supply warmth in the rooms

The old cast iron, heavy radiator is a thing of the past — the modern standard heater is the steel panel radiator. Its surface is usually corrugated to increase the efficiency and there may be 1, 2 or 3 panels on each radiator. The convector radiator has a series of fins. Site a radiator under a window whenever possible. Do not cover with curtains at night. A shelf above a radiator deflects heat into the room and prevents unsightly wall stains.

The word 'radiator' is misleading — most of the heat is convected and not radiated (see page 29). You can buy convector heaters where all the warmth is obtained by convection. A fan-assisted model allows you to warm a room very quickly. A skirting-board model allows you to reduce draughts and improve the evenness of the heat around the room.

CONTROLS   The brains of the system — they make it do what you want

The purpose of controls is to allow the system to go on and off automatically at pre-set times and to maintain the desired air temperature in the heated rooms. Timers and programmers come in all shapes and sizes — their job is to switch the system on and off. The simplest just switches off the heating circuit at a desired time and then switches it on as required in a 24 hour cycle. The sophisticated ones have independent controls for heating and domestic hot water and have a wide range of settings. Make sure that you instal a programmer which has an override switch.

Thermostats switch off part or all of the system when a desired temperature is reached and not at a pre-set time. The boiler thermostat stops the water leaving at an undesirably high temperature — it also ensures that the return water is not too cool as this can lead to corrosion. A room thermostat in the living room switches off the system when the required temperature is reached. This can mean that other rooms may be too hot or too cold — it is better to have a thermostatic radiator valve (TRV) fitted to each heater. A frost thermostat is installed outside the house and switches on the system when the temperature falls below zero. This control is not necessary unless you plan to leave the house unoccupied for a long time in winter.

PIPEWORK   The veins and arteries of the system — they transport the water

In the standard system small bore pipe is used — this is mainly 15 mm tubing with one or more runs of 22 mm tubing. Mild steel is inexpensive, but copper is preferable as it is less likely to corrode. In this standard system there is the two-pipe circuit — one set of pipes taking the hot water to the radiators and another set returning it to the boiler.

Nowadays you can buy microbore pipe — 8 mm, 10 mm or 12 mm. The advantages are obvious — the piping can be bent and pushed between joists like electric cable. But there are drawbacks — it needs to be joined very carefully and blockages can occur. Installing microbore central heating is definitely a job for the professional.

AVOIDING CENTRAL HEATING PROBLEMS

● BLEED RADIATORS TWICE A YEAR

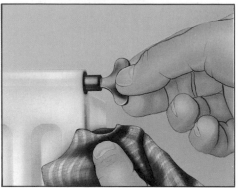

It is inevitable that some air will get into the system, and it is essential for it to be removed. A small amount of air will move into one of the radiators and cause it to be cool at the top — a large amount can seriously restrict the flow of water and so cut off heat to several radiators. Even worse, air will encourage corrosion and the by-products are hydrogen gas and rust in the radiators and black sludge throughout the system. Remove air and gas from the radiators as a matter of routine. Switch down the thermostat. Insert the radiator key into the valve nut and turn anti-clockwise. Hold a cloth under the key and close the valve as soon as water starts to escape. A hissing sound before this stage indicates that air was present. If a radiator feels cold at the top or if there is a gurgling sound within, bleed it immediately and don't wait for the routine treatment.

● SET THE THERMOSTATS & TIMERS CORRECTLY

There is no point in wasting heat when you are not around but it is often false economy to switch the system off on cold nights. It usually saves fuel in the long run to keep the house at a minimum of 50°F, and this means running the system with the thermostats at a low setting during mid winter nights. Make sure the boiler thermostat is at the setting recommended in the instruction book — the boiler will be damaged if the return water is too cool.

● OPERATE THE PUMP IN SUMMER

It is the pump and not the boiler which is the weakest part of the system. If not in use during the summer, run the pump for a few minutes at least once a month. Failure to do so can result in a build-up of sludge which may cause it to cease to operate.

● HAVE THE SYSTEM SERVICED REGULARLY

Never wait for trouble to occur before calling in a heating engineer. Have a regular service contract with a firm you can trust and this will give you the protection of a detailed examination plus any necessary repair work at least once a year. Of course, if something goes seriously wrong then you will have to ask for help immediately. Dangers to watch for are serious overheating accompanied by loud knocking or a hissing sound, and also water leaking from pipes or valves. In the case of a leaking radiator joint, try to tighten the nuts with 2 spanners before calling for help.

● USE A CORROSION INHIBITOR

If sludge and rust are present in the pipes and radiators it will be necessary to drain the system by opening the lowest draincock in the system. The system is then flushed with water until all the deposit has gone and the water from the draincock runs clear. This work can be done by the DIY enthusiast quite simply or it can be left to the service engineer on his next call. In either case make sure that a proprietary corrosion inhibitor is added to the feed-and-expansion cistern when it is refilled.

Cutting heating bills

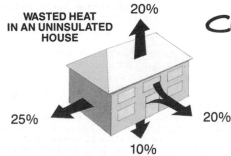

WASTED HEAT IN AN UNINSULATED HOUSE

20%
25%
20%
10%

Expenditure on fuel is a major item in your household budget, and most of the money goes in heating the air and water. Sadly you only receive the benefit of part of the energy you pay for — most of the heat is lost through walls, doors, roof etc. In a poorly insulated house about three-quarters of the heat is wasted in this way. This loss is not inevitable — according to the Energy Efficiency Office it is possible to halve the cost of heating — to do this you must carry out measures which either reduce heat loss or increase the efficiency of the fuel you use.

FUEL-SAVING MEASURE	TYPE OF SAVING	DETAILS	VALUE FOR MONEY SPENT
DRAUGHT PROOFING	More heat retained	See page 137	★ ★ ★
HOT WATER CYLINDER & LOFT INSULATION	More heat retained	See pages 10 and 137	★ ★ ★
CAVITY WALL INSULATION	More heat retained	See page 137	★ ★
DOUBLE GLAZING	More heat retained	See page 74	★
IMPROVED HEAT CONTROL & USE	Less fuel used	Set thermostats no higher than necessary — turning the setting down by 3°F can cut the fuel bill by 10%. Set the hot water cylinder thermostat at 140°F. Fit foil behind radiators. Draw curtains at night. Make sure that the heating system and the hot water system can be controlled separately. Fit time switches on room heaters if area is used for only part of the day	★ ★ ★ ★
BETTER BUYING OF FUEL	Less money spent	Use Economy 7 instead of full-rate electricity whenever possible. Compare prices from different oil and solid fuel suppliers — keep watch for off-season special offers	★ ★ ★ ★

★ ★ ★ ★ Most value
★ Least value

LIGHTING

Lighting can do much more than enable you to see at night. When properly used it will dramatically improve the appearance of the room as well as being able to provide a decorative feature in its own right. In addition, lighting can be used to deter burglars and to reduce the risk of home accidents by illuminating stairs and other danger spots.

Unfortunately most homeowners use lighting in a purely practical way and the average home has about 15 fittings. This is less than half the recommended number for a properly-lit house, and far too often the sole source of illumination in a room is a single pendant fitting hanging from the ceiling.

Much time and effort may be spent in choosing an attractive shade for this lamp but even if you pick a sparkling chandelier the light around the room will be uninteresting. The idea of multi-point lighting is to enhance the beauty of attractive features and to consign uninteresting parts of the room to the shadows.

There are three different types of illumination produced by light fittings. First of all, there is **diffuse illumination** which spreads upwards, sideways and downwards in an even fashion. Such fittings (paper lamp shades, fluorescent tubes etc) are used to produce general lighting in a room. At the other extreme there is **directional illumination** which is a wide or narrow beam of light. A spotlight is the classical example and such sources of illumination are used for all sorts of dramatic lighting schemes. The standard lamp shade is an example of the third type of light source — **semi-directional illumination**. Most of the light is directed downwards but some spreads outwards and upwards.

TYPES OF LIGHTING

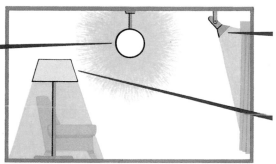

GENERAL LIGHTING illuminates the room — it is sometimes called background lighting. Aim for 20 watts per sq.yd of floor with tungsten lamps, 10 watts per sq.yd with fluorescent lamps

EFFECT LIGHTING illuminates a particular area for decorative purposes (e.g spotlight over curtains). Best combined with General lighting

SPECIFIC LIGHTING illuminates a particular area for practical purposes (e.g standard light by armchair). Best combined with General lighting

USING LIGHTING PROPERLY

- Begin outside the house. Bright lighting at the front and back doors will increase security against burglars and will provide a welcome to visitors. A timer or body-detector switch is useful.

- The hall needs warm but not over-bright general lighting. Remove dark shadows from stairs with carefully placed directional illumination. The rules for the kitchen are quite different — here you require strong general lighting. Choose diffuser-covered fluorescent tubes, downlighters (see page 37) or a ceiling made of illuminated panels. Miniature fluorescent tubes are effective when placed under wall units to light up the work surfaces below.

- The standard light fitting for the dining room is a rise-and-fall pendant over the table — for maximum effect instal a dimmer switch. The living room needs more care in design and a greater variety of lighting than other areas. First of all there should be a source of general lighting operated from a switch close to the door. Pendant lights and wall lights are suitable for this purpose. You will also need specific lighting for reading, watching TV etc plus effect lighting to add interest to curtains, pictures, house plants etc. Ideally you should be able to change the room by flicking a few switches from a brightly-lit practical area to a cosy and intimate room lit by pools of light and illuminated objects.

- Bathrooms need a safe source of general lighting — a closed ceiling-mounted fitting is the usual choice. Illumination is needed for the shaving/make-up mirror — make sure that the light shines on your face and not on the glass. Switches within the room must be of the pullcord type. Bedroom lighting is very much a matter of personal taste. Bedside lamps are essential if you read in bed — choose a narrow spotlight if your partner is not to be disturbed. Some general and dressing table lighting is required — use dimmer switch control.

- The light requirement depends on the colour and shininess of the surface to be illuminated. A dark wall may require 4 times the wattage of a light one to produce adequate brightness.

- Use fluorescent lighting with care. It is excellent for kitchens and some other areas, but the light tends to be 'cold'. Choose de-luxe warm white lamps.

- To make a high ceiling look lower, direct the light downwards. Use downlighters or a shade on a pendant light which permits little or no light to shine upwards.

- To make a low ceiling look higher, direct the light upwards. Use a pendant shade which diffuses the light or employ wall lights which shine upwards as well as downwards. Avoid placing pendant lights in the line of traffic if there is a chance of bumping your head.

- To make a narrow room look wider, direct spotlights on the shorter walls.

BULBS & TUBES

TYPE OF LAMP	DETAILS	EXAMPLES	NOTES
TUNGSTEN BULB Other names — Filament bulb, Incandescent bulb The thin metal filament within the bulb is heated by the current and glows brightly	**General Lighting Service (GLS).** By far the most popular form of electric lamp — pear-shaped, clear or pearl with a Bayonet cap and a range of outputs from 8 to 150 W. There are many variations. The white mushroom is better than the pear type for shallow light fittings. Shapes and types include pygmy, candle, globe and flickering flame		Life expectancy: Standard bulb 1000 hours Long-life bulb 2000 hours Bulb choice: 8 – 10 W Night light 40 – 60 W Bedside light 60 W Wall light 60 – 150 W Pendant light 75 – 100 W Table lamp 100 – 150 W Standard lamp Output: Long-life bulbs give 10% less light and coiled-coil bulbs give 15% more light than standard single-coil bulbs
	Crown Silvered (CS). The front of the bulb is silvered so that the light is reflected backwards to the reflector which then produces an intense narrow beam. The bulb to use if you want to light up a single object		A special spotlight fitting with a dish reflector is essential for use with this bulb. Usual cap is an Edison screw — Bayonet cap type is available in some sizes 40 – 100 W
	Internal Silvered Lamp (ISL) is the standard medium and wide beam bulb for indoor use — Bayonet cap and Edison screw cap are available. There is also the much more robust **Parabolic Aluminised Reflector (PAR 38)** made in toughened glass for both indoor and outdoor use		The glass front of the spotlight is clear — the rest is silvered to produce the beam ISL: 25 – 100 W PAR 38: 60 – 120 W No special type of fitting is required — these bulbs have their own built-in reflector
ARCHITECTURAL TUBE Other name — Strip light	An inexpensive alternative to the fluorescent tube for attaching to furniture and for picture lighting, but not where heat can be a problem		Available with Bayonet cap, Peg cap and Double cap fittings
FLUORESCENT TUBE The particles which coat the inside of the tube glow brightly (fluoresce) when the current is switched on	Available in various lengths (1½ – 8 ft) and 2 diameters (1 or 1½ in.). Miniature fluorescent tubes are ½ – 1¾ ft long and ⅝ in. diameter. Usual fitting is the Bi-pin type. An adaptor is available to allow use in a BC lamp holder. Several colour types are available — choose with care. Circular as well as straight tubes are available		Life expectancy: 6000 – 7000 hours Fluorescent lamps are cheaper to run than Tungsten ones, but only if they are not switched on and off at frequent intervals Failure to light — Firmly push starter into fitting. If it still fails, replace starter Light shimmering or dull — Change tube
ENERGY-SAVING BULB	The SL bulb is cylindrical, somewhat like an ordinary bulb. The 2 D bulb is quite different — it is tubular and requires an adaptor. Cool — a high intensity bulb can be used in a low-wattage fitting		Expensive — but they are cheaper in the long run These bulbs last 5 times longer than an ordinary Tungsten bulb, and only ¼ of the electricity is required

CAPS

Bayonet cap (BC)
The standard U.K. cap for Tungsten lamps. Pushed into holder and then turned. Small version (SBC) available

Edison screw (ES)
The standard U.S. & Continental cap for Tungsten lamps. Screwed into holder. Small version (SES) available

Bi-pin
The standard cap for Fluorescent lamps. Pushed into holder

Double cap
A fitting for Architectural tubes. Pushed into holder

Peg cap
A fitting for Architectural tubes. Pushed into holder

LIGHTING AROUND THE ROOM

CEILING-MOUNTED LIGHTING The fitting containing the holder for the lamp or bulb is attached to the ceiling. This type of light fitting is popular both in kitchens and bathrooms, and is also used where lack of height would make a pendant fitting a source of danger. The standard fluorescent tube fitting belongs here — so do the plastic and glass milky globes for tungsten bulbs. Ceiling-mounted lights tend to be utilitarian rather than highly decorative, but they still have a vital part to play in the lighting scene.

SPOTLIGHTING The fitting containing the bulb holder can be turned so that the beam produced is directed on to an object or area as required. The width of the beam depends on the fitting and the bulb — use a CS bulb for a narrow intense beam or an ISL or PAR 38 bulb for a medium or wide beam. Spotlights are made in various colours and styles, and a spotlight cluster can be used to replace a central pendant light fitting.

PENDANT LIGHTING The fitting containing the bulb holder is separated from the ceiling attachment by flex or a tube containing flex. The simplest form is a glass, plastic, fabric or paper shade covering a tungsten bulb — the illumination is diffuse and in most houses pendant fittings provide the basic source of general lighting. The range is enormous. There may be one or several bulb holders attached to the flex — styles vary from Tudor to Futuristic. Rise-and-fall types are useful for siting over tables and multiflexed models with lights at different heights are attractive in stairwells.

DOWNLIGHTING The fitting is fully recessed, partly recessed or mounted on to the ceiling, all of the light being directed downwards. Reflector lights of the ISL type or ordinary tungsten bulbs are used — the most versatile lamp is the eyeball spot which can be moved like a spotlight to illuminate a particular object or area. A series of downlights provide an effective means of general lighting in a modern setting. However, a dimmer switch and some additional form of lighting are essential in a living room.

TRACK LIGHTING The fitting consists of a metal or plastic channel which is screwed on to the ceiling or wall. Flex is carried within this channel and several spotlights are plugged into the track. The spotlights can produce beams of different colours and widths or can be used with ordinary bulbs so that a great deal of variety can be produced in the lighting scheme. Track lighting is useful in the kitchen to illuminate various surfaces and in the modern living room to add dramatic touches. Two warnings — do not fit track lighting in the bathroom and always angle spotlights away from direct view.

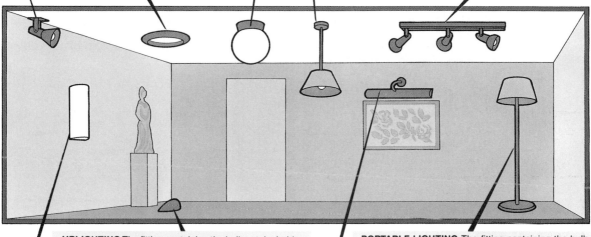

UPLIGHTING The fitting containing the bulb or tube holder is set on the floor or wall and all of the light is directed upwards. Uplighting is not commonly used, but the effect can be extremely dramatic. An uplight set at the base of an object such as a statuette or a specimen house plant will bring the details of the object into sharp relief — alter the angle and position of the light for maximum effect. Place the uplight behind the object for a quite different effect — the figure or plant is now seen in silhouette against a halo of light.

PORTABLE LIGHTING The fitting containing the bulb or tube holder is not attached to any surface and can be moved from place to place. Table and floor-standing (standard) lamps are the most popular examples — the illumination may be diffuse or directional. Models range from plain to highly ornate, and you should certainly think about a piece of furniture and not just a source of light when making your choice. The bulb in a table lamp should be about 3 ft above the ground and the light for reading should come from over your left shoulder if you are right handed.

WALL LIGHTING The fitting is attached to the wall and can be used in a surprisingly large number of ways. The usual approach is to attach bracket fixtures to produce diffuse or semi-directional illumination. Instead of following the traditional pattern you can fix individual spotlights or track lighting, or you can instal fittings which bathe the wall in light — a technique known as wallwashing.

STRIP LIGHTING The fitting containing the tube holder is attached to a suitable surface so that the light is directed as required. Fluorescent or tungsten tubes can be used — examples of strip lighting are picture lights, cupboard lights, lights inside pelmets and above kitchen work surfaces and lights within living room wall units. Purely functional and with no decorative value when switched off, strip lighting can be extremely effective when switched on.

SWITCHES

TYPE OF SWITCH	MODE OF OPERATION
STANDARD SWITCH	Move small bar (dolly switch) or rocker (rocker switch)
PULLCORD SWITCH	Pull cord — essential for bathroom lighting
TOUCH SWITCH	Touch switch plate — easier to operate than standard type
REMOTE CONTROL SWITCH	Press button on infra-red battery-powered unit
DIMMER SWITCH	Turn knob to dim lights for nursery, watching TV etc
LIGHT-SENSITIVE SWITCH	Expose to light — turns on at dusk and off at dawn
HEAT-SENSITIVE SWITCH	Approach fitting — body heat turns on light
TIMER SWITCH	Set times on switch for on/off cycle
DOOR SWITCH	Open door for on — close door for off

COOKING

Some people believe that the advent of television has killed the art of conversation and has reduced the interest in reading. But it has done nothing to diminish the joy of cooking — cookery books still feature strongly in the bestseller lists and today's home cook is much more adventurous than her (or his) counterpart before the war.

There has been a flood of new cooker models and other food-preparation equipment in recent years. If you plan to instal a new cooker or buy a new pan don't buy the first one you see in the showroom on the basis that "they must all be the same". They are not — this section will highlight the basic differences and you should always collect a number of leaflets before making your final choice.

The first step is to decide on the type of fuel, and the choice is nearly always between gas and electricity. **Electric** cookers are a little more expensive to run but they provide clean heat and the distribution of this heat in the oven is often thought to be superior to the gas version. On the other hand **gas** cookers have hobs with burners which respond immediately to the turn of a switch. For many the ideal would be an electric oven with a gas hob, and these days you can have this arrangement.

The traditional advantages and disadvantages of the two basic fuels have begun to disappear. Fan-assisted gas ovens have evenly-distributed heat — electric halogen hobs have instant controlability. So forget your prejudices and look at the leaflets.

In yesterday's kitchen there was the *conventional* free-standing cooker, but these days there is a wider selection. *Built-in* hobs and ovens can be sited together or separated (split-level) to give a fully fitted look to the kitchen. Alternatively you can buy a *built-under* oven to fit below a work surface. Finally you can instal a *slot-in* cooker which is a conventional-style model which is made with the width, depth and height of standard kitchen units.

Gas and electricity do not exhaust the fuel types — the solid fuel heater/cooker still remains and many people use bottled gas cookers where natural gas is not available.

CHOOSING A COOKER

Grill
Is it in the right position? The grill may be at eye or waist level — if you choose an eye-level one, make sure that you can see the contents of the grill pan without having to take it out. **Is the grill in the oven?** This is the standard arrangement in many cookers, but it does mean that you cannot use the oven when grilling. A separate grill chamber is desirable. **Is there a safety stop on the grill pan?** A useful safety measure, especially if there are children in the house. **Is there dual control?** A knob to allow you to use just half the grill is a money saver.

Hob
Are the rings or burners efficient? The advent of dual circuit rings, reflector plates and halogen hobs have improved the efficiency of electric hobs, but they have also added to the cost. **Is the hob easy to clean?** Radiant rings can be a problem — make sure that spillage bowls can be readily removed for cleaning. The ceramic hob is the ideal — just wipe the top like any other work surface. With gas cookers look for sealed burners. **Is there a lid?** Many cookers now have a hob lid — an extra work surface when not in use.

CONVENTIONAL COOKER
Wide range available. Economical — no extra fitting is required. The standard floor-standing cooker.

BUILT-UNDER OVEN
Most useful where space is limited — the oven slides under a standard worktop.

BUILT-IN COOKER
No dust traps behind the cooker. Smart in appearance, but there is the extra cost plus housing and fitting.

Controls
Do I need all the knobs and dials? Many clever automated features are now available — meat probes to switch off the current at a pre-set temperature, thermostatically controlled rings and burners, variable heat programmers for roasting, and so on. But all these aids add to the cost — don't pay for more than you need. A clock and timer are generally part of the standard equipment on a modern cooker — an autotimer which switches itself on and then off again at pre-set times is useful if you work during the day or want to use Economy 7 electricity at night.

Oven
Is it at the right height? Most of us are used to stooping down to reach the oven, but an eye-level model is a great boon for the not-so-young. **Can you see inside?** It is most useful to have a glass door and a strong light within — opening the door to see the food is no way to bake a cake. **Are there two ovens?** It is often very handy to have a small oven as well as the standard family-sized one. **Is it fan-assisted?** This modern innovation is a great boon for the keen cook — see page 39. **Is it self-cleaning?** The cookers now on sale are usually fitted with stay-clean linings.

SLOT-IN COOKER
Perhaps the best of both worlds for many — a free-standing model which fits between kitchen units for a fully fitted look.

THE ELECTRIC COOKER

Hobs

Radiant Ring The most popular type of boiling ring. The heating element is encased in a metal sheath and there is rapid heating up and cooling down. The major drawback is the amount of work necessary to clean up spillages.

Sealed Disc A flat circle of metal sealed into a hole in the hob. It takes longer to heat up and cool down than a radiant ring but it takes less time to clean. Thermostatically controlled versions are available in place of the usual simmerstat.

Ceramic Hob A major advance in cooker design — the hob is a smooth sheet of heat-resisting glass below which are installed the boiling rings. Their position is marked by etched designs which glow when in use. Attractive but also practical — the heat control is extremely precise and cleaning after use merely calls for a rub-down with a cloth. The hob can serve as a work surface when the rings are switched off. With ceramic hobs use pans which have machine-ground bases.

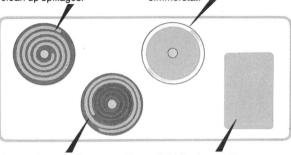

Dual Circuit Radiant Ring Frequently found in modern hobs — an energy-saving advance on the ordinary radiant ring. Heating can be restricted to the centre of the ring if a small pan is being used. The basic advantage and disadvantage of the radiant ring remain.

Griddle A useful but uncommon feature of the electric hob — a large rectangular metal plate which is controlled and fitted like a sealed disc. Some foods, such as hamburgers and griddle cakes, can be cooked directly on its surface.

Magnetic Induction Hob An advance in ceramic hob design, but without any important benefit. Instead of having to switch on or switch off with a knob, you merely lift the metal pan on or off the ceramic hob surface. Useful for forgetful people, perhaps.

Halogen Ring An advance in ceramic hob design with an important benefit. The standard boiling ring element below the glass surface is replaced by a tungsten halogen lamp. As with gas, heating response to the control knob is instantaneous.

Ovens

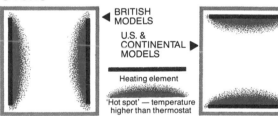

◄ BRITISH MODELS

U.S. & CONTINENTAL MODELS ►

Heating element

'Hot spot' — temperature higher than thermostat

◄ **FAN OVENS**
In a **fan-assisted oven** there is a fan at the back of the oven which circulates the hot air. There are all sorts of advantages — the oven heats up more quickly, you don't have to position food on shelves with care to avoid 'hot spots', food is cooked rather more quickly and a slightly lower temperature is needed than with a conventional oven. An excellent buy. A further advance is the **fan-ducted oven** — more expensive and much less common. Here there is a central heating element and the fan drives the hot air to the oven cavity through ducts.

Nearly all modern ovens are self-cleaning although it may still be necessary to clean the bottom plate and racks. The basic cleaning system is the **catalytic surface** — an occasional wipe-over is all that is needed. The **pyrolytic surface** is more expensive and much less popular. Deposits are burnt off at a very high temperature.

A rotating motor-driven spit is incorporated in some cookers where the grill is situated at the top of the oven. A rotating shaft and holding forks are turned by an electric motor — joints, poultry and kebabs can be cooked. This indoor barbecue method is thought to give a moister result with an attractively crisp exterior.

THE GAS COOKER

Cooking by gas maintains its lead — there are more gas cookers than electric ones. The instant response to turning up or turning down the boiling ring control knob is perhaps the main attraction, but gas is also slightly cheaper to use than electricity.

The modern gas cooker bears little similarity to the robust spartan models of 20 years ago. **Ignition:** The match or spark-maker has gone — choose between automatic ignition (flame appears when the gas-supply knob is turned) or semi-automatic ignition (flame appears when ignition button is pressed). **Hob:** Consider a lidded model which provides an extra work surface. Have one burner which is thermostatically controlled. **Grill:** Eye-level grills are more popular on gas cookers than electric ones. Some models allow you to choose between full-grill and half-grill operation. **Oven:** In the traditional gas oven the upper part is slightly hotter and the bottom slightly cooler than the regulo setting. The new fan-assisted gas ovens have even heat distribution throughout the oven and most models these days have self-cleaning linings. Ovens fitted with a rôtisserie are available.

Oven temperature

°F	°C equivalent	GAS MARK	DESCRIPTION	
225	105	¼	VERY SLOW	
250	120	½		
275	135	1	SLOW	
300	150	2		
325	165	3	MODERATE	
350	175	4		
375	190	5	MODERATELY HOT	
400	205	6		
425	220	7	HOT	
450	230	8		
475	245	9	VERY HOT	

THE PLUG-IN COOKER

MULTI-COOKER
An excellent piece of equipment where space is limited and the cooking need is small — alternatively it can be used as an extra cooker in a large household. The base looks like a frying pan — use it for frying by removing the lid. Put the lid back on for roasting, steaming or braising — the temperature is thermostatically controlled.

CONTACT GRILL
The food (bacon, steaks, chops, sausages etc) is held between 2 aluminium plates. Grilling takes place when the current is switched on, and there are advantages compared with ordinary grilling. Both sides are cooked at the same time and the surface is rapidly sealed by infra-red heat. Meat can go directly from freezer to grill.

SANDWICH MAKER
A popular adaptation of the contact grill. The non-stick aluminium plates are patterned to decorate and cut the sandwiches, and the edges of the plates are flanged in order to seal the sides of the bread. All sorts of fillings can be used to make toasted sandwiches — remember to butter the bread on the outside.

DEEP FAT FRYER
Despite all the appeals to cut down on fatty food consumption your family may be addicted to chips, fried fish, fried chicken etc. If so, the best way to ensure crispy food with a minimum of inner grease is to use a deep fat fryer. The secret is the depth of oil and the constant temperature maintained by the thermostat.

MICROWAVE OVEN

Advantages Microwave ovens have many advantages compared with standard types, but one feature dominates all the others — speed of cooking. Food from the freezer can be defrosted in a few minutes. A meal can be reheated without fear of drying out in about 4 minutes and as a general rule it takes about one quarter of the normal time to cook by the microwave method.

Linked with speed is the saving in electricity. Cooking smells are virtually eliminated and water-soluble vitamins are preserved.

Food can be cooked in serving dishes, which saves washing up, and the chore of oven cleaning is greatly reduced. Finally, the outside walls of the oven and the dishes inside remain quite cool — this lack of heating up makes cooking by children and handicapped people a much safer proposition and the kitchen a less oppressive place during a heatwave.

Disadvantages Ordinary microwave ovens do not brown food, but this drawback has been tackled in several ways. There are now browning dishes for hamburgers, sausages etc and in expensive models you will find browning elements for roasts. Lack of crispness can also be a problem if some form of grilling is not used as an after-treatment.

Uneven cooking is another problem with cheaper microwave ovens. Turning the food at regular intervals during cooking is a tiresome task — buy a model with some form of microwave distribution (see 'How it works' section).

Microwave ovens are not a health hazard. There is no chance of being affected by the waves if the door is opened accidentally — there is always an automatic cut-off. It is recommended that you should get the oven checked for leaks every 12 months, although problems are rare. There is one uncommon problem — some types of heart pacemaker are affected.

Adapting recipes from magazines and cookery books is not easy. Cooking times depend on wattage, quantity of ingredients, moisture content etc.

A microwave oven is a vital piece of equipment if you rely heavily on frozen foods or if you have frequently to warm up food because of irregular meal times. Even where these conditions do not apply it is a very useful addition to but not a substitute for a standard gas or electric cooker.

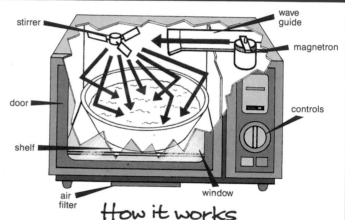

stirrer

wave guide

magnetron

door

controls

shelf

air filter

window

How it works

The magnetron at the top of the oven produces electro-magnetic waves (microwaves). These pass along a wave guide to a rotating stirrer which distributes them into the body of the oven. The microwaves bounce off the walls and into the food, in which the heating-up process starts.

The molecules of water in the top 2 in. of food start to move violently and this rapidly raises the temperature. The more moisture present in the food, the quicker the heating-up process. With dry ingredients and suitable containers there is little or no heat generated.

Standing (or equalisation) time is essential. This is the period when microwave activity is switched off and the heat in the outer layer of food is allowed to move inwards. In this way the food is cooked throughout and overcooking of the outside is prevented. Equalisation may be called for during or at the end of the cooking process — follow the instructions exactly.

Cover dishes with film recommended for microwave use (*not* clingfilm) if you want the food to stay moist. Prick the film before switching on the oven. Steam may build up under this film — remove with care after cooking.

Never switch on an empty oven. Keep a glass of water inside in case the oven is switched on by mistake.

Clean the inside occasionally. Place a bowl of water with a little lemon juice in the oven and switch on for 2 minutes. Wipe down the inner surfaces immediately after switching off.

When buying a new model, look for a microwave distributor (turntable or rotating antenna). If cost is not a problem, there are temperature probes and even an autocook which works out the correct time for you and switches off when cooking is completed.

Never use metal, metal trimmed or metal decorated containers. There are specially-made microwave utensils, but you can use any non-metal dish or pan if at the end of cooking the food is hot and the container is not.

Cookery Techniques

BAIN MARIE To cook by placing food in a pan which is stood in a shallow vessel (bain marie) filled with hot water.

BAKE To cook by exposure to the hot air and hot container within an oven. ROASTING meat is really a form of baking.

BAKE BLIND To bake a pastry shell without its final filling.

BARD To secure pieces or slices of fat to the outside of a joint or fowl before roasting. Not usually necessary. Compare LARD.

BASTE To spoon hot fat or other liquid over food roasting in the oven. Succulence and/or colour is improved.

BEAT To combine ingredients vigorously so that their identity is lost and air is incorporated into the mixture. Compare STIR, BLEND and WHIP.

BLANCH To place in boiling water for a few minutes. There are various reasons — to whiten meat (e.g tripe), to remove skins (e.g tomatoes), to remove salt (e.g ham) etc.

BLEND To combine ingredients so that their identity is lost. Blending is less vigorous than BEATING.

BOIL To cook in water or a water-based liquid at boiling point (212°F).

BRAISE To cook meat, poultry and/or vegetables etc by adding just enough water to moisten the food in the cooking vessel. Flavourings are included and the pan or casserole covered before cooking slowly. Similar to but not the same as STEWING.

BROIL An alternative term for GRILL.

BROWN To fry or grill meat before stewing or braising so as to seal in juices and improve colour.

CHOP To cut up meat, fruit, vegetables etc with a sharp knife into small pieces.

COAT To cover food before cooking with flour, breadcrumbs, coating mixture or butter.

CREAM To combine ingredients so that their identity is lost and a cream-like emulsion is produced.

CURE To preserve meat or fish by salting, drying, pickling or smoking.

DECORATE To improve the appearance and perhaps the flavour of a sweet dish by adding edible and/or non-edible items after cooking. Compare GARNISH.

DICE To cut up fruit, vegetables etc with a sharp knife into small cubes.

DISSOLVE To stir a solid into a liquid so that no trace of the solid remains.

DREDGE To coat lightly with flour, sugar, breadcrumbs etc.

DRESS To prepare food in a way which is pleasing to the eye as well as the palate — a vague term.

FLAKE To divide cooked fish with a fork into small pieces.

FLAMBÉ To flame food with a flaming spirit such as brandy.

FOLD To combine a WHIPPED ingredient or mixture with a dry or heavier one. This operation is done gently with a spoon.

FRY To cook in hot fat. In **shallow-frying** the fat does not cover the food — SAUTÉING is a type of shallow-frying. In **deep-frying** the fat does cover the food. **Dry-frying** means that the only fat used is that which runs from the food.

GARNISH To improve the appearance and perhaps the flavour of a savoury dish by adding edible items after cooking. Compare DECORATE.

GLAZE To make food shiny with egg, sugar, gelatine etc.

GREASE To coat the inside of a utensil or vessel with oil, fat, butter etc.

GRILL To cook by the radiant heat emitted from a glowing object — hot charcoal, electric element etc. Same as BROIL.

HANG To keep meat, poultry and game in a cool place for several days before cooking — the flavour and tenderness of the flesh is improved.

JUG To STEW game in the blood of the animal.

KNEAD To blend the ingredients of dough by pressing and working with the hands.

LARD To insert strips of pork fat or bacon by means of a larding needle into meat, poultry or game. Compare BARD.

MACERATE To soak in liquid — usually applied to fruit soaked in brandy or liqueur.

MARINATE To soak in an acid-based liquid to tenderise and perhaps to add flavour.

MIX To BEAT, BLEND or STIR.

PAN BROIL U.S. term for DRY-FRYING.

PARBOIL To boil food as the first step in the cooking process.

POACH To cook by placing food in SIMMERING liquid.

POT-ROAST To cook whole fowl or a large piece of meat by the BRAISING method. The food is BROWNED before pot-roasting.

PRESSURE COOKING To cook in super-heated steam kept under pressure in a special sealed vessel.

PROVE To allow dough to rise.

PURÉE To press food through a sieve and then blend with liquid.

REDUCE To thicken a liquid by boiling.

ROAST Strictly, to cook meat, poultry or game on a rotating spit in front of glowing heat. Nowadays, to cook meat, poultry, game and vegetables (with added fat where necessary) in an oven.

SAUTÉ To fry in a small amount of very hot fat. The food must be dry before cooking.

SIMMER To cook in water or a water-based liquid at just below boiling point (180–195°F). The surface should ripple slightly but not bubble.

SKIM To remove unwanted matter from the surface during the cooking process.

STEAM To cook by placing food over but not in boiling water or water-based liquid in a closed vessel.

STEW To cook meat, poultry, vegetables and/or fish in a liquid base within a covered pan or casserole. Similar to BRAISING, but the food is cut into pieces and more liquid is used.

STIR To combine ingredients into a mixture in which their identity is not lost. Compare BEAT, BLEND and WHIP.

STIR-FRY To fry finely-sliced or chopped ingredients very quickly in a small amount of hot fat. The ingredients are stirred constantly and a small amount of liquid added before removing from the pan.

STRAIN To separate solids from a liquid by use of a sieve or colander.

SWEAT To fry vegetables gently until their juices are released.

WHIP To beat egg whites or cream very vigorously to incorporate air and stiffen the mixture. Compare BEAT, STIR and BLEND.

WHISK An alternative term for WHIP.

LAUNDERING

In 1907 the first electric washing machine and the first detergent were offered for sale — together they have greatly reduced the chore of washday. More than four in every five British households have a washer, but it is not always essential. If there are just one or two adults in a small flat with very little kitchen space, it will cost no more over a period of years to go to a launderette than to buy and use a washing machine.

For most people, however, a washing machine is essential and it is simply a choice between a twin-tub or an automatic. Nearly everyone these days chooses an automatic — all you have to do is add the necessary powder in the dispenser, turn on the water and choose the right programme (see page 44). Switch on, and the machine washes, rinses and spin-dries the clothes without any help from you. The usual capacity is about 10 lb of laundry, and there are all sorts of extras to look for — pre-wash, superwash, crease-care, quick wash etc. If you have an inexpensive source of hot water, choose a hot-and-cold fill model rather than a cold fill one, and have the machine plumbed in rather than tying up the sink with trailing pipes.

Using a twin-tub is hard work compared to an automatic. The wet laundry has to be lifted by hand into the second tub for rinsing and spinning, and its capacity is small. Despite all the drawbacks, the twin-tub still has its disciples. Washing is both quick and efficient, and it spins at two or three times the speed of an automatic.

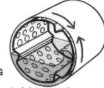

ROTATING DRUM
Inner perforated drum revolves — clothes tumble in and out of the water. Gentle action.

AGITATOR
Base-mounted spindle with paddles moves backwards and forwards through the wash. Gentle action.

ACTIVATOR
(Other name: Pulsator)
A small ridged disc spins at high speed at the side or bottom of the tub. Vigorous action.

THE WASHER

SINGLE-TUB
Once the only type of washing machine you could buy, now a thing of the past. The tub is fed by hose from the taps and washing takes up to ¼ hour once the water is at the correct temperature. Excess water is removed by means of the wringer attached to the machine.

TWIN-TUB
The wash tub usually has an activator — washing time 4 minutes. The spin tub rotates at 1800 – 3000 r.p.m. — in 1 minute the clothes are drier than with most automatics. All the lifting, watching and refilling of the spinning water has made the twin-tub unpopular.

AUTOMATIC: FRONT-LOADING DRUM
By far the most popular type in the U.K. The door of the machine opens directly into one end of the horizontal drum, which rotates for washing and spinning. It can be placed under a worktop or used to carry a tumble-drier on top. A low-foaming washing powder must be used.

AUTOMATIC: TOP-LOADING DRUM
The horizontal rotating drum is fed from the top and not from the front. Compared to the more popular front-loader there are advantages — it is narrower and you can interrupt a programme. The main drawback is that it cannot be housed under a worktop. Washing powder must be low-foaming.

AUTOMATIC: TOP-LOADING TUB
Popular in the U.S. but not in Britain. Washes by agitator in a stationary tub — tub revolves during spin-dry phase. There are advantages — you can buy large-capacity models for home use, any type of washing powder can be used and you can interrupt a programme to add more laundry.

AUTOMATIC: WASHER-DRIER
The all-in-one machine — washer, spin-drier and tumble-drier. At first glance the complete answer — dirty clothes in, clean and dry clothes out. But there are drawbacks. Only half the full wash load can be tumble-dried at one time, so part-emptying of the drum is necessary. Also, drying speed is slow.

THE DRIER

WET — spin dry → DAMP — hang in dry air *or* place in airer-drier *or* tumble-drier → DRY

Getting from the wet to the damp stage is easy these days — the spin-dry action of the modern washer replaces the old mangle or wringer. But moving from the damp to the dry stage can be difficult. Hanging the clothes outside is not practical on wet days or if you live in a flat, and hanging damp laundry indoors can create problems. If you use an airer-drier you must tackle the condensation problem — instal an extractor fan or open the window. A tumble-drier should be vented through a window or outside wall — if this is not possible you can buy a condenser drier which retains the moisture.

So you must choose between a simple clothes line in the garden or a sophisticated tumble-drier. If you do buy a tumble-drier, do consider the sensor type, which automatically switches itself off when the correct degree of dryness is reached.

SPIN-DRIER
A useful piece of equipment if you wash only by hand, but now almost entirely replaced by the twin-tub and automatic washing machine. Extracted water goes into the sink (pump type) or into a bowl (gravity type). Further drying will be necessary before ironing or wearing.

AIRER-DRIER
The principle is simple — damp laundry from the spin-drier or automatic washing machine is hung on racks above a heater. There are free-standing and wall-mounted models — inexpensive compared to a tumble-drier but slower and more troublesome.

TUMBLE-DRIER
If you have the space and the money, a tumble-drier is the best buy. The damp clothes are tumbled in warm air and then in cold air for a brief spell. Use the venting kit to take moisture and tiny fluff particles out of the room. Clean the filter after use.

THE IRON

There are 3 basic types. Choose an iron which is comfortable to hold — don't be influenced by the weight as a light iron will do just as well as a heavy one if the temperature and dampness are correct.

DRY IRON
Cheapest, simplest and usually the lightest. Quite satisfactory if the amount and range of fabrics is small. Make sure that there are easy-to-operate controls, different settings for various fabrics and an indicator light.

STEAM IRON
Irons which emit steam are now much more popular than dry irons. Laundry need not be sprayed before ironing and garments can be pressed without a damp cloth. Buy a model which has a visible water gauge and can use tap water — the water drips down on to the hot sole plate and turns into steam.

STEAM/SPRAY IRON
Most expensive, but well worth the difference. At the touch of a button a fine spray of water is emitted — better than using a spray bottle but still to be avoided on fabrics marked by water. Some models produce a burst of steam on pressing a button — useful when ironing dry and difficult areas.

Choose an ironing board with care. Place an iron on it — the handle should be the same height as your elbow. There should be an asbestos or asbestos-impregnated rest for the iron — there is no health hazard and they are more stable than wire ones. There are many useful optional extras, such as flex supports, sleeve boards and sheet rails. One safety point — do not leave an iron unattended if you have something else to do. Switch off as the thermostat may fail and the sole plate melt.

FABRIC	IRONING TEMPERATURE	SIDE FOR IRONING	NOTES
COTTON	● ● ● Hot	Right side	Should be damp
EMBROIDERY, CORDUROY	● ● ● Hot	Wrong side	Place a thick towel between cloth and ironing board. Use a damp cloth — iron quickly and gently
LINEN	● ● ● Hot	Wrong side for dull finish	Should be damp
RAYON (VISCOSE)	● ● ● Hot	Wrong side	Do not spray or steam. If garment is too dry, roll in a damp towel for a few minutes
POLYESTER + COTTON	● ● Warm	Right side	Should be slightly damp
SATIN, SILK	● ● Warm	Wrong side	Do not spray or steam. If garment is too dry, roll in a damp towel for a few minutes
WOOL	● ● Warm	Wrong side	Press very lightly with a steam iron — do not stretch. Iron only if necessary
ACETATE, TRIACETATE	● Cool	Wrong side	Should be slightly damp
ACRYLIC	● Cool	Wrong side	Should be dry. Iron only if necessary
NYLON, POLYESTER	● Cool	Right side	Should be slightly damp
VELVET	–	–	Do not iron — hang up in a steamy bathroom

Look at the Care Label

At the neck, waist or side seam of a garment you will find a Care Label — this bears symbols which are part of the International Textile Care Labelling Code. The basic symbol is the Washing Code — arrange your wash into piles of similar numbers. If you want to wash a load of mixed numbers, you must set your machine at the highest programme number (1 is lowest, 8 is highest — 9 is a special case). Remember 'wash separately' means what it says.

Typical Care Label:

WASHING CODE
See below

DRYING CODE

⬜ Tumble drying is beneficial

⊠ Do not tumble dry

BLEACHING CODE

△ Household (chlorine) bleach can be used

✕ Household (chlorine) bleach must not be used

IRONING CODE

Cool (120°C) Acrylic, nylon, acetate, triacetate, polyester

Warm (160°C) Polyester mixtures, wool

Hot (210°C) Cotton, linen, viscose or modified viscose

Do not iron

DRY CLEANING CODE

(A) Any solvent may be used

(P) Perchloroethylene, white spirit, Solvent 11 & 113 may be used

(F) White spirit and Solvent 113 may be used

⊠ Do not dry clean

WASHING CODE

OLD SYMBOL	NEW SYMBOL	USED IN U.K.	FABRICS	WASHING TEMPERATURE		AGITATION	RINSE	SPINNING/ WRINGING
				MACHINE	HAND			
1 95	95	YES	**White Cotton programme** For white cotton and linen without special finishes. The most vigorous washing conditions are provided — the results are maximum whiteness and stain removal.	Very hot (95°C) to boil	Hand-hot (50°C) or boil	Maximum	Normal	Normal
2 60	60	YES	**Colourfast Cotton programme** For coloured cotton, linen and viscose without special finishes — colours fast at 60°C. Vigorous washing takes place at a temperature which maintains the colours.	Hot (60°C)	Hand-hot (50°C)	Maximum	Normal	Normal
3 60	60	NO	**White Nylon programme** For white nylon and white polyester + cotton. The wash temperature is high enough to prolong whiteness — cold rinsing and short spinning time minimise creasing.	Hot (60°C)	Hand-hot (50°C)	Medium	Cold	Short spin or drip dry
4 50	50	YES	**Synthetics programme** For nylon, polyester, cotton and viscose with special finishes, acrylic + cotton, polyester + cotton. Similar to 3 but with cooler water to safeguard colours and finish.	Hand-hot (50°C)	Hand-hot (50°C)	Medium	Cold	Short spin or drip dry
5 40	40	YES	**Non-colourfast Cotton programme** For coloured cotton, linen and viscose — colours fast at 40°C but not at 60°C. Agitation, rinsing and spinning as 2, but lower wash temperature to safeguard colours.	Warm (40°C)	Warm (40°C)	Maximum	Normal	Normal
6 40	40	YES	**Acrylic and Wool + Synthetics programme** For acrylics, acetate and triacetate (with or without wool) and polyester + wool. A gentle programme to preserve colour and shape and to minimise creasing.	Warm (40°C)	Warm (40°C)	Minimum	Cold	Short spin
7 40	40	YES	**Wool and Silk programme** For wool and wool mixtures with cotton or viscose, and for silk with colours fast at 40°C. Low wash temperature, minimum agitation plus normal rinsing and spinning preserve colours, size and handle (the feel of the fabric).	Warm (40°C)	Warm (40°C)	Minimum (do not rub)	Normal	Normal spin — do not wring
8 30	30	NO	**Non-colourfast Silk and Acetate programme** For silks and printed acetates with colours not fast at 40°C. The gentlest of all programmes — cool water with minimum agitation and spinning. Colours are maintained.	Cool (30°C)	Cool (30°C)	Minimum	Cold	Short spin — do not wring
9 95	95	NO	**Special finish Cotton programme** For cotton with special finishes which benefit from high temperature washing to ensure maximum whiteness but need drip drying to preserve crease-resistant finish.	Very hot (95°C) to boil	Hand-hot (50°C) or boil	Minimum	Cold	Drip dry
🖐	✋	YES	Do not machine wash — hand wash only					
⊠	⊠	YES	Do not wash					

For further details on FABRICS, see pages 112 – 113

For details on STAIN REMOVAL, see pages 126 – 127

CLEANING

The use of electrically-powered machines can make the task of cleaning much easier. This concept is universally accepted for carpets — 96 per cent of British homes own a vacuum cleaner. Floor coverings are kept cleaner and last longer, but you must empty the bag regularly. The performance of a standard vacuum cleaner starts to decline once it is half full.

The attitude towards washing dishes is quite different. Only a small minority of British homes possess a dishwasher, and it is not just a matter of cost. Shortage of kitchen space can be a problem and so can worry about the noise it might make. But there is also a psychological barrier — many people and some textbooks still regard it as a luxury. Washing dishes by hand is regarded as the 'proper' thing to do, uniting the family around the sink.

A floor polisher is a useful item if you have a large area of uncarpeted flooring, but a carpet shampooer is a machine to hire rather than to buy.

THE VACUUM CLEANER

UPRIGHT

It is not necessarily a good idea to buy the largest model you can afford. Lightweight cleaners are much easier to carry upstairs and are more manoeuvrable. If, however, you have large areas of fitted carpets then a large upright is the best vacuum you can buy. It cleans more quickly than a cylinder model because there is brushing as well as suction action. Some models have a beater bar and there are all sorts of refinements available — air fresheners, illuminated fronts, variable suction etc. There are some drawbacks — cleaning under tables and into corners can be tricky and you have to buy attachments for cleaning curtains, stairs etc.

CYLINDER

The great virtue of the cylinder cleaner is its versatility. The attachments supplied allow you to clean smooth floors, soft furnishings and so on. In addition, reaching under low objects is no problem. On the negative side it takes longer to clean a carpet with a cylinder than with an upright model. True 'cylinders' are a thing of the past — modern versions are streamlined flattened boxes with a variety of extra features — automatic flex rewind, variable suction power etc. Pick up metal objects before vacuuming and renew the filter every few months. For maximum efficiency buy a model with a power head which is fitted with brushes.

WET/DRY

The wet/dry or multipurpose type is the latest introduction to the vacuum cleaner range. At the pick-up end there is a hose and a range of tools as with cylinder models, but dust or other waste material is collected in a large metal canister rather than a bag. It deals with wet as well as dry waste — water in blocked drains, wood shavings, dead leaves, broken glass etc as well as ordinary fluff and dust on carpets and furnishings. It is rather awkward to use and is noisier than an ordinary vacuum cleaner — regard it as an extra piece of equipment for heavy duty use indoors after decorating or major spillages and outdoors for the garage and path.

THE DISHWASHER

If you have a large family or entertain frequently, a dishwasher is a near-essential piece of equipment. Washing-up in the average home takes an hour a day, and the scalding hot water used in a machine ensures cleaner and more hygienic dishes. Dirty crockery and cutlery can be put away immediately, which means a cleaner kitchen.

Most dishwashers are fitted under the work surface although there are small models which can be table-mounted. The usual size is 12 place settings (a place setting is the amount of cutlery and crockery required for a 3 course dinner). The machine will have to be plumbed into the water supply. The features of the models available vary widely — study a range of leaflets before you buy.

It is up to you to choose the most suitable routine. A popular plan is to fill the machine with dishes, pans, cutlery etc during the day and then switch it on at bedtime.

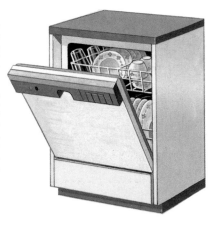

You will have to use a special dishwasher detergent. Don't use an ordinary detergent — it will not be strong enough and it is not designed to break up food deposits. You will also need a rinse aid to prevent water marks forming on glasses and dishes. Many dishwashers have a built-in water softener — top up with salt as recommended by the manufacturer.

Not suitable for dishwashing
Lead crystal glasses
Fine or hand-painted china
Gold- or silver-decorated china
Wooden-, plastic- or
bone-handled cutlery and pans
Polythene dishes and utensils
Silver plate next to
stainless steel cutlery

WASHING & BATHING

In your home there are a number of receptacles designed to hold water from the hot and cold taps, releasing this water to the drainage system once the plug at the bottom of the receptacle has been removed. Sinks hold water for kitchen use, basins allow us to take water to our bodies whilst baths allow us to take our bodies to the water.

Occasionally it is necessary to replace an old installation or to put in a new one. Take a great deal of care when choosing the unit — make sure it is the best one for your purpose and have it installed properly. Some home items such as curtains, wallpaper and the TV may be changed every few years, but a major plumbed-in structure is often expected to last for decades. So think ahead. Make sure that the hand grips on or near a new bath would help someone at least ten years older than you are now!

THE BATH

The standard bath is rectangular — 66 in. long x 28 in. wide x 20 in. high. This may not suit you. Choose a longer one if you are tall and have the space, or a shorter one if the bathroom is small. A 36 in. sit-in hip bath is an option for the infirm or if the room is tiny. If you want to be different there are baths in many weird and wonderful shapes.

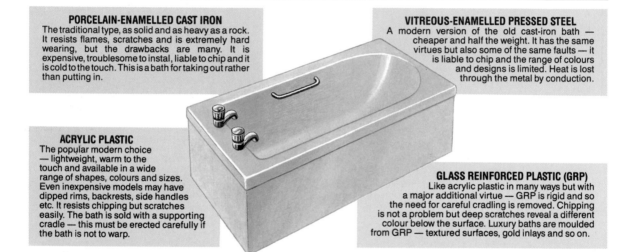

PORCELAIN-ENAMELLED CAST IRON
The traditional type, as solid and as heavy as a rock. It resists flames, scratches and is extremely hard wearing, but the drawbacks are many. It is expensive, troublesome to instal, liable to chip and it is cold to the touch. This is a bath for taking out rather than putting in.

VITREOUS-ENAMELLED PRESSED STEEL
A modern version of the old cast-iron bath — cheaper and half the weight. It has the same virtues but also some of the same faults — it is liable to chip and the range of colours and designs is limited. Heat is lost through the metal by conduction.

ACRYLIC PLASTIC
The popular modern choice — lightweight, warm to the touch and available in a wide range of shapes, colours and sizes. Even inexpensive models may have dipped rims, backrests, side handles etc. It resists chipping but scratches easily. The bath is sold with a supporting cradle — this must be erected carefully if the bath is not to warp.

GLASS REINFORCED PLASTIC (GRP)
Like acrylic plastic in many ways but with a major additional virtue — GRP is rigid and so the need for careful cradling is removed. Chipping is not a problem but deep scratches reveal a different colour below the surface. Luxury baths are moulded from GRP — textured surfaces, gold inlays and so on.

The usual choice is a vitreous-enamelled pressed steel or an acrylic bath — the acrylic type is the favourite one for the DIY enthusiast. Break up an old cast-iron tub in the bathroom to facilitate removal — cover with a cloth, wear goggles and take care. For many, a sunken bath sounds like real luxury but it is difficult to instal. A better idea is to raise the floor to the rim of the tub, with steps leading to the bath of your dreams. However, you will need a bathroom with a high ceiling to make it all possible.

THE SHOWER

A shower has none of the lazy indulgence of a hot bath, but it has many other advantages. It takes only 20 per cent of the hot water, it is often safer for elderly and handicapped people, and it is quicker, more hygienic and invigorating.

The simplest type of shower is fitted over the bath — the base of the bath under the shower head should have a non-slip surface. You can use a Y-shaped flexible hosepipe which pushes on to the taps, but it is much more satisfactory to instal a bath/shower mixer in place of the existing taps — a flick of the lever and the water is diverted from the bath to the shower.

There are problems with these simple arrangements. If someone turns on a tap elsewhere in the house there is a drop in pressure and a change in water temperature which can be dangerous. In addition, the force of the spray will be inadequate if the distance between the shower head and the bottom of the cold water cistern is less than 3 ft.

A good answer to these problems is to instal an instant electric shower. There is a temperature stabiliser to ensure no cooling or overheating when a tap is switched on, and there is no pressure problem as the water is drawn from the rising main.

A wide range of shower cubicles is available. An excellent addition to any home — look for a thermostatic shower mixer, tight-fitting doors and a shower tray which is non-slip, at least 6 in. high and more than 30 in. square.

THE BASIN

Basins for bathrooms and bedrooms are available in a wide range of colours and shapes. The traditional washbasin was a rectangle — 24 in. wide and 16 in. deep, but today you will find ovals, circles, quarter-circles, scallop shells and so on. Materials as well as shapes have been extended. Once all basins were made of vitreous china, and this type of bowl remains the most popular. It is heavy and hard wearing, easy to clean and resistant to scratches, but it can be chipped or cracked.

The increasing popularity of vanity units has resulted in the production of both enamelled pressed steel and plastic basins for inclusion in decorative storage units.

PEDESTAL BASIN

A popular form of basin — the unsightly pipes are hidden from the front by the hollow leg. This pedestal takes some of the weight of the bowl, but it must never be the sole means of support. A firm wall fixing is necessary. There are one or two drawbacks — the height of the bowl rim is fixed at about 32 in., which may be too high or too low for your family. Another disadvantage is the need to cut the floor covering around a somewhat difficult shape.

WALL-HUNG BASIN

Many types are available in addition to the standard rectangular pattern which is hung on brackets fixed to the wall. There are corner units and semi-recessed types which are partly set into the wall. Both save space, and so do the 1 ft deep mini-basins used in cloakrooms. With wall-hung basins there is no pedestal to clean and there is unimpeded foot room, but the plumbing is exposed unless the pipes are taken through the wall.

VANITY BASIN

A vanity unit is a low cupboard with a basin set in or on the upper surface. This structure is generally more expensive than buying a simple bowl, but there are several advantages over an ordinary basin. There is storage space, an extended work surface, a built-in look and completely hidden plumbing. In the lay-on type the basin unit forms the whole of the top surface — in the inset type the basin is mounted in a hole cut in the top of the vanity unit.

THE SINK

A distinctive feature of the pre-war British kitchen was the Belfast sink. Deep and rectangular, its stout white-glazed body was borne on large brackets. On the wall behind were the bib taps — on one side was a wooden draining board. About 30 years ago the sink revolution took place — the age of the sink unit had begun.

The unit provides drawer space as well as storage space below. Plumbing is hidden and there is a place for cleaning materials — the sink unit is usually the centre-point of the built-in arrangement. In nearly all cases it is placed under the window, but this is not essential unless there are small children to watch. The key point is that it should be close to the cooker.

The sink itself is nearly always stainless steel or vitreous-enamelled pressed steel. Stainless steel is often dearer and it may show water marks after draining dishes. There are no attractive colours from which to choose, but stainless steel still remains the popular choice. The enamelled pressed steel sink is catching up — modern ones are much less liable to chip. There are plastic sinks available, but damage by hot utensils can be a problem.

LAY-ON SINK

This is the standard stainless steel 'sink top' — the sink fits over the top of the base unit and so provides the whole of the work surface. The lay-on sink is generally the least expensive, but it is also the most limited in versatility and range of designs. Depending on the space, you can choose a single- or a double-bowl model with a single or double drainer. The bowl depth is usually 7 in.

INSET SINK

Here the sink is set into a hole cut in the work surface — take care to make the seal between the sink and worktop watertight. Many designs are available, and there is no need to seal between the unit and the wall. Round, square or rectangular bowls, deep or shallow, stainless steel, enamel or plastic — go to a DIY superstore to see the large range which is now offered. A waste disposal unit will need a wide outlet.

WORK CENTRE SINK

A development of the ordinary inset sink — the dividing line between the two is rather vague. A work centre always has more than a standard bowl and a drainer — the usual additions are an extra shallow bowl and drainer basket for washing up, plus a cutting board cover for the bowl. There are also half bowls for waste disposal, cutlery holders, washing-up brushes and so on. Clearly the sink of the future.

FREEZING

Thirty years ago less than one home in ten had a fridge — now almost every house has one, and about half of Britain's households have a deep freeze. Gone are the days of daily visits to the corner store for meat and vegetables — the once-a-week shopping trip to the supermarket is now a feature of present-day life.

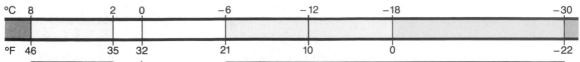

°C	8		2	0		−6		−12		−18			−30
°F	46		35	32		21		10		0			−22

REFRIGERATOR
An appliance which keeps perishable food fresh and safe to eat for a limited period

Don't guess the temperature — keep a thermometer in both the refrigerator and the deep freeze

FROZEN FOOD COMPARTMENT
An appliance fitted in a standard refrigerator which makes ice cubes and preserves shop-bought frozen food for a limited period. The length of this period is denoted by a star rating — see below

DEEP FREEZE
An appliance which preserves shop-bought frozen food for up to 3 months. It can also be used to freeze and store fresh and kitchen-prepared food. The storage period depends upon the food — see page 49

THE REFRIGERATOR

Buy as large a refrigerator as your pocket and space will allow. As a general guide, 1 cu.ft per person plus an additional cu.ft will be required. Check that the door swings the right way for your needs and make sure that tall bottles can be housed.

Set the refrigerator 2-3 in. away from the wall so that heat can escape. If placed under a work surface, there must be a space on either side. Set it away from the cooker or other source of heat and make sure that it is level and not in contact with any other unit or piece of equipment.

Do not put hot food into the refrigerator — always cover dishes to prevent the transfer of smells and flavours. Space out the items to allow cold air to circulate.

Defrost every few months. Turn off, empty the shelves and place a bowl of hot water inside. When all the ice has melted, empty the drip tray and switch on. A semi-automatic defroster operates by pushing a button, but you still have to empty the drip tray. With an automatic defroster you have to do nothing at all.

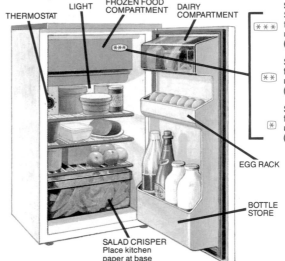

THERMOSTAT LIGHT FROZEN FOOD COMPARTMENT DAIRY COMPARTMENT

STAR RATING
*** Shop-bought frozen food can be kept for up to 3 months (Temperature 0°F/−18°C)

** Shop-bought frozen food can be kept for up to 1 month (Temperature 10°F/−12°C)

* Shop-bought frozen food can be kept for up to 1 week (Temperature 21°F/−6°C)

EGG RACK

BOTTLE STORE

SALAD CRISPER
Place kitchen paper at base

STANDARD REFRIGERATOR
The main body of the refrigerator stores perishable items at above-freezing temperature. The thermostat is used to maintain the temperature in the 2° – 8°C range — a different setting will be needed in summer compared to winter. At the top there is a frozen food compartment which is maintained below freezing point — the temperature is indicated by the star rating on the front flap.

LARDER REFRIGERATOR
In homes where there is a deep freeze as well as a refrigerator it is usually found that the refrigerator is filled to capacity much more often than the deep freeze. In such cases it is sensible to buy a larder refrigerator when the standard model has to be replaced. There is no frozen food compartment, which means that all the capacity is used to store perishable items at above-freezing temperature.

FRIDGE-FREEZER
The ideal answer where you haven't the space or need for a separate refrigerator and deep freeze. The single compressor model has the freezer on top of the fridge. The temperature of one unit can affect the efficiency and running costs of the other — it is better to buy the more expensive but also more satisfactory double compressor type with the fridge on top of the freezer. Here the two units run independently.

THE DEEP FREEZE

DEEP FREEZE MARK
This star rating indicates that the appliance is a true deep freeze. It is capable of storing shop-bought frozen food and at the same time freezing both fresh and kitchen-prepared food.

Every year thousands of people buy a deep freeze (or freezer) for the first time. If your needs are modest — packs of frozen foods from the shops, a loaf or two for emergencies and meat or fish for the weekend, buy a small model. But a deep freeze can do much more. Vegetables from the garden and from the shops when prices are low can be stored. Meat and fish can be purchased in bulk, and cooked in large quantities and then stored in meal-sized portions for later use. To make full use of a deep freeze in this way, buy one with a net volume of 2 cu.ft for each person plus an extra 2 cu.ft (1 cu.ft of net volume = 20 lb of food). When freezing from room temperature the maximum amount during a 24 hour period should be 2 lb per cu.ft of net volume, unless the instruction book states otherwise.

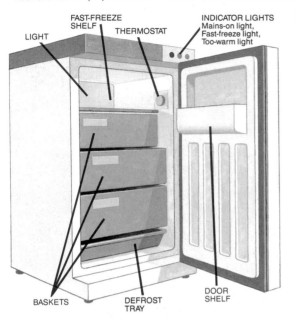

LIGHT · FAST-FREEZE SHELF · THERMOSTAT · INDICATOR LIGHTS Mains-on light, Fast-freeze light, Too-warm light · BASKETS · DEFROST TRAY · DOOR SHELF

A deep freeze works by keeping food at −18°C(0°F) — at this temperature both harmful and spoiling bacteria are completely dormant and food-spoiling enzymes in the food are de-activated. To freeze fresh food and made-up dishes, place the items in the fast-freeze compartment and press the fast-freeze button. This will lower the temperature below −18°C, but not to the −30°C of commercial freezing installations. After 4 – 24 hours (depending on the quantity of food being frozen) switch off the fast-freeze button and place the food in one of the baskets or storage trays.

Freezing Tips
- Use suitable containers, such as heavy gauge polythene bags, waxed containers, plastic boxes with lids, aluminium foil and foil dishes.
- Freeze food at peak freshness — fish should be frozen on the day it is bought.
- Make up dishes in convenient-sized portions and fill the container properly. Drive out as much air as possible with solid foods before sealing thoroughly — liquids should have a ½ in. head space.
- Double wrap items such as bread, meat, fish, poultry etc to prevent the transfer of smells and the danger of freezer-burn (loss of colour and flavour due to dehydration).
- Slightly undercook and underseason food for the freezer. Leave out garlic altogether. Cut off excess fat. Cool all food to room temperature or below before placing in the deep freeze.
- Label and date all packages. Buy special labels and a freezer pencil for this purpose. Always keep the freezer reasonably full.
- Consider open-freezing for some items — they can then be used individually as required. Spread the items (small cakes, mushrooms, fruit etc) as a single layer in a plastic or non-stick baking tray. Place in the fast-freeze compartment and when frozen, remove each item and package individually. Store in the deep freeze in the usual way.
- Food removed from the deep freeze should be allowed to thaw and then eaten at once, cooked at once or placed in the refrigerator. Thawed food which has been kept at room temperature for even an hour or two should not be refrozen.

Not for Freezing
Whole eggs in shells · Single cream · Bananas · Avocados · Salad vegetables · Stuffed poultry · Cooked potatoes · Jelly · Cream cheese · Whole strawberries

Defrosting
Defrost twice a year when stocks are low. Remove and wrap food in newspaper — place in a cool spot. Switch off and place newspapers or rags on the floor. Remove the excess ice with a wooden or plastic scraper and leave the door open. Place a large bowl at the base to catch the water. When all the ice has gone, remove any food stains with bicarbonate of soda solution. Wipe the inside, re-connect and set at the lowest temperature. Replace food and alter the thermostat to the normal setting.

Emergencies
Tape the plug to the socket to prevent accidental removal. In the case of a power cut, never open the door. The food inside will stay frozen for 12 hours — a full freezer will remain cold for much longer than a half empty one. Once power is restored put on fast-freeze for 6 hours.

CHEST FREEZER
Space is the main problem — chest freezers are often placed in garages or outbuildings as kitchens are generally too small. There is also the problem of arranging the various food items and then readily locating them when required — organising packages vertically is more difficult than horizontally. But there are advantages — chest freezers are less expensive to buy and run, and less cold air is lost when the door is opened. Large items such as turkeys and sides of beef are easier to store.

UPRIGHT FREEZER
More popular than the chest freezer. It takes up no more floor space than an ordinary refrigerator — in fact, it is sometimes possible to place one on top of the other. The front-loading arrangement makes frozen items much easier to arrange and locate, and the top can serve as a work surface. The main problem is that a bulky object such as a large joint or turkey cannot be housed unless one or more of the shelves are removed. In addition cooling down occurs more rapidly if the power supply fails.

MAXIMUM STORAGE TIME (months)											
1	2	3	4	5	6	7	8	9	10	11	12
Milk Prawns Ice cream Sausages	Bread Cream Offal	Soup Butter Mince (beef) Cheese	Cakes Mushrooms Fish Chop (pork)	Duck Goose Fruit juice Beaten egg	Joint (pork) Pastry	Joint (veal) Turkey Steak (beef) Biscuits	Chop (lamb) Game Fruit purée	Rabbit Fruit	Joint (lamb)	Chicken	Joint (beef) Vegetables

CHAPTER 4
INSIDE THE HOUSE

In each room of your home there is a basic framework — floor below, ceiling above and walls, windows and doors in between. Their size and surface coverings largely determine the overall feel and character of the room — furniture and furnishings can enhance the effect, but they cannot fully compensate for basic deficiencies which exist in this framework.

There will be times when changes will be necessary. Minor maintenance jobs have to be done — hinges oiled, sinks unblocked, taps re-washered, shelves erected and so on. These are simple jobs which anyone can tackle by following the instructions in this book. But redecoration calls for time, equipment and a degree of expertise — only you can decide whether to tackle the job yourself or to call in a professional. There are, of course, both advantages and disadvantages for DIY compared to employing a skilled Contractor, but it is worth underlining the point that if you do tackle the job then you must learn the correct techniques *before* you start, and you must prepare the surfaces at least as thoroughly as would a skilled professional.

The DIY boom continues and about nine in every ten households do at least some decorating for themselves. There is, of course, nothing wrong with this — but the situation is different if a major structural change is planned or a complex repair problem has arisen. In most cases it is wise to seek outside help — moving walls or installing new pipes or electric cables can lead to disaster if you do not know what you are doing. Choose a builder, decorator, plumber etc with care — check that he belongs to the appropriate trade organisation, see examples of work done for others wherever possible and listen to the recommendations of your friends.

WHAT THE WORDS MEAN

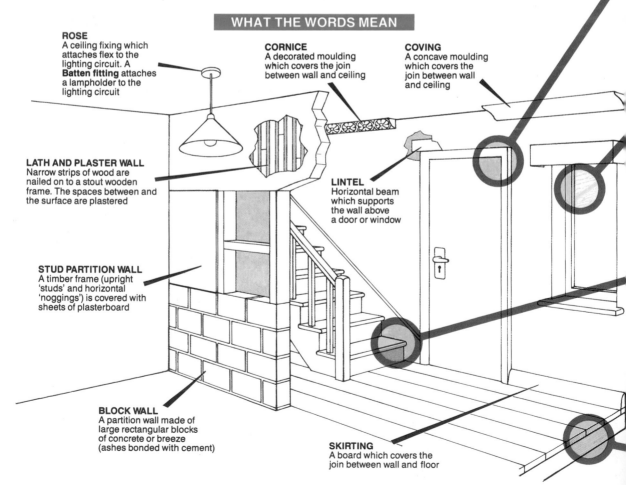

ROSE
A ceiling fixing which attaches flex to the lighting circuit. A **Batten fitting** attaches a lampholder to the lighting circuit

CORNICE
A decorated moulding which covers the join between wall and ceiling

COVING
A concave moulding which covers the join between wall and ceiling

LATH AND PLASTER WALL
Narrow strips of wood are nailed on to a stout wooden frame. The spaces between and the surface are plastered

LINTEL
Horizontal beam which supports the wall above a door or window

STUD PARTITION WALL
A timber frame (upright 'studs' and horizontal 'noggings') is covered with sheets of plasterboard

BLOCK WALL
A partition wall made of large rectangular blocks of concrete or breeze (ashes bonded with cement)

SKIRTING
A board which covers the join between wall and floor

DOOR

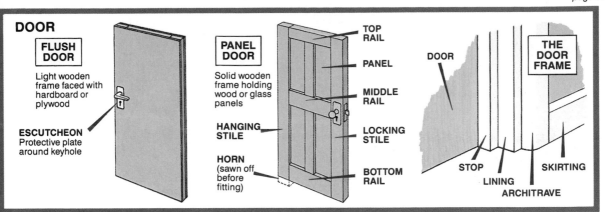

FLUSH DOOR

Light wooden frame faced with hardboard or plywood

ESCUTCHEON
Protective plate around keyhole

PANEL DOOR

Solid wooden frame holding wood or glass panels

HANGING STILE

HORN (sawn off before fitting)

TOP RAIL

PANEL

MIDDLE RAIL

LOCKING STILE

BOTTOM RAIL

DOOR

THE DOOR FRAME

STOP

LINING

ARCHITRAVE

SKIRTING

WINDOW

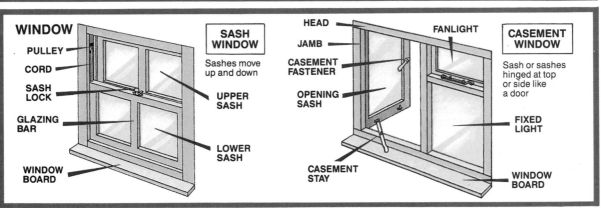

PULLEY

CORD

SASH LOCK

GLAZING BAR

WINDOW BOARD

SASH WINDOW

Sashes move up and down

UPPER SASH

LOWER SASH

HEAD

JAMB

CASEMENT FASTENER

OPENING SASH

CASEMENT STAY

FANLIGHT

CASEMENT WINDOW

Sash or sashes hinged at top or side like a door

FIXED LIGHT

WINDOW BOARD

STAIRS

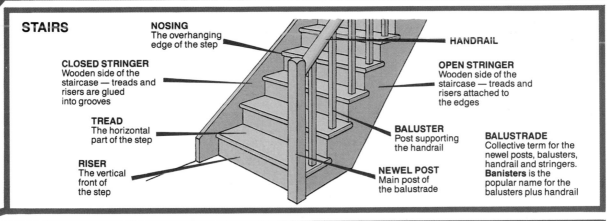

NOSING
The overhanging edge of the step

CLOSED STRINGER
Wooden side of the staircase — treads and risers are glued into grooves

TREAD
The horizontal part of the step

RISER
The vertical front of the step

HANDRAIL

OPEN STRINGER
Wooden side of the staircase — treads and risers attached to the edges

BALUSTER
Post supporting the handrail

NEWEL POST
Main post of the balustrade

BALUSTRADE
Collective term for the newel posts, balusters, handrail and stringers.
Banisters is the popular name for the balusters plus handrail

FLOOR

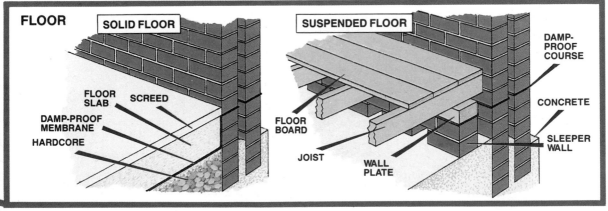

SOLID FLOOR

FLOOR SLAB

SCREED

DAMP-PROOF MEMBRANE

HARDCORE

SUSPENDED FLOOR

FLOOR BOARD

JOIST

WALL PLATE

DAMP-PROOF COURSE

CONCRETE

SLEEPER WALL

Floors & Flooring

Before the start of World War II both downstairs and upstairs floors were of the **suspended** (or hollow) type. Floorboards were laid on stout wooden joists set about 16 in. apart — on the ground floor these joists were stood on an open brickwork wall (sleeper wall). Since the war the standard ground floor has been of the **solid** type — a block of concrete laid directly on the ground, and upstairs floors are often made of chipboard or plywood rather than floorboards.

In nearly all cases it is desirable to cover this wood or concrete with flooring material. Fifty years and more ago it was all so simple — stained floorboards with a carpet square for the living and entertaining rooms, bodywidth carpet up the stairs and lino sheeting in the kitchen. Now it is not so simple. There is a staggering variety of flooring materials, ranging from the very cheap to the amazingly expensive and from the practical to the distinctly delicate.

The advantages and disadvantages of the six basic types are set out on page 54. There are additional types, such as vegetable matting, rubber tiles, thermoplastic (asphalt) tiles and bricks. In making your choice the aim must be to balance an attractive appearance with several practical considerations. Use the check-list below.

- **Appearance:** Personal likes and dislikes play a strong role — some people cannot stand patterned floorings whereas others find plain surfaces far too dull. The flooring type should be in keeping with the style of the room.
- **Comfort and safety:** Warmth and quietness are highly desirable in the living room, bedrooms and playroom. Even in working areas such as the kitchen it is worth considering high-density flocked carpet or cushion-backed vinyl rather than a solid vinyl. Safety is an extremely important factor if there are old people and small children around — always pick a non-slip surface and whenever possible choose a 'soft' flooring material which has a good deal of resilience.
- **Durability:** Areas near outside doors must be able to withstand dirt and grit. Kitchen coverings must not be damaged by fat-laden spills, and bathroom flooring must stand up to moisture-laden air and wet patches. Hard wear is bound to occur in living rooms and kitchens — durable coverings are essential here.
- **Ease of laying:** See page 55.

THE UNCOVERED FLOOR

TURNING IT INTO
A SUITABLE SUB-FLOOR

A sub-floor is the basic floor structure on which a decorative flooring material such as carpet, vinyl or parquet blocks is laid. There are 3 basic requirements — this sub-floor must be level, dry and firm. If it is not level the imperfections may be an eyesore and the flooring material may either crack or wear badly. A weak sub-floor will creak and sag — it is either difficult or impossible to tackle this problem once the flooring has been laid. Finally, the sub-floor must be dry — dampness will make adhesion difficult and can lead to the destruction of most floor coverings.

Wooden sub-floor: Rot, woodworm or damp must be cured before you start. Fix all loose floorboards and cure creaks — fill gaps and drive in protruding nails. The main problem is to obtain a level surface — old floorboards are often bowed, and hollows may appear here and there. Sanding is the answer if the surface of the sub-floor is basically smooth — if it is markedly uneven then a covering with hardboard is the answer (see page 53).

Solid sub-floor: Call in a builder to relay the floor if it is wet — you can deal with slight dampness by painting with damp-proofing material or laying down a sheet of building paper. Hollows in a solid sub-floor can be cured with a self-levelling compound (see page 53), but if the surface is badly pitted and cracked you will need to have the floor re-screeded by a builder.

TURNING IT INTO
A DECORATIVE FLOOR

It is not always necessary to cover the floorboards in order to produce a decorative floor. Stained and polished floorboards in the dining room can be a most attractive feature.

The boards will have to be sound, reasonably level and free from unsightly holes and gaps. Don't worry about old stain or grime — this will be removed by the first step of the operation. Sanding is the essential start, and you will need to hire the proper equipment (see page 53) rather than trying to use a hand sander.

After sanding all dust must be removed. When the surfaces have been thoroughly cleaned it is time to stain the floor, if staining is necessary. Treat small test areas to find the right colour — choose spots which will be hidden by rugs or furniture.

Apply the first coat of a polyurethane varnish when the stain has dried. This will seal the surface, and should be put on as soon as possible before dust gets into the grain. Use a cotton pad for this first coat of varnish — rub it well into the wood and leave it to dry for a day. Rub down the surface with fine steel wool, then dust and apply a second coat with a good quality paint brush. When dry apply a third and final coat.

DEALING WITH FLOOR PROBLEMS

● **LIFTING A FLOORBOARD** Mark board or boards to be lifted. Switch off electricity if there are cables below. Remove screws if present.

① Use a padsaw to cut through tongue on one side

TONGUE AND GROOVED

② When sawing is completed proceed to ③

SQUARE EDGED

③ Start at one end. Tap bolster chisel in at an angle with a hammer

④ Lever upwards until nails are loosened

⑤ Lift up board with claw of hammer. Insert an iron rod and push forward

⑥ Press down with foot to loosen nails at other end of the board

⑦ Push bar forward — remove floorboard

● **FILLING GAPS BETWEEN FLOORBOARDS**

There are several reasons why gaps appear between floorboards. Shrinkage is a common cause — so is splintering due to pest or disease attack. If the wood is diseased, replace the board with a new one. Where the boards are healthy, there are several ways of dealing with the problem.

Tiny gaps Fill with wood filler. Smooth surface with sandpaper when dry.

Small gaps Fill with papier-mâché (shredded newspaper pulped with thick wallpaper paste, plus appropriate stain if boards are exposed). Smooth surface with sandpaper when dry.

Large gaps If there are just a few gaps, drive in strips of wood — tap down until level with the surface. Sometimes gaps are numerous, making the floor quite unsuitable for covering. The perfectionist lifts all the floorboards and relays them, but it is easier to cover the surface with hardboard.

● **CURING LOOSE AND SQUEAKING FLOORBOARDS**

① Drive in extra brads close to the existing ones

② Sink heads below surface with a nail punch

If squeaking persists, dust talcum powder into the cracks. If all else fails, remove the offending floorboard and plane the edge to get rid of the protrusion.

● **CURING WEAKENED JOISTS**

When walking over the floor you may find that some of the floorboards are springy — a linked problem is sagging joists when a new piece of furniture is introduced. The usual answer is to strengthen or replace the joists.

If you are not a handyman, call in a reputable builder. The joist may be broken or rotten, or the sleeper wall (see page 51) may have cracked. Serious problems are generally best left to the professional, but if you are a DIY enthusiast it is worth looking under the floorboards to see if you can tackle the problem. You may find that although the joists are free from insect or fungus attack there is one which is not firm and can be moved up and down by standing on it. Fix a strengthener to it — a stout piece of wood which is securely bolted to the side of the weakened joist. Make sure that the top of this strengthener is no higher than the top of the joist.

● **LEVELLING FLOORS** Sometimes nailing down loose boards or replacing a warped floorboard or two is not enough — the whole surface must be levelled. There are two alternative methods — sanding or sheeting.

Sanding

Hire a floor sander with a 20 cm drum, and also an edge sander. You will need a dust mask.

Prepare the floor carefully before you begin sanding. Remove all bits of metal, protruding tacks etc and drive all floorboard nails below the surface.

① To begin, tilt floor sander backwards and switch on. Gently lower on to the floor and allow to move forward slowly. Never allow the machine to operate without moving

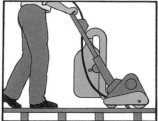

② Begin with medium-grade paper — finish with fine-grade paper

③ Work along the length of the floorboards, never along the line of the joists. Keep cable over shoulder. If the floor is rough or the boards are warped, begin at 45° to the floorboards and finish parallel to them as noted above

④ Use the edge sander close to the skirting boards. Once again work parallel to and never across the floorboards

⑤ When finished, clean up thoroughly with a vacuum cleaner and then with a dry cloth

Sheeting

Buy tempered hardboard — the standard size is 8 ft × 4 ft. Condition for use by sprinkling the rough side with water and leaving the sheets in the room for a couple of days.

Prepare the floor carefully before laying hardboard. Remove all bits of metal, protruding tacks etc and drive all floorboard nails below the surface.

① Cut boards into 4 ft × 4 ft and 4 ft × 2 ft pieces. Start at the centre of the room — stagger the joins

② Nail down with hardboard pins at 6 in. intervals

Levelling solid floors

Hollows in solid floors can be removed by using a self-levelling compound. It is mixed with water and poured over the floor — it spreads and settles to form a smooth and horizontal surface. This method is not suitable for wooden floors

FLOORING MATERIALS

TYPE OF FLOORING	DETAILS
CARPET	Carpeting is everybody's favourite for living areas, bedrooms and stairs. In dining rooms it competes with wood and rugs — in bathrooms and kitchens it is rivalled by vinyl tiles. The variety of colours, patterns and surfaces is enormous — the prices range from fairly cheap to very expensive and the wide assortment of fibres now available mean that there are carpets which are ideal for every room in the house. Deciding which one to buy is difficult — read pages 56-57 before making your choice. There are 'bargains' everywhere, but price is nearly always a sound indication of quality.
LINOLEUM	The ingredients of linoleum are cork, wood-flour and linseed oil with a hessian backing. Once the darling of the kitchen and bathroom but now a thing of the past. Although now only made for the industrial market, linoleum in both sheet and tile form is still to be found in homes scattered about the country. This flooring material had several good points — it was inexpensive, easy to clean, hard-wearing and fairly resilient. But now vinyl tiles have taken over completely from their former rival for kitchens and bathrooms — they are softer than linoleum tiles and they do not readily curl up at the edges when water gets into the seams.
VINYL	A popular covering for kitchens and bathrooms, but regarded as rather austere for living rooms, bedrooms and stairs. Vinyl sheet is not easy to lay, but tiles are straightforward. Printed vinyl is popular and colourful, but the 'wear layer' is thin and so signs of wear occur after a few years. Cushioned vinyl is softer to walk on and will also take up minor floor irregularities, but again it lacks durability. If you want a vinyl which will last for many years, then solid vinyl tiles are the answer but they can be slippery when wet. Vinyl asbestos tiles are long-lasting, inexpensive and tolerant of slightly damp floors, but they are inflexible and can crack if the floor is uneven.
WOOD	In the right setting polished wood has an elegance and richness which nothing can match. It can be noisy, expensive and sometimes tricky to lay, but it is also extremely durable and a good investment. If you are lucky you may be able to sand and polish the existing floorboards (see page 53), although you are much more likely to have to buy either strips, blocks or mosaic panels. Wood strips are high-quality narrow floorboards which are laid at right angles to the floorboards. Wood blocks are laid in a parquet pattern. Most popular of all are mosaic panels — a basket weave of miniature strips of wood on a backing. These tile-like panels may be hardwood or veneered, unfinished or surface-coated. All wood floors must be sealed after laying.
CORK	Cork is nearly always bought as tiles rather than in sheet form. These tiles are not difficult to lay and are suitable for both wooden and solid floors. You are most likely to find them in the bathroom or playroom, where their warmth, softness and quietness are highly desirable features. The drawbacks of cork are few — it is not as durable as hardwood and can be marked and dented by sharp objects. Direct sunlight can cause bleaching but the main disadvantage is the very restricted range of colours. Two types are available — unsealed and plastic-coated. Coated tiles can be slippery — where this could be a problem it is better to lay unsealed tiles. Treat later, if necessary, with a polyurethane sealer.
CLAY & STONE	Quarry tiles have long been popular for porches, their waterproof, stone-like and easy-to-clean surface providing an excellent bridge between the outdoors and inside. Made by baking unrefined, silica-rich clay, these tiles are unglazed and nearly always 6 in. squares in reds or browns. Most people cannot see the appeal of quarry tiles indoors, as they are cold, noisy and completely unresilient. Yet they do have their adherents for kitchens, bathrooms and hallways. Their more glamorous cousins, the ceramic tiles, are available in a wide range of colours and shapes and can be used to provide a shiny, exotic look to rooms. Marble is the most luxurious (and expensive) stone tile — all these 'hard' tiles can be used on solid (not wooden) floors fitted with underfloor heating.

LAYING FLOORING MATERIALS

LAYING SOFT TILES (cork, carpet, wood and vinyl)

(1) Stretch chalked string across centre of room from wall to wall — stretch another chalked string at right angles (check with a set square)

(3) Place a tile where the 2 lines cross — set out other tiles from all 4 sides to reach walls

(5) Tiles may be self-adhesive or need glue. Work out from centre line in pyramid fashion. If using glue, stick down about 6 at a time

(7) Place second tile on top of loose tile close to wall. Place third tile and cut as shown

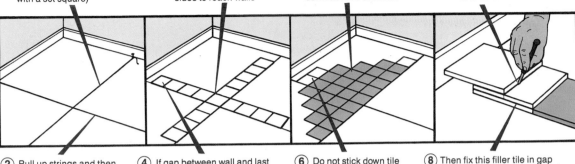

(2) Pull up strings and then release to leave chalk lines. Remove strings

(4) If gap between wall and last tile is very narrow, adjust chalk lines to aim for at least ⅓ tile width as the space at the end of each arm

(6) Do not stick down tile row closest to wall

Key: ☐ loose tile
▨ stuck-down tile

(8) Then fix this filler tile in gap formed when the bottom tile is moved and fixed against the wall. Note: with wood block and panels leave narrow expansion strip at wall edge — fill with cork strip

HINTS & TIPS

- Buy about 5 per cent more than the measured area of the room — increase this amount if the flooring material has a large pattern.

- Some floorings (vinyl, cork, wood etc) should be conditioned before laying. This calls for spreading them out in the room for about 2 days before starting work.

- Not all floorings are suitable in rooms with underfloor heating. Insulators (rubber, foam-backed carpets etc) and thermoplastic tiles are out of the question — seek advice before making up your mind.

- Do not attempt a job which is beyond your capabilities. Quarry tiles and stone floors should be laid by a flooring contractor, and laying fitted carpets calls for a good deal of experience as well as the right tools.

SHEET OR TILE?

A number of floorings are available in both large sheet (up to 15 ft width) and small tile form. Each has its own advantages and disadvantages.

Sheet: The great advantage here is that there are few joins, so there is no network of narrow spaces to spoil the luxury appearance (an important point with carpets) or to absorb water, dirt and spills (an important point in kitchens and bathrooms). But sheet is awkward to handle and even more awkward to lay. Wastage is inevitable, especially in irregular-shaped rooms.

Tile: The great advantage here is that the basic material is easy to handle and easy to lay even by the inexperienced do-it-yourselfer. There is little waste and a mistake is not costly — all you have to do is to cut another tile. Worn areas are quite easily replaced, but there are drawbacks. Carpet tiles do not have quite the same overall fitted appearance of broadloom carpeting, and the choice of colours and patterns is more limited.

LAYING VINYL SHEETS

(1) Place sheet about 2 in. from side wall — leave 3 in. overlap at ends

(3) Push sheet against side wall — fit should be exact. Leave overlap against end wall

(5) Pull sheet back so it is about 2 in. from end wall. Keep sheet flush against side wall

(7) Run scriber along end wall from the second mark. Cut along the scratch mark

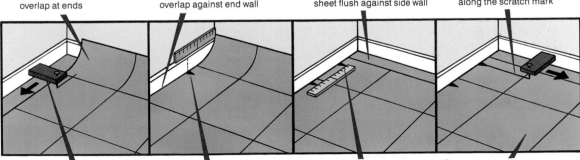

(2) Then run scriber (wooden block with a protruding nail) along side wall to mark the surface. Cut along the line

(4) Then mark side of sheet 9 in. from end wall

(6) Then make second mark 9 in. in front of first

(8) Then push sheet forward to fit end wall. Stick down sheet according to instructions

CARPETS

All of the flooring materials described in this chapter have a part to play in the modern home, but carpeting has a charm which nothing else can match. There is a feeling of warmth and comfort, and in the second half of this century the carpet square has been replaced by the fitted carpet.

Carpets are available in various widths. There is **broadloom** (6 – 15 ft wide) for fitted carpets, **bodywidth** (2¼ – 3 ft wide) for hallways and stairs, **squares** of various widths to cover part but not all of a room and **tiles** (1 – 1½ ft wide) for kitchens and bathrooms. These tiles are often made of hair rather than natural or synthetic fibres.

Many fibres are used for making broadloom carpeting these days, and the composition of a carpet helps to determine its suitability for the room you have in mind. The way in which the fibres have been transformed into a carpet will also influence its properties.

Your new carpet will shed fluff for a few weeks — this is nothing to worry about. Vacuum carefully. With all-wool or velvet carpets use a hand brush during this period and snip off any 'shooting' tufts (groups of fibres which are standing above the surface). After about a month you can vacuum in the normal way. To prevent localised wear try to move chairs and tables about from time to time.

Rugs and matting are close relatives to carpeting. Rugs are small carpets which can be readily moved from one spot to another — make sure that there is a non-slip underlay on a slippery surface. Matting is generally rough on the feet but kind on the pocket — woven vegetable fibre such as sisal, coir, seagrass or rush is used to cover passageways and spare bedrooms.

BUYING — WHAT TO LOOK FOR

Department stores and flooring specialists offer an enormous range of colours and qualities, but most of the carpets will not be right for you when you decide to look for a carpet for a particular room.

Before you go shopping, think of the amount of wear and the amount of dirt which the carpet will have to suffer. Also write down the amount you can afford to pay. At the store, check for labels which will suit your purpose — a medium wear grade would not be good enough for a living room filled with children. For hallways and kitchens look for a fibre or fibre blend which will resist stains.

Now it's down to money. If your budget is strictly limited then there is no point in looking at all-wool woven carpets — you will have to choose something cheaper. Do remember that most of the wear grades come in a wide range of prices. The general rule is to buy a carpet which is as densely packed with tufts as you can afford. The more tufts, the dearer the carpet as denseness is a key feature of quality. To test for denseness, bend a sample of the carpet back on itself. If the base is easily seen then the pile is not very dense.

Finally there is colour and pattern, and nobody can help you here. Choose the style which makes you happy, but remember that pale colours without a pattern make a room look larger but patterns and bright colours are better at hiding dirt and minor imperfections. Try to obtain a sample to take home — it may look quite different next to your curtains and in your lighting. Remember to buy underlay. If fitting is extra, get a written quotation.

LOOKING AT THE LABEL

There is no universally-accepted system for labelling carpets. However, most British-made carpets are labelled according to British Standard 3655 and so you will find the following information:
Method of construction — Tufted, Axminster etc
Yarn material — Nylon, Wool, Rayon etc
Width
Laying instructions
Care instructions

There may also be a CP (Carpet Performance) Rating. These ratings are awarded on the basis of laboratory tests and durability assessments carried out by the British Carpet Manufacturers' Association. Most high-quality carpets bear a CP Rating label, but it is a voluntary scheme and so the absence of a label does not necessarily mean poor quality.

A	EXTRA HEAVY WEAR	Contract use only — for extremely heavy wear areas such as shops
B	VERY HEAVY WEAR	The most durable domestic grade — for stairs and much-used living rooms
C	HEAVY WEAR	The standard grade for busy areas at home — living rooms, main hallways etc
D	GENERAL WEAR	The grade for average wear — dining rooms, entertaining rooms etc
E	MEDIUM WEAR	The bedroom grade, suitable for rooms which get used for only part of the day
F	LIGHT WEAR	The grade for rooms which are used only occasionally, such as the spare bedroom

UNDERLAY

Some carpets have a built-in underlay, but these foam-backed types are not meant for heavy-duty wear. With all other carpets you should always use a separate underlay — softness is increased, insulation is improved and life expectancy is extended. Foam rubber is the most resilient — the ripple type is spongier than flat foam rubber. The other sorts of underlay (crumb rubber, needlefelt and latex-impregnated felt) are less comfortable. Never use old underlay or old carpeting as underlay — uneven wearing of the carpet is bound to result.

SHADING

Shading is a peculiar phenomenon. Light and dark areas appear on the carpet, due to the tufts leaning in different directions, and the effect on a plain carpet can be an eyesore to some people. It is a feature of cut pile carpets with straight fine-textured yarns — velvet piles are most affected. It is more noticeable on plain carpets than patterned ones and the effect is heightened by pastel shades rather than strong colours. Pressure marking is perhaps easy to understand — the area along traffic lanes tends to be affected by shading. But true shading remains a mystery — in some (but not all) velvet carpets an irregular-shaped patch will suddenly appear to turn a darker shade as the tufts change direction, and nobody seems to know why it happens.

COATINGS

Stain protectors: Scotchgard protector is available as an aerosol for treating new or shampooed carpets. The coated fibres do not absorb stains and dirt penetration is inhibited. The need for frequent cleaning is reduced, and the protective film will withstand several shampooings.

Anti-static sprays: Most synthetic fibres generate static electricity in a dry atmosphere, and the result is a mild shock when a metal object is touched. This can be unpleasant — increase the humidity of the room or spray on an anti-static product which contains metal particles which earth the fibres.

CARPET CONSTRUCTION

There are several ways in which the pile may be attached to the backing. The traditional method of making carpets is to weave them — the pile and backing being created at the same time. Two methods are involved — Axminster and Wilton, which are types of weaving and not brand names nor indications of quality. Tufted carpets are a modern and less expensive alternative to weaving, and so are bonded carpets. Needleloom carpets do not have a standard pile — fibres are punched into the backing and secured with an adhesive.

				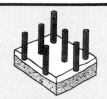
AXMINSTER The pile is woven in as a series of tufts, the tufts being cut during the weaving process. The main features are a wide variety of colours and patterns with a smooth cut pile. Multi-coloured luxury carpets are Axminster — backing is jute or plastic yarn.	**WILTON** The pile is woven in as a continuous length rather than as a series of tufts. The main features are a carpet with 1-5 colours and an absence of complex patterns. The pile is nearly always looped, but may occasionally be cut.	**TUFTED** The pile is stitched into the primary backing, coated with latex and then secured with a second backing. The main features are a vast range of colours and patterns with either a cut or looped pile.	**BONDED** The pile is stuck on to the backing with an adhesive, producing a surface ranging from an almost flat pile to a soft and velvety one. Loops may be cut or uncut. The main features are plain colours and absence of fraying when cut.	**FLOCKED** A form of bonded carpet — the short fibres (usually nylon) are electrostatically fixed into the adhesive on the backing. A flocked carpet does not fray when cut. High-density flocking produces kitchen-grade carpets.

TYPES OF PILE

CUT PILE Each tuft is cut off at the top so that the pile is made of single and not looped fibres. Standard cut pile is neither velvety nor shaggy 	**VELVET PILE** Carpet with short and densely packed fibres, giving a distinct velvety look. More likely to show shading and tracking than other types — note that all strips must be laid the same way. The velvety effect is less pronounced in Velour, Plush and Saxony carpets
	TWIST PILE Carpet with tufts made from tightly twisted yarn. These tufts lie at various angles — less likely to show shading and tracking than straight pile
	SHAG PILE Carpet with tufts at least one inch long. Luxurious, but the pile is not dense and so mats down very quickly with heavy traffic. Needs regular cleaning and combing
	STRAIGHT PILE Carpets with tufts made from untwisted yarn. Less 'pebbly' than twisted yarn, but increased tracking is the cost of this smoother look
LOOPED PILE Each tuft contains loops of fibres which are left uncut. The looped tufts are less likely than cut pile to crush down under pressure, but they are more difficult to clean 	**BRUSSELS PILE** Carpet with long loops — a Wilton carpet
	CORD Carpet with very short loops — a Wilton carpet. Woolcord is made from sheep's wool — haircord is produced from the hair of goats, pigs or horses. Cords are hard-wearing — cheaper cords are bonded (not woven) carpets
	BERBER Carpet with a number of distinctive features — thick yarn, dense pile, looped tufts and 'natural' colours such as cream or grey. Wool is the usual fibre
CUT & LOOPED PILE Both cut and looped tufts are present	**SCULPTURED PILE** Carpet with distinct areas of cut and looped tufts giving a distinct pattern. The terms 'figured pile' and 'embossed pile' are used to describe this effect, although the sculptured look can be obtained by combining straight and twisted yarns or by using tufts of different lengths

CARPET FIBRES

FIBRE	PROPERTIES
WOOL	The traditional carpet fibre with many advantages — unmatched appearance and feel, excellent resistance to flattening, static electricity and staining plus the ability to dye well. It cleans easily and is flame resistant, but there are 3 basic drawbacks. It is expensive, it requires moth-proofing and it is not as durable as nylon. As a result blends are now very popular — see below
ACRYLIC	This is the man-made fibre which looks and feels rather like wool. It is easy to clean and stains can be removed very simply. Unfortunately it does flatten although it is hard-wearing
NYLON (Antron, Timbrelle)	This is the hardest wearing fibre, easily cleaned and with good stain resistance. With ordinary nylons there is none of the soft feel of wool and there can be both static and cigarette-burn problems. It is the 4th generation nylons (Antron, Timbrelle) which are rather wool-like and resist flattening
POLYESTER	Soft and easy to clean, but with the usual static and cigarette-burn problems. Its resilience is not good — blending with other materials is necessary to produce a hard-wearing carpet
POLYPROPYLENE	A hard-wearing synthetic fibre which is used in blends. On its own it crushes easily and has a harsh feel, but it is waterproof and inexpensive. The range of colours is limited
VISCOSE & MODIFIED VISCOSE	A cheap fibre which was once the standard blend with more expensive materials. It does not wear well and it is not particularly resilient
BLENDS	Blends of fibres are popular — synthetics can reduce the price of wool and also add other features. The classic blend is 80 per cent wool/20 per cent nylon, but there are many other types

Walls & Wall Coverings

One painted or papered wall may look very much like another, but the structure behind them can be quite different. There are times when it is necessary to know the make-up of the inner walls — when you are putting up shelves and wall units or repairing holes prior to papering etc. It is absolutely essential to know the wall structure if you plan to make any structural alterations to it. It may be a loadbearing wall, supporting either the roof or some other structure upstairs. In that case, you will have to obtain planning permission from your local council before starting work.

The outer walls of your house may be constructed in various ways, depending on its age and style. Once it was just a matter of brick, stone or wood, but in modern houses you will usually find either a supporting wall of bricks with an inner skin of concrete blocks, or a supporting frame of timber with an outer skin of bricks (see page 100). In all cases, both outer and internal walls carry inner linings which form the rooms of the house.

This lining is nearly always either plaster or plasterboard, providing fire insulation, heat insulation and noise reduction as well as a smooth surface for decorating. The range of wall coverings these days is truly enormous, but for most people it remains a matter of choosing an appealing paper which may or may not be painted after hanging.

INNER WALL TYPES

SOLID WALL
Plaster on masonry (brick, stone, concrete, blocks etc). A common form of lining on the walls of old houses — bricks are covered with 2 or 3 coats of plaster. Such walls are the easiest in which to secure fixings.

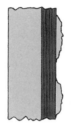

LATH AND PLASTER WALL
A common form of lining on the walls and ceilings of old houses until 50 years ago. Plaster was laid on a framework of narrow wooden laths — such walls are difficult to attach heavy objects to and are often uneven.

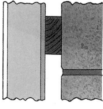

DRYLINED WALL
Plasterboard on masonry. Plasterboard began replacing plaster about 70 years ago — today it is the standard wall lining. It is easier and quicker to use than plaster. Fixing battens may or may not be present.

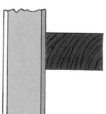

PARTITION WALL
Plasterboard on stud. Wooden frames of upright studs and horizontal noggings are used for both external and internal walls in modern houses. The frame is covered with plasterboard — the wall is hollow.

Identifying your wall type

The first step is to tell whether it is a hollow partition wall or if there is a backing of wood or masonry behind the plaster or plasterboard. The usual advice is to tap the wall and see if there is a hollow sound, but this can be deceptive — some concrete block walls sound hollow when tapped. Undoubtedly the best way is to drill a small test hole in an inconspicuous place — if there is white dust, little resistance to the bit and the drill soon shoots forward, you are dealing with a partition wall. Wood dust in the bit would suggest a lath and plaster wall.

With more solid walls examine the bit after drilling — this will tell you the material behind the plaster or plasterboard. Brick gives red dust and only moderate resistance to the drill, breeze blocks produce dark grey dust, and strong resistance to the drill plus light grey or cream dust reveals concrete or stone.

PLASTER
Plastering the walls of rooms has been going on for thousands of years, but there have been many advances in recent years to make the job easier and more successful for the amateur. Old-fashioned cement plaster is still widely used for rendering outside walls or damp walls inside, but for standard work gypsum-based plasters are a much better choice. They are easily worked, set quickly and produce a smooth finish.

Don't buy more than you need — gypsum plaster quickly deteriorates when stored. Choose the correct grade — this will depend on the surface to be plastered and the job the plaster has to do. An **undercoat** plaster is applied quite thickly to remove the unevenness of the surface. This coat has several alternative names — undercoat, base coat, browning coat, backing coat or floating coat. **Finish** plaster is finer-grained and is applied as an 1/8 in. layer over undercoat plaster or as a 1/5 in. layer over plasterboard. This layer is carefully smoothed to produce a surface which can be papered or painted.

For the DIY enthusiast there are **one-coat** plasters which can be used for both the undercoat and finish layers. More convenient, but also more expensive.

DEALING WITH WALL PROBLEMS

● SMALL HOLES AND CRACKS IN PLASTER

(1) Remove all loose plaster with a filling knife. Sides of the damaged area must be sound

(3) Brush away all dust from the damaged area

(5) Press the filler into the damaged area, moving the knife at right angles to the crack

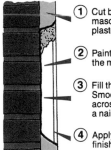

(7) With deep cracks it may be necessary to apply 2 separate layers to fill the hole

(2) Undercut edges, if possible, so filler can key into plaster

(4) Dampen the sides of the crack or hole with a paintbrush

(6) Remove excess filler by drawing the knife along the crack

(8) When dry the surface should be sanded with fine glasspaper to produce a flush finish

● HAIRLINE CRACKS IN WALLS AND CEILINGS

Long and straight hairline cracks are caused by the movement of plasterboards. These cracks are extremely difficult to fill — plaster or filler soon drop out. You can widen the crack to provide a more satisfactory key, but it is better to cover the affected ceiling or walls with a thick textured paper.

● GAPS BETWEEN CEILING AND WALLS

These are caused by slight movements of the house, and there is no point in trying to fill them. Cover instead with a coving to bridge the gap.

● LONG AND WIDE VERTICAL CRACKS

These may indicate a serious structural fault such as subsidence. Seek professional advice.

● DAMP PATCHES OR MOULD GROWTH

See Chapter 7.

FILLERS

Cellulose fillers are available in both powder form for mixing with water and in ready-to-use form. The advantage of a powder product is the ability to produce different consistencies. Deep cracks and wide holes need a stiff paste — fine cracks call for a cream-like mix. Add the recommended amount of water and stir thoroughly — an uneven mixture will produce disappointing results.

● REPAIRING PLASTERBOARD

Small holes can be repaired with scrim (see below) and plaster, but it is more usual to repair plasterboard by fixing a patch. The damaged board is cut away to the joists or studs on each side. A new piece is fitted and the edges covered with scrim and plaster before applying a thin finish layer of plaster over the whole area.

● LARGE HOLES IN PLASTER

When a piece of plaster falls away, tap the wall. If it is a solid wall but sounds hollow over a large area, call in a builder to replaster the wall. If the wall is basically sound and only a limited area is affected, you can try patching.

(1) Cut back to sound plaster and down to the masonry if necessary. Remove all loose plaster and dust

(2) Paint the hole with PVA bonding agent if the masonry below is absorbent

(3) Fill the hole with undercoat plaster. Smooth off by drawing a straight board across the plaster. Score the surface with a nail. Leave to dry

(4) Apply a thin layer of finish plaster

PLASTERBOARD

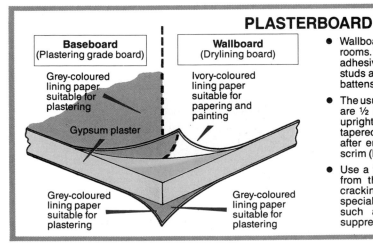

Baseboard (Plastering grade board)

Grey-coloured lining paper suitable for plastering

Gypsum plaster

Grey-coloured lining paper suitable for plastering

Wallboard (Drylining board)

Ivory-coloured lining paper suitable for papering and painting

Grey-coloured lining paper suitable for plastering

● Wallboards are the most popular material for lining rooms. They can be stuck directly on to masonry with an adhesive or nailed with plasterboard nails on to the studs and noggings of a partition wall or on to wooden battens fixed on a masonry wall.

● The usual sizes are 8 ft × 4 ft and 6 ft × 3 ft — the widths are ½ in. and ⅜ in. Store boards flat but carry them upright. The best type to use for decorating have tapered edges. The slight hollows left between boards after erecting are filled with plaster or filler in which scrim (bandage-like fine hessian) is embedded.

● Use a fine-toothed saw for cutting wallboard — work from the ivory side. Support the board to prevent cracking. Several non-standard types are available for special purposes — these have an improved feature, such as fire resistance, water resistance, noise suppression or heat insulation.

WALL FIXINGS

There always seems to be something which has to be fixed to a wall. If the wall is a solid one you have no problem — there are satisfactory fittings for any weight from small pictures to large cupboards. But lath and plaster walls and partition walls do pose a problem — a heavy-duty fixing is not possible here. The only answer is to locate a support (usually wooden but occasionally metal) behind the plaster or plasterboard and then screw or bolt into it.

SELF-ADHESIVE PAD
Double-sided, self-adhesive pads made of PVC foam can be used on a clean and non-fibrous surface to hold lightweight pictures. Adhesion is strong, but the fixing is no stronger than the bond of the paper or paint to the wall

WALL PLUG
The plug should be large enough to go to the back of the hole and wide enough to fit the hole tightly. As the screw is driven in the plug expands to grip the hole tightly. Plastic wall plugs have largely replaced fibre ones

PICTURE HOOK
Brass picture hooks can be used for hanging framed pictures and small mirrors to solid walls. There will be 1, 2 or 3 hardened pins — use a pin hammer to drive them in. Picture hooks are not suitable for heavy frames or large mirrors

MASONRY NAIL
These extra-hard nails are driven directly into masonry — there should be at least 1 in. penetration into the brick, block etc behind the plaster or plasterboard. Drive in with a series of light taps. Hit the head squarely — wear goggles

PLASTIC FILLER
Sometimes a hole becomes too large and ragged to hold a plug. Widen the hole at the back and moisten filler. Ram it into the hole and insert the screw. Do not tighten fully until the filler has hardened

WALL ANCHOR
This is the fitting for heavy-duty work in solid walls, especially if there are any doubts about the strength of the masonry behind. As the bolt is tightened, the metal 'wings' open to grip the sides of the hole

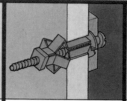

HOLLOW-WALL PLUG
A fixing for hollow walls. As the screw is tightened, the metal, plastic or rubber casing inside the cavity flattens against the inside surface, thereby forming a firm anchor. The screw should be turned gradually

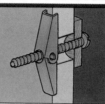

SPRING TOGGLE BOLT
A fixing for ceilings and hollow walls. Two spring-loaded wings open when the bolt has been inserted — these wings grip the inside surface. Make sure there is enough space for the wings to operate. Strong, but not removable

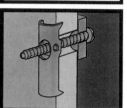

GRAVITY TOGGLE BOLT
A fixing for hollow walls. A bar drops down when the bolt has been inserted — this bar grips the inside surface as the screw is tightened. Make sure there is enough space for the bar to operate. Strong but not removable

Choosing the right fixing

	LIGHT LOAD eg Pictures 　　Skirting boards 　　Plaques	MEDIUM LOAD eg Large mirrors 　　Shelves for plates 　　Small wall units	HEAVY LOAD eg Cupboards 　　Shelves for books 　　Large wall units
SOLID WALL	Masonry nail or Picture hook or Wall plug	Wall plug (Use a cellular block plug if masonry behind is breeze block or aerated concrete block)	Wall anchor or No. 10 or 12 wall plug if masonry behind is brick or concrete
LATH AND PLASTER WALL	Toggle bolt or Nail or screw into stud or joist behind plaster	Toggle bolt or Screw into stud or joist behind plaster	Screw into stud or joist behind plaster
DRYLINED WALL	Masonry nail or Wall plug (Make sure the nail or plug goes into masonry behind plasterboard)	Wall plug (Make sure the plug goes at least 1 in. into masonry behind plasterboard)	Wall anchor (Make sure the wall anchor goes 1 – 2 in. into masonry behind plasterboard)
PARTITION WALL	Hollow-wall plug or Nail or screw into stud or joist behind plasterboard	Hollow-wall plug or Toggle bolt or Screw into stud or joist behind plasterboard	Screw into stud or joist behind plasterboard

LOCATING WOODEN SUPPORTS

If you plan to put up a heavy object on either a lath and plaster or a partition wall or ceiling you will have to find a wooden support which can bear the retaining screws. The simplest way is to tap the wall with the handle of a screwdriver or chisel — a change in sound to a dull thud indicates that a wooden joist, stud or nogging has been reached. Sounds simple, but it doesn't always work. Other methods are to use a magnet or hand metal detector to locate the plasterboard nails; or to measure from the corner of a partition wall, remembering that studs are usually erected at 18 in. intervals.

BORING THE HOLE

Use a masonry bit for boring into walls — an 8 – 12 mm bit is suitable for most jobs. Use a slow speed, removing the bit occasionally to allow it to cool and to remove dust. When making this withdrawal do not switch off or the bit may jam in the hole. Aim to make a hole which is 1 – 2 in. deep in the masonry and keep the bit at right angles to the wall. Do not let it wander or a conical hole will result. When drilling through tile always cover the site of the hole with masking tape before you start. For concrete walls you will need a hammer-action drill. If in doubt, check with a portable metal detector that there are no cables or pipes behind the plaster.

WALL COVERINGS

ROLLS

TYPE	DETAILS
LINING PAPER for painting or papering over	It is not generally necessary to line the walls before papering or painting, but a plain lining paper is sometimes needed to provide a smooth and even surface. Lining is essential if you plan to paper a painted wall. Rolls are usually longer and wider than standard wallpaper — the strips of paper are laid horizontally. Buy **Medium Grade** to hide cracks and other imperfections — lightweight grade tends to stretch when pasted. **Linen-backed Lining Paper** The best choice if the wall is subject to movement and cracking. **Extra-white Lining Paper** The best choice if the surface is to be painted rather than papered.
RELIEF COVERING for painting over	If the surface is uneven and somewhat bumpy, it is often better to use a pre-painting lining which has a raised rather than a plain surface. There are numerous types — they are generally easy to hang but are difficult to remove. **'Anaglypta'** Two layers of paper embossed with a low-relief pattern. Many types available. **'Supaglypta'** Two layers of cotton-based paper embossed with a high-relief pattern. **'Vinaglypta'** Paper with a vinyl surface, embossed with a high-relief pattern. Hard-wearing and scrubbable. **Foamed Vinyl** The raised pattern is spongy and not embossed — the paper backing is flat. There is no danger of squashing the pattern when hanging. Expensive. **Woodchip Paper** Paper in which wood chips and sawdust have been included to produce an oatmeal-like surface. Inexpensive.
STANDARD WALLPAPER	Despite all the innovations of recent years, standard wallpaper in 33 ft × 20½ in. rolls remains by far the most popular type of wall covering. The paper bears a printed pattern and the surface is either smooth or embossed. Choose an embossed paper if the wall is uneven. The advantages of standard wallpapers are economy and the enormous range of colours and patterns. However, they are not resistant to scuffing or soiling, and they cannot be washed. Look at paper quality and not just colour and pattern when buying. Cheap and lightweight papers tend to stretch and tear easily when wet with paste. To avoid problems choose a medium- or heavy-weight paper. **Ordinary Wallpaper** is machine-printed — **Hand-printed Wallpaper** is made by block- or screen-printing — the result is exclusive, expensive and often in non-standard roll sizes.
WASHABLE WALLPAPER	A thin plastic coating is placed on standard wallpaper during manufacture — the result is a surface which has good stain resistance and can be wiped clean with a damp cloth. It is not as easy to hang as standard wallpaper and is also more difficult to strip.
VINYL	Vinyls (also called **Paper-backed Vinyls**) are an excellent choice for kitchens, bathrooms and children's rooms. A thick layer of PVC which contains the pattern is fused on to a paper backing. Vinyls are waterproof, scrubbable and easy to hang. They are also dry-strippable (the plastic layer can be easily pulled away from the backing paper which remains as a lining paper for redecoration). They are stain- and scuff-resistant, but they are also expensive. **Smooth Vinyl** is available in many colours and patterns — **Relief Vinyl** is embossed and many tile-like designs are available.
FLOCK PAPER	Plastic fibres or silk ones are stuck on to a wallpaper or vinyl base. The result is a wall covering with a velvet-like pile. For ease of hanging and upkeep, buy a ready-pasted type with a vinyl base.
FOIL PAPER	Patterned and coloured foil is attached to a paper backing to give an unusual and light-reflecting wall covering. There are more problems than advantages — it is difficult to hang and expensive to buy, and small imperfections on the wall surface are highlighted. Foils should not be used in bathrooms or behind light fixtures.
READY-PASTED COVERING	Removes the need for a pasting table. The back of the paper is coated with dry adhesive — this turns into paste when the ready-pasted wall covering is drawn through water in a trough. A number of the wall coverings described on this page are available in ready-pasted form.
FOAMED POLYETHYLENE	Removes the need for a pasting table. The wall is pasted, not the wall covering. You work straight from the roll — a sheet of lightweight plastic which is textured and patterned. **'Novamura'** is easy to hang and strip, feels warm to the touch and can be sponged down.
FABRIC & CORK	A variety of luxury papers is available in which either a fabric or a thin layer of **Cork** is bonded on to backing paper. **Hessian** is the cheapest — unbacked hessian is even less expensive but it is more difficult to hang. **Grasscloth** and **Silk** are difficult to handle and with all of them it is better to get a professional to do the work unless you have the skill and experience. The rolls are wider than wallpaper and it is usual to paste the wall rather than the paper.

Lining paper

'Anaglypta'

Standard wallpaper

Washable wallpaper

Vinyl

Flock paper

Foil paper

'Novamura'

Hessian

Ceramic tile

Mosaic tiles

Mirror tile

Stone tile

Cork tile

Polystyrene tile

Wood cladding

TILES

TYPE	DETAILS
CERAMIC	The basic tile, made of clay which is coloured, glazed and fired. The surface may be plain or patterned, smooth or textured. The tiles are durable, stain- and water-resistant, making them a good choice for kitchens and bathrooms. Choose heat-resistant tiles for fixing around a fireplace, boiler or cooker. Numerous sizes and shapes are available — hexagons, oblongs, ornate provencales etc. Squares are the most popular, and the basic sizes are 4¼ in. × 4¼ in. and 6 in. × 6 in. Ordinary tiles without rounded edges are called field tiles — an RE tile has one rounded and glazed edge for finishing off a border and an REX tile has 2 rounded and glazed edges for finishing off a corner. A narrow space has to be left between tiles — if you are new to tiling you should buy ones which have built-in spacing lugs around the edges. Universal tiles make fixing easier — edges are bevelled so that you don't have to leave a space when fixing.
MOSAIC	Smooth ceramic tiles are mounted on a sheet — this paper or mesh may be on the back of the tiles or on their face, depending on the manufacturer. Mosaic tiles are fixed in the usual way (see pages 67 – 68) — remove surface sheeting (if present) when the adhesive is dry. Grout between the tiles as with ordinary ceramics. Quite expensive, but useful for tiling small or awkwardly-shaped areas.
PLASTIC	Thin tiles which are made to look like ceramic ones but which have several advantages — they are warm to the touch, can be cut with scissors and bent round corners, and can be attached with double-sided, self-adhesive pads. Standard sizes are 4¼ in. × 4¼ in., 6 in. × 6 in. and 12 in. × 12 in. Good for the not-so-handy, but they do not have the durability nor the scratch-resistance of ceramic tiles.
METAL	Attractive in the right situation — gold, silver or copper with a shiny or matt surface. They are easily fixed and can be cut with scissors, but do not fix them under light fittings and never use an abrasive cleaner.
MIRROR	Squares of silvered glass, which may be clear or tinted, are attached to walls with double-sided, self-adhesive pads. A good way of increasing the apparent depth of an alcove, but the wall must be perfectly flat or the distorted reflection will be unsightly.
BRICK & STONE	Thin slices of real or simulated brick or stone can be used to provide a real-wall effect. More realistic than brick or stone wallpaper or vinyl, but you can't remove them with ease if you later change your mind. Make sure that you buy a suitable adhesive for the brick or stone tiles you have chosen.
CORK	Sheets of cork in a variety of shades, usually 12 in. × 12 in. Cork provides good heat and noise insulation, and is warm to the touch, but do buy a steam-proof grade if you intend to use them in the bathroom. Seal cork tiles with a polyurethane varnish after fixing.
CEILING	**Polystyrene Tiles** are the cheapest and the most popular. Lightweight, easy to fix and available in both smooth and embossed forms, they do pose a fire risk in certain situations. Don't use them in the kitchen and do not cover with an oil-based paint. **Fibre Tiles** are thicker and have better insulating properties. Edges are usually tongue-and-grooved so that you can pin an interlaced sheet to the ceiling joists. The usual sizes for ceiling tiles are 12 in. × 12 in. and 18 in. × 18 in.

WOODEN PANELS

TYPE	DETAILS
CLADDING	Tongue-and-grooved or shiplap boards provide a warm and durable wall surface with a touch of luxury. Whitewood (for staining) and knotty pine are the least expensive — hardwood boards such as mahogany are the dearest. The usual board size is ½ in. × 3½ in. × 8 ft, but there are other sizes available.
SHEET	Decorative-faced sheets of plywood or hardboard can be used to cover walls quickly — the standard sheet size is 4 ft × 8 ft. Panels with an embossed grain can be especially effective. There is a wide range of prices. At one end of the scale are sheets faced with luxury hardwood veneers such as rosewood — at the other end are sheets of thin plywood faced with printed plastic or paper.

WALLPAPERING

BUYING

● MAKE SURE THE TYPE AND DESIGN SUIT THE ROOM
The type you choose should be right for the room — washables where steam or stains can be a problem, embossed or woodchip papers for poor quality walls and so on — see pages 61 – 62 for guidance. The choice of colour and pattern should also be influenced by the room. There are a few general rules. If you want to create a feeling of space, choose a plain or small-patterned, light-coloured paper — dark colours and large patterns will make a room look smaller. Horizontal stripes will make a wall look longer — vertical stripes will make a ceiling look higher. Bright primary colours create interest and excitement, pastel shades induce relaxation.

● BUY THE RIGHT TYPE FOR YOUR SKILL
Avoid thin papers, foils, flocks and fabrics if you are inexperienced and plan to do the work yourself.

● FIND OUT HOW MANY ROLLS YOU WILL NEED
Cut a piece of wood or string to provide a 20½ in. measure. Working round the room use this to find out the number of full-length strips you will need. Now work out how many strips you will get from each roll — measure the length from ceiling to skirting, add 4 in. and divide this length into 33 ft. You can now calculate the answer — for example, you will need 7 rolls if the total number of strips required is 28 and you can get 4 strips from each roll. Always buy an extra roll if you are inexperienced or have chosen a large pattern.

● BUY WISELY
It is usually worth shopping round once you have chosen the paper from a pattern book — prices do vary from shop to shop. Always check that the batch number on each roll is the same — failure to do so can lead to annoying differences in colour. Also beware of the label 'Shade before hanging' if you are a beginner — it means that there can be colour variations in the same batch.

PREPARING

● GET THE ROOM READY
Remove as much furniture as possible. Roll back or cover the carpet with newspaper. Cover chairs, tables etc with dustsheets as wall preparation can be messy work.

● GET THE WALLS READY
The basic objective is to obtain a clean, dry and flat surface. This surface must be rough enough ('keyed') to grip both paste and paper, and firm enough not to move away from the undersurface after wallpapering. It must also be impervious enough not to soak up the paste. Holes and cracks must be filled. Mark screw holes by inserting matchsticks into them. There are different types of preparatory treatment — the right one depends on the surface.
Wallpaper: Paper over it only if it is smooth paper (not plastic) and firmly attached to the wall. Otherwise it will have to be stripped — a long and difficult job. Soak with a solution of a proprietary stripper in warm water. Remove paper with a stripping knife held at an angle to the wall — avoid gouging out holes. Rub off remaining scraps with a glasspaper block. Washable and painted papers are very difficult to remove — score with a serrated scraper before soaking. For large areas hire a steam stripper. To make the job much easier next time, hang a dry-strippable wall covering.
Plaster: You should leave at least 6 months between plastering and papering. New plaster which has not been papered before should be treated with a primer/sealer — use size on old plaster.
Plasterboard: Treat with primer/sealer.
Paint: Wash down emulsion paint — if some washes off you will have to remove all of it. Rub down gloss paint with coarse glasspaper — get rid of all blisters and use lining paper if the prepared surface is uneven and the chosen paper is smooth-surfaced.

EQUIPMENT

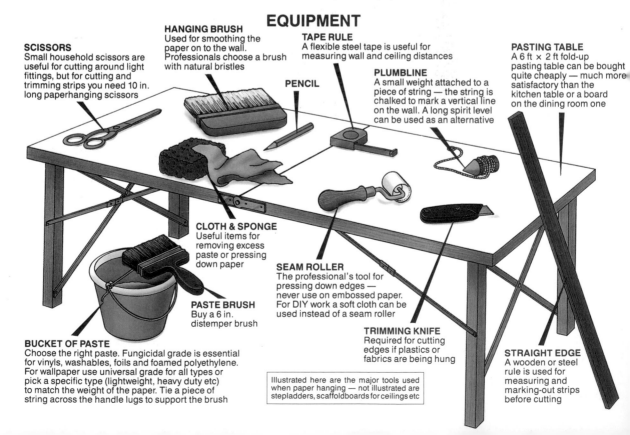

SCISSORS
Small household scissors are useful for cutting around light fittings, but for cutting and trimming strips you need 10 in. long paperhanging scissors

HANGING BRUSH
Used for smoothing the paper on to the wall. Professionals choose a brush with natural bristles

PENCIL

TAPE RULE
A flexible steel tape is useful for measuring wall and ceiling distances

PLUMBLINE
A small weight attached to a piece of string — the string is chalked to mark a vertical line on the wall. A long spirit level can be used as an alternative

PASTING TABLE
A 6 ft × 2 ft fold-up pasting table can be bought quite cheaply — much more satisfactory than the kitchen table or a board on the dining room one

CLOTH & SPONGE
Useful items for removing excess paste or pressing down paper

SEAM ROLLER
The professional's tool for pressing down edges — never use on embossed paper. For DIY work a soft cloth can be used instead of a seam roller

PASTE BRUSH
Buy a 6 in. distemper brush

BUCKET OF PASTE
Choose the right paste. Fungicidal grade is essential for vinyls, washables, foils and foamed polyethylene. For wallpaper use universal grade for all types or pick a specific type (lightweight, heavy duty etc) to match the weight of the paper. Tie a piece of string across the handle lugs to support the brush

TRIMMING KNIFE
Required for cutting edges if plastics or fabrics are being hung

STRAIGHT EDGE
A wooden or steel rule is used for measuring and marking-out strips before cutting

Illustrated here are the major tools used when paper hanging — not illustrated are stepladders, scaffoldboards for ceilings etc

1 Start at one side of the largest window in the room and work towards the door

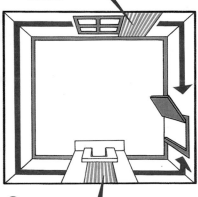

2 Exception: Start at the centre of the chimney breast if the paper has a large pattern

3 Use a plumbline to mark a true vertical. Chalk the string — use coloured chalk if necessary. Pin end to top of wall one roll width less ½ in. from window frame

4 Let weight come to rest. Hold string against the wall and then pluck to leave chalk line

5 Measure the height from ceiling to the skirting board

6 Unroll paper on the pasting table and mark out this length plus 4 in. Cut at right angles to the edge

7 Paste the paper: Cover one half at a time — paste strip A first, then paste out to B and C. Make sure edge overlaps table when pasting

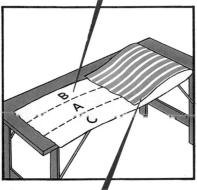

8 Fold pasted half of paper as shown — then paste second half. Wipe off any which has got on to the table

9 Leave paper to soak for time recommended on package. Make sure all strips are left to soak for the same time

10 Carry the strip to the wall, as shown. With experience, you can have one strip pasted and soaking whilst hanging a previous one

11 Open top half. Holding both edges place the paper so that it touches the chalk line and overlaps ceiling join by about 2 in.

12 With the palm of one hand move the paper so that the edge lies along the chalk line

13 Brush down the middle holding the paper slightly away from the wall

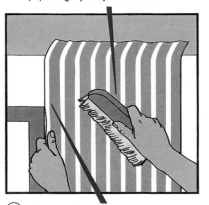

14 Then work towards the edges, brushing well into corners. Wipe the brush frequently

15 Crease the paper along the edge, using the tip of the scissors

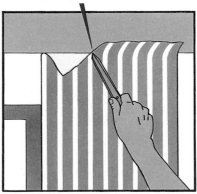

16 Pull the paper back gently. Cut along the crease and then brush back in place

17 Unfold the bottom half of the strip. Smooth down with the hanging brush

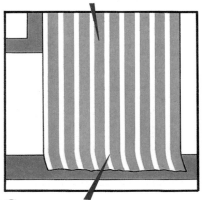

18 Carry out stage ⑮. Wipe off any paste on the ceiling and skirting board

(19) Lay the roll on the floor and measure out the next strip. Make sure the pattern matches and that there is at least a 2 in. overlap at the top and bottom

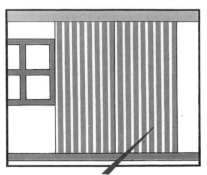

(20) Carry out stages ⑦ to ⑱. This second strip should butt neatly and tightly against the first one

(21) **Room corner:** Cut the last strip vertically so that there will be a ½ in. overlap on the unpapered wall. Keep the offcut

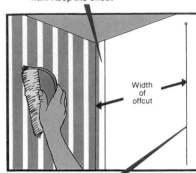

Width of offcut

(22) Follow stages ③ and ④ to make a vertical chalk line. Hang the offcut to the chalk line — lifting up or down to match pattern

(23) **Protruding corner:** Cut the last strip vertically so that there will be a 1 in. overlap on the unpapered wall. Keep the offcut

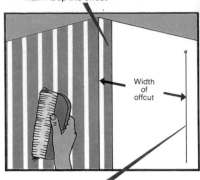

Width of offcut

(24) Follow stages ③ and ④ to make a vertical chalk line. Hang the offcut to the chalk line — lifting up or down to match pattern

(25) **Light fittings:** Switch off at mains. Unscrew fitting and pull forward — trim, leaving a narrow margin inside the area covered by the plate

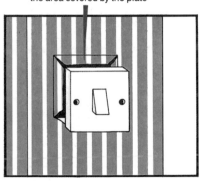

(26) Where the cover cannot be removed, make a series of triangular cuts around the fitting and trim back neatly

Ceiling: Paper ceiling before walls. The techniques for measuring, pasting and trimming are basically the same as for wall hanging, but the work is more tiring. You will probably need someone to help

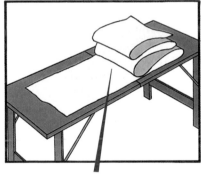

Paste paper as stage ⑦, but fold the pasted portions into concertina-like pleats about 1½ ft long

Erect a stout platform using 2 ladders and a board directly under where you will have to work. Begin at the window and work inwards

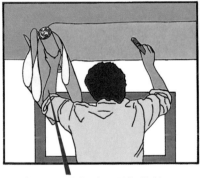

Overlap walls by about ½ in. Hold up all folds with a spare roll of wallpaper — brush into place as you move along the platform

Ready-pasted paper: Cut each strip to the required length (see stages ⑥ and ⑲) and roll loosely with pattern inside. Leave paper immersed in the trough for recommended time

Raise paper gradually and place in position. Smooth down with a sponge, working from the centre to the edges. Have a little ordinary paste handy to secure unstuck edges

WALLPAPERING PROBLEMS

● BUBBLES
A common fault — the usual cause is careless brushing out. Areas are allowed to stick to the wall before all the air behind them has been removed. Brush out steadily from centre to edges — this is a job not to be rushed. Bubbles can also be caused by lumpy paste and insufficient soaking time. If the paste is still wet, lift the paper and smooth out properly. If the paste has dried, cut a cross at the centre of the bubble and then stick down the flaps.

● BUMPS
Unlike bubbles, there is no air within. The cause is poor preparation — some papers highlight wall imperfections. Consider a high-relief textured paper if the wall is in poor condition.

● TEARS
An annoying problem usually associated with poor quality paper, careless handling and/or leaving the paper to soak for longer than necessary.

● PAPER NOT ADHERING
There are numerous possible causes — the usual ones are damp walls, porous walls which have not been sized and the application of too little paste.

● EDGES NOT ADHERING
The usual cause is either too little paste applied to the edges or drying out due to spending too much time over stages ⑬ and ⑭. Even properly-pasted paper will not stick along the seams if you fail to press down with a seam roller or cloth.

● PATTERN NOT MATCHING
The usual cause is irregular stretching due to strips being allowed to soak for varying times. Other causes include allowing part of a long length of pasted paper to drop suddenly when hanging, and brushing out too vigorously.

TILING

BUYING

- **MAKE SURE THE MATERIALS SUIT THE ROOM**
  A vast range of tiles is available — your pocket must decide whether you buy cheap, mass-produced tiles or expensive, hand-painted ones. There are other considerations — a glazed surface is essential if the surface is to be regularly washed and heat-resistant tiles should be used for the area around a boiler, cooker or fire. You must also pick a suitable adhesive — a water-resistant grade for kitchen or bathroom or a heat resistant grade where high temperatures are likely to be a problem.

- **BUY WISELY**
  It is more economical to purchase tiles by the box rather than singly. Make sure you have enough RE and REX types (see page 63) if you are not using universal tiles. It is always wise to buy a few extra ones, and a few very cheap tiles in order to practice cutting. Always check for breakages and imperfections before leaving the shop and buy the required number of plastic spacers if the tiles do not bear their own spacer lugs.

SETTING OUT

The vital first step, when the tiling pattern is carefully worked out before fixing begins. The purpose of setting out is to find both the correct starting point and the correct level for the first row. This ensures that the lines between the tiles will be truly horizontal and vertical. In addition, the aim is to have the body of the tiled area and the top row made up entirely of whole tiles. This means that the cut tiles will be at the sides and the lowest level. A gauge stick (see below) and spirit level are used for setting out. The standard pattern is to have the first row of tiles at one tile's length (or less) above the skirting board, and equal-sized cut tiles at both edges of the tiled area.

PREPARING

- **GET THE WALL READY**
  The surface to be tiled must be dry, level and free from grease. In addition it must be rigid and must also be capable of carrying the weight of the tiles. This means that wallpaper has to be removed and gloss paint should be carefully examined for soundness.

  Plaster: A suitable tiling surface provided it is at least 6 weeks old and has a finish coating (see page 58). Fill cracks and holes, remove bumps and then paint with a plaster primer. Tiling can begin when this is dry.

  Paint: Check carefully. With gloss paint, test that it is firmly bonded on to the wall by pulling at the surface with a strip of adhesive tape. If the paint pulls away, the surface will have to be removed or covered with plywood before tiling. If the paint is sound, remove any loose patches or blisters with a scraper and apply primer to any bare areas. Wash down and rub with coarse glass-paper. Emulsion paint should be removed before tiling.

  Wallpaper: Wallpaper and other wall coverings must be removed before tiling. It is necessary to get down to the plaster or plasterboard. Wash down with water after stripping.

  Wood: Narrow panels are not really suitable for tiling, but wood sheeting, plywood, hardboard and chipboard sheets can be tiled provided they are firmly attached to the wall. Use a flexible tile adhesive.

  Brick: This surface can be tiled as long as it is smooth and dry. Brick walls are, however, usually too rough for tiling — it is generally necessary to line with plywood.

  Tiles: Tiles make a satisfactory base. Fix any loose tiles and rub down with a suitable abrasive paper to provide a key. Wash down thoroughly before tiling begins.

EQUIPMENT

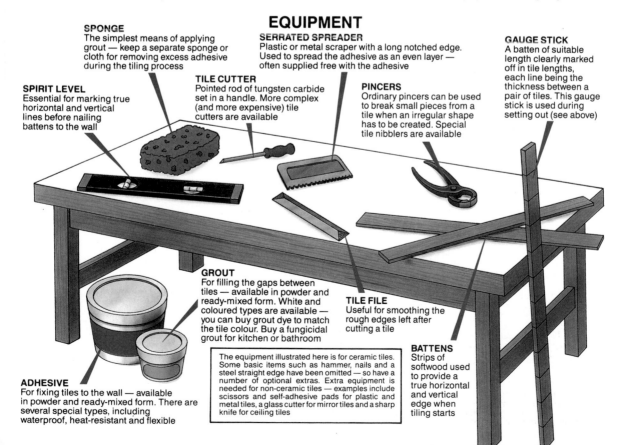

SPONGE
The simplest means of applying grout — keep a separate sponge or cloth for removing excess adhesive during the tiling process

SERRATED SPREADER
Plastic or metal scraper with a long notched edge. Used to spread the adhesive as an even layer — often supplied free with the adhesive

GAUGE STICK
A batten of suitable length clearly marked off in tile lengths, each line being the thickness between a pair of tiles. This gauge stick is used during setting out (see above)

SPIRIT LEVEL
Essential for marking true horizontal and vertical lines before nailing battens to the wall

TILE CUTTER
Pointed rod of tungsten carbide set in a handle. More complex (and more expensive) tile cutters are available

PINCERS
Ordinary pincers can be used to break small pieces from a tile when an irregular shape has to be created. Special tile nibblers are available

GROUT
For filling the gaps between tiles — available in powder and ready-mixed form. White and coloured types are available — you can buy grout dye to match the tile colour. Buy a fungicidal grout for kitchen or bathroom

TILE FILE
Useful for smoothing the rough edges left after cutting a tile

BATTENS
Strips of softwood used to provide a true horizontal and vertical edge when tiling starts

ADHESIVE
For fixing tiles to the wall — available in powder and ready-mixed form. There are several special types, including waterproof, heat-resistant and flexible

The equipment illustrated here is for ceramic tiles. Some basic items such as hammer, nails and a steel straight edge have been omitted — so have a number of optional extras. Extra equipment is needed for non-ceramic tiles — examples include scissors and self-adhesive pads for plastic and metal tiles, a glass cutter for mirror tiles and a sharp knife for ceiling tiles

(1) Nail a batten along the wall to form the horizontal support for the first row. Check with spirit level

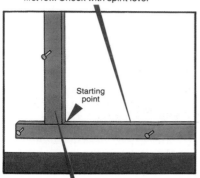

Starting point

(2) Nail second batten on top of this horizontal batten. Check that it is truly vertical

(3) Spread adhesive as an ⅛ in. layer over an area of about 1 sq. yd. Use a serrated spreader

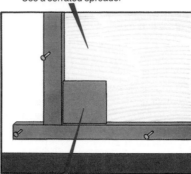

(4) Place first tile in position. Press against adhesive

(5) Work in horizontal rows, pressing (not sliding) tiles into position. Wipe off adhesive which oozes to the surface

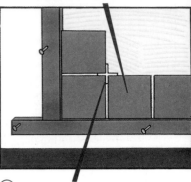

(6) Insert plastic spacers (or matchsticks) if spacer lugs are not present on the tiles. Not necessary if universal tiles are used

(7) Check occasionally that rows are truly horizontal. Remove battens and spacers when all whole tiles have been laid and the adhesive has set (12 – 24 hours)

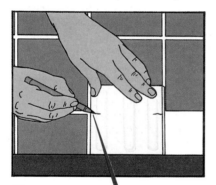

(8) Cut and fit remaining tiles as required. Hold the tile to be cut back to front in the space to be fitted. Mark the edges with a pencil

(9) Reverse the tile and mark the front. Firmly score the tile with the tile cutter and a steel straight edge

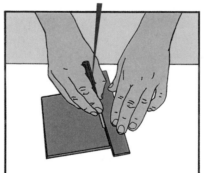

(10) Place a matchstick at both edges of the tile directly under the scored line. Press down on each side to snap the tile

(11) L-shaped and irregular cuts require different treatment. Mark and then score the area to be removed. Make extra score lines

(12) Use pincers to 'nibble' (remove small pieces of tile) until the line is reached. Clean edge with the tile file

(13) Rub grout into the spaces with a sponge once all the tiles have been laid and the adhesive has set

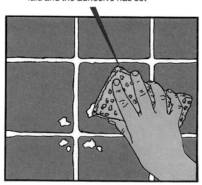

(14) Run a rounded stick or wet finger along the lines to produce a smooth finish. Rub the surface briskly with a soft cloth when the grout is dry

Mirror tiles: A perfectly smooth surface is required. Fix with self-adhesive pads — never use ordinary tile adhesive

To cut tiles, follow stage (9) using a glass cutter in place of the tile cutter. Irregular-shaped cuts are very difficult to make

Polystyrene ceiling tiles: Mark the ceiling with 2 chalk lines, crossing at right angles near the centre

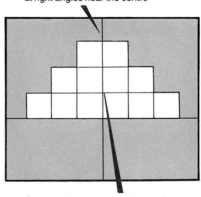

Spread polystyrene adhesive on the back of each tile, going near to but not reaching the edges. Press into place, working to the edges in pyramid fashion. Cut tiles with a sharp knife

Windows & Curtains

The basic purpose of a window is to let light into the room, and here you must strike a balance. Too little glass will make the room dingy and depressing — too large an expanse of unshaded glass will result in soaring temperatures in summer. There are no hard and fast rules — the experts say that the window area should be about 15 per cent of the floor area.

Windows also provide ventilation, which is so vital for dispelling stale air, preventing mould, reducing condensation and so on. Here there are strict rules — the Building Regulations insist that the area of openable glass must be at least 5 per cent of the floor area if the room is to be lived in for part of the day.

A window cannot be simply lifted out and replaced like a rug or cupboard. Despite the large amount of work and expense involved there are still times when it is necessary to have one or more replacement windows installed. The wooden frame may have rotted or you may wish to have a larger window in the living room in order to enjoy the beauty of your garden. You may wish to modernise the outside appearance of your home or you may be tired of having to paint steel-framed windows every few years. It is, of course, sensible to instal double-glazed replacement windows when such needs arise, but to put in double glazing solely as a means of cutting down on heating bills is not really worthwhile.

Consider all the factors before deciding to tear out your windows. If the house was built before the war then the windows will not be standard size and you won't be able to buy a replacement off the shelf. Pick a suitable style and construction material — there have been great advances in recent years, but also check with your local authority that they won't object. Finally make sure that the glass is sufficiently strong for the site and the size of the glazed area. Read pages 72 – 73 as well as the sales leaflets — always insist on safety glass in any high-risk zone such as patio doors or child-high panes of glass. Many thousands of people go to hospital each year because this simple rule is ignored.

In addition to providing light and ventilation, windows give a view of the world outside. This means that during daylight hours a window is a focal point, and interior decorators spend a great deal of time thinking about this aspect. If the view is attractive then the window covering should do nothing to detract from the scene — if the view is an eyesore or open to public gaze then there are blinds, net curtains etc to make life more comfortable. Picking the right curtains is more difficult than most people think — see page 76 for basic guidelines.

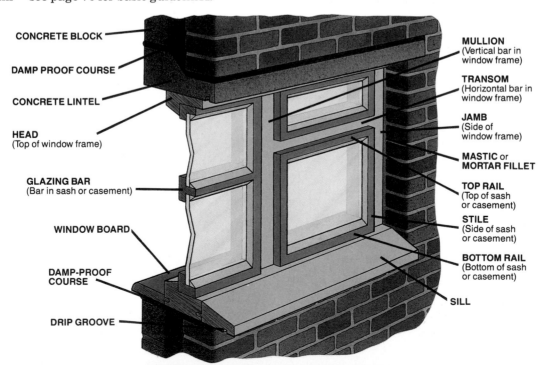

CONCRETE BLOCK

DAMP PROOF COURSE

CONCRETE LINTEL

HEAD
(Top of window frame)

GLAZING BAR
(Bar in sash or casement)

WINDOW BOARD

DAMP-PROOF
COURSE

DRIP GROOVE

MULLION
(Vertical bar in
window frame)

TRANSOM
(Horizontal bar in
window frame)

JAMB
(Side of
window frame)

MASTIC or
MORTAR FILLET

TOP RAIL
(Top of sash
or casement)

STILE
(Side of sash
or casement)

BOTTOM RAIL
(Bottom of sash
or casement)

SILL

WINDOW TYPES

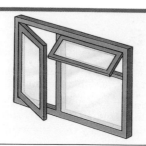

CASEMENT WINDOW
The casement window has taken over from the traditional sash window as the most popular type. A large number of styles and sizes are available — all have at least one hinged piece of framed glass (the casement) and the usual pattern is one side-hung casement plus a fixed pane of glass and a top-hung fanlight. Look for easy-clean hinges — they allow you to get behind the casement to clean the glass. For casement windows which act as doors, see page 78.

SASH WINDOW
Stout sash windows with 2 wooden sashes which slide up and down were once the basic type. There are advantages — good ventilation and it's safe to open the top sash for ventilation when children are around. But there are also problems — they can rattle, stick and sash cords can break. In modern windows spring sash balances have replaced the old system of cord-carried weights and pullies. Don't regard them as old fashioned — modern aluminium sash windows are excellent.

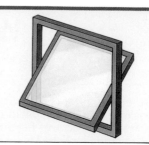

PIVOT WINDOW
The answer to outside window cleaning — the window can be reversed for washing and such windows can be a boon where cleaning from outside would be impossible. Wood is the usual construction material and both horizontal and vertical pivot types are made. The pivot window can be attractive in a modern setting but has not become popular. When open part of it projects into the room and there is also the danger aspect. Small children can easily crawl through.

LOUVRE WINDOW
Strips of glass are fitted into a metal frame which contains an open-shut lever. When closed the glass panes press together — when open there is a large space with very little obstruction to the air outside. Not very popular — the view outdoors is obstructed and they can be draughty when closed. An added drawback is the security risk as panes can be removed. You can buy casement windows which have a louvred section instead of a fanlight.

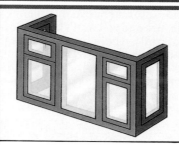

BAY WINDOW
Once part of every architect's stock in trade and a basic feature of the Victorian villa. Nowadays, however, the bay window has lost much of its appeal. There are several styles — square bays which are block shaped, splayed bays with sloping sides, curved bays etc. The roof above the bay may be flat or pitched, and the projection may involve one floor only or the whole height of the house. A Georgian variation is the bow window — a curved bay with many glazing bars.

SLIDING WINDOW
Until the appearance of aluminium as a construction material, horizontal sash windows (Yorkshire lights) were not popular. Lightweight sliding windows are now seen everywhere — in office blocks, hotels and in houses. When open there is no projection either outside or inside, and there is good control of ventilation. Sliding windows are usually double glazed, and the patio door (the type giving access to the garden) has become very popular.

WOOD
Despite the growing interest in aluminium and plastic, timber remains the most popular material for window construction. An off-the-shelf softwood window is the cheapest type you can buy, and its insulation properties are excellent. Of course there is the problem of bulky frames and sections, and the much more serious drawback of regular maintenance. The rule is to choose carefully. Make sure any softwood used in the construction has been pressure-impregnated with a preservative. Choose a hardwood frame if you can afford it — at least make sure the sill is made of hardwood.

STEEL
Galvanised steel windows were popular between the wars. They were fixed in a wooden subframe and adorned semi-detached villas everywhere, but the drawbacks have pushed them into bottom place for replacement windows. Regular maintenance is necessary to prevent rust, and heat insulation is poor. Condensation can be a problem and the wooden subframe will need occasional maintenance. The steel window did introduce one major advantage to window construction — slim sections in place of the stout frames of wooden windows.

ALUMINIUM
The double-glazing boom has increased the popularity of aluminium windows. They are available in anodised or acrylic colours as well as the traditional silvery-grey, and very little maintenance is needed — merely rub down with water and a little detergent twice a year. Some manufacturers fit a thermal break which reduces heat loss and condensation. Another way of reducing heat loss is to buy an aluminium/uPVC composite window. A hardwood subframe is nearly always needed for aluminium windows.

uPVC
Unplasticised polyvinyl chloride has been widely used for some time on the Continent, and at last the advantages of plastic frames have become apparent in Britain. The white, grey or wood-effect frames and casements are rigid, require no maintenance and have the heat-insulating properties of wood. A timber subframe is not usually required and the cost of a made-to-measure window should be no more than for an aluminium one. Drawbacks are few — the surface can be scratched and it will be damaged by a naked flame.

DEALING WITH WINDOW PROBLEMS

● GENERAL MAINTENANCE

Wooden windows should be painted once every 4 – 5 years. Prepare carefully before you begin to paint — if rot is present, carry out remedial treatment (see page 132). Metal windows should also be painted regularly — if rust is present you should cure the problem as soon as possible (see page 133). Do not apply too much paint — avoid a build-up which can cause sashes or casements to stick or fail to close properly. Oil hinges regularly and tighten loose screws. The exception here is the pivot window — do not oil.

● RATTLING WINDOWS

This is a problem of ageing sash windows. Because of movement and shrinkage the beads (strips of wood between and in front of the sashes) no longer fit properly. Wind causes the sashes to move in the space and a rattle is the result. Wedges can be used to hold the sashes tight but this is not a satisfactory solution. It is better to fit nylon-pile draught excluder between the sash edges and the beads. If this fails then the beads will have to be moved — a job for a joiner or DIY enthusiast.

● REPAIRING A BROKEN WINDOW

(1) Wear gloves to remove broken glass. Use a screwdriver or chisel to get rid of all old putty. Remove any glazing sprigs, metal clips or beading and then brush away dirt and dust

(3) The new pane should be 1/8 in. smaller than the minimum width and height of the opening. Make sure you buy the right grade and thickness — see pages 72 – 73 for details

(5) Place new glazing sprigs in position if the frame is a wooden one. Knock the sprigs into the rebate with the side of an old chisel — slide the blade along the surface of the glass — do not use a hammer

(7) Use a putty knife to smooth the putty as a neat bevel. Mitre the corners and then remove all excess putty from glass surface and glazing bars

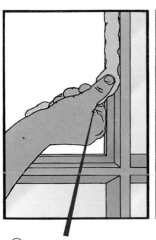

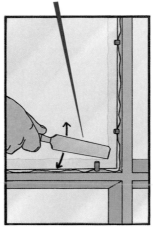

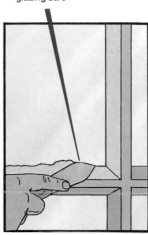

(2) Buy the right grade of putty — linseed oil putty for wood, and metal casement putty for metal. Mould the putty in your hands until it is soft — squeeze a 1/4 in. thick strip into the rebate

(4) Press the glass into the putty until it is firmly bedded in place. Put the bottom of the pane into position first and then press forward — always press the edges and never the middle of the glass

(6) In a metal window use glazing clips. Run another strip of putty in the angle between the new pane and the wooden frame. Only a small amount of putty will be needed if beading is to be fitted

(8) Wipe off remaining traces of putty and fingerprints with a cloth soaked in methylated spirits. Run a moist brush along the putty surface and leave for 2 weeks. Paint, covering all putty

● STICKING WINDOWS

If a sash is shut tight and will not move, tape the glass so that it will not shatter. Then use a mallet to tap a block of wood placed against the wooden or metal rail or stile. Move the block all round the window until the seal is broken. Once opened, rub the inner channels with a block of beeswax or spray with a silicone lubricant. This simple technique may not succeed — the cause may be a build-up of paint, which calls for stripping and then repainting, or it may be due to swelling which requires planing down. The cause of sticking of a casement window may be quite simple — stiff hinges, loose hinges or too much paint. Check all these points.

Unfortunately the cause of sticking of both sash and casement windows may be more serious. The joints of the frame may be loose or the sash may have warped. Another possible reason is that the sash cords have broken, and in all of these cases you should call in a joiner unless you are a knowledgeable DIY enthusiast.

● DRAUGHTS

Hold a lighted candle close to the edges of the window — a flickering flame will reveal that you have a draught problem. The cause may be a break in the mortar fillet between the window frame and the wall — this should be filled with mastic sealer. It is much more likely, however, that the draught is due to a space between the sash or casement and the window frame. The answer with a casement window is usually quite simple — apply self-adhesive foam strip all the way round the rebate of the frame. Sash windows require plastic or nylon-pile draught excluders.

● REPLACEMENT WINDOWS

Numerous DIY books indicate that taking out old windows and installing new ones is a straightforward job provided the diagrams are followed. This advice is best avoided — either leave it to a builder or a replacement window company. If you wish to do it yourself then get someone who is experienced in such work to help you.

GLASS

For most of us panes of glass are things to be washed and not seen, but this desire for invisibility was not really satisfied until the early 1960s. Before that time **sheet glass** was used for house windows — smooth and clear but with varying thicknesses along the panes. The result was some distortion of the view outdoors — this could only be overcome by using **plate glass.** Unfortunately this polished glass was expensive and so was restricted to areas such as shop fronts. Both types have now largely been replaced by **float glass** which is perfectly flat, free from distortion and inexpensive enough to use for all windows.

In general we don't want to notice window glass, and yet it can be a material to add either decorative charm or personal tragedy. Patterned or decorated glass can enhance the appearance of a room, especially when used in internal doors or room dividers. But there is also the danger element — ordinary (or annealed) glass will shatter with razor-sharp pieces when broken. So when putting in new windows keep both the beauty and safety aspects in mind.

Thickness (Imperial)	Thickness (Metric)	Recommended uses
24 oz	3 mm	Only for very small windows — do not use in a high-risk zone
		Picture framing
32 oz	4 mm	The best choice for windows up to 1 sq. yd in area — do not use in a high-risk zone
$\frac{3}{16}$ in.	5 mm	The best choice for windows 1–2 sq. yd in area — do not use in a high-risk zone
$\frac{1}{4}$ in.	6 mm	The best choice for windows 2–3 sq. yd in area — up to 2 sq. yd in a high-risk zone
		Patio doors. Table tops
$\frac{3}{8}$ in.	10 mm	The best choice for very large windows — 2–3 sq. yd in a high-risk zone
		Patio doors. Table tops

Glazing for safety

The rule of thumb is to use 4 mm window glass for small areas and 6 mm for larger areas — but this only applies for sites where there is negligible risk and where high winds are unlikely to be a problem. Where there is some risk of breakage or if the window is exposed to high winds, you should use thicker glass than standard — raise the rule of thumb to 6 mm and 10 mm glass.

In truly high-risk zones this is not enough. You should use some form of safety material — toughened glass, laminated glass or wired glass. Typical high-risk zones are doors with large panes of glass, large glass panels next to doors, glassed-in balustrades and shower screens. Always use safety glass if the glazed area extends below 31 in. from the floor and is likely to have children running nearby.

Of course, you may have a high-risk zone which has been glazed with ordinary window glass and so you have to face the problem of reglazing for safety. One solution is to cover the existing glass with self-adhesive transparent film which will prevent the glass from shattering in case of an accident. Solar-control film has the added advantage of reducing the entry of the sun's heat in summer.

Breakage is not the only problem — children (and the absent-minded) do walk into closed patio doors and the result is a bad bruise rather than lacerations. One answer is to have some form of sticker or central strip on a large expanse of glass, but the protection afforded should not be exaggerated.

CUTTING GLASS

(1) Place the glass on a flat and even surface which has been covered with felt or layers of newspaper

(3) Clean the glass with turps and then place a straight edge between the 2 nicks

(5) Put the straight edge under the glass with one side along the scored line. Do this immediately after cutting

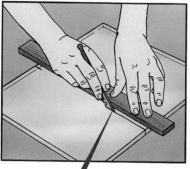

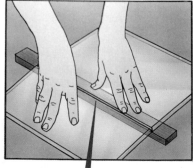

(2) Mark out the line to be cut by nicking both edges with the glass cutter. With patterned glass keep smooth side uppermost

(4) Draw the glass cutter along the straight edge from one side to the other in a single motion, applying firm pressure

(6) Hold the glass firmly with both hands as shown above. Press down lightly until the glass breaks

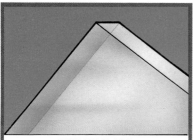

WINDOW GLASS
For most glazing purposes you will need ordinary window glass which is perfectly clear and distortion-free. The standard choice these days is float glass and the thickness may be 4 mm, 5 mm or 6 mm — see the table on the previous page. For some purposes you will need one of the special glasses shown on this page, but they will cost more than float glass. You can save money by ordering 3 mm glass for small windows which are well away from small children.

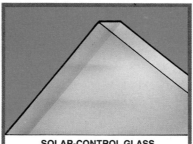

SOLAR-CONTROL GLASS
A large expanse of glass can make a room unbearably hot in summer — one answer is to use solar-control glass. With the most successful types the heat entering the room is cut by 80 per cent and glare is greatly reduced. Most brands are tinted bronze or grey and some can provide a high degree of privacy by serving as a one-way mirror. Solar-control glass is available in all popular thicknesses and for doors there are both toughened and laminated grades.

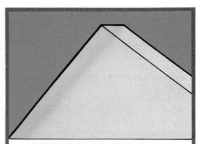

DIFFUSE-REFLECTION GLASS
Plain window glass has the annoying property of reflecting bright objects (lamp bulbs, sunny windows etc) when used for framing pictures. The answer is to use diffuse-reflection (popularly known as non-reflective) glass. The surface has been treated to form a very slightly roughened texture which does not impair transparency to any noticeable extent. The roughened surface, however, has very poor reflective powers. The thickness of this glass is 2 mm.

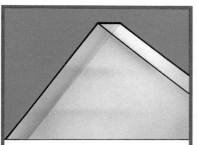

TOUGHENED GLASS
The strongest of the standard safety glasses — toughened (or tempered) glass has been subjected to a special heat treatment which makes it about 5 times stronger than ordinary window glass. When hit hard enough it crazes rather than shatters, and the tiny pieces are rounded granules rather than jagged spears. Good for doors and table tops — obscure and clear grades are available. It cannot be cut or drilled — you will have to order the size you want.

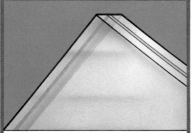

LAMINATED GLASS
The panes sold as laminated glass are not toughened — they are just 2 ordinary sheets of glass which sandwich a sheet of tough plastic between them. The result is glass which may crack but will not shatter, and there are grades which are burglar-proof and even bullet-proof. The standard thickness is 5.4 mm and there are many variants — solar control, patterned surfaces, tinting and so on can be introduced. You will have to order the size required as it is difficult to cut.

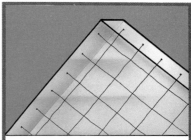

WIRED GLASS
The glass here is no stronger than the ordinary window grade — the safety factor is a welded wire mesh which is embedded within the pane. The square- or diamond-shaped pattern of wire holds the glass fragments together in case of breakage. Wired glass is widely used where a high degree of fire-resistance is required, such as in fire doors. Clear and translucent grades are available — the standard thickness is 6 mm. Use where safety is more important than appearance.

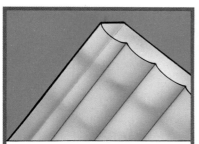

PATTERNED GLASS
One side has a textured pattern — the other side is plain. Patterned glass is chosen for either its decorative effect or ability to obscure the view. All too often it is chosen for the bathroom window only as a means of privacy, with no thought of the beauty it can provide. These days there are scores of patterns in clear or tinted glass, and you should look at a number of samples before making your choice. Both 4 mm and 6 mm grades are available — buy the toughened type for doors or shower screens.

DECORATED GLASS
Included here are all the decorative effects other than patterned glass on which the texture is produced by a roller at the time of manufacture. Amongst the decorative glasses is stained glass, once decried as old fashioned but now staging a minor comeback. There is also sandblasted glass with a variety of shaded effects, and engraved glass which is used to produce highly-decorated screens. Most decorated glass is in the luxury class, but a plain glass door bearing a transparent transfer belongs here.

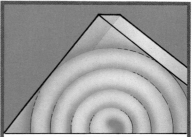

BULLION GLASS
A few panes of bullion glass are used in multi-pane windows to provide an old-world touch to neo-Georgian houses these days, and they do have a long history of decorating windows. Bullions were once made by a hand-spinning process — such authentic bullions are expensive. Modern bullions are made by rollers, like patterned glass, and both clear and amber-tinted types can be bought in a variety of sizes ranging from 6 in. × 6 in. to 28 in. × 18 in. Don't overdo it with bullion glass — too many panes will mar the view.

DOUBLE GLAZING

A room without a window is a dingy place indeed, but inserting panes of glass in the fabric of the wall does create its problems. Glass is a poor insulator — letting heat out and noise in. In winter cold air enters through faulty frames, and pockets of cool air form against the surface of the glass.

Double glazing has been heavily promoted in recent years as an answer to these difficulties. Double glazing simply means having 2 panes of glass instead of a single sheet of glass. It is the air between the panes and not the glass itself which acts as the insulator — this air should be dry, still and the space between the panes must be the correct width for the job which has to be done.

Installing double glazing is an expensive and disruptive business and you should think carefully before going ahead. As pointed out earlier, your motive should not be solely to cut down on fuel bills — it will take many, many years to pay for itself. You should only go ahead if at least some of the other advantages appeal to you — reduced draughts, reduced condensation, improved window appearance, increased security and so on.

Points to remember

- A single-glazed house loses about 20 per cent of its heat in winter through windows and the cracks around doors. Double glazing can reduce this by about a half, but only if it is efficiently constructed and installed, and if the panes are ¼ – 1 in. apart. A smaller gap is less efficient in conserving heat — a wider gap is slightly less efficient.

- Double glazing can cut down noise from outside, but the glass should be thick and the gap between the panes has to be 4 – 8 in. wide.

- Double glazing makes entry and exit more difficult. Breaking and entering through 2 panes of glass is an effective burglar deterrent, but secondary windows can also prove to be a fatal barrier in case of fire. Make sure that the windows can be opened in an emergency and show each member of the family what to do if the need arises.

- You may qualify for a grant towards double glazing — ask your local authority. Make sure the installer is a member of the Glass and Glazing Federation.

SEALED UNIT

Two panes of glass are joined by an airtight seal. This unit is used **in place of** an existing pane.

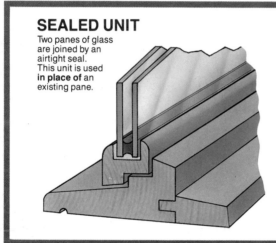

There are 3 advantages compared with secondary windows. Sealed units do not have a condensation problem between the panes, they are suitable for all types of window and they are unnoticeable. The gap between the panes is ¼ – ½ in., which means they will reduce heat loss but will do little to reduce noise.

If the rebate in the window is wide enough you should buy spaced units in which the 2 panes are the same size. In most cases you will have to use stepped units in which each outer pane is larger than the inner one and so fits outside the rebate.

Sealed units (sometimes called insulating glass) are available in many sizes and varieties. The glass may be as thin as 3 mm or as thick as 10 mm — it may be toughened, patterned or wired. Low E (low emissivity) glass improves insulation by reflecting heat back into the room and also cuts down the amount of ultra-violet light entering the room from outside.

SECONDARY WINDOW

A sheet of glass or plastic is placed inside (or sometimes outside) an existing window. This sheet is used **in addition to** an existing pane.

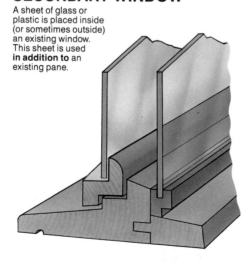

The simplest form of secondary window is a sheet of **plastic film** stretched over the window and fixed with self-adhesive tape. Condensation will be reduced or eliminated, but the insulating effect is often slight and the overall appearance is usually unsightly.

You can use acetate sheet in a simple frame, but the most satisfactory simple method is the **plastic channel** which contains a pane of 4 mm float glass and is attached to the sash or casement with clips. The window is opened and closed in the usual way.

With the **secondary sash** the second sheet of glass is fitted against the window frame and not against the sash or casement. This secondary sash is made of aluminium or plastic and may be fixed or hinged. The space between the original pane and the secondary one may be quite large, so this arrangement is suitable for noise insulation.

The basic secondary sash system described above is not difficult to fit but it does not make for easy opening. The sliding type with the glass moving in horizontal or vertical channels provides much easier access to the outside but it also increases the incidence of condensation between the panes.

BLINDS

Blinds have been used traditionally in bathrooms and kitchens where curtains may be inconvenient. They have also been used on tiny or sloping windows where curtains could be impractical. Of course, blinds are not used where a highly decorative effect is required ...

You can forget these prejudices nowadays — blinds can be as luxurious as any curtain. There are all sorts and styles available, ranging from no-nonsense roller and Venetian blinds to billowing Austrian blinds with exaggerated flounces. Kits can be bought which require no special skill for construction — you can also buy made-to-measure blinds or fabric and the necessary accessories from your department store. The darling of the interior decorator is the curtain and blind combination. Dress (or non-closing) curtains are used to frame the window, and so there is a saving in fabric cost compared with standard curtains. The role of the blind is to provide privacy and light control — in addition it can provide extra colour and interest to the room.

Blinds are fitted either inside the window recess (especially when part of a curtain and blind combination) or outside on the ceiling or wall. Most types are easy to instal, but you must use a spirit level to make sure that the fall is perfectly vertical.

Choose the fabric for roller or Roman blinds with care. Avoid flimsy material which will stretch easily and also heavy fabric which will not roll or fold properly. Plastics and synthetic fibres are frequently used, but perhaps the best choice is stiffened cotton or cotton blends. You can buy specially prepared blind fabric, or you can treat ordinary closely-woven cloth with a liquid or aerosol stiffener. Fabric is not the only material for blinds — wood, metal, plastic and paper are all widely used.

Illustrated here are the main varieties of blinds, but there are others. An example is the slatted blind — strips of wood or cane woven together with cotton. The colour range is not large, but then neither is the price.

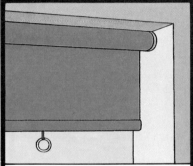

ROLLER BLIND
A roller blind kit consists of a spring-loaded roller (which can easily be cut to fit the exact space) plus a bar for the bottom of the blind. There are also brackets and a pull cord. The fabric can be chosen to match the wallpaper, curtains, carpet or any other feature, and the bottom edge can be plain, fringed, braided or shaped. Where money is no object, you can have the fabric hand-painted to match your room decoration.

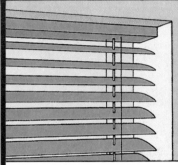

VENETIAN BLIND
Slats of plastic or metal are controlled on a 2-pulley system, one to tilt the slats and the other to move the blind up and down. Once associated with offices and public buildings, Venetian blinds are being increasingly used in the home. The colour range has been greatly extended, and this style fits in well with a curtain and blind combination. There are no kits available — you must either buy a standard model or have the blind made to measure.

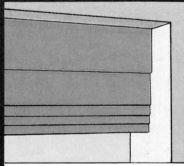

ROMAN BLIND
When fully extended a Roman blind looks somewhat like a roller blind. Pull the cord and the difference is seen immediately — the fabric rises up in a series of flat folds. The pleats are formed by horizontal wooden slats which are sewn in at intervals. When fully open the pleated fabric forms a pelmet. The fabric is always lined, which means that it keeps out light and cuts down on draughts better than a roller blind.

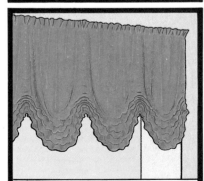

AUSTRIAN BLIND
As the cording raises the lightweight fabric a series of ballooning swags appear at the base. With a festoon blind these swags are apparent even when the blind is fully closed. These blinds are at home in an ornate living room or bedroom where the billowy effect of the half-closed blind adds a welcome touch of luxury. Buy them ready-made or you can make your own by using a special track and Austrian blind heading-tape.

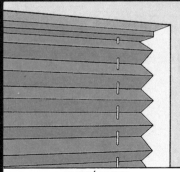

PLISSÉ BLIND
The plissé or pleated blind is at the other extreme from the Austrian blind. Thoroughly practical, limited in both style and colour, its sole purpose is to provide privacy whilst allowing some light to enter. The aluminium-backed version also provides heat insulation. The plissé blind looks a little like a Venetian one, but is in fact a sheet of folded paper or stiff fabric which is raised by side cords which pass through punched holes.

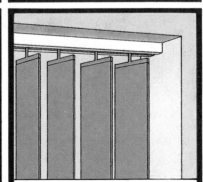

VERTICAL BLIND
Wide strips of stiffened fabric hang from the headrail — as with a Venetian blind the 'vanes' can be swivelled by one cord and the whole blind moved aside by means of another. The advantages over Venetian blinds include less dust on the strips and less interruption of the view, but they are expensive and the range is quite limited. The vertical louvre blind is highly recommended where a large picture window is to be clothed.

CURTAINS

Not all windows have to be curtained. The experts tell us that windows by the stairs and areas of decorative glass are best left uncovered, and in some cases blinds may be a better choice. But for the vast majority of homeowners a window without a curtain is shamelessly undressed.

Curtains can, of course, add beauty to a room. They are used to add both height and width to a window and also to add colour and perhaps a touch of luxury. Yet there is more to it than decoration — curtains keep heat in on winter nights and out during summer days, draughts are reduced and outside noise minimised. Undesirable views outside can be hidden and privacy inside can be preserved.

Buying new curtains means that several decisions have to be made. The curtain rail is probably already in position — if not, look at the pictures on this page. Tracks should have 4 gliders per foot — poles require 4 rings per foot. Length is an important consideration — full-length curtains are always elegant but are not always practical. They can overpower a tiny room, can cost the earth in an expensive fabric and there may be a radiator under the window. For most situations the choice is between sill- and apron-length — the experts frown on mid-length curtains which are half-way between sill and floor.

The decisions go on — Which heading? Which fabric? To line or not to line? Pull-cord or free-running? Pelmet or exposed rail? It is *much* easier to pick a new car than choose the right curtains!

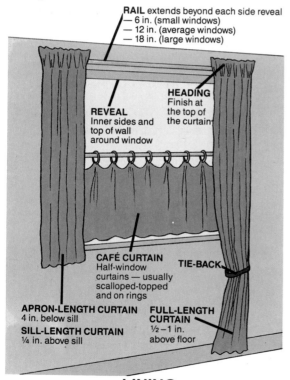

RAIL extends beyond each side reveal
— 6 in. (small windows)
— 12 in. (average windows)
— 18 in. (large windows)

HEADING
Finish at the top of the curtain

REVEAL
Inner sides and top of wall around window

CAFÉ CURTAIN
Half-window curtains — usually scalloped-topped and on rings

TIE-BACK

APRON-LENGTH CURTAIN
4 in. below sill

SILL-LENGTH CURTAIN
¼ in. above sill

FULL-LENGTH CURTAIN
½ – 1 in. above floor

LINING

Lining may not be worthwhile for cheap and cheerful curtains in some of the rooms, but it certainly is needed for the main windows. Lined curtains hang better and the fabric is protected from the sun. Cotton sateen is the usual lining material. Heat insulation is improved (use Milium for top efficiency) and early morning light is kept out of bedrooms (use rubberised lining for top efficiency). Most linings are sewn to the curtain fabric but there are advantages in having loose linings which are attached to the heading tape and only tacked to the fabric. Such loose linings can be washed separately and shrinkage is not a problem.

RAILS & CORDING

Choose the curtain rail with care — if a pelmet or valance is not to be fitted then the face of the rail should be either decorative or not noticeable when the curtains are open or drawn. The usual choice of rail is a track rather than a pole, and the popular material is plastic. For heavy curtains, however, you should buy a metal track. Ceiling- and wall-brackets are available and there are brands of plastic track which can be bent around corners. For heavy curtains buy overlapping tracks which allow one curtain to pass about 6 in. in front of the other when drawn. A pull-cord to close the curtains will prevent wear and tear through handling — choose a ready-corded rail or fit a cording set to an existing track.

GIRDER TRACK
The traditional type of track, made of metal or plastic. The gliders run along the bottom of the girder — the track is usually exposed when the curtains are closed and so a pelmet is generally used

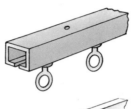

BOTTOM CHANNEL TRACK
The gliders run along the channel at the bottom of the track. Decorative-faced types can be used without a pelmet. Lightweight ceiling-mounted versions are available for fitting within the window recess

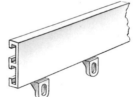

CONCEALED GLIDER TRACK
The gliders run along a channel at the back of the track. Very popular — Swish Deluxe, Luxaflex Pacemaker etc. Decorative-faced types can be used without a pelmet

EXPOSED GLIDER TRACK
The gliders which run along the face of the track have built-in hooks at the front. At the base of each of these glider-hooks is a small ring which can be used to carry a separate lining

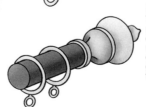

POLE
True poles are made of wood or metal with decorative finials at the ends. Large gliding rings carry small rings at their base to carry the curtain hooks. Imitation poles have gliders attached to the rings and these run along a track at the back

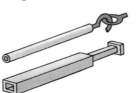

COVERED WIRE & ROD
Expandable wire is the traditional rail for net curtains. It is supported by means of hooks fitted into eyes which are screwed into either the wall or the window frame. Telescopic rods are very useful for putting up net curtains — the rod fits inside the window reveal

BUYING CURTAINS

Before buying or ordering curtains you must measure the exact length of the rail and also the drop from the hook rings on the pole or track to the length desired. You should also know the type of heading you want.

Buying ready-made curtains makes the job easy. There is a large range these days in a wide variety of widths, but the choice of lengths is strictly limited. There are advantages — you can see what you are getting and you know that the material is suitable as curtaining. But ready-made curtains are not always such a practical choice — the fabric type, colour or pattern you have in mind is so often not available, especially at the more expensive end of the range, and the heading type or length may not be suitable.

Custom-made curtains are often the answer. Get a detailed quote before placing your order. You can sew your own but making complex or patterned curtains is not a job for a beginner.

The golden rule when buying curtain material is to make sure that they will look full even when drawn. It is better to buy ample cheap material which will show off its folds than expensive curtaining which has to be pulled tight to close. Choose material carefully, and think of practical considerations as well as purely decorative ones. Pale curtains or ones which blend in with the wall will show off the view — bright fabrics and large patterns will show off the curtains. Thick curtains will effectively reduce outside noise — bedrooms will need properly lined curtains.

Take home a sample before ordering — the material may look quite different in your room. The choice of materials is enormous. Sheer and semi-sheer fabrics such as net, lace, openweave etc provide privacy without darkening the room. Cottons and linens are excellent but silk tends to disintegrate in bright sunlight. Velvets, velveteens, brocades, moirés, satins . . . the choice of luxury fabrics is a wide one.

PELMETS & VALANCES

The purpose of a pelmet or valance is to hide the rail as well as the heading of the curtains. It can vary from a simple stained plywood frame to elaborate sweeps of fabric above the curtains with draped tails on either side. There are no strict rules for the correct depth of a pelmet — 1/8th of the length of floor-length curtains is the usual recommendation.

Pelmet A 4 in. wide pelmet board is fitted a few inches above and on either side of the curtains. This board is either faced with wood for staining, painting or polishing or covered with stiffened fabric. The lower edge may be straight, scalloped or curved

Pelmet board

Valance A short unstiffened curtain is gathered or pleated using standard heading tape. The material can match or contrast with the curtains and the lower edge may be straight or ruched. The valance is attached to a pelmet board or to a second rail in front of the curtain one

HEADING

Heading tape is usually but not always used — cased and scalloped curtains do not employ tape. But if you want a gathered or decorative heading then you will need to buy the appropriate tape for the style chosen. Drawstrings are present to produce the gathering or pleating and there are slits to carry the curtain hooks. Use deep heading tape (3 in. wide) for heavy fabrics and standard tape (1 in. wide) for light ones.

HEADING TYPE	WIDTH OF FABRIC REQUIRED	NOTES
GATHERED	1½ – 2 times the length of the rail	Used on unlined curtains for small windows and/or in rooms not in regular use — also suitable where a pelmet or valance hides the curtain track. Buy standard heading tape — choose the lightweight grade for sheers such as net curtains
PENCIL PLEAT	2¼ – 2½ times the length of the rail	Used on lightweight and medium weight fabrics — suitable for either track or pole. Straight and narrow pleats are produced along the whole length of the material — especially effective on full-length curtains. Decorative, but less so than pinched pleats
PINCHED PLEAT	2 times the length of the rail	Used on all types of fabrics, ranging from fleecy nets to heavy velvets. Pinches of 2- or 3-fold French pleats are separated by smooth cloth. Suitable for either track or pole — buy deep heading tape for maximum effect; narrow tape for sheer fabrics
CASED	1¼ – 1½ times the length of the rail	Unloved, often unmentioned, but still the basic type on lightweight and net curtains in millions of homes. A 2 in. hem is sewn at the top — this wide hem is divided by a row of stitching along the centre. The rod or wire is threaded through this open hem
SCALLOPED	1¼ – 1½ times the length of the rail	Used on café curtains where a pole is used without a pelmet or valance so that the heading can be clearly seen. Economical — too much fullness would spoil the effect. Use firm material — do not line and attach curtain rings as shown on page 76

Doors

A stranger's first impression of your house is usually gained on the doorstep. A poor quality front door in need of decoration says a great deal about the occupants, and this image can only be partly removed by an impressive interior. This does not mean that you should buy the grandest front door you can afford — a highly ornamental door bedecked in brass would be out of place as the entrance to a cottage-style house — the golden rule is to make sure that the front door is regularly maintained and is in keeping with the style, size and surroundings of the house. Inside doors also have an important part to play in interior decoration, and so do the doors of wardrobes, cupboards etc. But doors also have a number of practical jobs to do, and none more so than the front door. This must keep out weather, noise, intruders, insects, domestic animals, dust and draughts. Internal doors have a simpler job to do — they cut down the passage of noise from one area to another and they provide a barrier for rooms such as bathroom and bedrooms where privacy is essential.

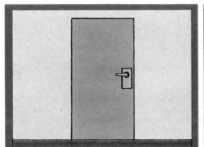

FLUSH DOOR

The most popular type of room door — unfinished or veneered facings cover a lightweight wooden frame. A recent innovation is the embossed flush door which looks like a panel one. The inner core may be empty or filled with cardboard, wood strips, plasterboard or asbestos depending on the weight and use required. The edges of the door are covered (lipped) with thin strips of wood and the position to attach hinges and the lock is usually marked on the appropriate lip.

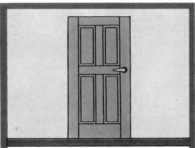

PANEL DOOR

The basic structure consists of 2 vertical wooden stiles with 3 or more horizontal rails. The open spaces are filled with wood, plywood or glass. Panelled doors are nearly always made of softwood when designed for indoor use, but front doors are usually constructed from hardwood so that they can be sealed and varnished rather than painted. If you buy a front door which has a softwood base, make sure that it has been treated with a preservative to prevent rotting.

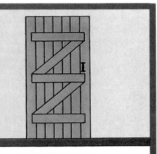

BOARDED DOOR

A sturdy door which belongs on a country cottage, shed or garage rather than an urban home. Strong but plain, the simplest version (ledged and braced) is made up of tongued and grooved boards held together by horizontal ledges and diagonal braces. The stable door version has an upper and lower section. The best type of boarded door is the framed, ledged and braced door. A stout frame constructed with mortise and tenon joints surrounds the boards. A mortise lock can be fitted.

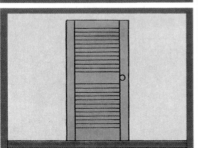

LOUVRED DOOR

A timber frame holds numerous wooden slats which are set at an angle. The number and the angle of the slats ensure that air passes freely through the door but the view is blocked. A wide range of sizes for cupboard and room doors is available — softwood is usually used and louvre doors are often sealed and varnished to preserve the natural wood appearance. Paired louvred doors are occasionally used to produce Western-style swing doors. Built-in wardrobe doors are often louvred.

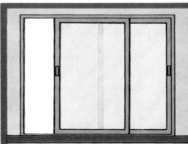

PATIO DOOR

Aluminium alloy is the usual frame material, although plastic and wooden versions are available. The fully glazed floor-to-ceiling panel or panels slide horizontally, bringing the living room and garden together in summer. For many people it is the favourite window, but it is also a favourite for burglars and accidents. Use safety glass for glazing (see page 72) and have some form of decoration on the glass to indicate that the window is not open. Fit high-security locks.

FRENCH WINDOW

Glazed casement doors, fitted singly or in pairs, have long been the traditional way of stepping from the living room into the garden, but their role is now being steadily taken over by patio doors. Wooden French doors keep their place in period houses, although they tend to be draughtier than patio ones and stays must be fitted to keep them open. In addition they lack effective control over ventilation. Use safety glass for at least the lower panes and fit a stout lock.

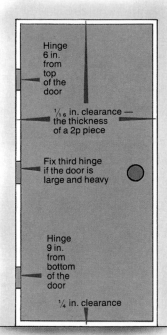

Hinge 6 in. from top of the door

⅛₆ in. clearance — the thickness of a 2p piece

Fix third hinge if the door is large and heavy

Hinge 9 in. from bottom of the door

¼ in. clearance

EXTERNAL DOOR

Usual size: 6 ft 8 in. × 2 ft 9 in. × 1¾ in.

Make sure that the door you buy is constructed for exterior use. Aluminium and plastic (uPVC) doors are guaranteed to be weatherproof, but the usual choice is a wooden door. The popular one is a panelled door made from hardwood, or a softwood base covered with a hardwood veneer. The glue used will be exterior grade and the panels will be made of plywood (not hardboard). The stiles should be at least 4 in. wide so that a proper security lock can be fitted and safety glass should be used if the area for glazing is large. Alternatively you can buy a flush door, but do make it clear to the supplier that it is for exterior and not interior use. This means that it will be more strongly built with facings of water-resistant plywood and a central block to hold the letter plate. Use brass or stainless steel hinges to hang the panel or flush door. At the bottom of the frame a door sill (or threshold) must be present to keep water away from the frame/wall join, and the door will have a weatherboard to keep rain out of the narrow gap between door and frame.

INTERNAL DOOR

Usual size: 6 ft 6 in. × 2 ft 6 in. × 1⅜ in.

The choice is much greater when you require a room door rather than an external one. Both softwood and hardwood panel doors are available for staining, although cheaper softwood types are generally painted rather than varnished. Flush doors for internal use range from cheap ones with hardboard facings and a hollow core to luxury ones with veneered facings and a wood-filled core. Before fitting a new door you should check the regulations with the local council if you live in a flat — it may be necessary to fit a fire-resisting door with a self-closing mechanism. Most internal doors are either panel or flush ones, but there are other types which should be considered. Louvred doors are popular for wardrobes and cupboards rather than as room doors, although they are widely used as pairs in folding form as room dividers. Another form of room divider is the concertina door — a folding door made up of numerous narrow sections which take up very little room when open. Sliding doors are an alternative where space is restricted. Small sliding doors need no special tracking — full-sized doors need a wheeled track at either the top or bottom of the frame.

LOCKS

It is essential to understand the difference between a catch, a latch and a deadbolt. A **catch** is a closure which can be simply released by pulling the knob or handle forward. A **latch** is more secure — a handle, knob or key has to be turned to open it, but the latch is *not* locked inside the striking plate. This means that an intruder can force it open by inserting a credit card or screwdriver between the frame and the door. A **deadbolt** is the most secure of all — it is opened and closed by a key and cannot be forced back when closed.

RIM LOCK A lock which is mounted on the inside face of the door.

NIGHTLATCH

Traditional front door lock — opened and closed from the inside by a knob and from the outside by a key which operates a cylinder-type lock. The latch is not deadlocked and so the security rating is not high.

DEADLOCKING NIGHTLATCH

Basically similar to the ordinary nightlatch, but turning the key from either the inside or outside turns the latch into a deadbolt. The lock should be made to British Standard 3621.

MORTISE LOCK A lock which is set within a mortise or slot cut into the door.

MORTISE DEADLOCK

The second security lock which is often fitted to the front door near to the nightlatch. It is a lever-type lock with a traditional-type key — make sure that there are at least 5 levers. A double-throw lock moves the bolt further forward with a second turn of the key.

SASH LOCK

A combined lock for back doors. The latch is operated by a handle or knob and the deadbolt is closed by means of the key at night or when the house is unoccupied.

CYLINDRICAL LOCK A lock which is installed through 2 holes bored into the door, one for the handle/lock and the other for the latch/bolt.

Easier to instal than a mortise lock. The latch is reversible with an automatic deadlocking mechanism. The key operates a cylinder-type lock fitted inside the handle. The simpler latch-only version for interior use is known as a tubular lock.

HINGES

Hinges are simple things, but you can easily buy the wrong sort if you don't take care. Tell the supplier the size, type and thickness of the door and the way it has to open. If there is no one to help, check the wording on the package carefully to make sure the set of hinges will be satisfactory. Several materials are used to make hinges — brass, stainless steel, cast steel, nylon etc. The size range is 1–6 in. — the recommended sizes are 3 in. (internal doors) and 4 in. (external doors). Screw the hinges first on to the door and then on to the frame.

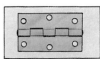

BUTT HINGE

The standard type for all sorts of doors except fire-resisting ones, where self-closing hinges are required. The two leaves of an ordinary butt hinge cannot be separated, but you can buy loose-pin (or lift-off) hinges.

RISING BUTT HINGE

The door lifts when it is opened — not enough to notice but sufficient to carry it over a thick carpet. The top of the frame may have to be slightly chamfered. This type of hinge is often self-closing.

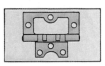

FLUSH HINGE

This hinge does not have to be recessed like a butt hinge. It is used for lightweight flush doors — simply screw on to the surface of the door and then on to the side of the door frame.

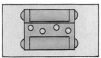

HELICAL SPRING HINGE

The spring loading of this hinge makes the door return to the closed position after it has been opened. Two-way spring hinges are often used on restaurant kitchen doors.

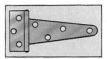

T HINGE

The standard type for boarded doors — practical but not decorative. They are made of galvanised or painted steel to withstand the elements — for heavy doors a stronger version (hook and band hinge) is required.

CONCEALED HINGE

This type of spring-loaded hinge is fitted inside a cabinet so that the set-in door can open and move in line with the side of the unit.

DEALING WITH DOOR PROBLEMS

● SQUEAKING DOOR

The usual cause is hinge stiffness. Apply just a drop of light oil at the top of each metal hinge — wipe off excess oil immediately. Rising butt hinges should be oiled regularly but do not oil plastic hinges. If oil does not cure the squeak, the door must be catching in the frame — read the 'Sticking Door' sections on this page.

● RATTLING DOOR

A rattling door indicates an improper fit — with an outside door it is usually linked with a draught problem. Fitting a self-adhesive foam strip may cure the problem, but not if the lock and the striking plate on the frame are out of position. The latch should fit snugly through the space on the plate — it may be necessary to move the plate slightly.

● HINGE-BOUND DOOR

A door is hinge-bound when either the door and frame or the hinge screws come together before the door is closed. Projecting screws can be the problem — drive them home firmly or use shorter screws

The cause may be that the hinge has been set too far into either the door or the frame. Unscrew hinge leaf and pack recess with a strip of cardboard. Rescrew. Pack out other side of hinge if still not cured

● SIDE-STICKING DOOR

Doors can stick at the sides or top for a number of reasons. The point of sticking is sometimes obvious — if not, carry out carbon paper test. Hold paper at various points — black smudge reveals sticking area

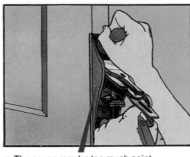

The cause may be too much paint — rub or plane off the excess. In bathroom and outside doors the wood may have swollen. Plane sticking area on the door on a dry day. Take care not to remove too much wood

● BOTTOM-STICKING DOOR

If the problem is only slight, you might be able to remove excess wood by opening the door several times over coarse abrasive paper. If the problem is more severe, remove door and plane bottom

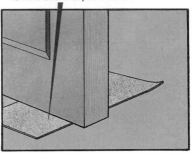

A common cause of bottom sticking is the introduction of a thick carpet in place of a thin one. Planing the bottom of the door may not be possible with a flush door. Cure the problem by using rising butt hinges

● WARPED DOOR

Doors warp and twist for a number of reasons — radiator too close, unseasoned wood, marked heat difference on either side of the door etc. If the warp is at the top or bottom and the door can be kept closed, force back, close and insert small wedge between door and frame. Leave for 7 days

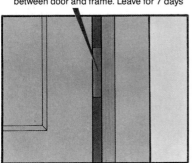

If centre of the door is bowed, remove door and straddle between chairs, with curve facing upwards. Place bricks at centre to press down wood — leave for 7 days. If the warp is at hinge side of door, fit additional hinge midway between existing hinges

● DROPPED DOOR

There are several symptoms of a dropped or sagging door — squeaking, sticking and failure to close properly. Loose hinges are the usual cause — tighten screws. If this fails, use longer screws or insert dowels in holes before rescrewing

The trouble may be more serious. In old panel doors the joints may have opened. The answer is to hire a sash clamp to pull the door back into shape. Strengthen by drilling holes at each joint and inserting pieces of dowel

● LOOSE FRAME

The proper way to repair a loose frame is to remove the door and architrave, replace the packing between the frame and wall and then drill deep holes through the wood and into the masonry. The holes are plugged and then screws are fitted

If only one side of the frame is loose and is truly vertical, you can try a much simpler remedy. Drill holes through the offending side and at least 2 in. into the masonry. Plug and screw firmly

● STIFF LOCK

Do not squeeze oil into the lock. With a cylinder-type lock such as a nightlatch, spread a little light oil over the latch and dust the key with powdered graphite. Turn the key several times in the lock. With a lever-type lock such as a mortise deadlock again add a little oil to the extended bolt but apply a little light oil and not graphite to the head of the key. Open and close the lock several times.

● LOST KEY

You should be able to force back the latch of a nightlatch from the outside (see page 79) — you will certainly be able to open it from the inside. Outside or inside, you have a difficult problem with a bolted mortise lock if the key is lost. The only answer is to call in a locksmith. It is a wise precaution to have duplicates of all external door keys. Keep the spare in a safe place in case of an emergency — but *not* under the carpet or anywhere close to the door.

Shelving

Putting up shelves is one of the easiest DIY jobs and one of the most rewarding. There is instant access to the items being stored and there is maximum exposure of decorative items. Basically there are two types — wall-mounted and side-mounted. Shelves used for *very* heavy loads should be both wall- and side-mounted with wooden battens or strong brackets. Wall- and side-mounted shelves can be fixed directly on to the wall or may be part of an adjustable shelving system. The great value of a shelving system rather than fixed shelves is that shelves can be moved and new ones introduced to meet changing demands. Whatever type of shelving is used, there are several basic rules. The fixing must be strong enough for the type of wall — see page 60. Also, the shelf must be able to bear the weight of its load without sagging — see the table below. Make sure that shelves for frequently-used items are 2½−5½ ft above the floor. Finally, provide more shelving than you need at present — you will be surprised at just how many more items you will accumulate over the next year or two!

Wall-mounted

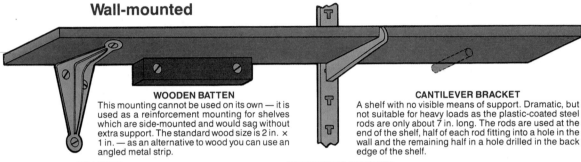

WOODEN BATTEN
This mounting cannot be used on its own — it is used as a reinforcement mounting for shelves which are side-mounted and would sag without extra support. The standard wood size is 2 in. × 1 in. — as an alternative to wood you can use an angled metal strip.

CANTILEVER BRACKET
A shelf with no visible means of support. Dramatic, but not suitable for heavy loads as the plastic-coated steel rods are only about 7 in. long. The rods are used at the end of the shelf, half of each rod fitting into a hole in the wall and the remaining half in a hole drilled in the back edge of the shelf.

BRACKET
Metal L-shaped brackets are not expensive and are available in a variety of finishes, both practical and decorative. Buy the correct size brackets — the tip should be 1 in. or less from the edge of the shelf. Screw directly on to the wall or on to wooden uprights.

ADJUSTABLE BRACKET
Shelf-supporting brackets ranging in size from 6 in. to 2 ft fit into the notches or are locked in the continuous channels which are found on the face of the uprights. The aluminium or wooden uprights are made in a variety of finishes and are cut to fit and then screwed against the wall.

MATERIALS

The most popular material is **chipboard** — inexpensive and available in a wide range of widths and lengths. A major advantage is that you can buy chipboard in a variety of finishes — wood veneers to match your furniture or white and imitation wood melamine to provide easy-to-clean surfaces. The major drawback is that supports must be set more closely together than with other shelving materials. **Blockboard** and **plywood** are strong and stiff materials which are useful for shelving — **medium density fibreboard (MDF)** is the man-made board to choose if you intend to paint the shelves. **Solid wood** is the traditional material — it is less likely to sag than the materials listed above. **Glass** is an excellent shelving material for showing off choice items, but it should not be used for heavy loads. Tell your supplier that the glass is for shelving.

The table below is for shelving to carry books, which means that it is suitable for reasonably heavy loads		
MATERIAL	**THICKNESS**	**DISTANCE BETWEEN SUPPORTS**
CHIPBOARD	12 mm (½ in.) 18 mm (¾ in.)	300 mm (12 in.) 500 mm (20 in.)
FACED CHIPBOARD	12 mm (½ in.) 18 mm (¾ in.) 25 mm (1 in.)	400 mm (16 in.) 600 mm (24 in.) 800 mm (32 in.)
PLYWOOD	18 mm (¾ in.) 25 mm (1 in.)	800 mm (32 in.) 1,000 mm (40 in.)
MDF	18 mm (¾ in.) 25 mm (1 in.)	600 mm (24 in.) 800 mm (32 in.)
BLOCKBOARD	12 mm (½ in.) 18 mm (¾ in.)	500 mm (20 in.) 800 mm (32 in.)
FINISHED WOOD	15 mm (⅝ in.) 21 mm (⅞ in.)	600 mm (24 in.) 900 mm (36 in.)

Side-mounted

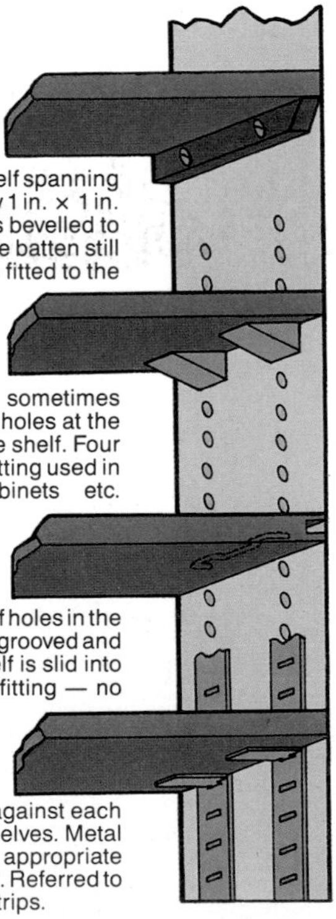

BEARER BATTEN
The standard method for fixing a shelf spanning an alcove. The size used is generally 1 in. × 1 in. or 1 in. × 2 in. and the front edge is bevelled to improve the appearance. To hide the batten still further an overhanging strip can be fitted to the front of the shelf.

PLUG
Wooden, plastic or metal plugs, sometimes called pegs or studs, are fitted into holes in the sides of the unit which will carry the shelf. Four plugs hold each shelf. A standard fitting used in home-assembly bookcases, cabinets etc. Heavy-duty plugs are available.

INVISIBLE WIRE
A strip of wire is firmly held in a pair of holes in the uprights. The edges of the shelf are grooved and they house the wires when the shelf is slid into place. A cupboard and bookcase fitting — no support is visible.

METAL STRIP AND STUD
A pair of metal strips are screwed against each side of the carcasse to carry the shelves. Metal studs are inserted in slots at the appropriate height — 4 studs holding each shelf. Referred to in some catalogues as bookcase strips.

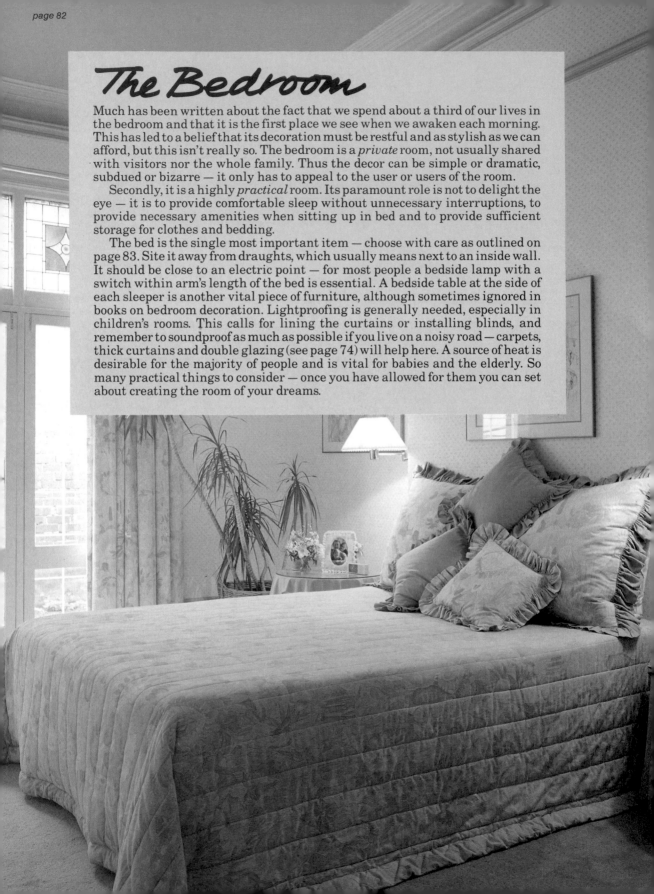

The Bedroom

Much has been written about the fact that we spend about a third of our lives in the bedroom and that it is the first place we see when we awaken each morning. This has led to a belief that its decoration must be restful and as stylish as we can afford, but this isn't really so. The bedroom is a *private* room, not usually shared with visitors nor the whole family. Thus the decor can be simple or dramatic, subdued or bizarre — it only has to appeal to the user or users of the room.

Secondly, it is a highly *practical* room. Its paramount role is not to delight the eye — it is to provide comfortable sleep without unnecessary interruptions, to provide necessary amenities when sitting up in bed and to provide sufficient storage for clothes and bedding.

The bed is the single most important item — choose with care as outlined on page 83. Site it away from draughts, which usually means next to an inside wall. It should be close to an electric point — for most people a bedside lamp with a switch within arm's length of the bed is essential. A bedside table at the side of each sleeper is another vital piece of furniture, although sometimes ignored in books on bedroom decoration. Lightproofing is generally needed, especially in children's rooms. This calls for lining the curtains or installing blinds, and remember to soundproof as much as possible if you live on a noisy road — carpets, thick curtains and double glazing (see page 74) will help here. A source of heat is desirable for the majority of people and is vital for babies and the elderly. So many practical things to consider — once you have allowed for them you can set about creating the room of your dreams.

BED

Compact single bed	2 ft 6 in.	× 6 ft 3 in.
Small single bed (called 'Single' in some stores)	3 ft	× 6 ft 3 in.
Standard single bed	3 ft 3 in.	× 6 ft 6 in.
Compact double bed	4 ft	× 6 ft 3 in.
Small double bed (called 'Double' in some stores)	4 ft 6 in.	× 6 ft 3 in.
Standard double bed or Queen size bed (called 'King size' in some stores)	5 ft	× 6 ft 6 in.
King size bed	6 ft	× 6 ft 6 in.
Super king size bed	7 ft	× 6 ft 6 in.

Choose carefully. Get the **size** right — a single bed should be at least 3 ft wide, a double bed should be 5 ft or more wide for comfort. The length should be at least 6 in. longer than the sleeper.

Get the **firmness** right. Forget what you have heard about 'orthopaedic' beds being good for back trouble — a really hard bed can make matters worse. People with a back problem and overweight sleepers need a bed which is firmer than average — youngsters need a mattress which is softer than average. You must test a mattress for yourself. Lie on it in the store — if it is for two, both of you lie on it. Carry out the National Bedding Federation test. Lie on your back and slip your hand into the small of your back. If the space is empty, the bed is too firm. If you find it difficult to push your hand through, it is too soft. If in doubt, err on the firm side — mattresses soften a little during the first few weeks.

You can buy a **bedstead** (a wooden or metal frame with springs, slats or wire mesh to support the mattress) but the usual choice these days is a **divan**. The **base** of a divan is a cloth-covered box which is either **sprung-edged** (springs right to the edge, expensive, mattress lasts longer) or **firm-edged** (springs in a wooden frame, cheaper, useful if the bed is used for seating). Note that the base does not have to be springy for comfort — its main purpose is to allow the mattress to breathe.

On top of the base goes the **mattress,** the essential feature for comfort. You can still find **stuffed** mattresses containing horsehair etc, but the choice these days is between **interior springing** and foam. A **pocket-sprung** mattress is the most expensive — each spring is in its own cloth cover and when one is depressed it does not automatically pull down the nearby springs. An **open-sprung** mattress has all the springs interlinked and is cheaper — a **continuous-sprung** mattress has the springs in a continuous web. Do not assume that a pocket-sprung mattress is best — the number of springs is as important as the type of springing. An expensive double bed should have at least 500 springs. **Foam** has advantages — it doesn't need turning, it doesn't collect dust and it is lighter than springing. Look for the following high-quality points — latex foam, thickness 4 in. or more and 2 or more layers of foam in the mattress. High density foam lasts longest.

Turn interior-sprung mattresses every 3 months and buy a new bed every 10-15 years. Always buy a new mattress and new base at the same time.

GUEST BEDROOM

The average home cannot afford to have a fully equipped bedroom set aside for guests — the guest room usually has to double as a sewing room, study etc. It does not have to look like a bedroom (its secondary function) — make it look like a sitting room by using a bed-settee or a single bed against a wall with a row of cushions at the back. A cheap **bed-settee** can be torture for the unsuspecting guest — the mattress should be at least 4 in. thick.

SHEETS

Available as either **flat** (20 in. required all round for tucking in) or **fitted** (for tucking over the corners of the mattress). Linen is best, but is now extremely expensive. Pure cotton is also excellent, but is also pricey. Pure nylon sheets are the cheapest, but they hold moisture and therefore feel hot in summer. The popular choice is a cotton/polyester mixture — comfortable, hard-wearing and laundering is made easy with no need to iron.

BLANKETS & DUVETS

Half of Britain sleeps under sheets and blankets, the other half under duvets (also called continental quilts or sleeping quilts). **Blankets** still have advantages, despite the move away from them. They look neat and you can adjust the number according to the temperature. But they do mean that bed-making is a chore and in mid winter can feel restrictive. You need about 15 lb of conventional covering to keep you as warm as a 4 lb duvet. Wool blankets are best, but are expensive. Acrylic blankets are therefore a more popular choice. Lightweight cellular blankets are extremely effective if placed under a standard blanket. With all blankets you will need about 20 in. all round for tucking in.

Duvets can be used practically all year round. They are graded in togs — the usual choice is tog 8-11. The best (if you do not have an allergy) are filled with down and/or feathers — warm, light and expensive. Polyester-filled duvets are much more popular — it is advisable to look for one where the brand name of the filling is given. A duvet should be at least 18 in. wider than the bed.

ELECTRIC BLANKETS

An **underblanket** is placed on the mattress under the sheet. It is turned on for about an hour before bedtime and then switched off when you get into bed. Only the heavy-duty type can be left on all night. An **overblanket** is used over the top sheet — it is designed to be left on all night. There is thermostatic heat control — double blankets may have separate controls.

CHILDREN'S BEDROOM

Here you must think about all the practical problems. Washable walls are recommended and floors must be quiet — the experts recommend sealed cork or carpet tiles. Shelves and free-standing furniture are important — they must change or adapt as the child or children get older. Make sure cupboards etc can't be pulled over. **Bunk beds** are a popular choice, but think and inspect before buying. The upper-bunk occupier should be at least 5 years old and there should be a nearby light to allow safe middle-of-the-night journeys. The top safety rail should be firm and the ladder should not slip when pushed. Make sure that the lower-bunk child can sit up without having to stoop.

WALL COVERING

There is no need to use a washable covering. You can go for one of the luxury ones such as cork, grasscloth or silk. Many people like a co-ordinated look in the bedroom, with wallpaper, curtains and/or bedding having the same pattern. Pay attention to the ceiling — the bedroom is the one room in the house where it is studied for long periods!

FLOOR COVERING

Warmth is the prime requirement, but it need not cost a great deal. Carpeting is the first choice, but a high-quality grade which will stand hard wear is not necessary. Outside dirt will not be tracked in, so you can choose a light colour. Velvet and shag pile are popular.

STORAGE

The choice is between **free-standing** and **built-in** furniture. Free-standing pieces (dressing table, wardrobe, bedside tables etc) have the advantage of giving the room a traditionally furnished look, being movable when we get bored with the arrangement, and being transportable when we move. The trend, however, is to have at least some built-in furniture in the bedroom. A great deal more can be stored in this way, and built-in wardrobes can be amply supplied with drawers, shelves, mid-height hanging rails etc. Leave at least 2 ft between doors and the back wall. There are several ways of installing built-in furniture. Many suppliers have a fitting service, or you can buy pieces and instal your own. The simplest idea is to fit ceiling and floor tracks at one end of the room and cover the whole area with sliding doors. A mirrored front to these doors will make the room look much larger.

The Bathroom

In recent years there has been a tremendous change in our attitude towards the bathroom. Once it used to be a clinical and purely functional place — white fittings, frosted glass windows and white tiled walls. Nowadays it is a place full of colour and decoration, either in reality if we can afford it or in our daydreams if we can't. Bathroom suites are now available in all sorts of colours and shapes with simple or garish decoration. Baths, basins and WCs are sleek and streamlined — no wonder so many bathrooms have been remodelled in the past ten years.

But a few words of caution. Before rushing out to buy that wonderful new suite, have a word with a qualified plumber. It may not be suitable for your plumbing (changes in pipework can be very expensive) or there may be laws or regulations which say no to a bidet or the taps you have chosen. A dark-coloured suite may seem a good idea, but in a hard-water area the white deposit which forms can make it unsightly.

It is sound advice to avoid being too daring with suite colours but to be as outrageous as you like with the easy-to-change decorations. Bathrooms are usually small, so you can create a feeling of luxury for less than elsewhere in the house. Let the carpeting and tiles run up the side of the bath, think about 'soft' walls of cork or relief vinyl instead of tiles, and put the array of toothpaste tubes, aftershave, hand lotions etc in a cabinet and use the shelves and walls for decoration. Fancy jars, pictures, ornaments — it's up to you. Remember that the bathroom is a superb place for house plants — they thrive in the steamy atmosphere.

BATH

If you are working to a tight budget, an acrylic bath is the one for you. The choice is wide, but if you have the money and desire to keep up with the Joneses you will pick either a custom-made glass reinforced plastic bath or a whirlpool type which produces a multitude of swirling air bubbles below the surface. In the right setting an old bath can be left exposed in all its Victorian glory, but boxing-in is needed for a modern bath. Baths can be bought with matching sides — if not, you will need a wooden frame and a suitable covering. Hardwood panels for sealing and varnishing, hardboard for painting or blockboard for tiling. For further details about baths, see page 46.

BASIN

The various types are described on page 47. Choice is a matter of personal preference, but do think of the practical considerations if you are remodelling the bathroom. A vanity unit is so useful if you have the space — there is a work surface for decorative items or the tools of the trade for shaving and making-up, and also storage space below. Also consider a double-bowl unit — waiting one's turn is a common cause of family friction!

BIDET

A commonplace item on the Continent but still something of a rarity in British homes. Some experts believe that it is only a matter of time before we catch up with the Europeans, and there are many models (both floor-standing and wall-hung) to choose from in the catalogues and larger stores. You may have the room for this missing link in your bathroom, but think of the difficulties before buying one. The waste water must be routed down the soil pipe and not the waste water one, and be careful to pick the right type. The usual and less-expensive bidet is the **over-rim** type which has 2 taps and generally raises no problems with the water authority. The **flushing-rim** type, however, can create problems — your local water authority will insist on the pipes going directly to the cold water cistern and hot water tank, which can be an expensive and disruptive job.

SHOWER

The choice is between an **instant** and **mixer** shower. Instant showers have become very popular — they work off the mains supply and the water is heated by electricity within the unit. You can fit an instant shower over the bath or in a separate cubicle. Check that the water pressure is high enough for the shower you have chosen — the hotter the shower, the slower the water flow. With a mixer shower you have a different problem — the water is drawn from the cold water cistern and the hot water tank, and the cold water cistern must be at least 3 ft above the shower head. If the distance is less, you will need a pump. A mixer shower can be nothing more than a pipe and shower head leading from the hot and cold taps, but taps turned on elsewhere in the house can lead to a sudden change in water temperature — do instal some form of temperature control.

WALL COVERING

Ceramic tiles are the traditional covering for bathroom walls. These days you can buy some beautiful tiles, but they still give a cold look to the room and encourage condensation. The same criticism applies to gloss paint and so there is a move to alternative wall coverings. The chosen material has to stand up to steam, splashing and condensation, which means that the choice is limited. Wood panelling is sometimes used — other recommended materials are cork tiles, vinyl, PVC and foamed polyethylene. You can use ordinary wallpaper, but it must be sprayed after hanging with a transparent waterproof finish.

FLOOR COVERING

Ceramic and quarry tiles are still widely used, but you really should look for something warmer. You can use cushioned sheet vinyl, but perhaps the 2 best materials are sealed cork tiles and non-absorbent nylon carpet with a rubber or synthetic backing and underlay.

WC

There are 2 basic parts to a WC or water closet. There is the **pan**, usually made of vitreous enamel and bearing a movable wooden or plastic seat and cover, plus a **cistern** to hold the flushing water. The usual capacity of the cistern is 2 gallons, but there are 1 gallon dual-flushing cisterns available.

The pan and cistern must, of course, be connected. Before the modern bathroom revolution we lived with the **high-level** cistern — a cast-iron or pottery tank with a chain. You can still buy high-level cistern WCs — in the right setting and opulent surroundings the Victorian lavatory gives a feeling of style, but in a small home it can give a feeling of poverty. The choice these days is therefore for a **low-level** cistern which operates by means of a handle and which is joined to the pan with 1 ft or less of flush pipe. Conversion from a high-level to a low-level cistern posed a major problem until recently — the pan had to be moved forward to accommodate the cistern. Now you can buy a **slim-line** cistern or flush panel which allows you to have a low-level system without having to move the pan. The most up-to-date WCs are **close-coupled** — the cistern and pan have an internal connector so no pipework is visible.

Pans, like cisterns, are available in several basic types. They are generally **floor-mounted**, but you nowadays can also buy cantilevered or **wall-hung** models which appear to hang in mid-air. Clever, but some people feel uncomfortable. There have also been advances in the flushing action. The traditional pan has a **washdown** action — cleaning depends on the weight and movement of water round the pan. Many modern WCs have a **siphonic** action by which waste is removed by suction as well as the weight of the water. The advantages are increased efficiency and noise reduction (a double-trap siphonic WC is even quieter than a single-trap one), but they cost more and are more prone to blockage.

WCs, however modern and well-made, occasionally go wrong. A blocked pan can be difficult to clear — see page 13. If plunging does not cure the problem, call in a specialist drain cleaner who will have the proper equipment. Cistern overflow pipes may drip or pour — see page 11. Failure to flush properly usually means that the flap valve needs replacing — a cistern filling-time of over 3 minutes indicates that the wrong ball valve has been fitted or it has become partly clogged.

LIGHTING & HEATING

Pay careful attention to both of these features. A cold bathroom in winter is unpleasant no matter how luxurious the surroundings. There must be no exposed elements which can be splashed nor switches which can be reached with wet hands. In a tiny bathroom consider a combined light/infra red heater.

You will need 2 types of lighting. There should be a good source of general illumination — usually a ceiling-mounted fluorescent or glass-covered tungsten lamp. You will also need spot lighting for shaving, making-up etc. Such lighting should ideally be on either side of a mirror — if it has to be above a mirror then it should be directed on to the face and not towards the glass.

VENTILATION

An essential feature of bathrooms. You can open a window to remove smells and steam — train the family to do so. Some form of mechanical ventilation such as an extractor is desirable — it is required by law if a WC is present and there is no outside window.

TAPS

Standard baths and basins have tap holes drilled in the centre of the far side — you can order units with holes in a different location but you may have to pay extra. Also remember that bath and taps are usually displayed together in catalogues and showrooms, but the taps have to be bought separately. The choice is enormous — mixer taps are popular for baths because it is easier to gauge the water temperature at filling time. There are no particular snags about buying taps, but if they are Continental ones you must check with the store that they conform with U.K. water regulations — some do not.

The Living Room

Living room, drawing room, sitting room, lounge … a variety of names for the room which is the heart of the house, the room which people do not think they have to leave when a particular activity is over. It is, therefore, an area which is primarily for relaxation, and both the furnishing and decoration should reflect this role.

Millions of homes do not have the space to provide a room solely for relaxation. The living room has to perform an extra function — it may include a dining area (living/dining room) or a bed (bed/sitting room). If possible, aim to separate these areas with a room divider such as a modular unit or folding door where practical. If not, provide independent lighting which can be switched off when the secondary function is not in use.

You must design and arrange your living room to suit the activities which take place there (shelves for books, drawers for sewing and other hobbies, cupboards for toys, etc) and to suit the occupants (high-level storage to protect ornaments from busy young fingers, ample heating for the elderly, etc). Furnishing is a matter of taste, but there are a few general precautions. Try out all items (especially armchairs) before buying. Remember that chairs and tables will look bigger in your home than in the store, and keep all cleaning tags for future reference. Try to keep things in proportion — a large 3-seater settee or a barrel-sized lampshade will overwhelm a small room. As detailed on page 87, the experts have quite firm views on the way a living room should be decorated, but it is your room and not theirs. There are no actual rules except one — the surfaces should be hard-wearing as well as attractive if you have an active family.

DESIGN & DECORATION

If you are re-designing your living room, the first step is to make a list of items which you have to or want to include — hi-fi, seating for 6, coffee tables, bookcase, table lamp etc. Next, go round the stores with a tape-measure to find the size of items you fancy — collect a number of catalogues. Then, draw a plan of the room (you don't have to be an artist!) and start to think where the various items will go.

Your first thought should be the seating. You will probably know by now the type and number of chairs you want and it's time to position them to maximum advantage. The rule is that they should all generally face towards the focal point of the room. Every living room needs a focal point — once it was the fireplace in every case, but not any more. Today it is generally the television set but in the absence of TV it can be a large architectural plant, illuminated picture, modular unit or attractive coffee table.

The experts feel that large areas of bright primary colours should be avoided, but it is up to you. Do listen to them, though — you will have to spend hours each day looking at the walls and it does make sense to leave your more adventurous ideas for the bathroom, dining room or bedroom.

The classic approach is to pick a fairly neutral colour for a fixed feature of the room. This colour must strongly appeal to you and the colours of other large areas should be related to this hue — blending but never sharply contrasting. Brightness and colour are then added through cushions, pictures, flowering plants, curtains etc — be prepared to change these brighteners occasionally.

HOUSE PLANTS

One of the easiest and cheapest ways of adding colour. Avoid having a plain foliage plant standing alone — group plants together for maximum effect. For details see The House Plant Expert.

STORAGE

A place is required for drinks, ornaments, records, books, letters and the rest. There are two distinct types of storage — cupboards, drawers etc where objects can be put away and shelves, glass-fronted cupboards etc where they can be prominently displayed. Avoid intermediate storage where plain or unsightly objects are left lying about.

The right type of storage will depend on the room. Ornate cupboards and glass-fronted bookcases are right for a Georgian or Victorian room, but a modular unit would be much more at home if the decor is distinctly modern. The advantage of a fixed modular unit is that shelves, cupboards, glass-fronted display units and desk units can be added as required. With any storage unit test the drawers and doors before buying — don't assume that they will get easier with use.

TABLES

Tables close to chairs are vital for holding newspapers, snacks, drinks, books etc — they can either be left in the same spot (essential for heavy coffee tables) or moved out when required — a nest of tables is useful if space is short. Tables can be highly decorative as well as functional. An ornamental table makes a good focal point for a group of chairs — make sure that the space between chairs and table is wide enough for comfortable passage. There are no rules about height, but do not have tables too low if they are to be used for holding cups and plates.

TV & HI-FI

The TV, video recorder and hi-fi make up the focal point in many living rooms these days. There is no criticism here — the room is for *your* relaxation and enjoyment. Still, there are some rules for comfort and safety. Avoid trailing wires and have at least one side light when viewing TV at night. Do not have a table or other piece of furniture between you and the TV unless you have remote control and do remember the neighbours. Having speakers on the wall you share can be a nuisance if you insist on having the volume at a high level.

SEATING

The prime role of the living room is to seat all the family and have some spare seating for guests. The number of spare seats will depend on the size of the room and the money available. Don't forget the importance of folding chairs and large cushions as spare seating if space and cash are tight.

Don't immediately turn to the traditional 3-piece suite — it is rarely the right choice. In a small room it is much better to use unit seating on 2 walls with a corner piece to join them together, or buy a 2-seater settee and one or more compact armchairs. Three-seaters really belong in large rooms, and are not ideal for conversation. In a small room it may be impossible to avoid a round-the-wall arrangement for the chairs, as it is a cardinal sin to turn the living room into an obstacle course. But if there is room you should seek a better arrangement — create one or more conversational areas (depending on the size of the room) with the chairs at right angles or facing each other.

Looking around the furniture store you will find chairs which appeal and others which do not. Obviously the chair should be attractive but it is essentially a practical object which must let you relax or work in comfort. It's not just a matter of comfort — hours spent in a chair which is wrongly designed for you can aggravate a back problem.

Always carry out the **chair test** before buying. Sit as far back in the chair as you can. Hold the arms. Are both feet flat on the floor? If not, the chair is not right for you. If you plan to spend long hours in a chair, look for a high back and rather low arms.

Testing quality is more difficult — everything is hidden by the covering. Sit down once again and press down hard on the arms and seat. You should not be able to feel the wooden frame. Repeat the exercise with the cushions removed — you should not be able to feel the springs nor webbing in the base. Finally, test the cushions. Push down firmly and then remove your hand — it should spring back into shape. Put your hands on both sides and press — if you feel your fingers on the other side then there is insufficient filling present.

A few practical points. You will not want to hide the beauty of a leather suite but washable slip covers are a good idea if there are children in the family. Remember to arrange chairs so that everyone can watch TV — moving seating every night is a chore and can cause excess wear to the carpet. Turn seat cushions occasionally. An abundance of scatter cushions on the chairs gives a feeling of relaxation and comfort to the room.

FIREPLACE

The fireplace and its mantelpiece were the traditional focal point of the living room until the advent of central heating and TV. An open fire still remains unrivalled — the gas log-effect fire (page 31) can be used where the hard work of a real fire is unacceptable. Modern fireplaces are more than surrounds for the beauty of glowing coals or burning wood — they are highly decorative in their own right. Once again you must keep a sense of proportion — large imitation-stone edifices have no place in a small room. The alcoves on either side of the fireplace are very important from the visual and storage point of view. Most designers seek to have some balance and symmetry between the 2 sides, but it is not essential if you have a good design eye. If in doubt, treat each alcove in a similar manner.

WALL COVERING

In the living room you have a wider choice of suitable coverings than in any other room. If money is short then an inexpensive wallpaper will do — if you want to impress the neighbours a fabric or flock paper should do the trick.

FLOOR COVERING

The choice is more limited than with wall covering. The floor must be warm and quiet with an air of comfort. There are two basic choices — you can either have fitted carpets or a polished wooden floor with a carpet or rugs covering part of it. Make sure that rugs are non-slip. All floor coverings used in the living room should be chosen not to show dirt or marks too readily — off-white carpets can mean constant cleaning. Other alternatives are carpet squares and vinyl squares but the paramount requirement for all types of floor covering is that it must be hard-wearing.

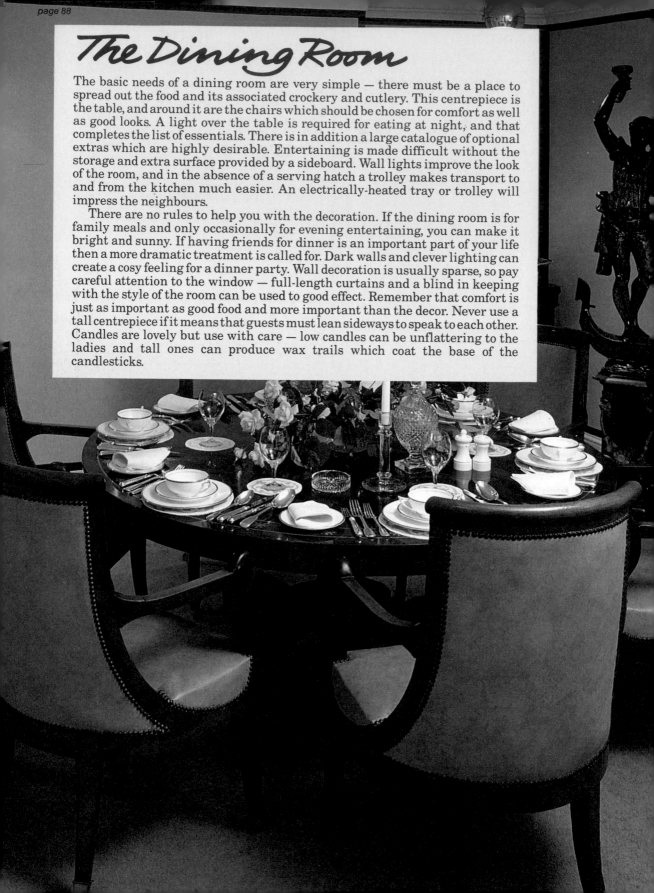

The Dining Room

The basic needs of a dining room are very simple — there must be a place to spread out the food and its associated crockery and cutlery. This centrepiece is the table, and around it are the chairs which should be chosen for comfort as well as good looks. A light over the table is required for eating at night, and that completes the list of essentials. There is in addition a large catalogue of optional extras which are highly desirable. Entertaining is made difficult without the storage and extra surface provided by a sideboard. Wall lights improve the look of the room, and in the absence of a serving hatch a trolley makes transport to and from the kitchen much easier. An electrically-heated tray or trolley will impress the neighbours.

There are no rules to help you with the decoration. If the dining room is for family meals and only occasionally for evening entertaining, you can make it bright and sunny. If having friends for dinner is an important part of your life then a more dramatic treatment is called for. Dark walls and clever lighting can create a cosy feeling for a dinner party. Wall decoration is usually sparse, so pay careful attention to the window — full-length curtains and a blind in keeping with the style of the room can be used to good effect. Remember that comfort is just as important as good food and more important than the decor. Never use a tall centrepiece if it means that guests must lean sideways to speak to each other. Candles are lovely but use with care — low candles can be unflattering to the ladies and tall ones can produce wax trails which coat the base of the candlesticks.

TABLE

There is an almost infinite range to choose from — tables in wood, brass, chrome and plastic with tops made of wood, tiles, laminate, glass and marble. Your choice, however, is quite narrow because there are a number of limiting factors. The style must be right for the house and the maximum shape and size is governed by the dimensions of the dining room. When the table is set for dining there must be at least 3 ft from the edge of the table to the wall at every spot where there is a chair, and each person will require at least 2 ft table space for comfort. A round table has no wasted corner space, but an 8-seater round table calls for a large room. A rectangular shape is usually chosen. The minimum width for seating on both sides is 30 in. — the minimum length depends on the seating required.

Seating required	Minimum length of table
4 people	4 ft 4 in.
6 people	6 ft 4 in.
8 people	8 ft 4 in.
10 people	10 ft 4 in.
12 people	12 ft 4 in.

The standard height of a table is 29 in. — if you buy an antique table which is lower than the standard you may find that there is not enough leg room if you use standard chairs.

CHAIRS

You must have a cushioned or upholstered seat if you expect your guests to linger over their coffee. Chairs with arms may seem a good idea, but they do take up a lot of space. Before buying, carry out the **chair test**. Sit down and hold the front of the table or some other object. Tilt backwards and gently rock to and fro. If the chair creaks and groans it is not sound enough for your needs.

TABLE LINEN

Tablecloths are no longer compulsory — many people prefer to use large table mats to show off the table surface and the cutlery. If hot dishes are to be stood on the table then heat-resistant mats made of cork, wood or melamine must be used. Napkins remain essential — paper ones for the family perhaps, but cloth ones when entertaining.

CROCKERY

Table crockery is usually made from plastic (unbreakable and dishwashable but not generally used for entertaining) or clay (traditional pottery, ranging from simple earthenware to ornate bone china). **Earthenware** is the cheapest type — the surface is glazed and coloured to provide our everyday 'china' — fairly thick-walled cups and saucers which chip easily to reveal the porous core. **Stoneware** is stronger and much less popular — black basalt ware and jasper are examples. At the luxury end is **porcelain** — fired at a very high temperature to produce delicate but very strong crockery with a glass-like non-porous core. This is 'fine china'. A British-only product is **bone china** — really a form of porcelain. Bone ash is added to the clay and the crockery is twice fired at a high temperature. The white glazed surface is translucent when held to the light, and bone china is *the* crockery for entertaining. Do not put bone china in the dishwasher unless there is a specific programme which allows you to do so. Standard dishwasher action will remove the surface decoration.

LIGHTING

The light should be centred over the table — if it is off-centre then the costly job of rewiring or the simple job of taking the flex to a central ceiling hook is called for. Finding the correct height for a pendant light is essential. Too high and you see the glare of the bulb — too low and your dinner partner opposite disappears in the gloom. A rise-and-fall pendant light is a sound investment.

Wall lights are very useful in the dining room. When they are fitted to a dimmer switch you can create a muted wall-washing effect when dining and a bright overall light at preparation and clearing-away time.

CUTLERY

Table cutlery should be hard-wearing and practical for everyday use, but gleaming and more decorative for entertaining. You can buy the score or more different forms of knives and forks for each place setting if you insist — coffee spoons, fish knives and forks, table spoons, asparagus tongs and so on. But these days it is felt that a basic set of 7 items should cover your needs, with perhaps a canteen of fish knives and forks kept for that special occasion. The arrangement below is for a meal of soup, prawn cocktail, main course and dessert.

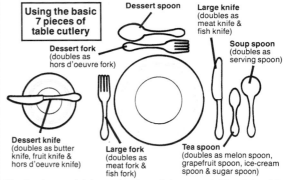

Using the basic 7 pieces of table cutlery

Dessert spoon
Large knife (doubles as meat knife & fish knife)
Dessert fork (doubles as hors d'oeuvre fork)
Soup spoon (doubles as serving spoon)
Dessert knife (doubles as butter knife, fruit knife & hors d'oeuvre knife)
Large fork (doubles as meat fork & fish fork)
Tea spoon (doubles as melon spoon, grapefruit spoon, ice-cream spoon & sugar spoon)

The basic material these days is **stainless steel**. Check that it is made to the British Standard (minimum 16% chromium) — high quality stainless steel contains 18% chromium and 8% nickel. **Silver plate** costs more, but is generally more decorative and is the cutlery used for entertaining. The silver coating should measure 20 microns, which means that the plating should last 20 years or more. Sterling or **solid silver** (92.5% silver) is hallmarked and very expensive. At the other end of the scale is **chromium-plated steel** which is inexpensive but with a coating which is not particularly long lasting.

GLASSES

Ordinary glasses are machine-moulded from soda-lime glass — they lack the weight and sparkle of crystal but they are at a price we can all afford. Crystal contains some lead — it is generally hand-made and is always expensive. Lead crystal contains a minimum of 24% lead oxide — full-lead crystal contains at least 30%. It is the lead content which provides clarity, brilliance and a ringing tone when tapped lightly on the rim. Lead also makes the glass more brittle — crystal glasses break more easily than soda-lime ones. Do not put crystal in a dishwasher.

Wine glasses are available in many shapes and sizes. Fashions come and go — champagne is now served in flutes rather than shallow saucers. The basic principles remain — stems shorter than average for good red wines, stems longer than average for chilled white wines.

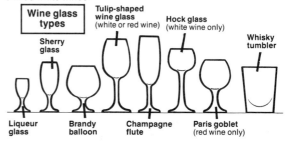

Wine glass types

Sherry glass
Tulip-shaped wine glass (white or red wine)
Hock glass (white wine only)
Whisky tumbler
Liqueur glass
Brandy balloon
Champagne flute
Paris goblet (red wine only)

Wine glasses should only be half-filled so that the aroma can develop — champagne glasses should be filled to the top.

FLOOR COVERING

The basic need is for an easy-to-clean material. Carpets are not really practical if there are small children, but for many people wall-to-wall carpeting is the indisputable choice. Look for a short pile, preferably with some form of pattern. In the right setting a polished wooden floor is the ideal surface for a dining room — noisy but elegant.

The Hall & Stairs

The hall leads us from outside the house to the rooms we use and which we want our guests to admire. All too often it is treated as a mere passageway, but it is the hall that people first notice on entering the house. It should be planned and decorated as well as your skill and funds will allow.

Of course, if you have a large square hall with an impressive staircase there is no problem. There is plenty of space for essential and decorative furniture, and a fine setting for richly-decorated walls and floors covered with fine carpet or polished wood. Unfortunately the standard British pattern is quite different and offers lots of problems — a long and narrow passage broken up by doors on one or both sides and a staircase at the far end.

So the average hall and staircase is quite a challenge for the interior decorator. Children and dogs mean push-chairs and muddy feet, so all surfaces should be hard-wearing and easy to clean. Try to choose colours and materials which are warm and welcoming, and avoid at all costs creating an obstacle course. Keep the passageway clear by reducing furniture to a minimum — consider a wall-phone if a telephone table will take up too much room, and make maximum use of the space under the stairs.

One way of solving the small hall problem is to have the wall between the living room and the hallway removed. Think carefully — noise insulation will be reduced, toddlers will have more ready access to the stairs and a porch to house coats, umbrellas, push-chairs etc will be essential.

WALL COVERING

If you have a large well-lit hall, there are no rules to follow. But if your hall is dark and narrow and you have a growing family, there are guidelines for making the best of a difficult situation. The basic aim is to ensure that the area will be as bright, spacious and durable as possible. This calls for using patterns with care — any bold pattern will bring the walls even closer together, and pattern on the walls must mean no pattern in the floor covering. The colour should be fairly light but avoid primary colours like the plague — go for soft pastel shades.

Toughness is vital — prams will bump into walls and little muddy hands will leave their mark. Vinyl is perhaps the best covering — an eggshell finish paint is also quite good. Avoid sharp contrasts between the colour of the woodwork and the walls — the bigger the difference, the smaller the hall will appear. Mirrored glass is an excellent way of making a small hall appear larger, but floor-to-ceiling mirror should be protected in some way if there are small children running about.

LIGHTING

The hall needs good lighting — a pool of light surrounded by shadows may be romantic in the dining room but it has no place in the hall. On the stairs it would be downright dangerous. Here the light must be strong and diffuse enough to cast a strong shadow so that it is easy to see where the riser ends and the tread begins on each step.

FLOOR COVERING

The floor areas around the front and back doors receive the hardest wear and tear of all. There is dirt, damp, regular coming and going, muddy boots and pram wheels, etc. The basic requirement for a hall floor is a covering which is hard-wearing and relatively easy to clean. Some people do lay ceramic tiles, but most householders prefer the surface to be quiet and fairly soft. A number of materials fit the bill — vinyl squares, rugs, sisal matting etc, but for the average home the first choice is carpeting.

Choose carpeting with care. The most attractive way to cover the hall and stairs is to have fitted or wall-to-wall carpeting. This is an expensive job — a very heavy wear grade should be used (see page 56) and for covering stairs it must be densely tufted. As a general rule foam-backed carpet should be avoided as fixing to stairs can be difficult.

In most houses it is a good idea to have the same carpet for both hall and stairs — a close-pile, hard-wearing fitted carpet is ideal. If a less expensive alternative is necessary, sisal or rush

matting will provide a satisfactory hall surface. These vegetable fibres do tend to be slippery, however, and should not be used on stairs — cord carpeting is a more suitable covering.

Bodywidth carpeting is 27 – 36 in. wide — a carpet runner laid down the centre of the stairs is both easier to lay and cheaper to buy than fitted carpet.

Use gripper fixing strips rather than carpet tacks or stair rods. A felt pad should be laid on each tread and around the nosing (see page 51) before the carpet is laid. Buy about 18 in. of extra carpet. Do not lay a felt pad on the bottom step — fold the extra carpet under the bottom riser and on the bottom tread. This will enable you to move the carpet when it begins to wear.

HOUSE PLANTS

About one third of the hallways of Britain are decorated with house plants. It is right that plants should be present in this transition zone between the garden and the rooms of the house, and their presence can improve the appearance of even the dullest hall.

The favourite spot is a difficult one for house plants. The table near the door receives draughts through the open door and is usually poorly lit. The choice of plants is limited, and you should pick from the 'easy' group listed in The House Plant Expert and other textbooks.

STAIRS

There are 3 basic types of staircase. In most homes you will find the standard tread and riser type (see page 51). In some modern houses you will find the open tread type — extra-thick treads are carried on stringers or are fixed directly into the wall. Some people find these open staircases rather frightening — if children under 5 years old are present the regulations state that the gap between the treads must be less than 4 in. Even more unusual than the open staircase is the spiral type, in which the treads are all attached to a single newel post.

You can buy staircases from major DIY suppliers, but erecting a new stairway is really a job for the professional. There are all sorts of building regulations which must be followed and special equipment is required.

DEALING WITH STAIR PROBLEMS

Creaking stairs are a common problem in old stairs. The first job is to isolate the problem by asking someone to walk up and down the staircase whilst you mark the offending areas. You may be lucky enough to solve the problem from the front of the staircase — dust talcum powder between the riser and tread at the point where the trouble occurs.

Unfortunately the trouble is not usually cured by this simple trick. It is necessary to get behind the staircase. Here you will find a series of wedges beneath each tread — tap home with a hammer if they have come loose. There will also be triangular blocks in the angle between each tread and riser — replace missing or loose ones. Finally, screw the back of the tread into the riser above.

Broken or **loose balusters** should be dealt with immediately. Small cracks can be glued — a large break may require a new baluster. A weak balustrade is a serious hazard — call in a joiner if you do not have the experience to fix it.

Loose carpets are another source of danger. You can buy clips which are attached to either the riser or tread and will hold the carpet in place. Another solution is to fix stair rods if carpet tacks are no longer holding the carpet runner securely.

HEATING

Efficient draught proofing around the front door will reduce your heating bills, but some form of background heating will still be necessary in winter. This is not just a matter of comfort in the hallway — an icy block of air at the front of the house will result in a cold draught every time you open the door of a heated room.

STORAGE

In the average home the hall is the place where coats, umbrellas, hats and perhaps boots and gloves are stored. These are not decorative items, so a free-standing wardrobe or fitted cupboard is used wherever possible.

The hall remains the traditional place for the telephone, although a narrow hallway is not really a satisfactory spot. A table is necessary to support it together with a notebook, and a chair is needed if your calls tend to be lengthy ones. Phones are now much more attractive and you can have plugs fitted in several rooms. Despite this, you may still feel that a telephone belongs in the hall. If space is really tight, you can consider a shelf instead of a table, or even have a wall-phone installed.

Wherever possible there should be a table or chest in the hall. There are so many things to find a home for — keys, letters, papers etc. It will also house ornamental items such as house plants, vases etc — a hall with no decorative touches at all is a stark place indeed.

Many people fail to utilise the space under the stairs. This can be boxed in as a wardrobe — put in lots of shelves rather than piling things on the floor.

WINDOWS

Curtains are not always the best way to decorate a hall window. If the area of glass is small you should consider a blind or even no covering at all — nothing should be done to cut down the amount of light entering the hall if only one small window is present.

If light is not a problem then attractive curtains can improve the appearance of the hall. One alternative is to place shelves across the window and stand pots of house plants on them.

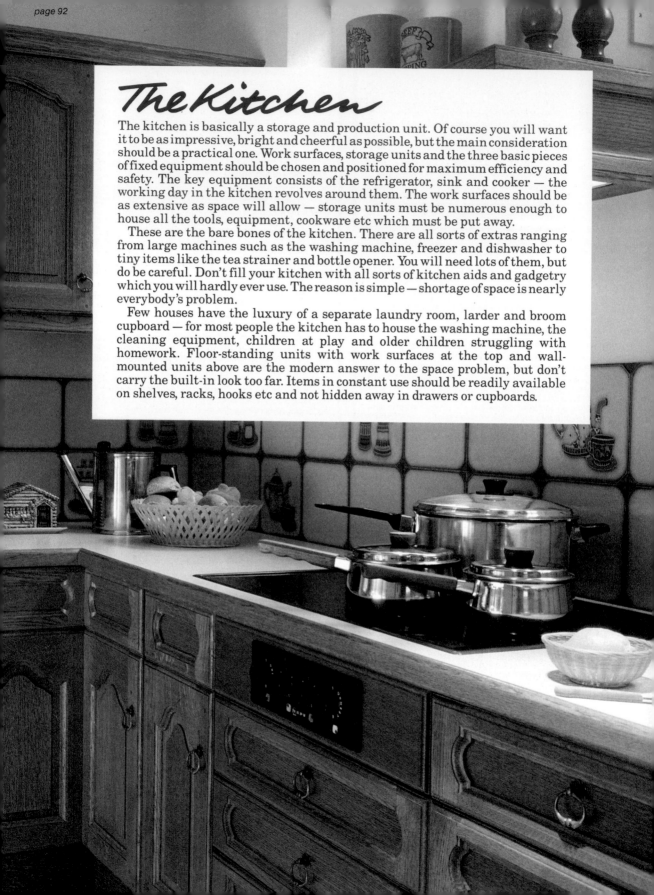

The Kitchen

The kitchen is basically a storage and production unit. Of course you will want it to be as impressive, bright and cheerful as possible, but the main consideration should be a practical one. Work surfaces, storage units and the three basic pieces of fixed equipment should be chosen and positioned for maximum efficiency and safety. The key equipment consists of the refrigerator, sink and cooker — the working day in the kitchen revolves around them. The work surfaces should be as extensive as space will allow — storage units must be numerous enough to house all the tools, equipment, cookware etc which must be put away.

These are the bare bones of the kitchen. There are all sorts of extras ranging from large machines such as the washing machine, freezer and dishwasher to tiny items like the tea strainer and bottle opener. You will need lots of them, but do be careful. Don't fill your kitchen with all sorts of kitchen aids and gadgetry which you will hardly ever use. The reason is simple — shortage of space is nearly everybody's problem.

Few houses have the luxury of a separate laundry room, larder and broom cupboard — for most people the kitchen has to house the washing machine, the cleaning equipment, children at play and older children struggling with homework. Floor-standing units with work surfaces at the top and wall-mounted units above are the modern answer to the space problem, but don't carry the built-in look too far. Items in constant use should be readily available on shelves, racks, hooks etc and not hidden away in drawers or cupboards.

KITCHEN PLANNING

With any room it is advisable to draw a scale plan showing the location of the fixed and heavy items before you set about the task of ordering and remodelling. With the kitchen it is more than advisable — it is essential. There are so many things to be fitted into the room and there are so many ways you can do the wrong thing. You can shift settees, tables and lamps in the living room, but you cannot just move a sink, cooker, and washing machine from one spot to another if you have made a mistake.

The first job is to write down all the factors which must be considered before drawing up the plan:

- Is the kitchen large enough? If not, can a wall be knocked down or an extension built? Take care — you should always consult a builder or an architect before moving kitchen walls.
- Who will use the kitchen? If children will be around, you *must* think of the safety factors described in Chapter 8. If the family is large you will need a lot of storage space.
- Are the services suitable? Remodelling is an opportunity to replace old pipes, have stopcocks fitted etc.
- Is cooking important? If meals are simple and entertaining is an uncommon event, it is not worth wasting money on a large and complex oven. If frozen food is frequently used you will certainly need a microwave oven.
- How often do you shop? Obviously you will need much more storage, refrigerator and freezer space if you shop weekly or fortnightly rather than daily.
- Do you plan to eat in the kitchen? Space may be a problem, but family meals in the kitchen make life much easier for the housewife, and even a small room can usually accommodate a breakfast bar.
- What fixtures do you plan to keep and what do you intend to replace?
- How much money can you afford? Left off some checklists in the textbooks, but a vital consideration for all of us!

There may be other points you wish to consider before getting down to the detail of planning. Once the plan is complete you should collect catalogues for the items of major equipment you propose to buy. Try to see the goods before you order. Shop around — check whether installation is included in the price.

Beginning the plan

Mark out the floor plan on graph paper — it is also useful to draw wall plans. Although the measurements on this page are given in inches, it will probably be better to work in metric units these days. The usual scale is 1/20.

Draw in doors, windows and the location of pipes, drains, electric points etc. Then mark the position of all appliances and units which are going to remain. The next step is to cut out pieces of card to represent the equipment and units you plan to instal. Before coming to a decision, carefully study the concept of the Work Triangle and the 5 basic kitchen styles.

The Work Triangle

The heart of the kitchen is the triangle formed by the refrigerator, sink and cooker — in a very small room this may be condensed to a line rather than a triangle. For the sake of safety avoid having the sink and cooker on either side of the line of traffic, especially if children and dogs are present. A door when opened should not enter this triangle. For the sake of efficiency keep the total length of the sides of the triangle to less than 20 ft.

Completing the plan

Having chosen one of the 5 basic arrangements it is necessary to site the main equipment and units. Illustrated right are the dimensions for standard units — on pages 94 – 95 are notes on a range of kitchen fitments. Read them carefully as each piece of equipment has its own positional needs. Following these needs as far as possible, move the cardboard shapes around to give you the ideal arrangement. If there is a piece of equipment which you want but cannot yet afford, leave a space and fill with a temporary unit.

Check the completed plan. Have you arranged for sufficient 13 A plugs (minimum 5) above the work surfaces? Have you positioned the tallest units (eg a broom closet) in a corner or at the end of a run of units? Have you put the sink, washing machine and dishwasher close together to make plumbing easy?

KEY

work triangle

cooker

refrigerator

sink

Kitchen layouts

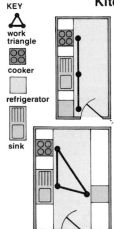

SINGLE LINE ARRANGEMENT
The only practical arrangement for a long and narrow kitchen. Go for as much floor to ceiling storage as you can. This arrangement is sometimes used in a larger room where a dining area is required. Cramped — not very efficient.

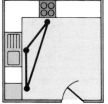

GALLEY ARRANGEMENT
The problem is to avoid a claustrophobic effect. Do not have a line of wall units on both sides and have at least one gap between the base units along one of the walls. This arrangement is often disappointing and is best avoided.

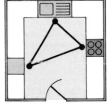

L-SHAPED ARRANGEMENT
The best layout for a large kitchen — the Work Triangle is not too large and there is ample space for food preparation plus a dining area which is away from the triangle. A popular and practical arrangement, especially if more than one door is present.

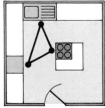

U-SHAPED ARRANGEMENT
The best arrangement for an average-sized kitchen — there is adequate room for the home laundry and kitchen units. Convenient, efficient and adaptable — in a large room a dining area can be arranged beyond one of the arms.

ISLAND ARRANGEMENT
One or more key pieces of equipment is located in a central island unit. The usual item is a large cooker — the other alternative is a sink-topped preparation unit. A stylish arrangement for the modern kitchen, but poses difficulties and perhaps risks where space is short.

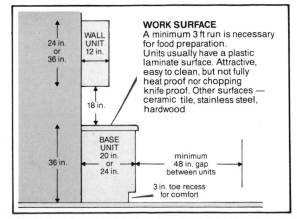

WORK SURFACE
A minimum 3 ft run is necessary for food preparation. Units usually have a plastic laminate surface. Attractive, easy to clean, but not fully heat proof nor chopping knife proof. Other surfaces — ceramic tile, stainless steel, hardwood

WALL UNIT 12 in.

24 in. or 36 in.

18 in.

BASE UNIT 20 in. or 24 in.

36 in.

minimum 48 in. gap between units

3 in. toe recess for comfort

FLOOR COVERING

There are certain obvious essentials. The floor covering must be hard-wearing — the back-door is usually located in the kitchen and there is regular traffic to and from the major items of equipment. The floor must also be easy to clean — a surface ruined by spilt food would be quite useless. It must not be damaged by water and it must be non-slippery. These essentials reduce the number of suitable flooring materials, but the choice is still quite wide. Flagstones, quarry tiles and ceramic tiles are traditional materials — all the key requirements are there but one highly desirable feature is missing — softness. The noise of clattering feet and the inevitable fate of dropped dishes or jars make these iron-hard surfaces out of place in the modern kitchen.

Sealed cork or rubber tiles are a good choice — so is cushioned vinyl. For maximum softness choose a bonded nylon carpet such as Flotex. It is extremely hard-wearing and stain-resistant.

WALL COVERING

A kitchen wall is subjected to steam, smoke, grease and perhaps occasional splashes. Above all other considerations it must be washable — the usual choice is between vinyl, ceramic tiles and a washable paper. Paint is popular — the best type is an eggshell- or silk-finish. Matt paint is not washable — gloss paint shows wall imperfections and enhances condensation.

The area directly behind the sink, boiler and hob are subject to the worst of all conditions — the heat and volume of steam are much higher than elsewhere. Tiling is popular here — so is gloss paint. The choice of colour for the wall covering is up to you, but remember that bright colouring can be tiring in a room where you have to spend several hours each day.

WINDOWS

The obvious rule is that you must never use curtains which get in the way or pose a fire risk by being too close to the hob unit, oven or boiler. Many experts believe that blinds are preferable to curtains in the kitchen — Venetian and roller types are popular.

VENTILATION

Working in the kitchen produces 3 types of air pollution. There is steam from pans, kettle etc, smoke (tiny, air-borne particles) from grill, oven, toaster etc, and food smells from the cooking process. In a large kitchen it may be possible to remove these unwanted air pollutants by opening a door and windows, but if the kitchen is used as a living or dining area then you will need a more effective means of removal.

An extractor fan fitted to the wall or window is one answer. Smoke and smells are removed and condensation is controlled — make sure that the model you buy will change the air in the room at least 10 times each hour. Another way of clearing the air is to fit a cooker hood. The hood can be purely functional or highly decorative, but for the sake of efficiency it must cover the whole of the hob area — the distance between the bottom of the hood and the top of the hob should be 26 – 30 in.

With a ducted hood the air is drawn through a filter which absorbs the grease and some other impurities. The filtered air is then blown along ducting to a grille on the outside wall of the house. This arrangement is not practical if the hob is not sited by an outside wall. Here you will need a recirculating hood. The fan draws the air through a filter — after the air has been cleaned it is recirculated into the room. In some models the air is dried before being returned to the kitchen. With all cooker hoods it is essential to wash or renew the filter regularly as instructed in the operating manual.

REFRIGERATOR & FREEZER

Read pages 48 – 49. Most people would like to have both a large refrigerator and a sizeable freezer, but space as well as money is often the limiting factor. When space is short the refrigerator has to be set under the work surface, and this means constant bending down. A combined fridge-freezer helps to overcome the space problem — for both convenience and efficiency choose one with the refrigerator at the top and the freezer at the bottom.

COOKER

The photographs and drawings on pages 38 and 39 amply illustrate the fact that a cooker these days need not be a free-standing unit with an oven below and a few rings on a hob above. The split-level concept will take the backache out of baking and roasting — the oven with its glass front is built into a unit so that the shelves are more or less at eye level. Eye-level grills have also become extremely popular in the same way that ceramic hobs (page 39) are starting to take over from the traditional rings. There really is a cooker revolution in progress — more and more ovens are fan-assisted and some contain a microwave unit. Self-cleaning is now a fairly standard feature and keen cooks sometimes choose an electric oven/gas hob arrangement.

Despite all the modern advances, the traditional rules for siting the cooker still apply. Do not put an oven or hob in the corner and don't put a cooker next to the door or under a window. There should be at least one work surface by the cooker. If the surface itself is not heat-proof, you will require a trivet or heat-proof mat for pans, trays etc taken off the hob or out of the oven.

DINING AREA

Dining areas within kitchens are of 2 basic types. There are breakfast bars which are built for convenience rather than comfort. Shortage of space dictates that the table top is narrow or even folds flat against the wall when not in use — seating is usually in the form of stools or narrow upright chairs. Not for luxury dining then, but it is a boon if breakfast and light meals can be eaten in the kitchen.

If room is available you can have the second type of dining area — a table with comfortable chairs which can be used for all family meals. This zone can be cut off by means of a peninsular unit, a light screen or by a trough of house plants. There should be independent lighting for the kitchen area and the dining area. This arrangement does require ample space — there must be at least 3 ft clear behind each chair.

DISHWASHER

Read page 45. You will already have made up your mind about a dishwasher — either it is a modern godsend which you already have or long for, or it is an unnecessary piece of equipment. There is a golden rule — if you do buy a dishwasher then make sure it is a good one and will deal with all your everyday crockery, cutlery and pans. It really is silly to buy one which can wash only small and simple things. Think carefully about siting — it will have to be close to a cold water supply and waste pipe, and it should be near the crockery/cutlery store and away from the fridge and freezer.

KETTLE

You don't *have* to own an electric kettle — about 25% of households do without. A pan or non-electric kettle takes longer to boil, however, and so your choice should be a well-made automatic electric kettle. This will take about 4 minutes to boil the recommended capacity of water — when boiling point is reached the current is switched off. With a non-automatic kettle there is a cut-out, which means that the current is switched off only when almost all the water has boiled away.

MIXER

Blender, mixer, food processor . . . there is much confusion over the names. A **blender** is a stout transparent container with a lid at the top and a set of blades at the bottom. These blades are driven by the motor in the base unit. Excellent for pulping, blending liquids and chopping soft materials but not man enough for tough mixing jobs. A blender is sometimes called a **liquidiser**. A **food mixer** may be a small hand-held model or a large table-standing unit. Here the motor is at the top of the machine — the beaters or other attachments are pushed into the mixer head. A good mixer can do many jobs — beating, blending, milling, shredding etc. These jobs can also be done by a **food processor**, but its mode of action is different. The power unit is at the base — a large transparent container houses the cutting attachment and the food entry tube.

POTS & PANS

Many materials are used these days for making cookware, and each material has its own set of advantages and disadvantages. When buying pots and pans it is necessary to understand the meaning of 3 terms. **Flame-proof** means that the container will withstand the fierce heat of a gas or electric ring as well as the temperature of an oven. **Oven-proof** ware can be used in an oven but not on a hob, and **non-stick** means that the surface has been coated with a material which makes cooking and cleaning easier. Non-stick pans, however, are harder to use than ordinary ones — they must not be over-heated, you should not use metal tools and they must be washed and dried thoroughly after use.

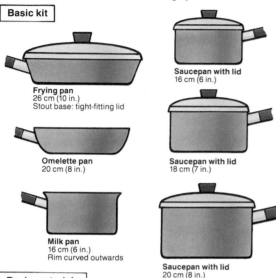

Basic kit

Frying pan
26 cm (10 in.)
Stout base: tight-fitting lid

Omelette pan
20 cm (8 in.)

Milk pan
16 cm (6 in.)
Rim curved outwards

Saucepan with lid
16 cm (6 in.)

Saucepan with lid
18 cm (7 in.)

Saucepan with lid
20 cm (8 in.)

Basic materials

ALUMINIUM Very popular, inexpensive and easy to clean. Thin pans warp — choose medium- or heavy-gauge. The outside may be polished or enamelled — the inside will pit if acid food is allowed to stand in the container.

ENAMEL-COATED STEEL Very attractive — available in many colours and patterns. Basic problem is uneven cooking — food tends to stick. For best results buy a pan with a metal-coated base and a metal-ringed rim and lid.

CAST IRON Loved by experienced cooks because it heats up slowly and evenly and then holds the heat — excellent for slow cooking, frying, omelettes etc. Hated by ordinary cooks because of the weight. Rub with oil after washing.

COPPER A set of gleaming copper pans is a showpiece in any kitchen, but they are expensive and must be frequently polished. Professionals use them because heat moves quickly and evenly — inner nickel or tin coating lasts about 5 years.

STAINLESS STEEL Stainless steel pans have the advantages you would expect — long-lasting, rust-proof, easy to clean etc. Heat conduction, however, is not good — look for a copper or aluminium base.

CERAMIC Earthenware and stoneware are used for casseroles — heat is distributed evenly and food can be served directly from the oven to the table. They are rarely flame-proof, however, so do not use on the hob.

GLASS Glass pots, pans, casseroles etc are available these days, made from borosilicate glass. Check that it is flame-proof before using on an electric or gas ring — nice to see things cooking but food tends to stick and burn.

SINK

The basic details are outlined on page 47. The usual place for a sink is under the window so that the view can be enjoyed, the children watched etc but there is no technical merit in the window spot — it is a matter of choice. Stainless steel is popular — a satin finish is more satisfactory than a shiny one in hard-water areas. If you do not have a dishwasher, choose a double-bowl model if you have the space. With all sinks it is essential to fill the gap between the edges and the surrounding units with a waterproof sealant.

KNIVES

Experienced cooks choose their knives with great care and spend the time needed to keep them properly sharpened and clean. Carbon steel holds its edge longest, but stainless steel is easier to maintain. Look for rivetted handles and store your knives on a rack rather than in a drawer. Place this rack near the preparation area but well away from children's reach.

Basic kit

Paring knife
Palette knife
Carving knife
Cook's knife
Bread knife
Utility knife
Serrated knife

LIGHTING

Effective general lighting is necessary to illuminate the whole kitchen at night — there should be no dark spots. Fluorescent tubes are frequently used for this purpose as they do not cast sharp shadows like tungsten bulbs, but the light can be a little harsh. There should be specific lighting for the sink and the hob — spotlights are useful but not if they shine in people's eyes. It is important that work surfaces should be well-lit — fit fluorescent tubes under wall units.

HEATING

For most of the year and for most of the day in the coldest months little or no heat is required in the modern kitchen. The oven, hob, kettle and central heating boiler usually supply adequate warmth, but there is often a need for a short period of instant heat on cold mornings. This can be supplied by a radiant fire or a fan heater.

STORAGE

Nowadays kitchen storage means a collection of units, giving the kitchen a built-in look. As warned on page 92, the uncluttered look should not be taken too far. Kitchen knives, mugs, cookery tools and so on should be stored on the walls or on the work surface.

Units of various types are available. Base units (full cupboard or drawer plus cupboard) 12 – 48 in. wide and wall units 12 – 40 in. wide are the main ones, but there are others. Sink units, of course, but also corner base units, corner wall units, hob units, open-ended units, drawer units and larder units.

When choosing the units remember that the most-used items should be stored at 2½ – 5½ ft from the ground. To determine the ideal height for the work surface, stand 18 in. from a wall and raise your arms slowly. The point where your fingertips touch the wall is the ideal height. Base unit cupboards are inefficient for storing a large assortment of small items — you will have to get down on hands and knees to reach to the back of the unit. It is a good idea to buy cupboards with wire drawers or fitted carousels for easy-reach storage. Units to be placed over a hob should have a fire-proof underside.

Units are available in 4 forms, depending on your needs, pocket and joinery skills. A **DIY unit** is made from basic materials — sawn wood, hinges, screws, glue etc as needed for your design. A **flat-pack unit** has the components pre-cut and packed for you to put together — the standard cash-and-carry model. A **ready-made unit** saves work but costs more — a **custom-made unit** made to an individual plan is, of course, the most expensive of all.

There are various finishes for doors and drawer fronts. At the economy end you will find whitewood for home painting or staining and chipboard coated with melamine. More expensive units have wooden frames and faces which are lacquered, veneered, varnished or covered with plastic laminate. A final safety point — read page 60 before putting up wall units.

CHAPTER 5
OUTSIDE THE HOUSE

Most of the money spent on home decorating goes towards improving the appearance and comfort of the rooms inside, and yet it is the outside which the world at large sees. Only a select few actually come through the front door, but a host of passers-by, casual callers and nearby residents judge us by the outside of the house.

Thus maintenance of the outer fabric is necessary to give a good impression, but there is much more to it than that. Neglect a spare bedroom and nothing frightening happens — neglect the outside and small problems can quickly become major headaches. A small area of rot on a door frame can be easily dealt with if caught in time, a missing roof tile is easily replaced . . . ignore these and similar problems at your peril.

Get into the routine of carefully inspecting the outside of your house each spring and after a gale. To do this properly you will need a ladder, and that calls for safety measures. The base should be at least a quarter of the height away from the house, and make sure that the foot of the ladder has a firm and level base. The ladder must be secure — tie the sides to stakes, place a heavy sack against the ladder or have someone hold the sides. If climbing a ladder is out of the question, inspect the gutters, roof, walls etc through binoculars.

Neglect is usually due to the fact that working on the outside is generally more difficult and often less pleasant than working indoors. An added problem is that you have less of a free hand — the decoration of a semi-detached or terraced house has to blend in to some extent with the neighbours.

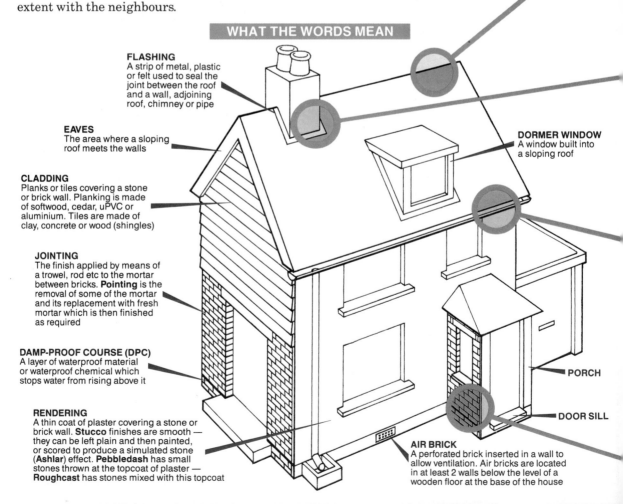

WHAT THE WORDS MEAN

FLASHING
A strip of metal, plastic or felt used to seal the joint between the roof and a wall, adjoining roof, chimney or pipe

EAVES
The area where a sloping roof meets the walls

CLADDING
Planks or tiles covering a stone or brick wall. Planking is made of softwood, cedar, uPVC or aluminium. Tiles are made of clay, concrete or wood (shingles)

JOINTING
The finish applied by means of a trowel, rod etc to the mortar between bricks. **Pointing** is the removal of some of the mortar and its replacement with fresh mortar which is then finished as required

DAMP-PROOF COURSE (DPC)
A layer of waterproof material or waterproof chemical which stops water from rising above it

RENDERING
A thin coat of plaster covering a stone or brick wall. **Stucco** finishes are smooth — they can be left plain and then painted, or scored to produce a simulated stone (**Ashlar**) effect. **Pebbledash** has small stones thrown at the topcoat of plaster — **Roughcast** has stones mixed with this topcoat

DORMER WINDOW
A window built into a sloping roof

PORCH

DOOR SILL

AIR BRICK
A perforated brick inserted in a wall to allow ventilation. Air bricks are located in at least 2 walls below the level of a wooden floor at the base of the house

ROOF

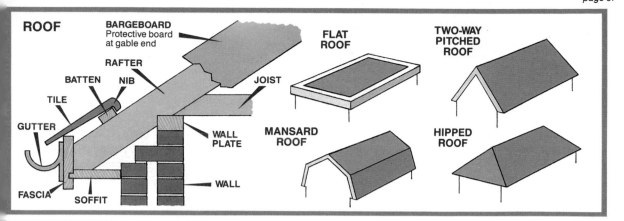

BARGEBOARD
Protective board at gable end

RAFTER

BATTEN

NIB

TILE

GUTTER

FASCIA

SOFFIT

JOIST

WALL PLATE

WALL

FLAT ROOF

TWO-WAY PITCHED ROOF

MANSARD ROOF

HIPPED ROOF

CHIMNEY

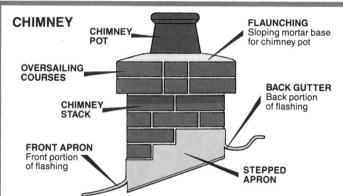

CHIMNEY POT

OVERSAILING COURSES

CHIMNEY STACK

FRONT APRON
Front portion of flashing

FLAUNCHING
Sloping mortar base for chimney pot

BACK GUTTER
Back portion of flashing

STEPPED APRON

A **FLUE** is the passage through which smoke and gases escape into the atmosphere. A **CHIMNEY** is the structure which forms the flue.

A **FLUE LINING** protects the body of the chimney from the hot and corrosive gases in the flue. Linings are usually made of fireclay or high alumina concrete.

A **COWL** is a hooded structure which is installed at the top of a chimney to aid ventilation and prevent the entry of rain.

GUTTERING

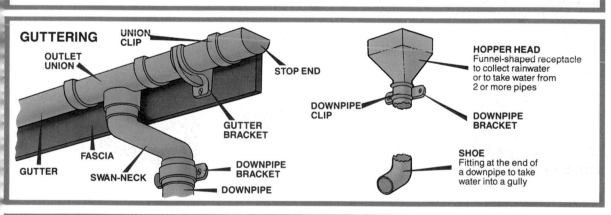

UNION CLIP

OUTLET UNION

GUTTER

FASCIA

SWAN-NECK

GUTTER BRACKET

STOP END

DOWNPIPE BRACKET

DOWNPIPE

HOPPER HEAD
Funnel-shaped receptacle to collect rainwater or to take water from 2 or more pipes

DOWNPIPE CLIP

DOWNPIPE BRACKET

SHOE
Fitting at the end of a downpipe to take water into a gully

WALLS

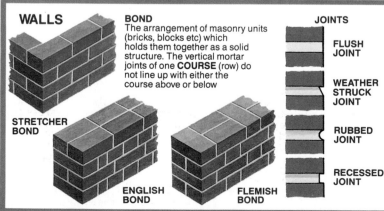

BOND
The arrangement of masonry units (bricks, blocks etc) which holds them together as a solid structure. The vertical mortar joints of one **COURSE** (row) do not line up with either the course above or below

STRETCHER BOND

ENGLISH BOND

FLEMISH BOND

JOINTS

FLUSH JOINT

WEATHER STRUCK JOINT

RUBBED JOINT

RECESSED JOINT

In a **CAVITY WALL** there are 2 parallel walls ('leaves') separated by an air gap which is at least 2 in. wide. The outer and inner walls are connected at intervals by metal **WALL TIES**.

There are 3 basic brick types — for details of brick qualities, see page 100. **COMMONS** are cheap and are used where appearance is not important. **FACINGS** are the standard type for walls which are not to be covered — they are more attractive than commons. **ENGINEERING BRICKS** are the hardest and strongest — they are not penetrated by water nor damaged by frost.

Bricks are laid with **MORTAR** — a mixture of sand with a binder (cement, lime or a cement/lime mix). The reserve of mortar is kept on a **SPOT BOARD** — the small quantity which is in use is kept on a hand-held **HAWK**.

Roof & Chimney

For most people, the roof is a no-go area. Routine inspections are not carried out, and the first sign of trouble is water dripping through a bedroom ceiling. This is worrying enough, but the hidden danger of a leaking roof is even worse — wet rot can take hold and ruin the roof timbers.

Despite the mystery, a pitched (sloping) roof is built on a simple principle. There are a series of parallel wooden triangles with rafters as the sides and joists at the base of each one. In all cases the triangles are joined by rows of horizontal battens which hold the roof covering. In traditional pitched roofs there is a stout ridge board joining all the triangles along the apex — in the modern trussed rafter roof there is no ridge.

Roofs do deteriorate with age and you should look at yours at least once a year. Look out from your neighbours' bedroom windows if you don't want to go up a ladder. Are the flaunching and chimney pots sound? Are there any cracks in the flashing? Can any broken slates or tiles be seen? Is the wood around the roof in need of painting? If there is a problem, tackle it at once. For major jobs call in a specialist roofing company — make sure that it is a member of the National Federation of Roofing Contractors or a similar association.

ROOF COVERING

The purpose of the roof covering is to prevent the entry of water and rapidly moving air despite the onslaught of heavy rain, driving snow and gales. It must last for many years despite bitter frosts and baking sun — roof replacement every 20 years is soon enough!

Many materials are used — thatch, wooden shingles, plastic and asbestos corrugated sheeting, wired glass, copper sheeting etc, but by far the most popular coverings are slates and tiles for pitched roofs and bitumen felt for flat ones.

You will still find slate on older houses — it was the most popular roofing material in Victorian times. Take care when buying second-hand slates — avoid chipped edges, flaking surfaces and enlarged nail holes. Clay tiles took over the crown from slate in this century, but since the war concrete has become the most important tiling material — it is less liable than clay to be damaged by frost. Tiles are available in many colours and surface textures these days, and also many shapes — waved pantiles, semicircular Roman tiles, exotic Spanish tiles, flat-faced plain tiles and so on. In older houses the visible roof covering is the only line of defence against the elements — in new houses there is a layer of felt or even boarding under the battens holding the slates or tiles.

PLAIN TILE
Each tile bears 2 holes near the top, but there are usually 2 nibs (projections) at the back, and the method of fixing is to hook the nibs over the battens and nail down every 4th row. As with slates, there is a wide overlap (double lapping) and the tiles in each row are staggered.

SLATE
Once very popular — now rarely used on new houses because of the price. Second-hand slates and artificial asbestos cement ones are often used for repairs. Slates come in many colour variations and sizes — check before buying. Each slate is nailed either along the upper edge or along the centre.

INTERLOCKING TILE
Most interlocking tiles are fixed like plain tiles, the nibs hooking over battens and every 3rd row being nailed down. Some interlocking tiles, however, must be secured individually. Many 3-D shapes are available, and because of the tight fit between neighbouring tiles they are laid with little overlap.

BITUMEN FELT
The standard material for flat roofs — the first layer is nailed to the wooden decking of the roof and the second layer is bonded to it with hot bitumen. A third layer of bitumen felt is bonded in similar fashion, and the surface is covered with stone chippings or reflective paint to reflect the sun's heat.

DEALING WITH ROOF PROBLEMS

WORKING ON THE ROOF

A small roof job, such as replacing a broken tile, can be carried out by the homeowner, provided the equipment and technique are satisfactory. If you are afraid of heights, leave it to someone else. If not, choose a still and dry day. Make sure the ladder against the roof is properly secured and at the correct angle — see page 96. Never lean it on the gutter — use a ladder stay and make sure that the ladder projects at least 2 feet above the gutter.

Few tools will be required for working on a sloping roof — make sure they are secured in some way and tie the top of the ladder to the wall or the fascia board by means of a rope through an eye-bolt. Put on rubber-soled shoes and you are ready to start work — provided the problem can be reached from the ladder. If you have to work on the roof itself, you will need a special roof ladder which can be hired quite cheaply for the day. The hook at the top of this ladder is placed over the ridge. Never walk on the roof and make sure that no workman such as a TV aerial fitter ever walks on your roof.

Flat roofs have their own rules. They are not designed to carry your weight which means that the surface should be protected. It is especially important not to walk across a chipping covered roof in hot weather — the chippings will be pressed into the surface and damage will result.

A ladder may not be suitable for extensive roof repairs. A scaffolding tower is necessary and many of the ladder rules apply — secure footing, fix to the wall with a rope through an eye-bolt, never stretch too far without moving the structure etc.

HIRING SOMEONE ELSE TO WORK ON THE ROOF

Apart from the need to find the money, it would seem to be an easy job to employ a roofing contractor to do the work for you. But there are pitfalls for the unwary. Get 2 or 3 quotes if the work is more than replacing a few tiles. Get the quotes in writing — make sure that they contain the details you want. If the roof leaks after repair you will only have yourself to blame if you did not insist that the quotation bears the words — 'the roof to be watertight after completion of the repairs'. The contractor has no obligation to remove the rubbish if the quote did not mention the requirement, and you can't expect a 10 year guarantee unless it was specified.

Choosing the right roofer by looking through the Yellow Pages is not easy. The best course of action is to find someone who has had a roof repaired recently and is pleased with the work. If this is not possible, check that the contractor is a member of a reputable association which will deal with any complaints which may arise.

REPAIRING A FLAT ROOF

The first sign of trouble is usually a damp patch on an upstairs ceiling. Don't expect the trouble to be directly above — water often travels some way before finding a weak spot in the plasterboard. Small repairs can be quite easily carried out. If there is a bubble, make 2 cuts at right angles and fold back the flaps to dry out the area. As with a crack, remove the chippings and clean the surrounding region. When dry, coat with a bitumastic compound and fold back the flaps. Retreat the area a day or two later and put back the chippings. Unfortunately the trouble may be more serious than a simple crack or bubble — the roof may have come to the end of its days. You will then have to have it reroofed by a specialist contractor or you can use one of the synthetic rubber products which are now available in DIY shops for sealing roofs. Follow the instructions exactly and don't expect a repaired roof to last as long as a replaced one.

BLOCKING OFF A CHIMNEY

About a quarter of chimneys designed for solid fuel are no longer in use. Leaving an open flue in a chimney which is never used can lead to problems — the simplest answer is to cap the top of the chimney pot with a half round tile. Rain is kept out but there is adequate ventilation.

REPLACING A BROKEN SLATE

The slate will be nailed to a batten — it is necessary to break off these nails by using a slate ripper.

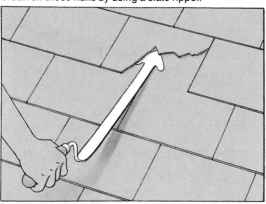

Hook one of the barbs of the ripper under a nail and pull downwards. Repeat with the other nail and then remove the slate. You now need to fix a tingle (1 in. × 10 in. strip of copper or lead) between the two slates which lay under the broken one.

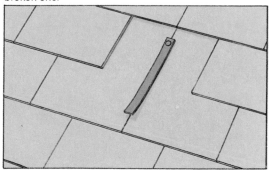

Push the new slate under the ones above. When it is aligned with the others on the same course, the bottom of the tingle should be bent upwards and then pressed down on to the lower edge of the new slate to form a firm hook. A loose slate should be reattached to the roof in the same way.

REPLACING A BROKEN TILE

It is usually easier to replace a tile than a slate. Lift up the tiles on the course above which lie on either side of the broken one. Insert small wooden wedges below them and then lift out the one to be replaced by unhooking from the holding batten. You may need a large bricklayer's trowel to help you to do this.

Push the new tile under the ones above until the nibs at the back hook over the batten. Remove the wooden wedges. A loose tile should be reattached to the roof in the same way, but a nailed-down tile which is either broken or loose will have to be treated in the same way as a slate.

REPAIRING FLASHING

Flashing may come away from the wall — scrape out old mortar, push the flashing into the gap and repoint the space between the bricks. If the flashing is torn the affected area should be cleaned and then treated with flashing strip primer. Cover the painted area with self-adhesive flashing strip.

Walls & Woodwork

A long car journey rather than a textbook will impress you with the wide range of wall types in this country. Wood, stone, concrete, but above all brick. Brick walls have evolved over the years, as the illustrations below clearly show. Once they were all solid walls — one brick-length (approximately 9 in.) or a brick and a half wide. Heat loss was high and weather resistance low, so in many cases the outer surface was rendered by coating with a plaster mix or cladded with tiles or planks of timber. Double cavity walls were known in Victorian times, but if your brick house was built before 1914 it almost certainly has solid walls — if it was constructed after World War II then there are cavity walls. The cavity wall has continued to evolve — once it was brick/brick — in the modern house it is either brick/concrete block or brick/timber (see below).

Whatever the construction, the outside needs regular inspection and maintenance. Check the walls for cracks, dampness, flaking, missing mortar between the bricks and discoloration. Clear rubbish away from air bricks and damp courses and look at the woodwork for signs of decay. Prod the bottom of the door and window frames — the standard danger points. If you are tired of your plain brick walls, you can clean, render or clad them . . . but don't paint them.

WALL STRUCTURE

Old-fashioned SOLID WALL
- Plaster
- Brick
- Mortar

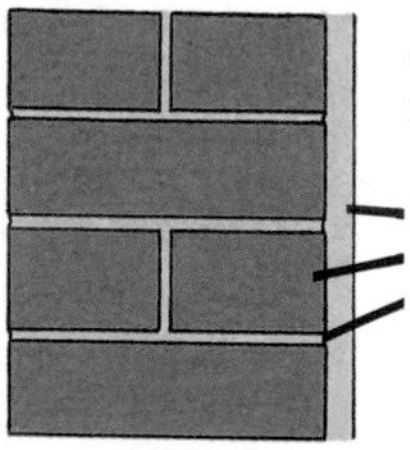

Traditional CAVITY WALL
- Brick
- Wall tie
- Mortar
- Plasterboard
- Batten

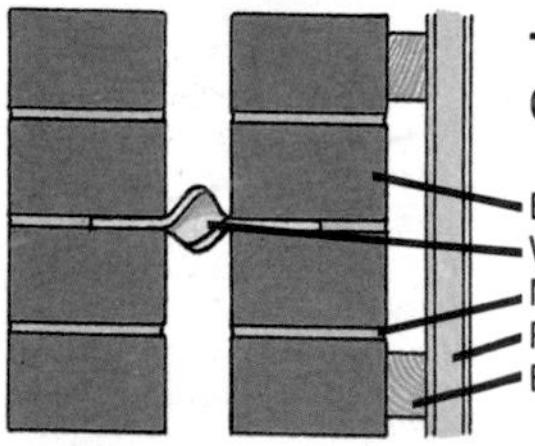

Modern BRICK & BLOCK
- Batten
- Plasterboard
- Concrete block
- Wall tie

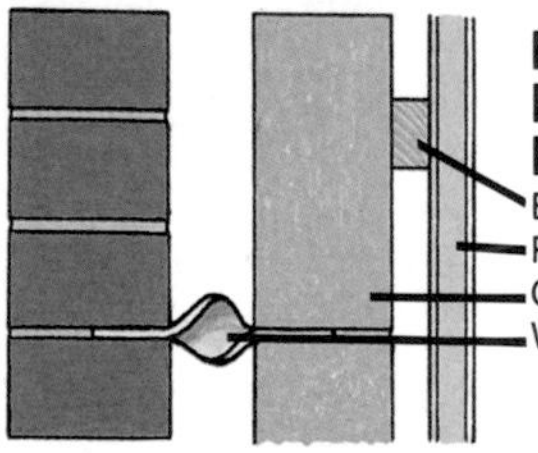

Modern TIMBER FRAME
- Plasterboard
- Vapour barrier
- Timber frame
- Wall tie
- Insulation
- Sheathing board
- Weatherproof membrane

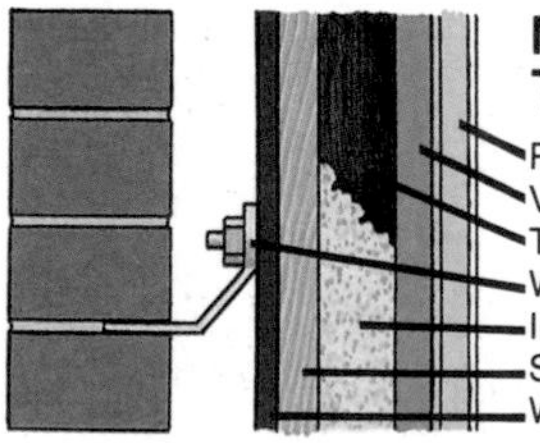

BRICKS
The standard brick

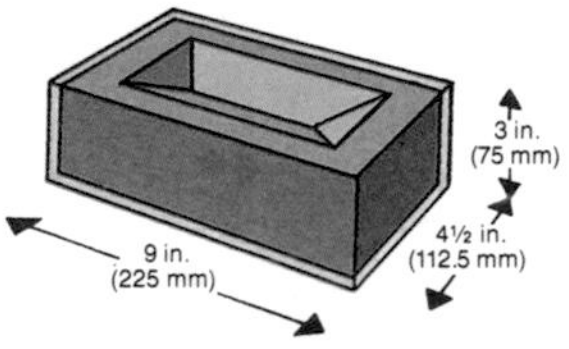

3 in. (75 mm)
9 in. (225 mm)
4½ in. (112.5 mm)

Nominal size allows for normal (10 mm) mortar layer.
Actual size is 215 mm × 102.5 mm × 65 mm.
Make sure you buy the right quality for the job:

Interior (O) — Not frost resistant — inside use only

Ordinary (M) — Moderately frost resistant — suitable for all outside work where water does not stand on surface

Special (F) — Fully frost resistant — all outside work including exposed situations, wall tops etc

STRETCHER (A brick laid lengthways)
HEADER (A brick laid sideways)

CONCRETE BLOCKS
The standard block

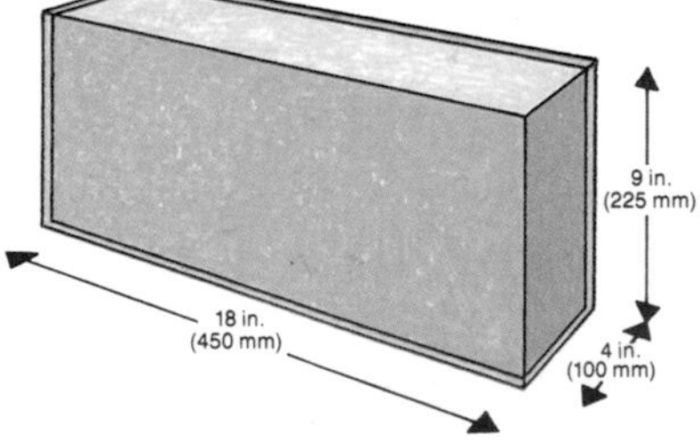

9 in. (225 mm)
18 in. (450 mm)
4 in. (100 mm)

Nominal size allows for normal (10 mm) mortar layer.
Make sure you buy the right quality for the job:

A — Strong, durable but expensive
B — The standard grade for outdoor work
C — Lightweight — internal, non-loadbearing walls only

Blocks have many advantages — quick to lay, good insulating properties, fireproof and the lightweight grades are easy to lift

MORTAR
For small jobs it is more convenient to buy dry-mixed mortar in a bag. For larger tasks you can mix your own — a standard mix is 1 part Portland cement, 1 part hydrated lime and 6 parts washed fine sand.

To mix mortar, turn over the dry ingredients until the mixture has an even colour. Flatten the heap and make a central crater with a spade or shovel. Pour water into this crater and slowly bring the outer wall into the centre. Mix and turn — add sprinklings of water until the pile is well mixed and thoroughly moist.

With regard to the craft of bricklaying itself, either watch a professional bricklayer at work or ask a skilled friend to show you how. It is not a craft you can acquire by reading a book.

DEALING WITH WALL & WOODWORK PROBLEMS

• CLEANING DIRTY WALLS
Examine the discoloration before you do anything. Moss and green slime often indicate dampness, which means that the basic problem must be put right or the trouble will return. White powder (efflorescence) is unsightly but is nothing to worry about — see page 128. There are several steps involved in cleaning rendered, exposed brick and stone walls. Begin by using a stiff brush to remove dirt and surface growths. Next, scrub with plain water — never use soap or detergent. If algae, moss or mould is present a proprietary fungicide or household bleach should be added to the water (1 part bleach : 4 parts water) — leave for about a couple of days and then wash off with plain water.

To renovate brickwork, rub the surface with a piece of similar brick. Stone should be treated with a stone 'sanding block' in the same way — keep the block wet at all times. A word of warning — wear goggles when using a brush or water containing an anti-slime chemical.

Mortar as well as masonry may be discoloured. Use an acid-based stone cleaner — follow the instructions.

• RESTORING POOR QUALITY WOODWORK
If door or window frames are in poor condition, you must do something about it or the problem is bound to get worse. Flaking paint must be removed and the area sanded down to bare wood before repainting. Read the section on Paint (pages 115 – 122) before repainting outside woodwork — there have been a number of recent advances, and the correct routine of preparation must be carefully followed.

You may find that part of the wood is rotten — there is little resistance to a steel point pushed into the surface. Treatment depends on the extent of the rot. If there is one large area, it will be necessary to cut out the rotten wood and replace with a section of new timber. The affected patch may be quite small — tackle the problem with a proprietary wood rot treatment as described on page 132. Unfortunately you may have waited too long and there are large areas of rot in several parts of the frame. Try one or other of the techniques above, but in the end you will probably have to replace the frame.

• REPAIRING CRACKS
It is quite normal for a few fine cracks to appear as a new house settles. These cracks may be quite long without giving rise to concern — fill with mortar when the movement stops.

Wall cracks can mean one of the most feared of all house problems — subsidence. Look for the danger signs — cracks running sideways from the corners of windows and doors, and cracks running downwards from the sides of windows or close to the corners of the house. Check to see if the house movement is continuing by using the glass slide test.

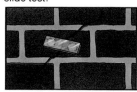

Glue a glass slide over the crack. Keep watch over the next few months. If it breaks you must consult a surveyor as quickly as possible as subsidence may be occurring — see page 129 for details.

• REPAIRING SPALLING
Isolated bricks may be unusually soft, allowing water to penetrate and then freeze in cold weather. The result is the surface breaking away, an effect known as spalling. Use a club hammer and cold chisel to remove the softened part of the brick. Cut a second-hand brick to fit the gap — mortar in place with a cement-rich mix (1 part cement : 3 parts sand). With a double cavity wall you can remove the whole brick — it is sometimes possible to reverse the brick and use it for refacing the wall. A word of caution — you must not allow mortar to drop into the cavity.

• REPOINTING
Sooner or later the combined effect of wind, rain and frost will loosen some of the mortar between the bricks. The effect is unsightly and the weatherproofing property of the wall is reduced. Repointing of the affected area is the answer. Remove the loose mortar to a depth of about ½ in. with a screwdriver, a club hammer and cold chisel or an electric drill fitted with a chasing bit. Make up mortar as described on page 100 — never mix more than you can use in 1–2 hours. Brush away all bits and dust with a stiff brush and then thoroughly soak the bricks and underlying mortar with water.

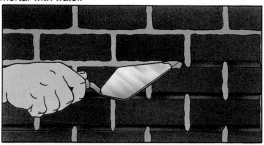

Use a pointing trowel to force the mortar into the gaps — start with the upright joints and then fill the horizontal ones. Now smooth the mortar — cut away the excess and follow the joint style (see page 97) which has been used on the wall. The final step is to brush off any traces of mortar when the repointed area is almost dry. These instructions are the standard ones you will find in any DIY book, but they can lead to an unsightly patch of wall. It is a wise precaution to make up a small amount of mortar and repoint the gap between a brick or two before starting on the whole area. You may find that the mortar has quite a different colour to the rest of the jointing — you can buy colourants for mortar mixes — experiment until you find the right colour and only then repoint the area requiring treatment.

• REPAIRING RENDERING
Use a club hammer and cold chisel to remove all the loose rendering. Rake out some of the mortar between the bricks and brush away all dust and chippings. Make up mortar (see page 100) and thoroughly wet the damaged area with a PVA bonding agent. Push mortar on to the area with a steel float (rectangular trowel) — if the patch is deep it may be necessary to apply 2 separate coats.

Level the surface by drawing a wooden batten across the wet mortar — use a sawing motion. Before the patch is dry smooth with a float for a stucco effect, cut in the required texture with a trowel, comb, roller or brush, or throw on stones and press in with a float to match a pebbledash effect.

Before painting a smooth or textured rendered wall it is necessary to repair all the damaged spots as described above. If in doubt, tap the surface with a trowel handle. A hollow sound means that the rendering has come away and so requires repair. Fine cracks are not a problem — they will be covered by the masonry paint.

Gutters & Downpipes

Gutters collect the rainwater and melted snow from the roof. There is a slight slope (at least 1 in 120) to the downpipes — vertical pipes which carry the water to the drains. Do not confuse with the drainage system which removes house waste — see page 12.

Before the war the standard material for gutters and downpipes was cast iron. Firm and solid, but also heavy and sure to rust if not regularly painted. The introduction of plastic uPVC has made a world of difference — lightweight, rustproof, easy to erect and maintain and so on. If you have a cast iron rainwater disposal system which is faulty, replace with uPVC. There are other materials — copper, asbestos cement (no longer available), aluminium, zinc, steel and so on, but plastic is the answer. Gutters are half round (held by brackets attached to the fascia board) or ogee-shaped (screwed directly on to the fascia board).

A breakdown in the system will lead to water pouring on the fabric of the house. Carry out an inspection once a year. Look for breaks and blockages — check that the gutters are not sagging. Remove debris from the gutters by means of a trowel — always work away from the downpipe union. When the gutters are clear use a hosepipe to flush the system.

DEALING WITH GUTTER & DOWNPIPE PROBLEMS

REPAIRING A SAGGING GUTTER
The usual symptom of a sagging gutter is an overflow of water from the gutter when it is raining. Of course, the displacement may be large enough to be visible from the ground. The problem is due to a broken bracket or loosened screws. The simple answer is to attach a new bracket using new screws close to the faulty bracket. With ogee guttering you will have to remove the screws and then attach at a slightly higher level so that the sag is removed.

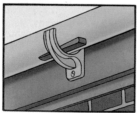 It is sometimes possible to repair a sagging gutter by inserting a small wooden wedge between the gutter and the bracket. Easy — but such a repair is best regarded as temporary.

REFIXING A LOOSE DOWNPIPE
You must secure a loose downpipe bracket — the pipe can easily work loose in high wind and come crashing down. Remove the pipe nails from the bracket, using a claw hammer with a piece of wood against the wall to improve leverage. Remove the lower section of pipe — if made of iron and a sealant is present you will have to use a blowlamp. The next step is to remove the old plugs in the wall — replace with new plugs made out of dowels. Extend the holes by drilling if necessary — hammer home the new plugs. Now refit the pipe and bracket — drive in new nails and reseal the joints of iron pipes.

REPAIRING A LEAKING DOWNPIPE
Look for the tell-tale signs of damp patches or green slime behind the pipe. Repair the leak with glass fibre bandage or self-adhesive flashing strip if you don't want to replace the section. With cast iron pipes the problem may be a break in the joint — remake the seal with a recommended mastic.

REPAIRING A LEAKING GUTTER
The first task is to find whether the leak is at a joint or in the body of the gutter. Most leaks are due to faulty joints — with a cast iron pipe you should ideally remove the section, scrape off the putty, apply fresh sealing compound and then rebolt the section back in place. But iron gutters are heavy, and the usual method of tackling the problem is to paint the leaking joint with a sealing compound or seal it with self-adhesive flashing strip. With plastic guttering it is a simple job to unclip the section and replace the defective seal.

The problem may be a hole in the body of the gutter — a common problem in old cast iron gutters where rust is an ever-present problem. If the hole is a small one it can be repaired with self-adhesive flashing strip — a general decay of the iron calls for a new section rather than simple patching. Prevention is so much better than cure when dealing with cast iron gutters and pipes. Whilst they are still sound the surface should be cleaned and treated with Rusty to convert existing rust and prevent further production. Apply a topcoat of gloss paint.

CLEARING A BLOCKED GUTTER
An overflowing gutter may mean that either the guttering or downpipe is blocked. Inspect the gutters — a thick cake of silt, leaves etc indicates a gutter blockage. Put a rag into the downpipe opening and remove the rubbish into a bucket suspended on the ladder. Brush away remaining silt and then remove rag from the downpipe. Pour water into the gutter — if it does not run away quickly you will have to now deal with a blocked downpipe.

CLEARING A BLOCKED DOWNPIPE
Put a bowl at the base of the pipe to stop debris getting into the drains. Poke a stiff wire up through the shoe to remove any lower blockage. Now work from the roof — remove any rubbish from the downpipe opening and then use a piece of stout hooked wire to lift up any debris from the upper part of the pipe. Push a long bamboo cane down the pipe if there is a straight run — if all else fails you will have to dismantle the pipe.

CHAPTER 6

MATERIALS

Ordinary householders cannot be expected to be scientists and yet they are exposed to an ever-increasing flood of technological products — polyurethane in varnishes, uPVC for window frames and gutters, Teflon on pans, polyesters to improve our cottons and fourth generation nylon to rival wool in our carpets. It would need a whole volume to deal adequately with all the materials used these days in household goods — this chapter can only touch on a few of the more common ones.

METAL

Some of the metals around the home are in their pure state. **Alloys** are more common — a metal blended with another metal or non metal to produce a material with improved properties. Other household articles are **electroplated** — an object coated with a thin layer of metal or metals by electrolysis so that the appearance or anti-corrosive property is improved.

METAL	DESCRIPTION	HOUSEHOLD USES
CAST IRON	Iron with 2 – 5% carbon. Cheap and tough but also brittle — a sharp blow can fracture it. Objects are moulded (cast) — metal cannot be drawn or twisted	Gutters, grates, boilers
WROUGHT IRON	Iron with carbon and slag. Can be worked in many ways — twisted, bent, shaped, cut etc. Suitable for welding and soldering — rusts relatively slowly	Gates, chains, screens
MILD STEEL	Despite the name, almost pure iron — carbon content is less than 0.1%. Easily worked, suitable for soldering and welding but it rusts quickly	Hinges, screws, brackets
ALLOY STEEL	Iron with other metals added, such as chromium, nickel, manganese, tungsten, molybdenum etc. Harder than mild steel, but again it rusts quickly	Chisels, saws, springs
STAINLESS STEEL	An alloy steel containing nickel and chromium. It is difficult to work but easily soldered. Widely used for kitchenware as it neither tarnishes nor rusts	Knives, sinks, pans
ALUMINIUM	Used where lightness is essential — easily worked and resistant to corrosion. It can be highly polished — major drawback is lack of strength	Foils, pans, beer cans
ALUMINIUM ALLOY	Aluminium rendered almost as hard as steel by adding small amounts of copper, manganese and magnesium. Lightweight and easily worked, but corrodes more easily than aluminium	Window frames, cladding, kettles
COPPER	An excellent conductor of heat and electricity. A soft metal, easily bent and shaped with many practical uses. Very decorative when polished, but darkens with age	Pipes, pans, cylinders
BRASS	An alloy of copper and zinc — a small amount of lead may be incorporated. A decorative metal, much used for ornaments and trimmings. Strong, bright, but darkens with age	Taps, screws, ornaments
PINCHBECK	A copper-rich brass with the appearance of gold. It was once widely used for making inexpensive jewellery, but is no longer used. Guinea Gold is similar	Antique jewellery, watches
BRONZE	Alloy of copper and zinc and resistant to corrosion. Easily worked and attractive but little used around the home. Much Victorian 'bronze' is really lead-treated copper plate	Door knockers, buttons, ornaments
ORMOLU	An alloy of copper, zinc and tin used to make decorative items — often gold-like. Originally, ormolu was brass gilded with gold leaf	Antique furniture, statuettes
PEWTER	An alloy of tin and lead. Dull, but can be highly polished. Once popular for kitchen and drinking utensils, but now ruled out because of lead content	Tankards, decorative plates, statuettes
LEAD	Heavy, soft, easily worked and highly resistant to corrosion. Once widely used for plumbing, but now replaced by copper and plastic because of poisoning risk	Waterproof flashing
ZINC	Somewhat similar to lead — soft, easily worked and resistant to corrosion. But it is lighter and less easily bent — not much used in the pure state	Substitute for lead flashing
SHEFFIELD PLATE	Silver sheet rolled on to one or both sides of copper sheet. Not the same as silver plate, which is done by electrolysis. No longer made	Trays, dishes, hollow-ware
NICKEL SILVER	Contains no silver at all — an alloy of copper, nickel and zinc. Nickel silver blanks are plated with silver to produce EPNS	Knives, trays, fittings
MAZAK	An alloy of zinc and aluminium, much used to produce die-cast blanks which are then brass plated to produce 'brass' objects. Check — real brass is heavy	Door knobs, ornaments, handles
BRITANNIA METAL	An alloy of tin, antimony and copper. Grey-coloured — much used by Victorians for teapots, tankards etc. Nowadays used as blanks for silver plating	Cutlery, trays, fittings
SILVER	A luxury metal — soft, easily worked but also easily scratched. Tarnishes with age — needs regular polishing. Sterling silver contains 92.5% pure silver	Cutlery, jewellery, containers
GOLD	The most prized of all household metals — reserved for rings and jewellery. Purity is measured in carats — 24 carats is pure gold, 22 carats is wedding ring gold	Rings, watches, jewellery
TIN PLATE	A coating of tin over mild steel sheet produces a metal which is easily cut, folded and soldered. The surface remains rust-free as long as the coating is not scratched	Tins, bakeware
ZINC PLATE	A coating of zinc over steel produces a rust-resistant metal known as galvanized steel or iron. It is used in sheet, rod or iron form	Wheelbarrows, wire netting, nails
COPPER PLATE	A coating of copper is frequently applied in electroplating, but it is used to serve as an undercoating for another metal such as chromium	Coating under chromium plate
CHROMIUM PLATE	Chromium has the advantage of producing a mirror-bright surface, and so is used where a gleaming finish is required — modern furniture, car trimmings, handles etc	Cheap cutlery, knobs, picture frames
EPNS	Electroplated nickel silver — the most popular type of silver plate produced in Britain. For domestic cutlery the silver thickness should be 20 microns	Cutlery, trays, fittings
SILVER PLATE	Silver coated on to any material — steel, copper, pewter, mazak, Britannia metal, plastic and even flowers and leaves. Most quality material is EPNS	Cutlery, trays, fittings
BRASS PLATE	A coating of brass on steel, mazak or plastic. Most 'brass' items are really brass plate — magnetism denotes that it is brass-plated steel	Door knockers, fire tongs, ornaments
GOLD PLATE	Tarnish-free and gleaming, such items are a sign of extravagance (e.g gold-plated bathroom fittings) or economy (gold-plated jewellery)	Jewellery, watches, taps
ROLLED GOLD	Gold sheet rolled on to one or both sides of a sheet of base metal — compare Sheffield plate. Once widely used for cases of pocket watches	Watches, jewellery, containers

WOOD

Everyone who is interested in the home needs to have some knowledge of wood and its properties. For the keen DIY enthusiast this is, of course, a fundamental requirement. He or she must buy the right type of timber at the keenest price, and it must be properly worked to produce that new cupboard, wall or bookcase. The casual handyperson may never pay a trip to the timber merchant, but driving in screws and repairing items of furniture are occasionally unavoidable. And for everyone there is the task of buying wooden fixtures and fittings — chairs, kitchen units, tables, desks and so on. The purpose of this chapter is to tell you about the range of woods available — the natural and the manufactured types, together with details of fixing methods and the basic principles of working with this satisfying material.

As a rough and ready guide, softwoods are used for general joinery — the joists, floorboards, cupboard carcasses etc. Where large sheets are required we turn to one of the manufactured boards, and for a decorative effect which will not need painting we buy boards which have a veneer of an attractive hardwood on the surface. For outdoors a naturally protected wood such as teak or cedar is used, or we use preservative-treated timber.

These are just general rules. If you are new to wood make sure you read this section before going along to buy your boards or sheets of wood. It may come as a surprise that the various woods nearly all have one drawback or other — it might be price, poor painting or staining quality, inability to soak up preservatives, resistance to standard tools ('hard to work') or softness. There are danger points to watch for when buying (page 108) and a confusing set of terms to understand. Still, your DIY store or timber merchant will have someone to give advice, but don't expect to find every type of wood mentioned on page 106. The wood world, like everything else, continues to change — there are now tropical hardwoods such as ramin which are almost as cheap and easy to work as some softwoods, and there are old favourites like English oak which have become prohibitively expensive.

SOFTWOODS

Softwood is cut from a conifer such as pine, larch, fir or spruce. The wood is usually lighter and softer than hardwood, but not always — yew is heavier and denser than some hardwoods.

A typical softwood comes from a cool or cold climate. It is pale in colour and there are resin-bearing streaks and a number of knots. It is cheaper than hardwood and is easier to saw, plane, nail etc. This is the wood which is used for nearly all general joinery and house construction work. When the home handyman wants to buy natural (not manufactured) boards or planks for a DIY job the usual choice is between redwood and whitewood — both commonly called 'deal'.

These two woods are widely available in both rough or planed form and in a series of standard widths and thicknesses. For outdoor use you will need wood which has been pre-treated with a preservative — for indoors you will usually require a hardwood-veneered surface if you plan to stain and polish rather than paint. Not always — Scandinavian redwood is now treated with clear polyurethane varnish to produce fashionable 'pine' furniture.

HARDWOODS

Hardwood is cut from a deciduous broad-leaved tree, such as oak, mahogany or teak. The wood is usually denser and harder than softwood, but not always — balsa is much lighter than any commercial softwood.

A typical hardwood is heavy and close-grained, which means that it will take a fine polish but is harder to work with than a softwood. It is also more expensive — sometimes much more expensive, and so hardwood is generally bought either in the form of mouldings or as veneers which are applied to softwood or manufactured boards. The exception is ramin, which is readily available in board form from DIY shops.

There are basically 2 types — temperate hardwoods and tropical hardwoods. The temperate types grow in Europe and other places with cool or cold winters — the result is generally a clearly distinct patterning due to the difference between winter and summer growth. The colour is usually pale and these woods are notoriously difficult to work. The tropical hardwoods are nearly always darker and the patterning tends to be less distinct. Working is generally easier but there may still be a need to drill pilot holes before nailing.

MANUFACTURED BOARDS

Manufactured board is made from wood in sheet, strip, shredded or pulped form with resins or glues bonding the pieces or pulp together. There are various types — plywood and blockboard are the most expensive; chipboard and ordinary hardboard are the cheapest. Make sure you always buy the right one for the job you have to do, and pay special care if the board will have to withstand outdoor conditions. Where water will be present you must specify an exterior or waterproof grade.

Manufactured board is sometimes regarded as an inferior material designed for people who can't afford 'real' wood. There is indeed a saving in price, but there are also other advantages. The main one is the availability in larger sheets — making up wide boards by gluing planks of timber together is not an easy task. Another point in favour of manufactured boards is the freedom from the standard defects you have to look for when buying natural timber.

For the production of finished furniture you can buy coated boards. Melamine coating is the most economical — laminate is very popular and at the top end of the range is board veneered with a decorative hardwood.

MANUFACTURED BOARDS

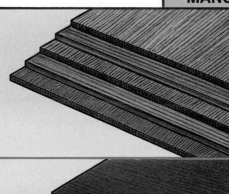

PLYWOOD

Thin layers ('plys') of wood are glued together to form a board which has neither the warping nor splitting tendency of natural wood. This property is due to each layer being laid at right angles to its partner and an odd number of layers being used to make up the finished board. The number of plys varies from 3 to 15 — the board thickness ranges from ⅛–1 in.

There are many grades: *INT* for indoor use, *WBP* (weather- and boil-proof) or *EXT* for outdoors, *aviation* for beading, *hardwood veneered* for high-quality appearance, *structural* for maximum strength and *plank-faced* for panelling.

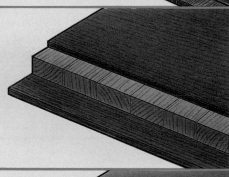

BLOCKBOARD

The inner core consists of strips of softwood glued together. The annual rings of the strips are at right angles to each other and this core is sandwiched between two thin layers of wood — usually birch. In top-quality blockboard these sheets are faced with decorative hardwood veneers. Board thickness is ½–1 in. and is worked in the same way as ordinary timber. A few words of caution: do not nail or screw too close to the end of the core strips and never paint just one face — treat both faces in the same way. Do not use blockboard outdoors.

Laminboard is a version of blockboard in which narrower strips of wood are used for the core.

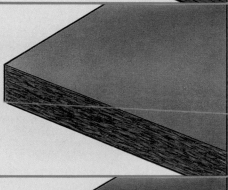

CHIPBOARD

Small chips of softwood are bound together with a resin adhesive and the sheet is squeezed between rollers to the required thickness (usually ½–1 in.). It is cheaper than plywood and blockboard and is widely used as a base for furniture because of its even texture and resistance to warping. For maximum strength buy the *multi-layer* grade, for painting buy *painting* quality which has densely-packed small fibres on the face and for underflooring look for the *flooring* grade. A multitude of *faced* varieties are available for making furniture and worktops.

There are problems. It will bow if the support is inadequate, the cut edge may be ragged, special screws or inserts must be used for fixing and it is not suitable for use outdoors.

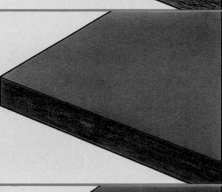

MDF (MEDIUM DENSITY FIBREBOARD)

The base material for fibreboard is made from the fibres produced when timber is subjected to a vacuum in a pressure chamber. These fibres are bonded with resin and then rolled — the pressure used has a profound effect on the quality of the fibreboard. Low pressures produce pinboard which is used for notice boards — high pressure produces panelboard for wall lining.

Medium density fibreboard is an exciting modern material which although very widely employed in the furniture industry is not often used by the home handyman. Rather similar to chipboard, but with the great advantage that it can be cut cleanly, nailed or screwed without problems and has a surface which can be stained, polished or painted.

HARDBOARD

Pulped wood is mixed with adhesives and rolled into sheets which are ⅛–¼ in. thick. This Cinderella of the manufactured boards is cheap and has little inherent strength, but has many uses around the home. *Standard* grade (smooth front face, roughened-mesh back face) is bought for covering doors, floors, drawer bottoms etc. There are *perforated* boards pierced with round holes (pegboard) or decorative shapes, and there is the *tempered* grade which has been impregnated with oil to make it water resistant.

Enamel- and *plastic-finished* boards are used where a decorative effect such as a tile or wood-panelling look is required.

SOFTWOODS

WOOD	DETAILS
CEDAR, WESTERN RED	Reddish-brown with a silky surface. Resists both rot and insects and so is popular outdoors for cladding, fences and sheds. It has its problems — colour fades with time, nails work loose and the surface is easily dented.
FIR, DOUGLAS	Popular with furniture makers and house builders — very strong and quite cheap, and also knot-free. Sometimes sold as British Columbian pine — pinkish-brown and even-textured but paints badly and cracks outdoors.
HEMLOCK	A general-purpose softwood from Canada and the U.S., used for doors, floors, joists etc. Strong and easily worked but not good for painting or outdoor use.
LARCH	A British wood, tough and difficult to work. There are 2 important characteristics — it has good rot resistance and holds nails well. As a result it is used for construction work indoors and fences etc outdoors.
PINE, PARANA	A fine-textured wood, attractively coloured in cream, brown or lilac and often knot-free. Very strong (used for staircases) but also temperamental — warps easily, splits outdoors and provides a poor surface for painting.
PINE, PITCH	A wood steeped in history — great halls, church roofs and barn walls are a testimony to its durability. Rich in resin, highly inflammable, rather difficult to work and even more difficult to find.
REDWOOD	The most popular of all woods for the home carpenter — inexpensive, reliable, easy to work, good for painting etc. Colours range from cream to reddish-brown — commercial names include Scots pine, Baltic pine, red deal and 'pine' furniture.
WHITEWOOD	Popular and inexpensive like redwood, but there are differences. It is softer with a finer texture, and the cream colour does not darken with age. Whitewood (other names — spruce, white deal) does not absorb preservatives — not for use outdoors.
YEW	The softwood that thinks it is a hardwood. Yew is very heavy and close-grained — the colour is orange or brown. It is a wood used by cabinet makers and craftsmen to produce high quality articles.

HARDWOODS

WOOD	DETAILS
AFRORMOSIA	A wood from tropical Africa. Close-grained and golden-brown like teak — used as a less expensive substitute in furniture manufacture. Available for the home carpenter in both solid and veneer form.
ASH	A pale-coloured timber with many uses — panelling, flooring etc. The 2 traditional applications are bentwood chairs and tool handles. The experts will tell you to avoid boards with brown streaks.
BEECH	A European wood which is often used in the furniture industry for making a stout and durable frame for veneering. The colour is ivory to pale brown and the grain is straight. Not recommended for outdoor use.
CHERRY	A wood with a wavy grain and a distinctive orange sheen — more often seen as a veneer than as solid wood. A material for the cabinet maker and craftsman, but American cherry is sometimes used for joinery work.
CHESTNUT, SWEET	Similar to ash but less expensive — used as a substitute for making office furniture. It is also used as a substitute for oak, which it quite closely resembles. No real drawbacks, but dark streaks can be disfiguring.
ELM	Coffins, wheelbarrows and Windsor chairs are traditionally made from this brownish rough-grained timber. European elm is very durable, but now scarce because of the ravages of Dutch elm disease. Japanese elm is less robust.
IROKO	A popular teak substitute — hard-wearing for both indoor and outdoor use at a significantly lower price. You will find its rich brown colour in parquet floors, furniture, garden seats etc. The texture is rather coarse.
JELUTONG	A wood to buy if you wish to try your hand at carving. Very pale, soft, straight-grained and even-textured. It is also useful for home carpentry — the surface is smooth and it is easily worked.
LIME	Like Jelutong, an excellent wood for carving and turning. The texture is fine and the grain is straight — the yellowish-brown colour has practically no figuring. Not a popular wood — you may have to search to find it.
MAHOGANY	One of the great woods, now more often used as a veneer than as solid timber. Not all mahoganies are the same — African has a rich orange-brown colour and a distinctive figuring — American is more even in appearance, more expensive and more lustrous.
MERANTI	A mahogany substitute from Malaysia — cheaper, redder and easier to work than real mahogany. It is quite widely available in sheet and veneer form and as mouldings — so is the closely-related lauan from the Philippines.
OAK	It is not just patriotism — British oak is the strongest, straightest and most durable of all oaks. Its toughness is legendary, but it is expensive, difficult to work and glue, and splits easily when nailed. European oak is a little softer — Japanese is even lighter and not suitable for outdoors.
OBECHE	Not a quality hardwood — it is a light, easily-worked timber used in the manufacture of whitewood furniture. The grain is open and the colour pale — obeche can be stained and polished.
RAMIN	A very popular hardwood which you will certainly find around the house in mouldings, picture frames, furniture etc. It is a straw-coloured wood, close-textured and easy to nail. A favourite material for the home carpenter.
ROSEWOOD	An expensive wood for the luxury look. The rosewood furniture you see is almost certainly veneered over a cheaper carcasse. Purples and browns swirl under the high lustre finish — you can buy boards as well as veneer but you will find it a difficult wood to work.
SAPELE	A mahogany look-alike — strength and colour are similar but it is less expensive. One drawback — it has a tendency to warp. Sapele is usually bought as a veneer — it polishes well but staining can produce a patchy finish.
TEAK	Teak is widely used in furniture manufacture these days both in solid form and veneer, its rich brown colour marbled with darker streaks. Apart from its visual appeal it resists rot, water and fire — teak is therefore used for outdoor furniture, ships' decks etc.
UTILE	Like sapele, one of the mahogany look-alikes. It has a pink-brown colour and an irregular grain — this wood is easily worked and is less inclined than sapele to warp. Widely used in the furniture industry.
WALNUT	Best of all is European (especially English) walnut — mid brown with dark streaks and swirling patterns beneath a lustrous finish. Long associated with antique furniture — today's walnut table will only be veneered on a cheaper frame. African walnut is easier to obtain but is less attractive.

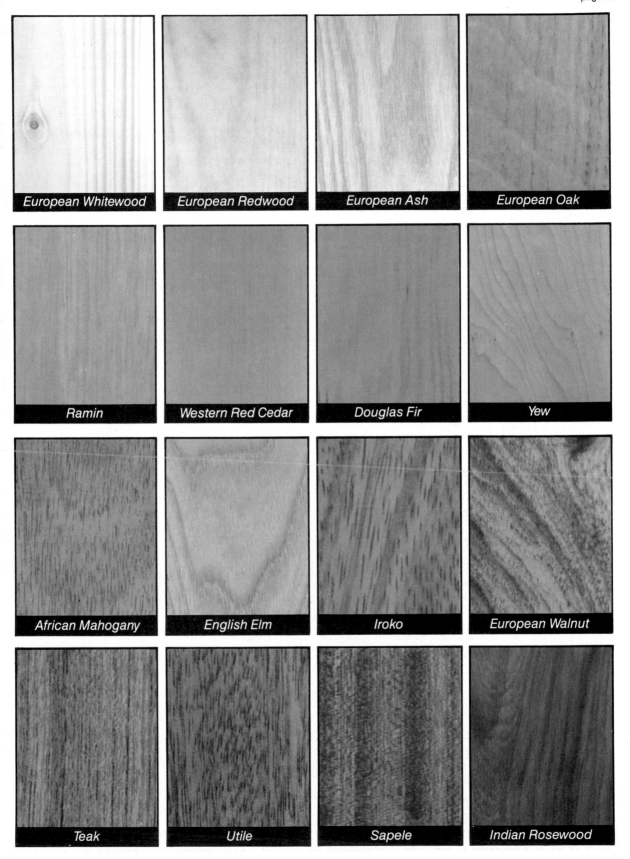

European Whitewood

European Redwood

European Ash

European Oak

Ramin

Western Red Cedar

Douglas Fir

Yew

African Mahogany

English Elm

Iroko

European Walnut

Teak

Utile

Sapele

Indian Rosewood

BUYING TIMBER

Wood can be bought from your local DIY shop, a builders' merchant or a specialist timber importer who produces a mail order catalogue. Obviously each source has a different role to play — you can't expect your local hardware store to stock rare hardwoods and it would be silly to buy large boards of ordinary redwood from a mail order company.

When buying timber from your chosen supplier there are a number of considerations — the 3 basic ones are size, quality and dryness of the type of wood you have chosen.

Size

Softwood is usually sold in confusing units known as metric feet. A metric foot is 300 mm — the standard length of softwood boards ranges from 6 metric feet (5 ft 11 in.) to 21 metric feet (20 ft 8 in.). The width and thickness is equally confusing. If the wood will be concealed it is usual to buy it in its cheapest form — **rough sawn**, which means that its surfaces are in the state left by the power saw. Shrinkage may have taken place, so that the *actual* width and thickness may be very slightly less than the size by which it is sold (the *nominal* width and thickness).

If the surface of the wood is to be seen it will be necessary to buy planed timber. This can be **PAR** (planed all round) or just **PBS** (planed on its two large faces only). Do remember that planing removes about 3 mm (⅛ in.) from the nominal size. All this means that the boards can be less wide and thick than stated on the label or the invoice — if you want an exact width and thickness then you have to order the wood to **finished** size.

Hardwood is not sold in standard widths and thicknesses. The width of boards is usually ½ – 1 metric foot and the thickness ¼ – ¾ in. It is usually sold as PAR. The timber is stored by the merchant as rough sawn boards and if you have a particular requirement these are then cut and planed to your specification. Do remember to specify what you want — rough sawn, PAR, PBS or finished size (see above).

Buying manufactured board is much more straightforward. The standard sheet size is 8 ft × 4 ft — cutting the sheet increases the price, but makes transport much easier.

Quality

Softwood is available in various quality grades but there is no single grading system for all types. As a general rule you will find that the wood stored by a builders' or wood merchant is offered in 3 grades. The cheapest is **carcassing** for joists, rafters etc — you must expect some knots and a moisture content of about 20 per cent. This means that some warping may occur as the wood dries out. **Standard joinery** is drier (15 per cent moisture content) and better quality — the wood to use for most DIY jobs. The top grade (**best joinery**) is expensive and should be purchased only if you intend to polish the wood (e.g a table top).

There are no standard hardwood grades — it is up to you to inspect the wood and judge quality for yourself. If you want to act like an expert in the timber yard, avoid wood from either the outside edge or the inner core of the tree, buy only old boards and select them from undisturbed stacks.

Make sure that wood for outdoor use is either naturally able or has been specially prepared to stand up to the elements. If it is not cedar or teak make sure that it has been treated with a preservative. Plywood should be marked EXT or WBP.

Dryness

Timber has to be dried before use — this increases strength, rot resistance, workability and cuts down the tendency to warp. Wood can be dried naturally by stacking it under cover in the open air (a hardwood board will take 3 – 4 years to dry after felling) or it may be kiln-dried. Furniture is made from kiln-dried wood with a moisture content of less than 13 per cent.

So buy properly dried wood, but this may not be the end of the problem. If the wood store has the same conditions as the place where you intend to use the wood, there is no difficulty. But if it is markedly warmer or colder, moister or drier, then you must leave the wood in its new surroundings for about a week before working with it.

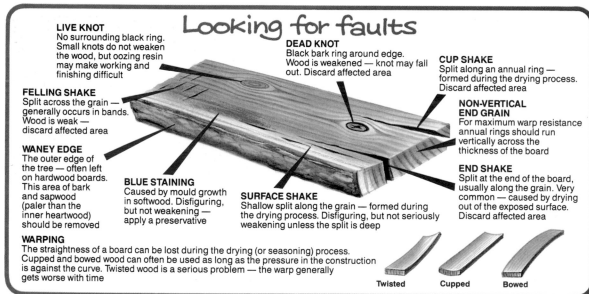

Looking for faults

LIVE KNOT
No surrounding black ring. Small knots do not weaken the wood, but oozing resin may make working and finishing difficult

DEAD KNOT
Black bark ring around edge. Wood is weakened — knot may fall out. Discard affected area

CUP SHAKE
Split along an annual ring — formed during the drying process. Discard affected area

FELLING SHAKE
Split across the grain — generally occurs in bands. Wood is weak — discard affected area

NON-VERTICAL END GRAIN
For maximum warp resistance annual rings should run vertically across the thickness of the board

WANEY EDGE
The outer edge of the tree — often left on hardwood boards. This area of bark and sapwood (paler than the inner heartwood) should be removed

BLUE STAINING
Caused by mould growth in softwood. Disfiguring, but not weakening — apply a preservative

SURFACE SHAKE
Shallow split along the grain — formed during the drying process. Disfiguring, but not seriously weakening unless the split is deep

END SHAKE
Split at the end of the board, usually along the grain. Very common — caused by drying out of the exposed surface. Discard affected area

WARPING
The straightness of a board can be lost during the drying (or seasoning) process. Cupped and bowed wood can often be used as long as the pressure in the construction is against the curve. Twisted wood is a serious problem — the warp generally gets worse with time

Twisted   Cupped   Bowed

VENEERS

Face veneers are thin sheets of decorative wood which are glued on to cheaper wood or manufactured boards. Laying a veneer on to a board is a skilled job, although it might look easy. It is usually much more satisfactory to buy veneer-faced plywood or chipboard for your construction work. Applying an edging with veneer is fairly straightforward — you can buy strips of sheet veneer which is much easier to work with as it can be cut and stuck without difficulty.

MOULDINGS

Boards, sidings, posts etc are cut with a square or rectangular cross section. Wood cut with any other cross section is known as a moulding. An enormous variety is available, ranging from narrow strips for edging or picture framing (half round, triangular, astragal etc) to tongue-and-grooved planks for panelling or flooring. Other mouldings are used for cladding outdoors, architraves and cornices indoors, plus window sashes, skirting boards and so on.

WOOD FIXINGS

Nails

ROUND WIRE NAIL (1–6 in.)
The standard general carpentry nail where appearance does not matter — head is unsightly. Liable to split wood

OVAL WIRE NAIL (1–6 in.)
The standard general carpentry nail where appearance does matter — head can be punched below the surface

LOST HEAD NAIL (½–6 in.)
Round or oval. Used in general carpentry and flooring — the small head is easily punched below the surface

PANEL PIN (½–2 in.)
A slender version of the lost head nail — widely used for fixing mouldings, attaching plywood and cabinet making

FLOOR BRAD (¾–6 in.)
Flat-tipped rectangular nail made for fixing floorboards to joists. Strong, unlikely to split wood but now hard to find

HARDBOARD PIN (½–1½ in.)
Copper-finished square-sectioned nail used for hardboard, thin plywood etc. Diamond-shaped head easily tapped below the surface

CLOUT NAIL (½–2 in.)
Short, galvanised nail with an extra large head. Used outdoors for fixing roofing felt, slates and fencing

TACK (¼–1 in.)
Small, sharply-pointed nail used to attach fabric to wood frames and carpets to floors. 'Improved' tacks are stronger

SPRIG (½ in.)
A headless tack with a number of special uses — fixing glass in wooden frames, lino to floorboards etc

Nailing is the most popular way of attaching one piece of wood to another — it is quick, inexpensive and all you need is a hammer and some nails. Simple — but not as simple as the novice may believe. There is a technique to learn and there are many types of nail from which you have to choose.

Most nails are made from mild steel wire — round or oval in cross-section. A blunt-pointed nail gives a more secure bond than a sharp one and oval nails should have the wide side running along the grain. Brad nails are rectangular in cross-section — the risk of wood splitting is reduced.

Not all nails are made of mild steel. There are galvanised and non-ferrous ones for use outdoors or in some hardwoods which are stained by mild steel. There are also steel ones for driving into masonry (see page 60).

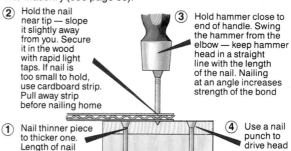

② Hold the nail near tip — slope it slightly away from you. Secure it in the wood with rapid light taps. If nail is too small to hold, use cardboard strip. Pull away strip before nailing home

③ Hold hammer close to end of handle. Swing the hammer from the elbow — keep hammer head in a straight line with the length of the nail. Nailing at an angle increases strength of the bond

① Nail thinner piece to thicker one. Length of nail should be 3 times the thickness of thinner board

④ Use a nail punch to drive head below surface

Screws

 Slotted head    Cross-head

The slotted-head screw is the traditional type, but a range of screwdrivers are necessary for different head sizes, and the blade can easily slip. Cross-head screws need a smaller range of screwdrivers, and a much more positive grip is obtained.

COUNTERSUNK HEAD SCREW (¼–6 in.)
The most popular type — the standard screw when you wish to attach wood to wood. The head can be driven below the surface and the hole filled prior to painting

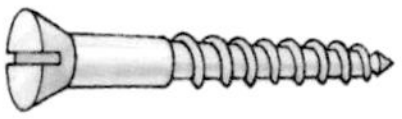

ROUND HEAD SCREW (¼–4 in.)
Mainly used to attach thin metal or plastic to wood — the standard screw for brackets and other hardware items which do not have countersunk holes

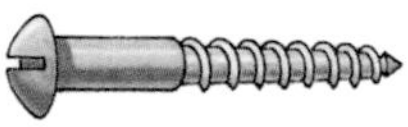

RAISED HEAD SCREW (¼–2 in.)
A hybrid of the countersunk and round screw — usually plated and used with decorative fittings which bear countersunk holes

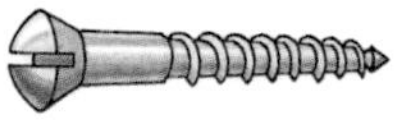

MIRROR SCREW (¾–2 in.)
A decorative chromium-plated domed cover hides the countersunk slotted head — used for mirrors, splashbacks and bath panels

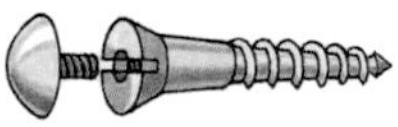

CHIPBOARD SCREW (½–2 in.)
A cross-head screw which has a very short parallel-sided shank. The extra-long thread is designed for chipboard

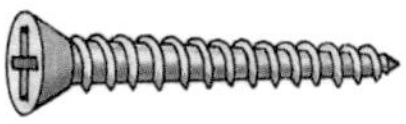

COACH SCREW (1–12 in.)
A heavy-duty screw for the joiner and builder rather than the home handyman. The head is turned with a spanner and not a screwdriver

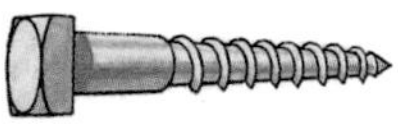

Screwed joints are stronger than nailed ones, and the parts can be readily dismantled by unscrewing. But there is more involved than brute strength — guide holes must be made before you try to screw two pieces of wood together. A bradawl will do for softwood and small screws, but a drill is usually required.

A screw is made up of 3 parts — the head, the smooth shank and the corkscrew-like thread. The size is the gauge number of the shank — for domestic use the range is from 4 (smallest) to 12 (largest). The length of a screw is the distance from the top of the head to the tip of the thread.

Most screws are made of mild steel, but you will often have to use other types. There are brass, aluminium and stainless steel ones for outdoors — plated finishes are for internal use only.

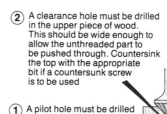

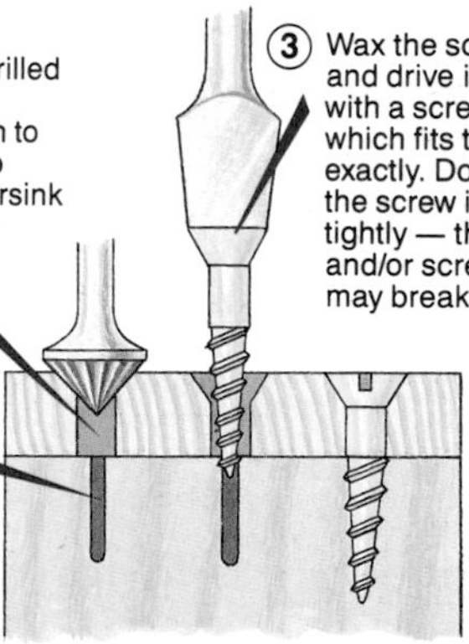

② A clearance hole must be drilled in the upper piece of wood. This should be wide enough to allow the unthreaded part to be pushed through. Countersink the top with the appropriate bit if a countersunk screw is to be used

③ Wax the screw and drive in with a screwdriver which fits the head exactly. Don't drive the screw in too tightly — the wood and/or screw may break

① A pilot hole must be drilled in the lower piece of wood. This should be half the thread length and also narrower than the screw gauge. Use a bradawl rather than a drill if gauge is less than 7

Other fixings

CORRUGATED FASTENER

ANGLE BRACKET

JOINT BLOCK — RIGID FITTING

JOINT BLOCK — KNOCK-DOWN (KD) FITTING

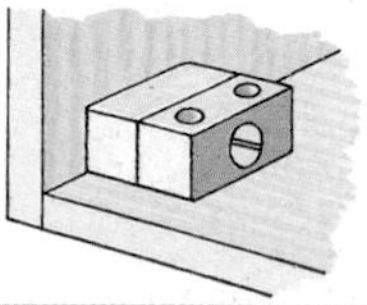

WORKING WITH WOOD

Using a saw

If you plan to work with wood it will be necessary to have more than one saw. There are 2 basic types which are readily distinguished — there is the 20–28 in. **handsaw** which is used for cutting planks, boards etc and the smaller **backsaw** with a brass, steel or plastic strip along the back of the blade to keep it rigid. A backsaw is used for cutting joints, small pieces of board etc.

There are a few general rules to follow whatever type of saw you use. Measure carefully, using a try square or a steel rule. Use a knife or sharp steel point rather than a pencil for marking — the cut fibres and very fine line will make sawing more accurate. If the cut line is hard to see, simply run a pencil point along it before you begin to saw. Widths are marked off with a marking gauge — the stock of the gauge is moved up or down to set the point at the desired width.

Always saw on the waste side of the line. Take care not to wander to the other side — excess wood can be easily removed with sandpaper or a plane, but wood which has been sawn off cannot be replaced.

Use the right saw for the job on hand. Obviously you will need a handsaw and not a backsaw if the whole blade is to travel through the wood, and the number of points (teeth) per inch (ppi) determines the type of cut — the smaller the ppi, the quicker but rougher the cut.

A carpenter has a range of handsaws. A ripsaw (26–28 in. long, 4–6 ppi) for ripping (cutting along the grain), a cross-cut saw (24–26 in. long, 6–10 ppi) for cutting across the grain, and a panel saw (20–24 in. long, 10–12 ppi) for cutting small planks and manufactured boards.

The householder needs only one — a panel saw. The piece of wood must be firmly secured on trestles or in a vice. If the board is allowed to bow when sawing the blade will jam.

Make the initial cut by drawing the saw back gently several times, using your thumb as a guide and keeping your eye on the line and not on the saw.

Now start to saw. Keep your index finger pointing downwards along the blade and apply pressure on the forward (not backward) stroke. The blade should be held at about 50°–60° and the cut should be wedged open with a small piece of wood if the blade begins to jam. Make sure you use the whole length of the blade and let the teeth rather than brute force do the work. Take care at the end of the cut to prevent splintering — with a wide plank it is a good idea to remove the saw and cut the last inch by starting again from the opposite side.

A carpenter or cabinet maker has a range of backsaws. The house-holder needs only one — a tenon saw.

The standard tenon saw is about 10–12 in. long with 14–16 ppi. The piece of wood must be firmly secured in a vice or a bench hook — a mitre box is used if an angled cut (mitre) is required.

Use your index finger as a guide — hold the blade horizontally and use the full length when sawing. For finer and more intricate work a dovetail saw (8 in. long, 18–22 ppi) is used. This looks like a small tenon saw — for model making there is the knob-handled gents saw (4 in. long, 32 ppi).

Choose your saw carefully if you plan to do a lot of woodwork — don't look for unbranded bargains. A hardpoint saw will stay sharp much longer than an ordinary blade, but they are more easily damaged. A PTFE-coated saw will not go rusty, and wooden handles are generally more comfortable than plastic ones.

Take care of your saws. When not in use hang them up rather than leaving them on a bench or in a drawer, and rub the blade with a little light oil to prevent rust. Most saws can be sharpened at home, but it is a job best left to the experts.

Using a chisel

Chisels are used for many jobs around the house, but do take care. Hold the tool properly, as described below, and never use the blade as a lever where the resistance is great. Many accidents are caused each year by people ignoring these simple principles.

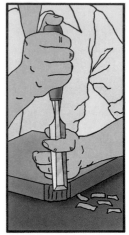

The best all-purpose type is the bevel-edge chisel. Buy one which is already honed and fitted with a protective guard. Paring (removal of thin strips of wood from the edge of a board) is a basic job for a chisel. The bevel is placed away from the board edge and both hands are kept behind the blade at all times. Pressure is applied with the right hand (if you are right-handed) and the left hand is used merely to guide the direction of the cut. Work slowly inward until the line marked on the board is reached. This paring technique is used for removing small areas of rotten wood from frames, cutting out housings for hinges etc.

A chisel is also used to make a mortise — a rectangular hole cut in the body of a piece of wood. Here hand pressure is not sufficient — you will need a mallet. Start work at the centre of the waste area, cutting out narrow ¼ in. deep wedges. Move gradually to the edges of the mortise — finish with the bevel of the chisel facing the cut-out area.

Using a drill

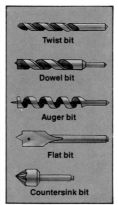

Twist bit

Dowel bit

Auger bit

Flat bit

Countersink bit

By far the most popular power tool is the electric drill, used for drilling, sanding and sawing. All sorts of improvements have been added in recent years, so deciding on the best buy is not as simple as it used to be. First of all, make sure there is a two-speed switch or a variable speed switch or dial — you need a slower speed (approx 1000 rpm) for glass, tile, metal etc than for wood (approx 3000 rpm). A hammer-action drill sounds like a good idea, but you would only need it for drilling through concrete. Finally, make sure that any attachments you require are suitable for the model you plan to buy.

There are a number of commonsense rules. You must drill at right angles to the work surface and make sure that the object you are drilling is held firmly. Do not exert too much pressure. Withdraw the bit occasionally to remove waste material during the drilling process. A drop in motor noise and a reduction in drill speed indicates that the motor is overloaded — withdraw the bit immediately and allow the drill to run at normal speed for a minute before recommencing work. Always keep the flex out of the way.

Look after your drill. Have it serviced at regular intervals if used frequently, and have it repaired immediately if sparking occurs during use.

PLASTIC SHEETING

RIGID ACRYLIC

Typical trade names: Perspex, Plexiglas, Oroglas

Rigid and almost unbreakable, clear or milky, flat or corrugated, acrylic sheet is the most popular glass substitute. When coloured it is also a decorative material, as the illuminated shop and garage signs on any High St. clearly demonstrate. Mark cutting lines and drilling holes on the protective paper cover before you begin to shape acrylic sheet — use a tenon saw for cutting and a hand drill (not a power one) for making holes. Smooth sawn edges by rubbing with glasspaper and then remove paper cover.

Acrylic sheet is softened by heat and can be bent or shaped by covering in metal foil and leaving exposed the area to be softened. The sheet is then held near an electric radiant heater until the area to be worked is rubbery — shape as desired and keep rigid until cool.

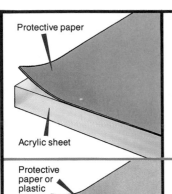

Protective paper

Acrylic sheet

RIGID PVC & OTHER PLASTICS

Typical trade names: Darvik, Novolux, Lexan

Rigid PVC (vinyl) sheet is a glass substitute which is designed for industrial and amateur use. It is employed as an alternative for the more popular acrylic sheet where very high heat resistance is required — for example light diffusers on fluorescent tubes. Corrugated PVC is used for roof lights where its fire resistance and high impact strength are important advantages. Polycarbonate is a lightweight, tough and transparent sheet.

Protective paper or plastic

PVC sheet

PLASTIC LAMINATE

Typical trade names: Formica, Warerite, Arborite

The introduction of plastic laminates has proved a great boon to both the furniture maker and the DIY enthusiast. Carcasses of chipboard, MDF or plywood (see page 105) are covered with it to provide most of the worktops and some of our kitchen and bathroom furniture. Each sheet is made up of several layers of resin-impregnated paper which are bonded together under heat and pressure to form a laminate 0.8 – 1.5 mm thick. Sheet width is generally 4 ft and it is cheaper to buy off-cuts than whole boards. The range of grades, colours and textures is enormous. Matt, shiny, plain, patterned, smooth, textured — you will find them all in plastic laminate.

There are 2 ways to cut the sheet — you can either use a fine-toothed saw held nearly horizontally or you can cut it in the same way as glass — see page 72. Cut the sheet slightly larger than the space to be covered. Use a contact adhesive which allows some adjustment after the 2 surfaces are brought together. Spread the adhesive on the back of the laminate and on top of the surface to be covered, and leave for about 15 minutes. Now bring them together, press firmly everywhere and leave to dry. Finally, remove the excess laminate with a plane or file from the edges.

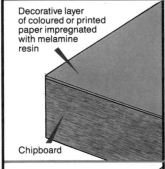

Decorative layer of coloured or printed paper impregnated with melamine resin

Backing layer of 5–6 sheets of kraft paper impregnated with phenolic resin

MELAMINE-FACED CHIPBOARD

Typical trade names: Contiplas, Aroplas

Melamine-faced chipboard is widely used to produce inexpensive furniture — it is cheaper than either wood covered with plastic laminate or veneer. The decorative layer is bonded under heat and pressure to chipboard — the popular finishes are white and woodgrain.

Shelves and simple pieces of furniture can be constructed quite simply at home. Melamine-faced chipboard is easily cut with a fine-toothed tenon saw and pieces are put together with KD fittings and chipboard screws (page 109). There is a range of board sizes — 3 – 8 ft long, 6 – 36 in. wide and ³/₅ in. thick. The boards are finished on both sides and edging strip is available which merely requires smoothing down with a warm iron. Melamine-faced chipboard is not as hard-wearing as plastic laminate — it is easily scratched and is not suitable for heavy-duty work surfaces.

Decorative layer of coloured or printed paper impregnated with melamine resin

Chipboard

FLEXIBLE PLASTIC

Typical trade names: Fablon, ConTact

The reasons for the popularity of stick-on plastic sheeting are the simplicity of application and the enormous range of colours, patterns, surface textures etc. No great skill nor experience is required to cover a shelf, tray, cupboard front or kitchen table top. The flexible sheeting is bought in 18 in. wide rolls and the decorative self-adhesive film is peeled away from the waxed paper backing after it has been cut to size. Almost any surface can be covered, but you must be careful to avoid creases and bubbles when pressing down the film. The surface is washable and stain-resistant, but it will not stand very high temperatures nor resist scratching by sharp objects. When covering a shelf, cupboard door etc make sure that there is at least a 1 in. overlap on the reverse side.

Plain colours, simple patterns and wood look-alikes are the favourite flexible plastics. Matt or shiny smooth surfaces are generally chosen, but there is suede-like film for drawer bottoms, milky film for frosting windows and transparent film for protecting book covers.

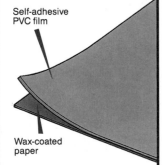

Self-adhesive PVC film

Wax-coated paper

FABRICS

ACETATE Silky fibre made from cellulose. Neither creases nor shrinks, but is not hard-wearing. Usually used in blends. Typical trade names: Dicel, Lansil.

ACRYLIC Woolly fibre made from an oil by-product. Crease-resistant and hard-wearing — used alone or in blends to add toughness to natural fibres. Typical trade names: Dralon, Acrilan, Orlon.

ALPACA Fine hair from S. American animal — Llama is shorter and coarser. Blended with wool or cotton.

ANGORA Soft and silky hair from Angora rabbit. Blended with wool or artificial fibre for knitwear.

ASTRAKHAN Fabric imitation of the curly fur of Astrakhan lamb.

BATIK Fabric bearing a pattern produced by dyeing, the areas not to be coloured being protected by a wax coating.

BATISTE Fine and smooth fabric made occasionally from wool but more usually cotton. Similar in texture to cambric.

BOUCLÉ Fabric made from 3-stranded looped wool or artificial fibre — used for ladies' suiting.

BROCADE Fabric with a raised pattern which is woven into the cloth — a popular curtaining material.

BRODERIE ANGLAISE Fabric, usually cotton, with a cut-out embroidered design which is nowadays machine-made.

BRUSHED NYLON Nylon fabric brushed to raise a fine nap of fibres — cloth has a warmer and softer feel than ordinary nylon.

BUCKRAM Stiffening fabric made of cotton or jute treated with gum.

CALICO Cotton fabric with a firm, close weave and a dull finish. It may be bleached or unbleached.

CAMBRIC Fine and smooth fabric made from linen or cotton. Similar in texture to batiste but the surface is shiny.

CAMELHAIR Brown woven wool imitation of fabric made from camel hair.

CANDLEWICK Cotton or artificial fibre fabric patterned with tufts of yarn. Used for bath mats and bedspreads.

CANVAS Strong fabric woven from coarse yarn — hemp, linen, cotton or artificial fibre. Unblended with a tight weave — more open weave used for embroidery canvas.

CASHMERE Soft and silky hair from Cashmere goat. Blended with wool for suiting and knitwear.

CELLULAR Cotton, wool or blended fabric with a honeycomb weave.

CHEESECLOTH Cotton or blended fabric with an open gauze-like weave.

CHENILLE Velvet-like fabric made of silk, cotton, wool or artificial fibre.

CHIFFON Semi-transparent fabric with a slightly crinkled surface. Very fine — made from silk, viscose or cotton.

CHINTZ Cotton woven fabric, always glazed on the surface and nearly always with a design of flowers and/or birds.

CLYDELLA Trade name for a popular blend of wool and cotton.

CORDUROY Ribbed woven fabric made from cotton or cotton blends. Hard-wearing — used for suiting.

COTTON Natural fibre from the seed pod of the cotton plant. Cotton fabric is absorbent, strong and dyes well, but creases easily if it is not resin-treated.

CRÊPE Crinkled fabric — various processes used on cotton, wool, silk, polyester etc.

CRÊPE DE CHINE Highly crinkled, glossy fabric made from silk originally but nowadays from artificial fibre.

DAMASK Jacquard-woven fabric with intricate designs and plain colours. Glossy — used for table linen and soft furnishings.

DENIM Twill-woven cotton fabric with a coloured warp and grey weft. Hard-wearing — used for overalls, trousers, skirts etc.

DRILL Coarse cotton fabric with a twill weave — used for uniforms, sails etc.

DUCK Heavy type of canvas.

FELT Fabric made of fibres (usually wool) bonded together by shrinking and rolling so that they interlock.

FLANNEL Woven woollen or woollen blend fabric which is both lightweight and soft.

FLANNELETTE Imitation flannel made from cotton or artificial fibre. Surface is brushed to produce downy finish.

FUR FABRIC Fabric made from cotton or artificial fibre to look like animal fur.

GABARDINE Hard-wearing, twill-woven wool, cotton or artificial fibre — recognised by its fine diagonal ribbing.

GEORGETTE Semi-transparent crêpe woven from fine yarn — silk or artificial fibre.

GINGHAM Cotton or cotton blend fabric with a distinct checked or striped pattern.

GROSGRAIN Silk (nowadays artificial fibre) fabric with a distinctly ribbed surface.

HESSIAN Strong and coarse fabric woven from hemp and jute. Used for upholstery, linings etc.

HOPSACK Loosely-woven fabric made from cotton, linen or artificial fibre. Used for suiting.

JACQUARD WEAVE Weaving process which produces intricate patterns on looms controlled by cards bearing a series of holes — an outstanding example of early automation.

JERSEY Knitted fabric made from cotton, wool, silk or artificial fibre.

LACE An intricately patterned fabric with an open weave. Once hand-made from cotton — now produced by machine from cotton or artificial fibre.

LAWN Fine and lightweight woven fabric made from cotton or cotton blend.

LINEN Natural fibre from the stems of the flax plant. Linen fabric is absorbent, very strong and lustrous but creases and shrinks unless treated. Nowadays used in blends.

MERCERISED COTTON Cotton fabric given added strength and lustrous finish by treatment of the yarn.

MERINO Soft and fine wool from Merino sheep.

METALLIC FABRIC Shiny fabric produced from plastic-coated aluminium 'yarn'. Typical trade names: Lamé, Lurex.

MODACRYLIC Type of acrylic which is flame-resistant. Typical trade names: Teklan, Dynel.

MODAL Viscose fabric which resembles cotton — absorbent and strong. Trade name: Vincel.

MOHAIR Fabric made from angora — often used as a blend with wool for knitwear and suiting.

MOIRÉ Fabric with watermarked swirling pattern and a ribbed weave — sometimes called watered silk.

MOQUETTE Carpet-like upholstery material with cut or uncut pile, made from wool, cotton or artificial fibre.

MUSLIN Plain-woven cotton with a somewhat loose weave.

NEEDLECORD Finely-ribbed corduroy.

NET A collective term for fabric loosely woven as a mesh.

NYLON Artificial fibre made from an oil by-product, famed for its strength, hard-wearing qualities and crease-resistance, but notorious for its non-absorbency. Typical trade names: Bri-nylon, Enkalon, Antron.

OILSKIN Fabric of natural or artificial fibre coated to make it waterproof.

ORGANDIE Delicate, semi-transparent fabric made from cotton or artificial fibre — silk version known as organza.

PERCALE Combed cotton or cotton blend fabric — closely woven like cambric.

PIQUÉ Stiff fabric, usually made from cotton, embossed with a ribbed or other patterned finish.

PLAIN WEAVE Weaving process without any frills. Warp and weft cross over each other in an over-under-over-under pattern.

PLISSÉ Puckered cotton fabric.

PLUSH Velvet-like material with a rather open weave.

POLYESTER Artificial fibre made from an oil by-product, widely used in cotton blends to improve crease-resistance and wear-resistance. Strong like nylon, but it does not stretch. Shrink-proof and moth-proof. Typical trade names: Crimplene, Terylene, Dacron.

POLYVINYL CHLORIDE Plastic coating (PVC) applied to fabric to make it waterproof.

POPLIN Closely-woven cotton or cotton blend fabric. Strong with fine ribbing.

RAYON Artificial fibre made from cellulose. Two types — acetate and viscose.

SAILCLOTH Stiff cotton canvas, strong and ribbed.

SATEEN Type of satin made from cotton.

SATIN Lustrous fabric with a smooth surface made from silk or artificial fibre blends.

SATIN WEAVE Weaving process where warp thread goes over-over-over-over-under the weft threads (compare plain weave).

SEERSUCKER Cotton fabric with crinkled stripes or checks.

SERGE Heavyweight wool or wool blend fabric, twill-woven and a popular material for uniforms.

SHANTUNG Silk or silk-like fabric with an uneven surface.

SHEER A collective term for thin, semi-transparent fabrics.

SILK Natural fibre from the cocoon of the silkworm. Strong, luxurious, warm, elastic but damaged by several things including sunlight and perspiration.

TAFFETA Shiny, closely-woven fabric — once made from silk but nowadays from artificial fibre.

TRIACETATE Artificial fibre made from cellulose and cotton. Somewhat similar to acetate but it is more resistant to wear, dirt and heat. Used in blends for weaving and knitting. Typical trade names: Tricel, Tricelon.

TULLE Net made from silk or artificial fibre — used for trimmings.

TWEED Coarsely-woven woollen fabric, often patterned with some form of check.

TWILL WEAVE Weaving process designed to produce diagonal ribbing. Herringbone is a variety of twill weave.

VELOUR Woven wool or cotton fabric with a velvety pile.

VELVET Fabric with a dense, smooth pile on one side. Made from many yarns — cotton, silk and a variety of artificial fibres.

VELVETEEN Velvet-like fabric made from cotton or cotton blend. The pile is short.

VISCOSE Silky fibre made from cellulose — sometimes called viscose rayon or rayon. Soft and absorbent but not hard-wearing and can be marked by water. Usually used in blends. Typical trade names: Darelle, Evlan.

VIYELLA Trade name for a popular twill-woven wool and cotton blend.

VOILE Soft, semi-transparent, plain-woven fabric.

WHIPCORD Cotton or woollen twill-woven fabric with distinct ribbing.

WINCEYETTE Soft twill-woven fabric made from brushed cotton or cotton blend.

WOOL Natural fibre from the fleece of sheep. Warm, elastic, crease-resistant, absorbent etc but shrinkage and matting after washing can be a problem. Nowadays often used in blends.

WORSTED Fabric woven from wool yarn which has been combed to produce a fine and smooth surface.

ADHESIVES

There is no such thing as a universal adhesive. There are a number of multi-purpose adhesives which will do a satisfactory job with many materials, but they all have their weaknesses. At the other end of the scale are the specific adhesives which are designed to stick just one type of material. Read the leaflet or label carefully — check that the product is suitable for the materials to be joined. You must also check that the product is suitable for the situation. Some adhesives are waterproof — others are not. Some are flexible — others are not. There are additional features to consider — cost, solvent dangers, setting time etc. Prepare the surfaces to be joined — they should be clean, dry and free from grease.

	Description	GENERAL PURPOSE	WOOD	FABRICS	PAPER & CARDBOARD	LAMINATES & VENEERS	LEATHER	CHINA	GLASS	RIGID PLASTICS	FLOOR TILES	VINYL SHEET	CEILING TILES	METAL
NATURAL GLUE	Made from animal bones or fish (Scotch glue). The traditional glue of the furniture maker, producing strong joints. Now out of fashion — smelly, slow setting time (4 – 6 hours) and not waterproof. Typical trade names: Certofix, Croid Universal Glue, Le Page's Liquid Glue		✓											
SUPERGLUE	The new cyanoacrylate adhesives have received much praise — most household materials can be joined by adding a thin film to one surface and pressing the other to it for a minute or two. Simple, but there are problems. There must be a close fit and Superglue is expensive. In addition care is needed. Keep off skin — keep a tube of Superglue Remover handy. Typical trade names: Super Glue 3, Ultrabond, Supalok	✓												
CONTACT	The standard contact adhesive is a solution of synthetic rubber in a volatile solvent. It has the great advantage (but sometimes the disadvantage) of making treated surfaces stick immediately on contact. The adhesive is coated on to both surfaces and left for about 15 minutes. The surfaces are then pressed together firmly. Typical trade names: Bostik 3, Evo-Stik Impact, Unistik. There are disadvantages. The bond is flexible but not very strong — not suitable for furniture. Also, instant bonding means no chance of adjustment. Some slight adjustment is possible with Thixofix and Time Bond. Also, inflammable vapour requires no smoking and good ventilation. There are now some non-solvent contact adhesives — Power Fix and Impact 2			✓	✓	✓	✓							✓
CLEAR	Like contact adhesives, the clear adhesives are rubber solutions. They are sold as multi-purpose fixatives for general household use. They are easy to use, but the bond is less strong than an epoxy or superglue one. Typical trade names: Bostik 1, UHU, Loctite Clear Glue	✓												
CELLULOSE	Crystal-clear and quick-drying — popular for repairing crockery and glass and for model-making. Flexible, heat-proof and waterproof, but the bond is not strong. Typical trade names: Durofix, Samson C110						✓	✓	✓	✓				
EPOXY	The most important of all household adhesives — a resin and hardener are mixed together to produce an adhesive which takes 3 – 30 minutes to harden and several hours to set to full strength. The bond is extremely strong and waterproof. Cramping may be necessary during the setting time — to speed up the setting process increase the temperature of the surroundings or use a quick-setting type. Typical trade names: Araldite, Bostik 7, Devcon, Dunlop Epoxy. Quick-setting types: Araldite Rapid, Borden Superfast	✓												
TWO-PART ACRYLIC	Similar to epoxy, but the resin is spread on one surface and the hardener on the other. Press together — hardening takes place in a minute or two. Typical trade names: Hyperbond, Multi-bond	✓												
PVA	Milky solution which sets in about 20 minutes and is fully dry in a day to produce a clear, strong bond. PVA has replaced glue as the standard woodworking adhesive — no unpleasant smell and no unsightly film. For indoor use only — not waterproof. Various formulations available — choose the right one for the job on hand. Typical trade names: Unibond, Bostik 8, Polybond, Evostik Wood Adhesive		✓	✓	✓		✓	✓						✓
LATEX	Milky solution which sets in 1 – 2 hours, to form a strong, clear waterproof bond. Washable in hot water but repaired fabrics should not be dry-cleaned. Typical trade names: Copydex, Jiffybind, Surestick			✓	✓		✓					✓		
UREA FORMALDEHYDE	A two-part adhesive for glueing outdoor wood — the bond is waterproof and resistant to heat. It also has excellent filling properties so it is the adhesive to use where a wood joint is loose. Typical trade names: Aerolite, Cascamite	✓												
RUBBER RESIN	A solvent-based synthetic rubber solution for fixing flooring materials. Setting time is 2 – 4 hours — the bond is waterproof when dry. Typical trade names: Evostik Flooring Adhesive, Dunlop Flooring Adhesive										✓			✓
VINYL ADHESIVE	A speciality adhesive which mends tears in vinyl (PVC) sheeting or welds pieces of flexible vinyl together. The bond is strong and flexible. Typical trade names: Vinylweld, PVX											✓		
GUM/ PASTE	An adhesive with a vegetable base, such as starch or cellulose. The range is limited but there are a large number of brands including many wallpaper pastes. Typical trade names: Polycell, Trufix, Solvite, Coragum				✓									
PASTE STICK	A convenient method of applying solid adhesive to paper or card — washable and non-toxic adhesive is packed in a lipstick-style case. Typical trade names: Pritt Stick, UHU Stic				✓									
GLUE GUN	Adhesive sticks are melted in the chamber of the gun — the trigger or thumb-button releases a strip of molten adhesive which sets in about a minute. Buy white sticks for wood and clear sticks for other materials	✓												

The adhesive kit

For many of the jobs you will have to do there will be a special adhesive — hanging wallpaper, fixing tiles, joining plastic pipes, laying cork tiles etc. But you will also need a general adhesive kit which will deal with repair jobs and emergencies. You will need an **epoxy** adhesive for fixing almost anything, provided it can be held together in some way until the bond has hardened. For instant fixing use **superglue** (for maximum strength) or a **contact** adhesive (for economy). Finally, a **PVA** adhesive is the one to use for woodwork or furniture repairs.

PAINT, STAIN & VARNISH

Paint is cheaper than wallpaper, and painting is by far the most popular DIY job. Every year about two-thirds of the adult population open a paint tin and use a brush or roller to provide a fresh new look to walls and woodwork indoors. The task is easier than it used to be — there are now non-drip paints, peel-off strippers and solid emulsions for simple roll-on application. Still, the age-old warnings remain — you must spend time and take care over preparation and you must choose the right paint system. Don't guess which system to use — read this section and check the manufacturer's leaflet. Bare wood may require a knotting-primer-undercoat-topcoat system — a sound wall which is to be painted in a similar shade may require just one coat of vinyl emulsion.

Painting outside woodwork is less popular — it is tackled each year by less than a third of the population. But it is more vital than indoor decoration — exterior paint has an important protective job to do as well as a beautifying one. It is certainly more time-consuming and less pleasant than painting indoors — some paint stripping is nearly always necessary and working near the top of a ladder is not for everyone. Repainting the outside woodwork is necessary every 2–5 years — call in a decorator if you do not plan to do it yourself.

Paint is made up of 3 basic parts. There is the *pigment* which provides colour and covering power. Next, the *binder* holds the pigment together and bonds it to the painted surface. It provides the paint's durability and the degree of lustre — once linseed oil was used but nowadays resins are employed. Finally there is the *liquid carrier* which holds the other ingredients — it is nearly always oil or water, but occasionally a volatile solvent is used. The 2 basic paint surfaces are *matt* (dull) and *gloss* (shiny), but you can buy *semi-gloss* paints with a range of sheens — silk, satin, eggshell, lustre etc.

The paint to use

There is a frightening array of types these days, but for most purposes the choice is quite simple. For wood and metal a gloss oil-based paint is the one to use — it will give the toughest and longest-lasting surface but it will also show up surface imperfections much more than a matt or semi-gloss type. The gloss you buy can either be liquid or non-drip. Each has its own advantages and disadvantages — see page 116.

If you are decorating stripped or new wood or an outdoor iron object you must use a primer. Painted surfaces do not need a primer — go straight on to the next step of putting on an undercoat. Finally, paint on the topcoat of liquid gloss — note that a non-drip gloss does not need an undercoat. The number of topcoat layers required will depend on see-through — one may do but you might need 2 if you are painting a light colour on a very dark one.

Walls and ceilings indoors are generally painted with a water-based emulsion paint — a roller is quicker than a brush. No undercoat is used — 2 or 3 coats of emulsion are applied.

Besides these standard paints there are a much larger number for special situations — painting outdoor walls, gutters, radiators and so on. See page 117 for details.

EQUIPMENT

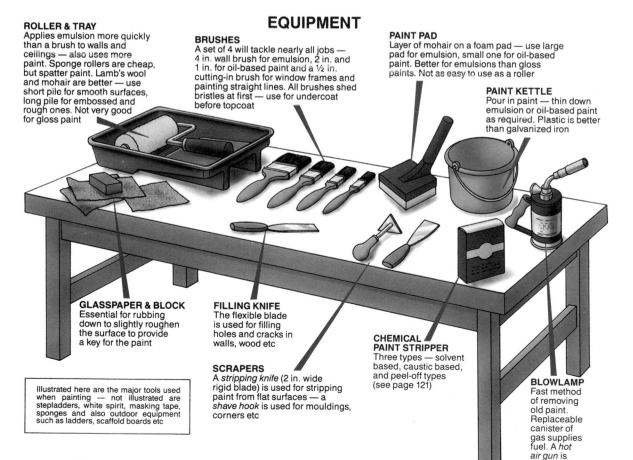

ROLLER & TRAY
Applies emulsion more quickly than a brush to walls and ceilings — also uses more paint. Sponge rollers are cheap, but spatter paint. Lamb's wool and mohair are better — use short pile for smooth surfaces, long pile for embossed and rough ones. Not very good for gloss paint

BRUSHES
A set of 4 will tackle nearly all jobs — 4 in. wall brush for emulsion, 2 in. and 1 in. for oil-based paint and a ½ in. cutting-in brush for window frames and painting straight lines. All brushes shed bristles at first — use for undercoat before topcoat

PAINT PAD
Layer of mohair on a foam pad — use large pad for emulsion, small one for oil-based paint. Better for emulsions than gloss paints. Not as easy to use as a roller

PAINT KETTLE
Pour in paint — thin down emulsion or oil-based paint as required. Plastic is better than galvanized iron

GLASSPAPER & BLOCK
Essential for rubbing down to slightly roughen the surface to provide a key for the paint

FILLING KNIFE
The flexible blade is used for filling holes and cracks in walls, wood etc

SCRAPERS
A *stripping knife* (2 in. wide rigid blade) is used for stripping paint from flat surfaces — a *shave hook* is used for mouldings, corners etc

CHEMICAL PAINT STRIPPER
Three types — solvent based, caustic based, and peel-off types (see page 121)

BLOWLAMP
Fast method of removing old paint. Replaceable canister of gas supplies fuel. A *hot air gun* is safer

Illustrated here are the major tools used when painting — not illustrated are stepladders, white spirit, masking tape, sponges and also outdoor equipment such as ladders, scaffold boards etc

TYPES OF PAINT

PRIMER/SEALER

A sealer prevents stains and other undesirable materials bleeding into the paint — a primer bonds tightly on to the surface and prevents the paint soaking into the surface. Most priming products serve both functions, adhering to metal, wood, brick etc and providing a smooth and satisfactory base for the undercoat or topcoat.

A primer is not always necessary. The main use is on bare wood and on metal surfaces, and also on asbestos, concrete, and stone.

UNDERCOAT

The second stage in a full paint system — it is applied immediately after priming to provide a dense and smooth surface which is soft enough for rubbing down to provide a key for the topcoat. Colour should be close to but not the same as the topcoat.

An undercoat is not always necessary. If the old paintwork is sound and is quite similar in colour to the new paint, you can rub down and apply topcoat. Non-drip gloss and emulsion paints do not need an undercoat.

TOPCOAT

The final part of the paint system — the layer which shows. It must be decorative but it must also be protective — strong enough to withstand knocks in the hall and condensation in the kitchen and bathroom. Outdoors it must keep out water and frost.

A range of textures can be produced by sponging with a second colour, dabbing with a rag or patterning with an embossed roller. Such techniques are often recommended, but they are best left in expert hands.

Standard paints

TYPE	NOTES
OIL-BASED	
Alkyd resin paint	Matt oil-based paints contain alkyd resins — gloss and semi-gloss ones may be made with alkyd or polyurethane resins. There are differences — alkyd resin paints are glossier and last a little longer outdoors than polyurethane ones. A basic paint for woodwork and metal indoors or out — make sure the undercoat is recommended for use with the chosen topcoat. Coverage is approx. 160 sq.ft per litre
Polyurethane resin paint	A basic paint for woodwork and metal indoors and out. Gloss is the usual form, drying more quickly than alkyds and providing maximum durability and water resistance. Coverage is approx. 160 sq.ft per litre
Polyurethane resin paint (non-drip)	Non-drip (also known as thixotropic or jelly) gloss paint is a boon for the inexperienced — it only turns into liquid when brushed out, so there are no irritating drips and runs. No undercoat is needed, but there are a few drawbacks. Coverage is less than with a liquid paint (approx. 120 sq.ft per litre), brush marks are more noticeable and it is more difficult to use in fine mouldings and around windows
Enamel	The proper meaning is a coloured glaze produced by heat treatment. Nowadays the word is used to describe a high-quality gloss paint in which the pigments are very finely ground. It is used without a primer or undercoat to produce a glass-smooth effect
WATER-BASED	
Vinyl emulsion or Acrylic emulsion	The basic paint for walls and ceilings indoors — often thinned with water before use. Easy to apply, but a gloss surface must be thoroughly rubbed down before applying emulsion. Matt dries quickly and is the preferred type where the surface is imperfect. Semi-gloss (silk or sheen) is recommended for kitchens, bathrooms, and on embossed papers. Gloss types are available, but the lustre is inferior to an oil-based paint. Coverage is approx. 120 sq.ft per litre
Solid emulsion	Matt and semi-gloss finishes are available in non-drip form, the rectangular tray containing a jelly-like formulation for roller use. Very useful for the beginner — the easiest of all paints to use
Distemper	The forerunner of all water-based paints — pigment, natural oil binder and water. Not very durable — still found on old walls but now replaced by modern emulsion paints
SOLVENT-BASED	
Lacquer	Paint dries as the inflammable solvent evaporates — finish is similar to enamel treatment. Commonest type is touch-up cellulose lacquer in aerosol form for car bodywork repairs

Specialist paints

TYPE	NOTES
Microporous paint	Microporous (or breathing) paint has caused quite a stir in the DIY field. Basically it is a water-based paint containing acrylic resin which is applied to bare wood. The great advantage claimed by the manufacturers is the ability of moisture trapped in the wood to escape, and the film is flexible. This means that the cracking and bubbling associated with traditional gloss paint when used outdoors can be avoided. Not all experts are yet convinced that microporous paints are the complete answer, but they are widely used in the U.S. and Scandinavia
Masonry paint	Ordinary emulsion paint should never be used outdoors — masonry paint is a special grade which can resist the effect of rain, frost, sunlight, ultra-violet rays etc. It usually contains sand, crushed stone or other aggregate to provide a surface texture and to fill small cracks. It provides a waterproof coating over brick, stone or rendering
Cement paint	A Cinderella product but it can be used on new brick, concrete and cement under damp conditions. It is bought as a powder and mixed with water
Anti-condensation paint	There are several brands which can deal with mild condensation and are recommended for kitchens and bathrooms. They work by insulating the surface — some also contain absorbent particles such as clay or vermiculite
Fire-retardant paint	Old oil-based paint is highly inflammable, thus posing a problem in high fire-risk areas. A number of paints are available which can slow down the combustion rate of the material on which they are painted. Emulsion type is useful for covering expanded polystyrene tiles
Bituminous paint	A black or brown paint which produces a waterproof layer — used for painting gutters, tanks, exposed walls etc
Textured paint	An indoor paint which forms a raised pattern surface after application, either automatically or by means of a roller or scraper
Floor paint	Brick, concrete, tile and stone floors can be painted with a special epoxy resin material. Do not use ordinary paint — it is not sufficiently durable
Radiator enamel	Ordinary white paint will turn yellow in time when applied to radiators. Use white radiator enamel instead
Heat-resisting paint	A boiler flue pipe is the only area where you are likely to need a paint which will withstand very high temperatures. Black and aluminium finishes are the only types available
Other paints	Anti-mould, blackboard, metallic (including gold, silver and hammered aluminium), anti-burglar for drainpipes and harmless phosphorescent paint for doorbells are manufactured, but some are hard to find in the shops

Primers/Sealers

TYPE	NOTES
Knotting	A shellac-based varnish which prevents resin from oozing out of the knots in softwood. If left untreated the resin would bleed into the paint
Multi-purpose primer	Other names include all-purpose and universal primer. This is the product to use on wood, metal and plasters unless there is a special problem. It blocks absorbency and forms a smooth layer which then requires an undercoat or topcoat. Coverage on wood is approx. 80 sq.ft per litre — more on metal, less on plaster
Wood primer	A white paint used as a single coat to prime bare wood and manufactured boards. Use neither the pink grade which contains lead nor red lead primer
Primer/sealer undercoat	A water-based acrylic material which seals, primes and undercoats wood or plaster in one operation. Unfortunately water tends to raise the grain of softwood, so rubbing down before and after priming is necessary
Aluminium wood primer	Use on hardwoods, highly resinous softwoods, badly stained surfaces, creosoted wood or wood stripped with a blowlamp
Zinc chromate primer	Use on metal before painting
Tannate primer	Sold as Rusty. Use on metal before painting. Added advantage is conversion of any rust which is present into harmless magnetite
Alkali-resisting primer	Use on new cement, concrete, brick or plaster before using an oil-based paint
Stabilising primer	Use on walls with a flaking or powdery surface — remove as much loose material as possible before treatment

PAINTING INDOORS | Preparation

Remove small pieces of furniture to another room — move larger items to the centre of the room and cover with a dust sheet. Curtains, pictures etc should be taken away and floor coverings which cannot be moved should be covered. Remove handles and keyhole covers from the doors.

Now you must prepare the surfaces in the correct sequence: ceiling → walls → woodwork/metal. Do not skimp this work — beginners are always amazed how long a professional takes to prepare a room for painting and how short a time he takes to do the actual painting!

CEILING

The job is simple if the existing emulsion paint is sound — merely wash down with dilute detergent or sugar soap, remove with plenty of clean water and let the surface dry thoroughly. Look for cracks — these must be filled flush with the surface (see page 59). Look for stains — these must be spot-treated with the appropriate primer/sealer (see page 117). Plaster and plasterboard do not present any problems — merely dust down thoroughly before painting and make sure that new plasterwork is left for at least 4 weeks before painting. Equally easy to prepare is wallpaper which is firmly attached to the ceiling. Never remove sound paper — dust with a soft brush and paste down any loose edges.

Unfortunately ceiling preparation is often more difficult than described above. Loose paper will have to be stripped away and all adhesive washed off. Wallpaper which has been painted with old-fashioned distemper will have to be removed, and any flaking emulsion paint will have to be scraped off and the surface smoothed before painting.

WALLS

Walls covered with wallpaper, emulsion paint, plasterboard or plaster are quite simple provided that the surface is sound. Follow the rules for ceilings described opposite — wash the walls with a sponge, moving upwards from skirting board to ceiling. When washing down you must avoid wetting light switches, wall lights etc.

All holes and cracks must be filled, and all loose paint must be removed. The surface should be thoroughly rubbed down with glasspaper after such work so that there is no 'stepping' between the old paint or paper and the patched or cleaned area. Spot prime all repaired or scraped parts of the wall. Gloss or semi-gloss paint must be rubbed down with glasspaper to provide a key for the emulsion paint or undercoat to be applied.

Preparation can be a lengthy job. Dampness or mould growth must be dealt with at this stage — see Chapter 7. The walls may have a large number of cracks or holes — it will be necessary to hang lining or textured paper after repairing the faults and before painting.

WOODWORK

Never strip away paint unless it is defective or if the layer is preventing doors or windows closing properly. If stripping is necessary, see page 121. If not, wash down thoroughly, rub down with glasspaper and finally remove all dust before painting. Holes and cracks should be repaired with wood filler and the surface spot-treated with primer after rubbing down.

IRON & STEEL

Rub with white spirit to remove grease. Wash thoroughly and allow to dry. If traces of rust are present, remove surface corrosion with a wire brush, rub down to a smooth surface and prime with Rusty.

Technique

Dip the brush into the paint so as to cover half the bristle length. Wipe off excess paint on the side of the tin. This is not necessary with non-drip paint.

A paint roller is loaded with paint by pushing it back and forth in the front of the tray and then again pushing it back and forth on the sloping back of the tray to spread the paint evenly over the roller. Paint the edges with a brush before you start — then roll slowly and evenly in criss-cross fashion until the whole area is covered. Remember to remove the roller gently from the surface to avoid splashing.

Matt emulsion

Laying on and brushing out
Apply a horizontal band of paint about 8 in. wide — brush out sideways

Laying off
Finish off with light upward strokes in a criss-cross pattern

Gloss paint

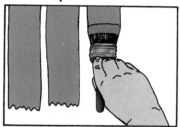

Laying on
Apply the paint from the brush in 2 or 3 vertical strokes

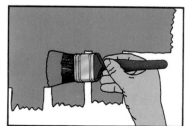

Brushing out
Spread out these vertical strips of paint by brushing sideways. Brush out sparingly with non-drip paint

Laying off
Finish off with light upward strokes. Lay off sparingly with non-drip paint

Tackling the job

The painting sequence

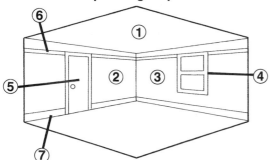

Holding the brush

Hold a small brush like a pencil

Hold a large brush like a table-tennis bat

CEILING

Work in 2 ft bands away from the window wall, these bands stretching from one wall to the opposite one. Work quickly so that the edge of each band is still wet when you start the next one. Start early in the day to ensure that the whole ceiling can be painted in one session.

WALLS

Work in 2 ft bands away from the window — start painting a wall in the top right hand corner (if you are right-handed) and end at the left hand corner above the skirting board. Start early in the day to ensure that the whole wall can be painted in one session. Paint ('cut in') the narrow strip around the door and window frames after the main body of the wall has been painted. Close the windows when you are working in order to cut down the drying rate.

WINDOWS

Start early in the day so that the edges will be dry before nightfall, thereby allowing the window to be closed. There is a clear-cut painting sequence. With a sash window the top sash is painted first, then the bottom sash and finally the frame and rebates. See page 121 for the casement window sequence.

Scraping paint off the glass with a razor blade is a tedious job — for a neat finish either stick masking tape around the outer edge of the panes before painting, or use a paint shield when painting. Remove masking tape as soon as the paint is dry.

BARE WOOD

New or stripped wood will need priming — softwood knots should be painted with knotting before applying a primer. Universal primer is quite satisfactory indoors, but blowlamp-stripped wood, hardwood, stained wood and preservative-treated wood should be painted with an aluminium primer. Fill in cracks and holes and then rub down. Spot prime the filled areas and then apply an undercoat, where necessary, or 1 or 2 applications of topcoat.

DOORS

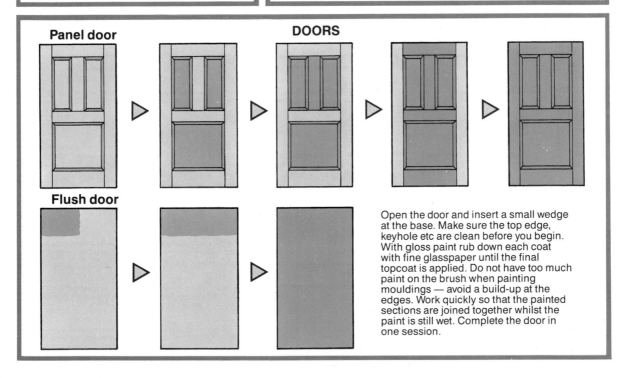

Panel door

Flush door

Open the door and insert a small wedge at the base. Make sure the top edge, keyhole etc are clean before you begin. With gloss paint rub down each coat with fine glasspaper until the final topcoat is applied. Do not have too much paint on the brush when painting mouldings — avoid a build-up at the edges. Work quickly so that the painted sections are joined together whilst the paint is still wet. Complete the door in one session.

PAINTING OUTDOORS | Preparation

The best time to paint the outside of the house is in early autumn — try to choose a settled spell in September or October and make sure that the work is finished before the onset of winter. If autumn is not possible, choose early summer. Successful house painting is threatened by rain (paint will peel and later blister), hot sun (paint will quickly blister if the wood is damp) and frost (gloss paint will dry with a dull finish and masonry paint will be damaged).

Before you can begin to prepare for painting it is essential to carry out any necessary repairs. Broken windows must be reglazed, rotten wood replaced or treated, brickwork repointed where necessary, cracked putty renewed, dampness eradicated and faulty gutters and downpipes repaired or replaced.

Ladders will be needed, but a scaffolding tower is a much better way of reaching the upper part of the house. Do take care — read pages 96 and 99 and make sure that children and pets are kept away from under the ladder. Tie a long board to the lower rungs if the ladder has to be kept in position overnight.

The basic principle is to prepare and then to paint from the top of the house down to ground level so that neither dislodged dirt nor paint will fall on to newly-painted work. There are 2 basic ways of tackling exterior painting — some experts recommend that you prepare and then paint each section in turn, but it is generally felt that it is better to do all the preparation first and then get on with the painting. The choice is up to you, but whichever way you decide the preparation and painting sequence shown below should be followed. Before you begin, cover plants, paths etc with polythene sheeting.

The preparation and painting sequence

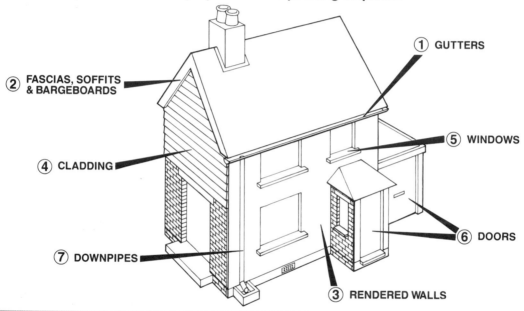

① GUTTERS
② FASCIAS, SOFFITS & BARGEBOARDS
④ CLADDING
⑤ WINDOWS
⑥ DOORS
⑦ DOWNPIPES
③ RENDERED WALLS

①	**GUTTERS**	Clear away all rubbish. Wire brush metal guttering to remove loose rust — paint with Rusty to provide an undercoat and to neutralise deep-seated rust
②	**FASCIAS, SOFFITS & BARGEBOARDS**	Rub down with glasspaper if the paint is sound. All flaking paint must be removed and the bare patches thoroughly rubbed down. Apply a primer after dusting. Work along the grain — double-coat the end grain. If flaking is severe, you will have to strip off all the paint — see page 121
③	**RENDERED WALLS**	Brush down the surface, working from the eaves to ground level. Repair cracks and replace loose rendering — see page 101
④	**CLADDING**	Rub down with glasspaper after filling cracks and holes. Replace or treat rotten wood — see page 132
⑤	**WINDOWS**	Wire brush metal windows — rub down wooden window frames with glasspaper. You must deal with flaking paint — see step ② above
⑥	**DOORS**	Treat as step ②. Hardwood doors are better stained and varnished than painted — see page 123
⑦	**DOWNPIPES**	Treat as step ①

Tackling the job

Make sure that the paint is recommended for exterior use. When working from a ladder use a paint kettle — it should be less than half full and suspended from a rung by means of a butcher's hook. Wait until the dew has gone before you start painting.

| ① GUTTERS | Treat the inside with 2 coats of bituminous paint or with gloss paint. The outside of the gutter should be painted with undercoat and a gloss topcoat. Plastic gutters can be painted if first thoroughly cleaned with a detergent solution |

| ② FASCIAS, SOFFITS & BARGEBOARDS | Start at the ridge and work downwards to the fascia boards (see page 97 for the meaning of the words). After priming all bare patches and replacing or treating rotten wood all of this exposed roof timber should be painted with undercoat and then 1 or 2 topcoats of gloss paint |

| ③ RENDERED WALLS | Start from the top right hand corner — use cement paint, exterior-grade emulsion or masonry paint. A 4 in. brush is the one to use, although you will find it quicker to use a roller than a brush. A roller with an extension pole will allow you to get to the higher reaches without having to take your ladder or scaffold there. Speed is important — you should paint the whole wall in a single session |

| ④ CLADDING | If previously painted, use undercoat and 1 or 2 coats of gloss paint. If stained use a reliable preservative — Woody provides non-fading colour and rot protection |

| ⑤ WINDOWS | See step ⑥ for general details. Windows should be painted in a set sequence, as shown below for casement windows and as described on page 119 for sash windows |

As with window interiors you should either stick masking tape around the outer edge of each pane before painting or use a paint shield when painting. The paint should go a few millimetres over the putty to prevent rainwater seeping in between the glass and putty

| ⑥ DOORS | The standard system for all wooden surfaces in exposed situations is undercoat plus 2 coats of gloss paint. Rub down between each coat. Bare wood will need priming and perhaps knotting before using the standard system. For new doors you can use one of the new one-coat microporous paints which require neither primer nor undercoat. As an alternative you should always consider staining and varnishing for hardwood doors |

| ⑦ DOWNPIPES | Make sure that the surface is properly primed — Rusty should have been applied to all rusted areas. Apply undercoat and gloss topcoats — hold a piece of cardboard behind the pipe to keep paint off the bricks. If you are changing from a bituminous paint to a standard oil-based one you will need to use an aluminium primer. Start at the top and work to ground level, applying the same undercoat and topcoat as in step ① |

Paint stripping

The quick and cheap way to remove paint is to use a **blowlamp**. Have a bucket of water handy and place a tray below the area to be treated. Hold the nozzle about 6 in. away from the surface and keep the flame moving by swinging the nozzle back and forth. When the paint has started to melt, scrape off with a stripping knife and shave hook. Always work from behind the blowlamp and scrape in the direction of the grain. There can be problems — lead paint should not be stripped in this way and wood can be charred if the flame is not kept moving. Glass can crack when window frames are treated and there is a danger of fire if a bird's nest is located under the eaves. For the home decorator a blowlamp should be reserved for large flat areas without mouldings and where there is no danger of fire.

A **hot-air gun** is safer — it works like a hair dryer. Despite the statement in some textbooks it is just as speedy as a blowlamp and by using directional nozzles you can remove paint from window frames without cracking the glass. It is heavy to hold and you do need an electric cable — but it is still the best choice if you have to strip a large area.

A **chemical stripper** is expensive compared to the other methods, but is the one to choose for a small area or for intricate mouldings. There are 2 basic types — solvent strippers and caustic ones, and there is now the peel-off type which allows you to remove all the paint by just peeling off the strip about an hour after treatment — no more scraping! Chemical strippers call for precautions — read the label carefully. Cover nearby surfaces which may be splashed and wear gloves, goggles and old clothes as instructed. The area must be washed down after stripping — use the liquid recommended by the manufacturer.

AVOIDING & DEALING WITH PAINTING PROBLEMS

● BEFORE YOU START PAINTING

If you are new to painting read this chapter and the instructions which come with the paint. Buy the right equipment and do not try to save time by ignoring the rules for preparing the surface prior to painting.

Stir paint with a broad piece of board or plastic — do not use a narrow cane or stick. Use a circular motion, moving the stirrer up and down. Do not stir non-drip paint.

Paint which has been stored for some time may pose a problem. A layer of water on top of emulsion paint should be poured away — a skin-like layer on top of an oil-based paint should be cut away and the contents strained through the fabric from a pair of old nylon tights.

Many paints can be thinned before use, but you must carefully follow the instructions on the can.

● BITTINESS

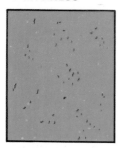

The cause of small pimples on the surface is dust. This dust may have come from the brush if not all of the surface was cleaned before you started or from the air when painting outdoors in an urban area. Another possibility is inadequate wiping after rubbing down the surface with glasspaper.

If bittiness is present, rub down with fine grade wet-and-dry glasspaper when the paint is dry. Wipe away all traces of dust and apply a fresh coat of paint.

● SAGS & RUNS

The tell-tale sign of a beginner. These tear-like streaks can be caused in several ways, but the usual reasons are loading the brush with too much paint and/or not spreading it out sufficiently. Sags and runs occur most frequently with gloss paint — with this type of covering you must lay on, brush out and lay off properly as described on page 118.

If the paint is still wet you may be able to brush out and lay off to remove the trouble. This is not usually practical — let the paint dry for several days and then carry out the treatment described for bittiness.

● BRUSHMARKS

Another common problem with several possible causes. The paint should form a smooth and even layer after laying off — the presence of clearly defined streaks when the paint is dry usually indicates that the bristles were sub-standard or the paint was too thick. Other possible causes are insufficient rubbing down of a gloss surface before painting and overloading the brush.

● SLOW DRYING

It is quite normal for paint to take a long time to dry in cold weather — have patience. Paint failing to dry at normal temperature is a serious problem — it usually indicates that the surface was either wet or greasy at the time of painting. There is no simple solution — you will have to strip off the paint, prepare the surface properly and then repaint.

● BLISTERS

A frequent sight on old gloss paint on wooden surfaces outdoors. The cause of the bubbles is a build-up of water vapour under the airtight and watertight skin formed by the paint. The water vapour arises from damp which was already present before painting or was able to creep into the wood after painting. In cold weather the dampness does not deform the paint — in hot, sunny weather the dampness vapourises and the blisters appear.

Isolated blisters can be cut out and the space filled with a fine surface filler. The surface should be rubbed down and repainted. If there are a large number of blisters, the only answer is to strip off the paint and begin again.

● LACK OF GLOSS

It is often difficult to pin-point the cause of dullness in gloss paint. It will occur if the work was done in frosty weather or if the film was affected by water — it also happens when too much thinner is added to the paint.

A common cause is poor priming or leaving insufficient time between coats. The answer is to rub down and repaint in warm weather.

● GRINNING

A technical term for see-through and the cause is usually obvious — too much thinning, too little stirring, overbrushing or the wrong undercoat. Rub down and apply another topcoat.

● WRINKLES

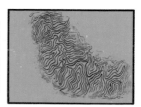

This crinkled effect is associated with gloss paint applied too thickly or to a badly prepared surface. Dampness or soft paint below the topcoat can also cause wrinkling. Strip off and repaint.

● FLAKING

The peeling or lifting of new paint shows that the surface was badly prepared. Dust is the usual cause with a water-based paint — dampness or a wet undercoat is the usual culprit with an oil-based paint.

Flaking of old paint has a different cause. It may indicate rot (test the soundness of the wood with a sharp point) or simply a break down of the film due to damp, frost, hot sun etc. Strip off, prepare thoroughly and repaint as soon as possible.

● AFTER YOU FINISH PAINTING

If you have to stop painting for a short time, merely wrap the brush in aluminium foil. Overnight the brush should be immersed in water or brush cleaner as appropriate. Never stand it in a jam-jar. Drill a hole in the handle of the brush, insert a piece of wire and suspend in the liquid so that the bristles do not touch the bottom of the container.

When the painting job is finished, scrape off excess paint from the brush by pulling a knife away from the handle to the tips of the bristles. Wipe off paint on newspaper, wash out paint with cleaner recommended on the container and then wash in warm water before hanging up to dry.

STAINS & VARNISHES

The purpose of **painting** is to provide an attractive and protective surface which obliterates the texture of the wood.
The purpose of **wood finishing** is to provide an attractive and protective surface which enhances the natural beauty of wood.

Materials

BLEACHES
Bleaches make the wood lighter. They are often used when the bare wood has been discoloured over part or all the surface. Buy a two-part bleach system and follow the instructions exactly. Once the surface has been brought to a uniform pale colour you can either finish the wood with oil, wax or varnish, or you can first change the colour with a stain.

STAINS
Wood stains (wood dyes) colour the surface and often enhance the grain. They usually approximate the shades of hardwoods, and a wide range of wood types is available. Purists claim that new wood should not be stained prior to polishing or varnishing, but for most people the somewhat insipid appearance of whitewood needs to be improved by the richness of a stain. For the adventurous there are stains in bright colours rather than hardwood shades — red, blue, green, yellow etc. These may look horrible or stunning, depending on the object which has been stained and the surroundings.
There are oil-, spirit- and water-based stains. Both the oil- and spirit-based ones can raise the grain — oil-based stains are the most popular. Buy the shade which is closest to the colour you want and buy the varnish at the same time — it should be produced by the stain manufacturer to ensure that the two will be compatible. Once the wood has been properly prepared you are ready to start work. Apply a dab of stain to an inconspicuous part or an unwanted piece of the wood to see if the colour is right. It may be quite different from the colour card — the shade depends on the nature of the wood. Stains can be mixed together to produce the desired colour.
Pour some stain into a saucer. Apply with a piece of soft, clean and lint-free cloth. Try not to put on too much liquid with the first coat — if the wood is too pale when dry, apply a second coat. If it is too dark, rub down with fine glasspaper.

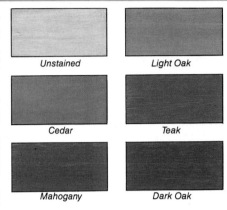

Unstained   *Light Oak*

Cedar   *Teak*

Mahogany   *Dark Oak*

OIL FINISH
The traditional finish for hardwood doors, window frames etc is a mixture of raw and boiled linseed oil with a little turpentine. There are several problems — the surface remains slightly gummy, attracts dust and darkens with age. It is much better these days to use teak oil or Danish oil which give a longer-lasting finish and a satiny sheen. Indoors an oil finish is marked by hot objects — outdoors it can provide excellent protection whilst maintaining a natural look.

WAX FINISH
The traditional wax finish is a mixture of beeswax and turpentine. Many coats are needed and wax finishing is not often recommended these days. The surface attracts dust and it is neither heat-resistant nor durable. It is a much better plan to apply a thinned-down coat of polyurethane varnish as a seal and then use a modern wax polish.

SHELLAC VARNISH
The traditional varnish which has been used on furniture for ages. It is thinned with methylated spirits and applied quickly over the surface. Each coat is lightly rubbed down with fine steel wool before the next one is applied, and the process is repeated until a smooth, glassy surface is obtained. French polishing is a skilled refinement of this simple technique and several brands of French polish for the amateur are available. All shellac varnishes, however, suffer from the drawback that the attractive surface does not stand up to heat, water stains, spilt alcoholic drinks nor hard wear. For wood which is to receive the spills and knocks of everyday living you should use either polyurethane varnish or two part plastic resin.

POLYURETHANE VARNISH
This is the type of finish you are most likely to find in your DIY shop. There are interior and exterior grades and gloss, semi-gloss and matt types. The finish is ideal indoors — hard-wearing, heat-resistant, water-repellant and so on. It is also recommended for outdoor use, but it is not particularly hard-wearing when subjected to bright sunlight.
Apply with a soft brush — it is vital that the first coat should be diluted with 10 per cent white spirit for softwoods (25 per cent for hardwoods). This coat sinks into the wood and should be left to dry for at least 12 hours in a dust-free atmosphere. Rub down with fine steel wool, remove the dust with a rag damped with white spirit and apply a second coat. About 4 coats are required to produce a satisfactory finish.
Indoors the effect may seem rather artificial. A more natural appearance can be obtained by using a matt grade which is then wax polished. Outdoors, yacht varnish grade is often recommended but there is little evidence of outstanding durability away from seawater.

TWO PART PLASTIC RESIN
Plastic resin (also called cold cure lacquer) is produced by mixing a resin with a hardener. The clear varnish forms an extremely hard and chip-resistant surface for table tops.

COLOURED VARNISH
With a coloured varnish the wood is stained and finished in one operation which, of course, saves time. There are gloss, semi-gloss and matt types. There are problems — if the surface is chipped after treatment then unstained bare wood is revealed. Also, you can't apply many coats — the surface gets darker with each additional coat.

MICROPOROUS STAIN   A stain for outdoor use with the same advantages as microporous paint (see page 117).

Preparing wood for finishing

All cracks and holes must be filled with a proprietary stopper. Keep this work to a minimum — stopping can be obtained in various wood shades but staining can result in the highlighting of these repaired areas. If the wood has an open grain the pores should be filled with a grain filler if you are aiming for a luxury finish.
The final step is to sand the wood until it is perfectly smooth. Wipe it down until it is completely free from dust.

CHAPTER 7

PROBLEMS

Problems, problems, problems . . . no matter how small your house may be or how recently it was built, there will be problems from time to time. It is not just a matter of the structure developing faults with age. Tower blocks are demolished with dwellings built centuries ago standing nearby — in the old days wood was thoroughly seasoned and basic techniques have stood the test of time. However, many materials have improved dramatically and the owner of a new house has the safeguard of the National House-Building Council's 10 year guarantee against major defects. Don't expect the builder to repair every fault which may develop during that period — your Agreement will show that his responsibilities are quite specific.

Problems are not always a matter of structural failure — they are more likely to be due to one of the services or a piece of equipment going wrong. Then there are all the living problems, ranging in size from tiny mites and fleas to noisy neighbours. So there will be problems, both large and small, and there are two golden rules to follow:

- PREVENT AS MANY PROBLEMS AS YOU CAN BEFORE THEY START

- TACKLE PROBLEMS WHICH DO OCCUR AS QUICKLY AS YOU CAN

So many troubles can be prevented with a little forethought and attention — frozen pipes, excess heat loss, foundations damaged by tree roots, house fires due to faulty electrical wiring etc. Some problems can't be prevented, but tackling the trouble promptly can stop it from becoming a major one. Rot in a door or window frame should be tackled immediately — so should unsteady furniture, loose roof tiles, pest infestations and so on.

Clearly the two golden rules given above are vital, and to follow them there are several steps you must take. A checklist is set out on the right — less pleasant reading than a page of design ideas or DIY tips, but much more vital in the long run.

1. Learn to know what to look for The way to spot problems is dealt with in several sections of this book. Service troubles — gas, electricity, plumbing, drains etc are dealt with in Chapter 2. Study Chapter 4 for the way to deal with general difficulties inside the house and Chapter 5 for exterior problems. This chapter brings together the remaining problems which can occur — a frightening array of minor and major headaches. Take heart — you will never experience most of them, but it is still necessary to know what to look for and what to do in case of an emergency.

2. Don't tackle the job yourself unless you know what to do This book tells you how to tackle many simple repair jobs for yourself but advises you to seek professional help when there is a serious and complex problem. DIY is a splendid hobby and can save you a great deal of money in maintenance and construction work, but most repair jobs call for experience, and that cannot be gained by reading a book. In particular avoid tasks involving tall ladders unless you have a head for heights.

3. Make sure that you use a qualified professional Never employ people who just knock on the door and offer to build a wall, resurface a drive or repair a roof because they have "material left over from the last job". Try to use someone who has done satisfactory work on a previous occasion for you or a friend, and who is a member of the appropriate professional body.

4. Locate the main taps and switches Find out how to turn off the main stopcock and gas tap before an emergency arises — instruct the other adult members of the family. Keep spare fuse wire or fuses and a torch in a handy place.

5. Have a house-saving kit In addition to a basic tool kit (page 148) and first aid box there should be waterproof tape for tackling leaking pipes, a selection of fuses for electric plugs, a fire blanket and fire extinguisher, and some form of emergency lighting and heating in case of a power failure. These are the basics — there are many more items for the keen and the cautious.

6. Have a list of emergency phone numbers This should include the electrician, police station, doctor, 24 hour plumbing service and the emergency gas service.

7. Have your equipment serviced regularly Major electrical and gas items need regular servicing — for some equipment such as central heating it is essential. If you have moved into an old house or if you have not had your wiring inspected for many years, ask the local Electricity Board to survey the plugs and circuits.

CONDENSATION

Everyone has seen the effect of **superficial condensation** in cold weather. The warm air in the kitchen or bathroom contains a large amount of water vapour. On contact with a cold surface, such as a mirror, window or ceramic tiles, condensation takes place and water droplets appear on the cold objects. Mirrors and tiles are easily wiped and so the problem is sometimes ignored, but if condensation is excessive you must take remedial action or the structure and its contents may be damaged. Water trickling on to woodwork can lead to rot — it will result in rust if left on steel window frames. Condensation can lead to mould growth on walls — on clothing in cupboards a musty smell develops. Less easily detected but much less common is **interstitial condensation** which occurs within the bricks of external walls.

The condensation problem is worse than it used to be. The reason is simple — an average family produces about 5 gallons of moisture in the air of the home each day, and this has to go somewhere. Cooking, washing and bathing are, of course, the main sources, but you produce 2 pints of water vapour per day simply by breathing and perspiring! The trouble is that in recent years we have done everything we can to stop heat from escaping — there is draughtproofing around doors, modern sealed windows, loft insulation, blocked-up chimneys and so on. The heat is kept in, but so is the water vapour. Wallpaper lets moisture escape to the bricks behind — modern vinyl and waterproof wall coverings keep the moisture in. For these reasons condensation has become a serious winter problem in the modern home.

Tackling the problem There is quite a lot you can do without having to spend any money. In a well-heated and insulated home the trouble is due to inadequate ventilation coupled with too much moisture in the air. In the kitchen do not let kettles and pans boil unnecessarily — close both the bathroom and kitchen doors when the rooms are steamy and open the windows slightly when they steam up. Open living room and bedroom windows for at least a few minutes each day to allow a change of air. Consider anti-condensation paint instead of gloss paint when next you decorate, and try cork tiles or carpet on the floor instead of cold ceramic tiles. Leave some space in wardrobes to allow air movement.

In an older house with little insulation the condensation problem is probably due to inadequate heat. Some background heat is necessary during the day — rooms which receive heat for just a few hours each day can be badly affected by condensation. Never use paraffin heaters if there is a dampness problem — a pint of paraffin or bottled gas produces a pint of water vapour.

Unfortunately, the most effective measures do cost money. A kitchen should be fitted with an extractor fan, a tumble drier should be vented to the outside and windows should be double glazed. There are ways to remove water vapour from the air. Containers of moisture-absorbing crystals can have only a small benefit — where the problem is serious (flats, bungalows etc) an electric dehumidifier may be necessary. Expensive, but it can remove several gallons of moisture from the air each day.

Trouble in the roof Loft insulation keeps the house warmer in winter but it also keeps the loft and its timbers much cooler. If water vapour is allowed to rise up into the loft and then not allowed to escape, condensation can occur on the structural timber and this may lead to rot. The answer is to place polythene sheeting on the loft floor before laying down the insulating material and then ensure that there is some ventilation through air bricks or tile vents.

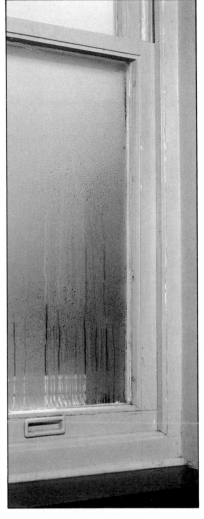

STORM DAMAGE

Winds below 50 mph rarely cause damage to a well-built house, but even moderate winds can blow over garden umbrellas, dustbin lids etc. It is not practical to take too many precautions against the risk of gale damage, but if your home is particularly exposed it would be wise to take some safety measures. Have the roof tiles, chimney and TV aerial inspected regularly — cut back tree branches which could break windows in a gale and keep a supply of sheet polythene handy.

During a gale-force storm close windows securely and unplug the TV if it has an outside aerial. If a window is broken, block it immediately with hardboard, tarpaulin or polythene sheet. If a roof tile is heard to fall, don't go out to inspect the damage until the storm has passed. A temporary repair of the hole in the roof may be possible by pushing a large sheet of polythene between the battens and the tiles surrounding the hole. At the end of the storm call a builder immediately if there has been damage — otherwise check the roof for slipped tiles and the gutters for blockages. After a snowstorm clear away any snow which may have collected in the loft.

SMELLS

There are two types of unpleasant odour which afflict the householder — temporary smells and persistent ones. Temporary smells include fresh paint and tobacco smoke (a bowl of vinegar is claimed to remove the odour), bonfire smoke (have a word with your neighbour — see page 129) and burnt food. For all temporary smells an air freshener block or aerosol is useful — but make sure that the aroma of the aerosol is not more unpleasant than the smell you are trying to mask. Rubbish in kitchen bins and outdoor dustbins should always be contained in plastic bags — use mothballs or a proprietary dustbin product if there is an odour problem with the bin in summer. Remove fish smells from pans by pouring in cold tea — leave for 30 minutes before washing.

Persistent odours are much more worrying. A foul lavatory smell usually indicates a blocked drain — seek expert help. A musty smell is caused by mould growth or rotting wood — locate and tackle the problem at once.

Smells are generally not a problem in the average home. Air fresheners are fine, but the prime way of achieving freshness is to air each lived-in room by opening the window for at least a few minutes every day.

STAINS

- The correct method of stain removal depends on the fabric, the material which has been spilt and the age of the stain. Never guess what to do — some treatments can do more harm than good. For example, soaking in hot water instead of cold may fix a stain in the cloth.
- Treat all stains as soon as possible — once they have dried removal may be very difficult. Dab or scrape off as much as you can and then take appropriate action. For spilt wine pour on salt — for spilt liquid on a carpet use a soda water syphon, taking care not to overwet the pile.
- With non-greasy stains on washable fabrics (except silk, wool and non-colourfast materials) rinse thoroughly in cold water. If the stain remains, soak overnight in a heavy-duty washing powder containing enzymes — make sure the fabric is suitable for soaking. Rinse and wash normally.
- With greasy stains, cover the area with talcum powder. Leave for 30 minutes and then brush off.
- A simple technique may be inappropriate or may not work. You have 2 choices. Firstly, you can take the item to a reputable dry cleaner or call in a specialist company for a carpet or upholstery. This is the preferred course of action for expensive materials, delicate fabrics such as silk and for materials you can't identify. Don't just hand the stained item over the counter — mark the stained area by tacking with cotton and tell the assistant the cause of the stain.
- The second alternative is to try to remove the stain yourself. There are numerous dry-cleaning fluids for greasy stains, Vanish bar for biological stains and the Stain Devils range for a variety of problems. In addition there are many common household products such as ammonia, methylated spirits, bleach etc which can be used to remove one or more types of stain. Consult the chart below.
- Use dry-cleaning fluids with care. Make sure the room is well-ventilated and don't smoke. Read both the instructions and precautions before use. Test the product first on a small and inconspicuous part of the fabric. Place the wrong side uppermost on an absorbent pad and dab (don't rub) with the cleaner. Work from outside the stain inwards.

STAIN	WASHABLE MATERIAL	NON-WASHABLE MATERIAL
ADHESIVES (see page 114)	**Contact, Clear** Dab with nail polish remover. Not suitable for acetates — use lighter fuel instead **Epoxy** Removal extremely difficult when dry. Dab with methylated spirits. Not suitable for acetates — use lighter fuel instead **Latex** If wet, wash off with cold water. If dry, peel off — remove residue with dry-cleaning fluid **PVA** Dab with methylated spirits — not suitable for acetates	Dab with nail polish remover. Not suitable for acetates — use lighter fuel instead Removal extremely difficult when dry. Dab with methylated spirits. Not suitable for acetates — use lighter fuel instead If wet, sponge off with cold water. If dry, peel off — remove residue with dry-cleaning fluid Dab with methylated spirits — not suitable for acetates
BEER	Cold rinse. Soak overnight in biological washing powder. Wash	Sponge with solution of 1 part vinegar/5 parts water. Sponge with clean water. Dab dry with kitchen paper
BIRD DROPPINGS	Scrape off as much as possible. Cold rinse. Soak overnight in biological washing powder. Wash. Bleaching of white fabric may be necessary.	Scrape off as much as possible. Take to the cleaners
BLOOD	If wet — soak in a strong salt solution. If dry — cold rinse. Soak overnight in biological washing powder. Wash	Sponge with solution of 3 drops ammonia/2 pints water. Sponge with clean water. Dab dry with kitchen paper
BUTTER	See GREASE	See GREASE
CANDLE WAX	Place cloth in the refrigerator — when cold scrape off as much as possible. Place blotting paper over and under wax — rub with warm iron. Repeat with fresh paper until clear	Cool area with ice cubes in a plastic bag. When cool scrape off as much as possible. Place blotting paper over wax — rub with warm iron. Repeat as necessary
CHEWING GUM	Place cloth in the refrigerator — peel off hardened gum. Remove residue with dry-cleaning fluid. Wash	Cool area with ice cubes in a plastic bag — peel off hardened gum. Remove residue with dry-cleaning fluid
CHOCOLATE	Scrape off as much as possible. Cold rinse. Soak overnight in biological washing powder. Wash	Scrape off as much as possible. Use dry-cleaning fluid
COFFEE	Cold rinse. Soak overnight in biological washing powder. Wash. If not removed, sponge with solution of 1 tablespoon borax/1 pint water. Wash	Sponge with solution of 1 oz borax/1 pint water. Sponge with clean water. Dab dry with kitchen paper
CRAYON	Sponge with methylated spirits — not suitable for acetates. Dab dry with kitchen paper. Wash	Sponge with methylated spirits — not suitable for acetates. Sponge with clean water. Dab dry with kitchen paper
CREAM	Cold rinse. Soak overnight in biological washing powder. Wash. If not removed, dab with nail polish remover — not suitable for acetates	Use dry-cleaning fluid or Vanish bar
EGG	Cold rinse. Soak overnight in biological washing powder. Wash	Use Vanish bar

STAIN	WASHABLE MATERIAL	NON-WASHABLE MATERIAL
FRUIT JUICE	If dry, rub with glycerine and leave for 1 hour. Cold rinse. Soak overnight in biological washing powder. Wash. If not removed, soak whites in solution of ¼ pint hydrogen peroxide/1 pint water/5 drops ammonia	Sponge with cold water. Rub with glycerine and leave for 1 hour. Dab dry with kitchen paper. Use dry-cleaning fluid
GRASS	Cold rinse. Soak overnight in biological washing powder. Wash. If not removed, sponge with methylated spirits or use Vanish bar	Use Vanish bar
GRAVY	Cold rinse. Soak overnight in biological washing powder. Wash	Use dry-cleaning fluid or Vanish bar
GREASE	Dab with dry-cleaning fluid. If stain persists, try Vanish bar. Wash	Use dry-cleaning fluid or Vanish bar
INK	**Washable ink** Cold rinse. Soak overnight in heavy-duty washing powder. Wash. If not removed, sponge whites with lemon juice and salt **Ball point, Felt tip** Sponge with methylated spirits — not suitable for acetates. Dab dry with kitchen paper. Wash	Sponge with dilute detergent. Sponge with clean water. Dab dry with kitchen paper Take to the cleaners
IRON MOULD	Sponge with lemon juice — leave for 30 minutes. Wash	Sponge with a proprietary rust remover
LIPSTICK	Scrape off as much as possible. Sponge with methylated spirits — not suitable for acetates. Dab dry with kitchen paper. Wash	Scrape off as much as possible. Take to the cleaners
MARGARINE	See GREASE	See GREASE
MILDEW	Cold rinse. Soak overnight in biological washing powder. Wash	Take to the cleaners
MILK	Cold rinse. Soak overnight in biological washing powder. Wash. If not removed, sponge with solution of 1 tablespoon borax/1 pint water. Wash	Sponge with solution of 1 oz borax/1 pint water. Sponge with clean water. Dab dry with kitchen paper
OIL	See GREASE	See GREASE
PAINT (see page 116)	**Oil-based** Scrape off as much as possible. Sponge with white spirit then soapy water. Wash **Water-based** Cold rinse. Soak overnight in heavy-duty washing powder. Wash	Scrape off as much as possible. Sponge with white spirit. Sponge with clean water. Dab dry with kitchen paper Take to the cleaners
PERSPIRATION	Sponge with solution of 2 tablespoons vinegar/1 pint water. Wash. If not removed, use Vanish bar	Sponge with solution of 2 tablespoons vinegar/1 pint water. Sponge with clean water. Dab dry with kitchen paper. If not removed, use Vanish bar
RUST	See IRON MOULD	See IRON MOULD
SCORCH MARKS	Soak in solution of 1 tablespoon borax/1 pint water. Wash	Sponge with solution of 1 tablespoon borax/1 pint water. Sponge with clean water. Dab dry with kitchen paper
TAR	Scrape off as much as possible. Sponge with eucalyptus oil. Wash	Scrape off as much as possible. Use dry-cleaning fluid
TEA	See COFFEE	See COFFEE
SHOE POLISH	See CRAYON	See CRAYON
SPIRITS	Cold rinse. Soak overnight in biological washing powder. Wash	Sponge with methylated spirits — not suitable for acetates. Sponge with clean water. Dab dry with kitchen paper
URINE	Cold rinse. Soak overnight in biological washing powder. Wash. If dried, soak first in dilute vinegar	Sponge with dilute vinegar. Sponge with clean water. Dab dry with kitchen paper
VOMIT	Scrape off as much as possible. Rinse under tap. Soak overnight in biological washing powder. Wash	Scrape off as much as possible. Sponge with water containing a few drops of ammonia. Sponge with clean water. Dab dry with kitchen paper. If smell persists, use Vanish bar
WATER	Spots on silk, velvet etc — hold in front of steaming kettle	Hard water spots on sinks, basins etc — wipe off with solution of 2 teaspoons vinegar / 1 pint water
WINE	Rub with lemon juice and salt. Leave for 1 hour. Wash	Sponge with warm water. Sprinkle with talc. Leave for 1 hour. Brush off

Most of the above remedies have been used for many years, but neither success nor safety to fabric can be guaranteed. Much depends on the age of the material, ingredients in the stain, etc. If in doubt, seek professional help

EFFLORESCENCE

A white deposit frequently appears on the surface of new brickwork. This is due to the water-soluble salts within the bricks being drawn to the outside as the walling materials dry out. Once at the outer face of the brickwork these salts crystallise and appear as a white fluffy film.

On outside brickwork there is no problem — efflorescence is quite normal and all you have to do is to remove the deposit with a wire brush until it ceases to appear. Never try to scrub it away with water — you will only make matters worse by bringing fresh salts to the surface. On inside walls it can be a problem by disfiguring or even dislodging the paper. To prevent efflorescence reappearing it is necessary to strip off damaged paper, leave the surface to dry, brush off the deposit and then treat the surface with a proprietary sealer before redecorating.

Efflorescence should not persist after 2 years. If it continues to appear you should consult a builder. It could mean that dampness is entering the wall from a leaking pipe, faulty damp-proof course etc and there could be serious trouble if the fault is left unattended.

MOULD

Patches of mould, usually greenish-black but occasionally brown or red, can occur on many surfaces in the home — furnishings, leather, clothes in a drawer, wallpaper and so on. The most likely areas to be affected are painted wood and window frames in the kitchen or bathroom.

Mould (referred to as 'mildew' on fabrics) receives scant attention in most homecare books — it is dismissed as harmless. This is regrettable. Firstly, it is not harmless. It is true that mould does not damage timber like the wood-rotting fungi but the air-borne spores of some types of mould can pose a health hazard by causing breathing problems. Secondly, the presence of mould indicates that the environment is not right — either damp is creeping through the walls or there is too little ventilation.

Remove mould when it appears. Wipe down the area with a solution of 1 part bleach/6 parts water and leave for a day before scraping away the surface growth. Remove and burn mouldy wallpaper. When redecorating use a fungicidal sealer and a fungicidal wallpaper paste. The long-term answer is to find and remove the cause — read the sections on condensation (page 125) and damp (pages 130 and 131).

NOISE

About 100,000 people complain about noise each year to their local authority. Little can be done about road traffic, trains, low-flying aircraft etc to stop the noise at source. It is up to you to lessen the problem by installing improvements in your home — sealing strips around windows and doors, wide-gap double glazing (see page 74), heavy curtains which are drawn at night, thick loft insulation and so on. If you live in a high-noise area you may qualify for a grant — see your local Citizen's Advice Bureau.

We accept the noise of our own equipment much more than that of our neighbours. Over 70,000 complaints are made each year — the main offenders are TV/radios, lawn mowers, vacuum cleaners and washing machines. By far the worst problem is the blaring stereo late at night — the only satisfactory answer is to persuade your neighbour to turn down the equipment, move it away from the party wall and/or close the windows. If the noise persists and is both regular and unreasonable, ask your local council to serve a noise abatement notice.

Noise can damage your health — for advice consult the Noise Abatement Society, PO Box 8, Bromley, Kent.

SUBSIDENCE

Subsidence occurs when the foundations of a house move downwards so as to cause structural damage. Upward movement is called *heave*. The possible causes are many and varied. First of all, the subsoil may move. Clays shrink and swell according to the water content, so that a very dry summer or a very wet winter may put a great strain on the foundations. A number of factors can attack the stability of the subsoil irrespective of its type — flooding, mine-workings, underground streams, uptake of water by tree roots, the presence of rotting wood or rubbish, insufficient settlement time prior to building and so on. Finally (and rarely), the foundations themselves may have been improperly laid.

After the causes, the symptoms. Doors may stick and windows fail to open but the characteristic feature is the appearance of cracks in the wall. If there is subsidence then you may face a serious problem. You will need to call in a surveyor immediately and the work involved will be expensive, disruptive and well beyond the skills of even the most ardent DIY fan.

Fortunately, not all wall cracks are caused by subsidence. In fact, only rarely do cracks indicate this frightening problem. In a new house you will find that fine cracks start to appear on some ceilings and internal walls — the main cause is shrinkage as the wood, plaster, mortar etc dry out. These shrinkage cracks are nothing to worry about — they are easily covered by decorating. Keep them to a minimum by maintaining the house on the cool side with good ventilation during the first few months after construction. In addition to shrinkage cracks there may also be settlement ones — fine cracks caused by the building settling down on its foundations. The builder is not responsible, but if cracks continue to appear after a year or so you should contact him as he may be liable for repairs under the guarantee scheme.

In older houses delayed settlement cracks sometimes occur. The problem is to determine whether you are dealing with a settlement crack, which can usually be dealt with quite simply, or with a subsidence crack, which calls for immediate attention by a surveyor. Look at the width of the crack — openings which measure less than ⅛ in. across are rarely worrying, but they may be the first sign of subsidence. Next, look at the location — cracks near a corner of the house or running diagonally from doors or windows can mean subsidence, especially if the crack occurs both inside and outside the house. Long cracks are much more worrying than short ones, and cracks along the join between an extension or garage and the house may indicate that the added-on building has subsided. Finally, carry out the glass slide test described on page 101.

If the signs point to subsidence or if you are in any doubt, call in a qualified surveyor. Leave any recommended works to a qualified builder. The work may consist of underpinning the foundations and some shoring up of the wall or walls. Steel tie rods may be sufficient to hold the affected wall, but with a badly affected house the only course of action may be to rebuild the damaged area. The cost will be high — with a new building there is the 10 year guarantee, and the National Coal Board will provide compensation if their mining has been responsible. Insurance cover depends on the wording of the policy — check it.

Obviously it is better to prevent subsidence than to try to remedy it. There is nothing you can do about the subsoil, foundation geometry etc but you can avoid the tree root trouble which can cause subsidence in clay soil. Do not plant a tree within 40 ft of the house if you expect it to grow to a considerable height. Even small trees should be at least 15 ft away. Instant removal may not be the answer — some trees are protected by law and the sudden change in the water content of a clay subsoil following felling may actually cause heave.

FLOOD

A flooded-out home is a terrible sight. If you live in an area which is prone to flooding you should have the necessary precautionary materials on hand — sacks and sand for making sandbags and some form of emergency lighting and heating.

When a flood alert is issued the local police helped by the fire brigade will take charge — follow their instructions. If they cannot get to you in time, follow the standard drill. Put sandbags (or soil in plastic carrier bags as a substitute) along the threshold of all outside doors and air bricks to impede the entry of water. Take as much as you can upstairs — drinking water, food, coats, torch, reading material, battery radio and valuables. Take up ground-floor carpets if possible. Finally, switch off the electricity at the mains and go upstairs.

The real headache begins once the flood water has receded. Do not switch on the electricity or drink the water until you are told to do so. Open windows and doors — wash down walls and remove carpets. Keep rooms heated — lift one or two floorboards to help the drying process. Drying out will take about 4–6 months — do not be in a hurry to redecorate.

NEIGHBOURS

Good neighbours are a joy but bad neighbours can make your life a misery. Sometimes your neighbours can cause annoyance or difficulty without meaning to do so. Point out that planting a tree too close to your house may cause trouble for which they will be legally responsible. If branches overhang your property you have a right to lop them off, but be polite and inform your neighbours first. Let your deeds resolve any boundary disputes — if the boundary is not clear then explain that a fence is considered to be yours if its posts are on your side. It may not have occurred to your neighbour that the proposed high wall or extension will cast a shadow on part of your house — simply explain that you have a legal 'right to light' if that part of your house has been unshaded for at least 20 years.

Unfortunately there are many neighbour problems which are due to pure selfishness. Bonfires, excessive noise, parking on your property, dangerous pets — the list is almost endless. If the problem is isolated (a noisy birthday party etc), grin and bear it. If it is persistent, do something about it. In the first instance, talk it over — be as friendly as you can. If that fails discuss the matter with the Environmental Health Department of your local council — you have a legal right to use and enjoy your home.

DAMP

At least 15 per cent of British homes show decoration damage due to dampness — it is a serious problem. The visible symptoms (damaged decoration, peeling wallpaper etc) are serious enough, but the hidden results can be even more worrying. Structural woodwork can be weakened by wet rot and the health of the family can be harmed by the mouldy, moist atmosphere when the temperature is low.

Take damp seriously. Learn how to recognise the types of dampness and how to detect the various sources of trouble. Inspect the outside of the house regularly to make sure the defences are sound. If you spot damp patches indoors, take remedial action. If in doubt, seek reputable and impartial advice — in many cases it will be necessary to seek professional help in order to cure the problem. Above all, don't wait until there is serious damage and rotten woodwork before taking action.

Types of damp

TRAUMATIC DAMP
Water from an **inside source** reaching the wall/ceiling

Recognition: Caused by leaking pipe, drain, tank or radiator. Size of patch steadily increases — not related to rainfall, temperature, season etc

PENETRATING DAMP
Water from **rain** or **snow** reaching the wall/ceiling

Recognition: Small or large patches may be some distance away from the point of entry, but patches around windows usually indicate poor sealing or faulty windowsill, and long vertical stain on upper floor indicates faulty gutter downpipe. Patches expand after heavy rain. Associated with exposed N and W facing walls and with old houses (no cavity walls)

CONDENSATION
Water from the **air** condensing on the wall/ceiling/room surfaces/ furnishings/clothing

Recognition: Water drops on windows, mirrors etc — damp and sometimes mouldy patches on walls. Less common on ceilings. Associated with steamy rooms, cold weather and poor ventilation — see page 125

RISING DAMP
Water from the **ground** reaching the floor/wall

Recognition: Wallpaper peeling away from skirting board, lifting floor tiles, discoloured patch on wall. Wall patch can rise up to about 3 ft — pronounced tidemark present. Patch expands in winter. Associated with old houses (damp-proof courses were rare before 1875, and old lime/sand mortar absorbs water)

Finding the cause of the trouble

Go outside just after a heavy rainstorm. Water will still be flowing through the gutters and downpipes but looking upwards will not be a problem once the rain has stopped. Take a notebook and pencil.

Testing for damp

Ideally you should detect damp before any visible signs are present. You can buy a battery-operated damp meter — 2 prongs are inserted into the mortar, plaster etc and a light indicates dampness. These instruments provide an indication only — they are not fool-proof.

Once a patch appears it may be easy to find the cause. However, it is often difficult — a wet patch at the bottom of the wall may be rising or penetrating damp, and in a cellar it is sometimes a combination of the two. Use the **aluminium foil test** to distinguish between condensation and other types of dampness. Dry the damp patch with a heater and then attach a piece of foil with adhesive tape. Inspect it some time later. Water developing on the surface indicates condensation — water on the back of the foil after removal from the wall indicates penetrating, traumatic or rising damp.

If the problem is serious you should call in a surveyor. Call in a damp-proofing company if you wish, but remember that the surveys of some of these companies tend to be unduly pessimistic. However, the location of a serious dampness problem by an independent survey still means that you will need the services of one of these specialist companies.

CRACKED FLAUNCHING
Repair needed

UNCAPPED CHIMNEY POT LEADING TO CLOSED-OFF FIREPLACE
Chimney breast may be stained. Fit half round tile — see page 99

DEFECTIVE FLASHING
Repair needed — see page 99 or call in a builder

DEFECTIVE TILES OR SLATES
Slipped, broken or missing tiles or slates will let in water — see page 99. Inspect from outside — also look for dripping by standing in loft on a rainy day

DEFECTIVE GUTTERING
See page 102

DAMAGED FELT
Look for bubbles and cracks. Carry out temporary or permanent repair — see page 99

DEFECTIVE WINDOWS
Gaps between frame and wall will let in penetrating damp — so will rotten woodwork or blocked groove under sill

DEFECTIVE DOOR
Gaps between frame and wall will let in penetrating damp — so will rotten woodwork or a defective weather bar at base

DAMAGED RENDERING
Cracked or broken rendering will let in water. Repair needed — see page 101

LEAKING DOWNPIPE
Can cause serious penetrating damp — see page 102

BLOCKED AIR BRICK
Remove leaves, soil etc

POOR BRICKWORK
Cracked bricks and missing mortar can lead to water entry — see page 101

BRIDGED DAMP-PROOF COURSE
Dpc may be bridged by earth or covered by a path. Gap between dpc and ground level should be at least 6 in.

Causes and cures

RISING DAMP

- **NO DAMP-PROOF COURSE** Rising damp is caused by water in the ground being sucked up through the brickwork and mortar by means of capillary action. If no damp-proof course is present (see page 51) then there is no waterproof barrier to stop the water rising up into the ground floor rooms. A damp-proof course (dpc) has to be inserted — see below. It is not easy to instal a dpc into a brick wall, but it is even more difficult to instal a damp-proof membrane under a concrete floor — many old houses have floors under which no damp-proofing was inserted at the time of building. In some cases the damp has come through and such concrete floors have to be lifted and remade to today's standards — a layer of concrete and then a screed over a stout damp-proof membrane of butyl rubber or thick polythene.

- **DEFECTIVE DAMP-PROOF COURSE** Builders have had to include a dpc since 1875, but some of the earlier ones were brittle and in older houses broken dpc can be found. If rising damp has resulted from a break in the dpc, use one of the 4 methods of replacement shown below. The problem area may be limited — don't repair more than you have to.

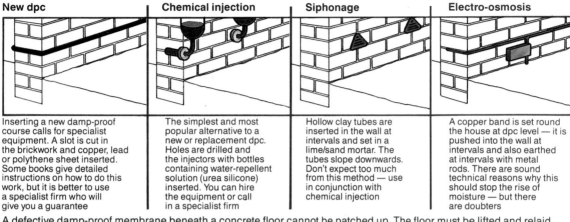

New dpc	Chemical injection	Siphonage	Electro-osmosis
Inserting a new damp-proof course calls for specialist equipment. A slot is cut in the brickwork and copper, lead or polythene sheet inserted. Some books give detailed instructions on how to do this work, but it is better to use a specialist firm who will give you a guarantee	The simplest and most popular alternative to a new or replacement dpc. Holes are drilled and the injectors with bottles containing water-repellent solution (urea silicone) inserted. You can hire the equipment or call in a specialist firm	Hollow clay tubes are inserted in the wall at intervals and set in a lime/sand mortar. The tubes slope downwards. Don't expect too much from this method — use in conjunction with chemical injection	A copper band is set round the house at dpc level — it is pushed into the wall at intervals and also earthed at intervals with metal rods. There are sound technical reasons why this should stop the rise of moisture — but there are doubters

A defective damp-proof membrane beneath a concrete floor cannot be patched up. The floor must be lifted and relaid.

- **BRIDGED DAMP-PROOF COURSE** The usual way of providing a link between the earth and the bricks above the dpc is to have earth piled against it in order to raise a bed or make a rockery. Remove the earth to create the statutory gap of 6 in. between ground level and the dpc. A raised path is a more difficult problem — but relaying may be the only answer. Less common ways of bridging the dpc are by rendering or plastering over it, thereby linking the moist earth with the upper bricks. Where possible, hack off to a line just below the dpc.

TRAUMATIC DAMP
Trace leak — it may be necessary to lift some floorboards to find it.

CONDENSATION
See page 125.

PENETRATING DAMP

- **DRIVING RAIN AGAINST A SOUND WALL** Rain should not penetrate through a sound cavity wall, but penetrating damp can seep through a solid brick or stone wall, especially if the mortar is a lime/sand mix. Large patches of damp on the inside face are the result, and waterproofing the exterior is the answer. The cheapest method is to paint on a silicone water-repellent — it will be invisible when dry. A masonry paint will change the appearance of your house, but missed patches at the time of application and cracking after use can be easily seen. Rendering is the traditional way of waterproofing exposed walls — very useful but it will do more harm than good if not properly applied.

- **DRIVING RAIN AGAINST AN UNSOUND WALL** Cracks in brickwork and missing mortar can let in water. Cracked and blistered areas on a rendered wall are even more serious — rainwater is trapped in the dislodged area and this serves as a reservoir for water which seeps through the wall. The cure is obvious — have the faults repaired.

- **DRIVING RAIN AGAINST A DEFECTIVE WINDOW** Damp patches on an internal wall around a window show that something is wrong outside. Dampness at the base usually indicates a sill problem — clean the groove under the sill and check the sealing. Dampness at the sides or at the top may indicate a damp-proof course problem — consult a builder.

- **ROOF & GUTTER PROBLEMS** See Chapter 5.

- **CAVITY WALL TIE PROBLEMS** The tell-tale sign is a line of regularly-spaced round spots on the wall which may be damp or mouldy. The ties may have been fixed wrongly by the builder, but it is much more likely that they have been covered by mortar carelessly dropped during the building operation. Don't try to cure the problem yourself — call in a builder.

Covering damp

There are many brush-on solutions and stick-on sheetings on the market for application to inside walls which are damp. These are sometimes described as damp cures. They are, of course, nothing of the sort — they merely prevent damp from getting through to the decorations. The problem of dampness in the wall remains and may as a result be driven to other parts of the structure and so extend the damage.

These masking agents do have an important role. They are useful when you wish to redecorate soon after curing a damp problem — leaving the walls to thoroughly dry out could take many months. They also have an important function when decorating a below-ground room where there is just no way of curing the inherent dampness. However, masking agents should not be used as a substitute for curing damp.

The simplest systems involve brush-on solutions. Bituminous emulsion is the cheapest treatment but the synthetic rubber products are more effective. Other types are available — whichever sort you use it is wise to check whether priming is necessary and what precautions are required. It is also wise to check if there is hydrostatic pressure against the wall — water will seep through a hole drilled through a brick. This is almost bound to be present underground — in this case use an epoxy damp-proofing system which involves mixing a resin with a hardener.

Some people prefer to use a lining material rather than a brush-on liquid. The popular one is aluminium foil — walls are washed down, cracks are filled and the lining foil laid using the recommended special adhesive. A popular alternative for cellars and basements is corrugated waterproof lathing which is bought in a roll. The old wet plaster is removed and the corrugated sheeting nailed to the wall. Plasterboard can be attached to the new surface and then painted or papered in the usual way.

The traditional way to cover a damp wall is by tanking — preservative-treated battens are nailed to the wall which is painted with an anti-mould solution. A vapour barrier and then plasterboard is attached to the battens so as to dry-line the damp walls.

WOOD DECAY

A house contains a large amount of wood — structural timber, furniture, mouldings, frames and doors. This wood is vulnerable to attack by both fungal diseases and insects.

There are many fungi which can infect wood, but the only two you have to worry about are dry rot and wet rot. In both cases air-borne spores infect the wood in the first instance and wood-rotting strands (hyphae) spread outwards. This initial attack only takes place if the wood is damp or wet and has been so for some time. There are no cures, so prevention is extremely important. Protect your home against damp and use preservative-treated wood in high-risk areas.

The only insect likely to trouble you is woodworm — the grub (larval) stage of a number of beetle species. Once again prevention is much better than cure.

Most softwoods have little or no natural resistance to attack by rots or woodworm, so a preservative is needed to bestow chemical protection. New softwood timber which is to be placed in an exposed or damp situation should be pressure-treated with a proven preservative. The purpose of a paint-on stain/preservative is to provide colour and top-up protection — Bio Woody is non-fading.

DRY ROT

Dry rot begins in a damp, poorly ventilated place — the favourite sites are suspended wooden floors, cellar timbers, leak-affected structural timber and the back of skirting boards. Unlike wet rot it prefers damp (20 per cent moisture) and not wet timber, and it does not affect wood outdoors. It is less common than wet rot but the effect is usually more serious because of the way it spreads. Once the fungus has taken hold a mass of cottony threads develop and from them long root-like strands appear which seek out fresh wood to attack. These strands can pass through plaster, mortar and even brick. In this way dry rot can move from basement to roof timber and from one semi-detached house to another.

Such extreme movement is not common. The long-held belief that these strands carry water to soften up dry wood does not seem to be true. There must be some moisture in the wood to render it susceptible.

Detecting dry rot is often not easy because it usually attacks timber which is hidden from view. There is a musty, mushroom-like odour and the wood is soft when prodded with a screwdriver. Woolly growths may be seen above a skirting board, and dried-out rotten wood has cracks both along and across the grain to form cube-shaped blocks which crumble when touched. After many months pancake-shaped fruiting bodies are formed on timber or plaster. Spores look like red dust — its presence is a sure sign that there is dry rot.

Don't try to tackle dry rot unless you have the necessary experience. All infected wood will have to be cut back 3 ft beyond the diseased area and all strands removed from plaster, brickwork etc. Dry rot fungicide is applied to the rest of the wood and the source of dampness discovered and eradicated. For the name of a nearby specialist company get in touch with the British Wood Preserving Association.

WET ROT

Wet rot attacks wet (at least 30 per cent moisture) and not moist timber. Unlike dry rot it will not spread to moist timber, and it is active outdoors as well as inside. The effect is often localised, but windowsills, window and door frames, doors and fenceposts can be destroyed. Rafters and joists in leaking roofs are sometimes attacked.

Detection of wet rot on visible timber is usually quite straightforward. Paintwork bubbles up and the timber below is soft. Rotten wood is dark brown with cracks along the grain — dark fungal strands are sometimes found on the surface of the wood.

Keep dampness out of the house in order to prevent the problem — make sure wood is allowed to dry out properly after a leak. Outdoor rot-susceptible timber should be properly maintained with paint or with a stain/preservative. Check that a 'preservative' actually contains a fungicide — its chemical name will be on the label.

To get rid of wet rot you will have to cut out the rotten timber and replace it with preservative-treated wood. For small areas of rot you can use the Ronseal wood repair system. This saves you having to insert a new piece of wood — all you have to do is cut away the rotten area and paint with hardener. The original level is restored with filler and preservative tablets are inserted into the surrounding sound wood.

WOODWORM

The presence of woodworm is all too obvious — a peppering of small round holes on the surface of the wood. These are the exit holes through which the adult beetles departed after spending several years as grubs tunnelling through the wood. Below the surface there will be a network of tunnels — on the surface there will be tiny piles of dust (frass) if the pest is still active.

The most usual type of woodworm is the furniture beetle — ¼ in. long with exit holes 1 – 2 mm in diameter. Other woodworms include the death-watch beetle (old hardwoods) and the house longhorn beetle (largest and most serious woodworm but restricted to parts of Surrey and Hampshire). The grubs of the furniture beetle prefer damp rather than dry wood, softwood rather than hardwood and are especially fond of plywood and glue.

The problem may start with a female beetle flying into your home and laying its eggs — unfinished wood is preferred and painted or polished wood is avoided. It is much more likely for the infestation to have begun with the introduction of wood which was already infested. Examine second-hand furniture carefully before purchase — examine plywood backs and drawers as well as the outer surfaces.

You can treat an infestation in furniture with an aerosol containing woodworm insecticide. After injecting the liquid into the holes with the special applicator, spray the surface thoroughly and apply a repeat spray a few months later. Call in a specialist company if structural timber has been affected — building societies insist on professional treatment if woodworm is present.

FIRE

Domestic fires are the most serious of all home problems. At best the result is upsetting with some damage — at worst there is loss of life and property. The advice is to stay calm and remember what to do, but the problem is that it is so often a time of panic which leads people to do exactly the wrong thing.

There are about 50,000 domestic fires each year attended by one or more fire brigades. Small fires which could have got out of hand exceed that number, so it is sensible to take wise precautions (see Chapter 8) and to practice what to do if a fire does occur.

The golden rule is to **tackle a small fire promptly and calmly if you have the equipment to do so, but to leave a large fire or a furniture fire with billowing smoke and call the fire brigade immediately.**

Dealing with small fires

The way to put out the flames will depend on the type of fire — water in some cases will do more harm than good. There are a few general rules:

- Get everybody out of the house
- Make sure you have a clear escape route
- Tackle the blaze, but if possible get someone to ring the fire brigade in case it gets out of hand
- If it does get out of hand or choking smoke is driving you back, close all the doors as you quickly leave and wait for the fire brigade outside the house

FRYING PAN FIRES are very common but fortunately are usually easy to extinguish. Switch off the burner if you can and then use either a fire blanket or a damp towel. Hold the blanket or cloth in front of you and drop it over the top of the pan to cover it completely. Turn off the stove if you haven't already done so and leave the pan undisturbed until it is cool. Two don'ts — don't ever use water and don't ever try to lift a burning pan.

ELECTRICAL FIRES are another common type of domestic fire. Switch off the supply and pull out the plug if you can. If you have been able to do this, then the flames can be dealt with by using water or a foam extinguisher. Water must never be used if the electrical supply is still on — use a dry powder extinguisher instead.

PORTABLE HEATER FIRES can be extremely dangerous. If the fuel is paraffin you should stand well away and extinguish with water. Never try to move a burning appliance. Tackling a bottled gas heater should be left to the fire brigade if you can't switch off the gas supply.

FURNITURE FIRES Water or foam can be used, but watch out for smoke. Modern cushions and upholstery often give off a highly toxic gas when burning — such fires should be dealt with by the fire brigade.

OTHER FIRES can be extinguished with water, earth, blankets, sand etc. The general principle when using an extinguisher is to direct around the edge of the fire rather than into its heart.

Dealing with large fires

If you are in the room, back quickly to the exit and close windows and doors if you can. The first priority is to get everyone out and having a pre-arranged drill can be a life-saver. Pull doors closed as you leave and call the fire brigade at once by dialling 999 — speak slowly and give them clear details. Keep everyone together outside the house — don't let anyone go back in to collect valuables, pets etc.

You may be unlucky enough to be trapped. If possible move to a room with a window facing the street and then close the door, blocking the air space at the bottom with a rug or other material. Shout for help from the window, but stay close to the floor at other times. Do not jump unless it is *absolutely* necessary. If there is no other choice, throw down as much soft material as you can, turn inwards and lower yourself down by your arms. Let go.

Dealing with a person on fire

Force yourself to do the right thing — it won't be easy. Push the person face downwards on to the floor and cover the burning clothing with any heavy material — a rug, coat, blanket etc to extinguish the flames. Tightly wrap burning hair away from the face with any material you can find. Don't try to remove the burnt clothing — apply cold water to injured areas of the body. Call for medical help immediately — every minute counts.

CORROSION

The surface of bare metal in contact with air forms a metallic salt which is different from the metal itself. Some of the metal is lost in the process — the metal has corroded. This corrosion layer may be very thin as with the tarnish of silver and the patina of bronze, or thick enough to weaken the metal as in the case of rust on iron and steel.

Most corrosive films are not harmful — this applies to aluminium, zinc, silver, copper, brass and bronze. It may, however, be unsightly — it can be prevented on decorative brass and copper ornaments by spraying with a transparent resin film or it is removed from tarnished objects by polishing. Aluminium is rubbed down before priming and painting — zinc should be painted without rubbing down.

The trouble with rust is that it develops on ferrous metals very quickly and the process continues as long as moisture and air are present. To prevent rust on new metal apply a rust-preventing primer and then an undercoat and topcoat. If rust is present you need a tannate-based rust converter such as Rusty. Brush away loose rust and rub down the surface until smooth. Paint on Rusty — this converts the remaining rust into harmless magnetite and forms a rust-preventing undercoat. Apply 2 coats and then a topcoat.

PESTS

You share your home perhaps with a family, perhaps with a pet or two, but quite certainly with thousands of unwelcome living things. Not all are harmful — spiders and silverfish do no harm within the house, but many people find them distasteful and so they get linked with all the others as 'pests'.

By far the largest group in number are the microscopic mites — by far the most frightening are the mammalian pests — rats, mice and bats. You will never have a pest-free home but by carrying out proper precautions and having the right remedies on hand you will not be troubled by their presence.

Precautions include good hygiene — old food scraps, crumbs left in drawers etc attract flies, mice, cockroaches and ants. Use plastic bags in kitchen rubbish containers and dustbins. Move compost heaps away from the house and fill gaps along skirting boards and around outside pipe entry points.

Cures come in many forms. As a standby have a general-purpose aerosol such as Kybosh on hand. Always read the label before you buy or use an insecticide or other pest killer. Do not spray food and store away from pets and children. A serious infestation of wasps, rats etc may be beyond you — get in touch with your local Environmental Health Department.

ANTS
Small insects less than ¼ in. long with a distinct waist — usually black but sometimes red. Spray ants and ant runs with Kybosh — trace back to nest if you can and pour in boiling water. Puff Anti-ant powder into the entrance.

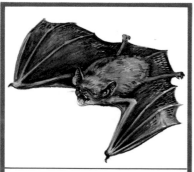

BATS
The bats in your room or behind the cladding are harmless and will not fly into your hair, but many homeowners are still afraid of them. The commonest type is the pipistrelle. Don't try to get rid of them or even block their access into your home — it's illegal. Contact the Nature Conservancy Council who will move them for you.

BED BUGS
Fortunately rare these days, but they may be there when you move house or buy second-hand bedroom furniture. The flat ⅛ in. round insects feed on human blood — irritating bites in the morning and a strange smell indicate their presence. Killed by insecticidal aerosols, but leave eradication to the Environmental Health Department.

CARPET BEETLES
The ⅛ in. long grubs of the carpet beetle and fur beetle attack carpets, woollens, fur etc — now more serious pests than clothes moths. Tell-tale sign is the presence of cast-off furry skins. Destroy birds' nests in roof (the favourite hiding place) and get rid of fluff in drawers, wardrobes etc. Spray with Carpet Beetle Killer.

CLOTHES MOTHS
A plain-looking moth, pale brown and ⅓ in. long. They do no harm — it is the ¾ in. white grub which eats wool and wool-mix blankets, carpets, clothes etc as well as fur. Perspiration and food residues act as an attractant. Store items in plastic bags with a moth repellent. Spray with an aerosol Moth Killer or Kybosh.

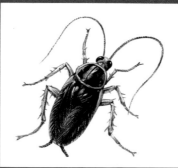

COCKROACHES
Brown beetles, ½ – 1 in. long, which come out of crevices at night to feed. They leave behind an unpleasant smell and perhaps food poisoning. Do not confuse with the harmless black beetle, which does not have the rapid scuttling movement of the cockroach. Spray kitchen nooks and crannies with Kybosh. Repeat treatment.

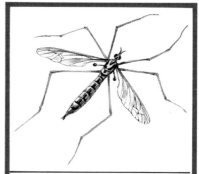

CRANE FLIES
Better known as daddy-longlegs — large spindly insects with gossamer-like wings. Harmless to you, but its grubs are the plant-destroying leatherjackets so hated by gardeners. The flies appear in late summer — they can be annoying and they should not be left to lay eggs on someone's lawn. Kill with a fly swatter or Kybosh.

FLEAS

Small red bites which are extremely itchy usually indicate a flea problem — your dog or cat will generally have been the carrier. Fit it with a Flea collar or apply a veterinary Flea powder. Burn infected bedding and vacuum carpets etc thoroughly. Spray cracks and crevices with Kybosh. Call in a contractor if the infestation is serious.

FLIES

The one you are most likely to see is the common housefly, but it can be a bluebottle (large, noisy, shiny blue), stable fly (housefly-like, but bites humans) or a cluster fly (housefly-size, but hairy and joins with others to form autumn swarms in upper rooms). Keep food covered and kitchen surfaces clean. Spray Kybosh.

MICE

The tell-tale signs are nibbled food and packages plus the presence of small droppings. Both the house mouse and the field mouse come indoors — tackle the problem quickly as both contaminate food, carry food poisoning and can gnaw through electric cables. May be difficult to control — use a Mouse bait, block entry points and use a trap if all else fails.

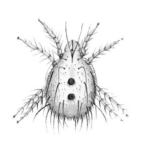

MITES

Tiny creatures just visible to the human eye — look like particles of dust on the move. The house dust mite lives on particles of dead skin — the furniture mite is found in upholstery. If you are allergic to the house dust mite you will start to wheeze — the asthmatic should use plastic filled pillows and vacuum bedrooms daily.

MOSQUITOES

A term loosely applied to tiny buzzing insects — midges are really flies, gnats are true mosquitoes which don't bite and there is the gnat look-alike which does. Biting mosquitoes are occasionally a problem — cover the surface of water-butts, guttering etc with a thin layer of paraffin. Spray insects with Kybosh.

RATS

The most frightening household pest of all for 2 reasons. The scurrying brown rat is about 9 in. long which makes it our largest trespasser, and it is a carrier of a number of serious (even fatal) diseases. Cables and pipes can be damaged — get in touch with your Environmental Health Department straight away. DIY control involves using Rat bait.

SILVERFISH

A pest of damp areas — silvery-grey, cigar-shaped, ½ in. long. Not often seen as it feeds at night, but sometimes trapped in baths and basins. Rarely causes any damage, but sometimes eats wallpaper paste. Silverfish are not a problem but the dampness they indicate could well be. Kill with Kybosh if they are a nuisance.

SPIDERS

All are harmless, but this is no comfort to people who are terrified of them. Cobwebs on wooden cladding often indicates dampness below — their presence indoors indicates nothing except the absence of regular dusting. Move spiders outdoors if you are not squeamish — squash them if you are.

WASPS & BEES

Wasps can be a nuisance in early autumn. Hornets (twice the size of ordinary wasps) are fortunately uncommon. Bumble bees may be more frightening than wasps but will rarely sting if not disturbed. Let bees escape through an open window — spray wasps with Kybosh. For nest removal consult the Environmental Health Department.

HEAT LOSS

Of course, *all* the heat produced by fuel is eventually 'lost' — the house cannot hold its warmth for ever. The purpose of insulation is to slow down the rate of loss so that you can gain as much benefit as practical before the warmth produced by gas, oil, electricity etc is dissipated to the air outside. This means that you will require less fuel to keep the rooms and water at the desired temperature.

In an uninsulated house about three-quarters of the heat you pay for is lost to the environment before you have derived the proper benefit from it. With proper insulation and the efficient use of fuel this loss can be halved (see page 34). This sounds most attractive, but do be clear on 2 points:

● You cannot cut down heat loss altogether by turning your house into an airtight box, nor would it be desirable to do so. There must be enough ventilation to keep condensation in check (page 125) and to allow gas and coal fires to burn efficiently.

● Not all forms of insulation are worthwhile unless you are seeking maximum heat conservation at any cost. It certainly pays to seal gaps and to draught-proof doors and windows, and you should always ensure that there is some loft insulation. Double glazing, however, is not usually a cost effective treatment — it will take many years before you will recover the purchase price in saved fuel.

The actual heat loss which takes place in a particular home depends on the situation. The prime controlling factor is the amount of insulation present — new homes are built to a much higher standard than old ones. A flat-roofed bungalow will lose considerably more heat through the roof than a 3-storeyed house with a pitched roof. Any apartment or terraced house will lose less heat through the walls than a detached house. But no matter what style of home you occupy there can be no doubt that some thought and a little money spent on insulation can cut your fuel bills.

It's not just a matter of cutting fuel bills. Draughts and cold corners in an uninsulated house can make life distinctly unpleasant in the depths of winter. Insulation can be expensive — if money is short begin with draught-proofing and then go on to lagging the hot water cylinder and insulating the loft. You may be eligible for a grant for the cylinder and loft work — ask your local council.

72°F

THE COMFORT ZONE

64°F

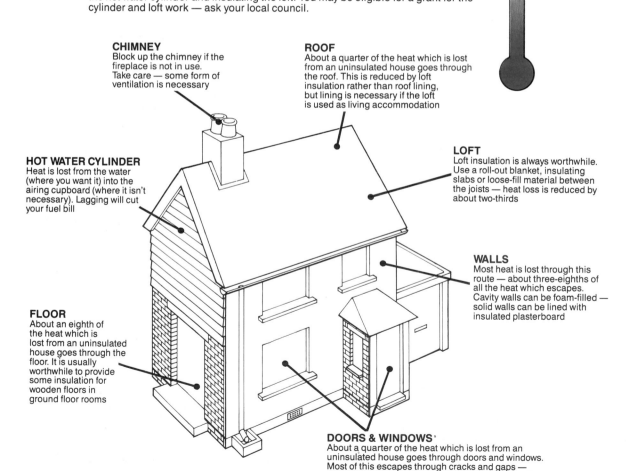

CHIMNEY
Block up the chimney if the fireplace is not in use. Take care — some form of ventilation is necessary

ROOF
About a quarter of the heat which is lost from an uninsulated house goes through the roof. This is reduced by loft insulation rather than roof lining, but lining is necessary if the loft is used as living accommodation

HOT WATER CYLINDER
Heat is lost from the water (where you want it) into the airing cupboard (where it isn't necessary). Lagging will cut your fuel bill

LOFT
Loft insulation is always worthwhile. Use a roll-out blanket, insulating slabs or loose-fill material between the joists — heat loss is reduced by about two-thirds

WALLS
Most heat is lost through this route — about three-eighths of all the heat which escapes. Cavity walls can be foam-filled — solid walls can be lined with insulated plasterboard

FLOOR
About an eighth of the heat which is lost from an uninsulated house goes through the floor. It is usually worthwhile to provide some insulation for wooden floors in ground floor rooms

DOORS & WINDOWS
About a quarter of the heat which is lost from an uninsulated house goes through doors and windows. Most of this escapes through cracks and gaps — draught-proofing is always worthwhile. Not a great deal goes through the glass — double glazing takes a long time to pay for itself

CHIMNEY

An unused fireplace is a significant escape route for warm air in winter. Unlike a badly fitting window you do not feel a direct draught, but an appreciable amount of heat is escaping. Blocking off the fireplace is the obvious solution, but to do so without blocking off the chimney is asking for trouble. The chimney pot must be capped, either with a half round tile (see page 99) or a special ventilator. Note that the chimney must not be blocked completely — some ventilation is essential to prevent condensation.

ROOF

Heat loss from the top of the house is reduced by insulating the floor of the loft rather than the surface under the tiles. There is an exception — if the loft is to be used as a room it is necessary to insulate the roof itself as well as the area between the joists.

There are several methods of roof lining. If there is already a sloping ceiling covering the roof battens you can cover it with expanded polystyrene sheeting or insulation slabs can be slid into the space between the ceiling and the tiles. You must not try to fill this space — there should be at least 2 in. air space for ventilation. If the roof is unlined you will need to cover the space between the battens with strips of roofing felt or polythene and then polystyrene slabs. The final step is to nail thermal plasterboard on the battens to form a ceiling.

You must not try to air-proof the loft — condensation will be a serious problem if there is insufficient ventilation (see loft insulation below).

HOT WATER CYLINDER

The easiest method of insulation is to fit a padded jacket — see page 10. This should be at least 3 in. thick and the cap and all cables should be left uncovered. It is sometimes not possible to fit a jacket — the answer is to build a hardboard box around the cylinder and fill the space with vermiculite.

LOFT

Vacuum the area between the joists before you begin, and replace rotten timber. Never stand or kneel on the floor — walk on the joists or on a stout board placed across them. Insulation will create a number of potential problems. Freezing-up will be more likely, so insulate pipes and the cold water cistern (see page 10) — do not lag the floor below the cistern. There will also be an increased risk of condensation — it is a good idea to place polythene sheet under the insulation to prevent the upward movement of water vapour. The vital step is to ensure that there is adequate ventilation despite insulation. If there are air gaps at the eaves or between the tiles then nothing more need be done. If the roof has been lined and the gap at the eaves blocked then you should drill a series of air-holes in the soffits — cover with fine wire netting.

METHOD 1
Roll-out blanket of 4 in. thick glass fibre or mineral wool — wear gloves, long sleeves and a face mask. Start at the eaves and unroll steadily to the centre of the roof. Push blanket under electric cables

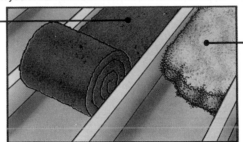

METHOD 2
Loose-fill granules of cork, vermiculite, expanded polystyrene or mineral wool. Easier than method 1, but more expensive and more difficult to keep in place. Use a piece of board to form a smooth layer 2 in. below top of joists

Flat roofs are difficult to insulate. The only practical method is to cut down heat loss by covering the ceiling below. Use expanded polystyrene tiles or thermal plasterboard.

WALLS

Filling the space in cavity walls will reduce heat loss — the cost is recovered in 4–5 years. This is not a DIY job and you must seek professional advice before you go ahead. Ask a surveyor or architect whether it is practical for your house — it may not be (timber framing, exposed location etc). If suitable, choose a firm which is registered with the appropriate body, and let them obtain the necessary local authority permission. There are several methods — mineral fibre threads, expanded polystyrene beads and urea-formaldehyde foam.

Solid walls call for different measures. Place aluminium foil behind the radiators to reflect heat back into the room. The easiest structural way to cut down heat loss is to dry-line the room with thermal plasterboard. There is a snag — it must be 2 in. thick to be worthwhile and that will reduce the size of the room.

DOORS & WINDOWS

Test for draughts with a candle — deflection of the flame indicates a draught. There is a wide range of draught-proofing systems and it is not easy to make the right choice. For hinged windows the cheapest way is to fit self-adhesive foam strips to the frames. When the window is closed the strip should be slightly compressed. Unfortunately these strips stay permanently squashed after a short time — metal strips and plastic compression seals are more satisfactory but they are more expensive.

Sash windows should be fitted with nylon pile draught excluders. The sides of doors can be fitted with inexpensive foam strip or with dearer but more efficient aluminium strips fitted with plastic seals. You will need a threshold strip at the bottom of the front door. There are numerous types and in general efficiency increases with price.

Look out for other problem areas. Fit a letter-box flap which fits tightly, seal gaps between door or window frames and walls, and block holes at the entry points of pipes into the kitchen.

FLOOR

You will find instructions in some textbooks for insulating suspended wooden floors — the boards are lifted and a blanket of glass fibre placed between the joists. As an alternative there is the technique of placing insulating slabs on the floor and covering with chipboard. In practise these methods are usually more trouble than they are worth — tackle the floor insulation problem much more simply by filling holes in the floorboards, sealing gaps between the floor and skirting boards, and by using a thick underlay beneath the carpet.

CHAPTER 8
SAFETY & SECURITY

This introduction contains statistics about home accidents and robberies. They make depressing reading, but there is a hopeful side to the story. Unlike some of life's problems neither accidents nor robberies at home are inevitable — most home injuries at home can be avoided without having to spend any money on safety measures, and many burglaries and break-ins can be prevented by care and commonsense rather than by installing a sophisticated alarm system.

Now for those statistics. Each year about 1 million people sustain injuries at home which need attention and about 6,000 die. There are about 200,000 burglaries annually in Britain — which represents 1 per cent of all households. Around these figures there are many myths and misconceptions — it is helpful to get rid of these mistaken ideas. Electrocution and fires are often thought of as the great killers. Take great care by all means, but only 1 per cent of fatalities are due to electricity, and fires account for 10 per cent of the home accident deaths in the U.K. Most deaths are due to falls by the elderly, suffocation and scalding of the very young, and accidental poisoning. The majority of burglaries take place in the daytime, not at night, and most of them involve entry through an open door or by gently forcing a defectively secured window or door. Few burglars like a challenge unless the house is known to contain valuables — they go elsewhere if the property is properly secured.

SAFETY
SAFETY MEASURES AROUND THE HOUSE

- Follow the **GLASS** safety code on page 72. Do not have loose rugs near windows.

- **FLOORS** cause many accidents. Lino, tiles and vinyl can be slippery — carpeting, cork and cushioned vinyl are safer. If there are children or old people in the house make sure that there are no loose rugs, heavy coatings of wax polish, frayed carpets or wet patches.

- **FIRE** can break out in any room in the house. The kitchen is the prime danger area, but read all of page 139 for the specific problems that may arise in each room of the house. There are some general points. Never drape clothes over a heater or in front of an open fire to dry, and have electrical and gas equipment serviced regularly. Cigarettes cause many fires — use a deep ashtray for stubbing them out and keep matches and lighters well away from children. Don't hang mirrors in front of fires and store all inflammable liquids away from sources of heat or bright sunlight.

  Each fuel presents its own problems. Read the safety measures for **electricity** (page 18), **gas** (page 21), **coal** and **wood** (page 22) and **liquid fuels** (page 23).

  There is a wide range of fire detection and fire fighting equipment available. A fire blanket stored in the kitchen is recommended — so are smoke detectors. There are mixed views about domestic fire extinguishers — you should have one in the car and a dry powder type in the garage, but some fire brigades consider that you ought to get out of a burning house rather than trying to deal with it by means of a small extinguisher.

  Despite all your precautions there may still be a fire. Read the instructions on what to do (page 133) **before** an emergency occurs.

- **TOXIC LIQUIDS** and **POWDERS** must be stored safely. Throw away all unlabelled packages and dispose of old prescriptions. Medicines should be kept in a locked cupboard away from children. Keep pesticides and DIY products in the garden shed or garage — never throw empty aerosols on the fire. Whatever the product, if there are precautions on the label you must read them before use.

- It is a sad fact that the growing interest in **DIY** has led to a disturbing increase in accidents. Half the injuries are due to either cuts from sharp tools or falls. Learn to use saws, chisels etc in the proper manner (page 110) and don't climb a ladder unless it is secure (page 96). A circuit breaker should be present when using electrical equipment outdoors (page 18) and buy a simple metal detector to test for cables and pipes before drilling into walls. The golden rule is to avoid all jobs with a potential hazard unless you know what you are doing and have the proper equipment and safety clothing to do it.

- Look for **SAFETY LABELS** when buying equipment and furniture.

- Learn the proper way to lift **HEAVY OBJECTS**. Bend your knees and not your back. Let your leg muscles do the work — not your shoulder muscles. Above all, know your limitations — use a cart or trolley when the object is too heavy for you.

- Have a properly equipped **FIRST-AID/MEDICINE CABINET** — see page 149. Learn the rudiments of first aid in case of an emergency but this does not mean that you have to be a skilled first aider. In case of a serious accident seek medical help immediately — this is no place for DIY.

SAFETY IN THE KITCHEN

- The oven and hob are the danger areas. The hob should be away from doors and curtains — and draughts if gas-fuelled. Don't fill a pan more than half way with oil, and dry food before placing in hot fat. Always turn handles so that they do not project beyond the hob or over a lighted burner. Do keep small children well away — fit a guard rail to the hob if you can't. Don't leave pans on the stove if you have to leave the room, and never let flex trail close to the hot plates or rings. Open oven doors slowly and use oven gloves to remove hot containers.
- Do not use either gloss paint or expanded polystyrene tiles on the ceiling. Lift up spilt food and mop up spilt liquid from the floor immediately.
- Never connect electrical equipment to a light socket.
- Take care with kitchen knives. They should not be kept loose — store in a wall rack placed well above little fingers or keep in a knife block. Always set downwards on a level and firm surface — keep your fingers well away. Take care when opening cans — especially corned beef ones.

SAFETY IN THE BEDROOM

- Do not smoke in bed. Take care with hot water bottles — do not use boiling water and remove from children's beds before getting in.
- Nightgowns should be made of flame-resistant material — keep all fabrics away from radiant fires.
- Electric blankets can cause problems — they should not be damp, creased or worn. Have them serviced regularly.
- A bedside lamp will avoid you stubbing your toe or tripping over things in the dark — never try to dim the lamp by putting cloth over the shade. Have a night-light in a child's room.
- If the windows are double glazed, make sure they can be opened by the occupant of the bedroom in case of an emergency.

SAFETY IN THE BATHROOM

- Don't take any electric equipment into the bathroom, apart from an electric razor or toothbrush. Switches should be the pull-cord type and both light fixtures and heaters must be well away from wet hands.
- Baths should have an anti-slip base — so should the shower. Turn on the cold tap in the bath before adding hot water. Read about showers on page 46 — a simple arrangement can be dangerous.
- Never put bleach and cleaner into the toilet at the same time — chlorine gas can be produced and the effect is most unpleasant and can be dangerous.

Safety for the elderly

Seven out of every 10 home fatalities involve people who are at least 65 years old. Falls are the problem. Use the following check list — no loose tiles or other floor coverings, good lighting near stairs, firm hand-rail on stairs, no climbing on chairs or stools to reach high objects and no wax polish on floors.

The elderly must also avoid vigorous exertion in cold weather after a period of inactivity. Spring digging and spring lawn mowing take their toll each year. More widely publicised is hypothermia — the room temperature must *always* be above 50°F for elderly people.

For the elderly who live alone there are help-summoning systems. Pressing the button on the neck-worn unit brings assistance. Some councils supply them free — check with the Social Services Department.

SAFETY IN THE LIVING/DINING ROOM

- Be careful with hot drinks — keep them well away from babies and toddlers, and do not rest a cup on the arm of a chair.
- Wear oven gloves to move oven-to-table dishes into the dining room — warn the family that the casserole or pan is hot.
- Make sure that toys are safe — no tiny detachable bits or sharp points for toddlers, no loose eyes on teddies etc. Watch your own safety — there are many accidents caused each year by adults tripping over playthings.
- Smouldering cushions can be lethal — look for the green match-resistant label when buying.
- Pull out the TV plug when not in use. This is especially important when you are going on holiday.
- Don't empty ashtrays into a waste-paper bin, and don't smoke if you often fall asleep in front of the TV.
- Avoid trailing flexes, multi-way plugs and flexes under carpets.

SAFETY IN THE HALL

- A staggering 100,000 people are hurt each year by falling down the stairs, and nearly half the injured are small children. Follow the rules — a firm hand-rail, nothing left on the stairs, good lighting, no loose mats near the stairs, a non-slip surface on the treads and no sharp-cornered objects near the top or bottom of the staircase.
- A gleaming hall floor may look nice, but it can be a menace for the young or very old.
- Remember the stairs and hallway are your escape route in case of fire — keep clear of hazardous objects, such as floor-standing oil heaters. Obviously you must do all you can to prevent the staircase burning in case of a fire when you are upstairs — do not store paper, rags, inflammable liquids etc under the stairs. On your way to bed at night, close all the doors along the hall. This will help to prevent flames and smoke from spreading in case of a fire.
- It is essential that the hall should be well-lit. Switches at the bottom *and* top of the stairs are most useful.

Safety for children

One out of every 10 home fatalities involves a child who is under 5 years old. Parental carelessness is the major problem before the toddler stage, and then childhood curiosity becomes a major factor.

Never use a pillow during the baby's first year. Never leave a baby alone in the bath or alone with a feeding bottle. Keep all small objects away — so many accidents are caused each year by babies swallowing beads, buttons, peanuts, crisps, sweets etc.

The toddler stage brings extra problems. You will need a safety gate at the bottom of the stairs and perhaps one at the kitchen door. Fit safety catches to upstairs windows and fit corner cushions to sharp furniture edges. Keep plastic bags out of reach and store dangerous liquids in a safe place. Obviously this means medicines, disinfectants, paints, pesticides etc but for young children it also means alcoholic drinks, detergents and many other apparently safe liquids. Fit a child-resistant catch on the door of the sink cupboard and cover electric sockets.

SECURITY

There are basically 2 types of housebreaker — the professional burglar and the sneak thief. The professional burglar will have generally chosen his target with care — he will know or strongly suspect that valuables are present. His first job will be to inspect the property to see the easiest point of entry, the safest escape route, signs of you being away and so on.

The professional usually likes to have ample time in which to work and does not leave a deliberate trail of destruction from room to room. Damage is done only if he has to break into things to get to the objects he is searching for. Once found, the burglar leaves as quickly as possible.

The often-repeated statement that there is no way of keeping the really determined burglar out of your home is basically correct, but that need only concern you if you keep a great deal of cash or a number of valuable objects in the house. There is still a great deal you can do. Report to the police immediately anyone who seems to be paying undue attention to your house. You will have to make your house secure, using the whole of the Security Plan on page 141.

For most of us the professional burglar is not the problem. The majority of break-ins are carried out by sneak thieves. Nearly 70 per cent of them are children or teenagers who are looking for easy access. If they can't find it, they move on elsewhere and the result is often senseless vandalism. Insurance cannot cover the deep sense of shock suffered by the unfortunate victim.

The answer is to make the sneak thief go elsewhere — he will not have made your home the object of his day's work. The house should look occupied at all times and entry must be made difficult at all times. To see if your house is secure, you can follow the excellent police advice — go out and lose your key! Of course you needn't *actually* lose your key, but do see how you could enter the empty house without a key and by causing little or no external damage to gain entry. You will probably find it can be done quite simply. Read the Security Plan on the next page.

What a thief looks for

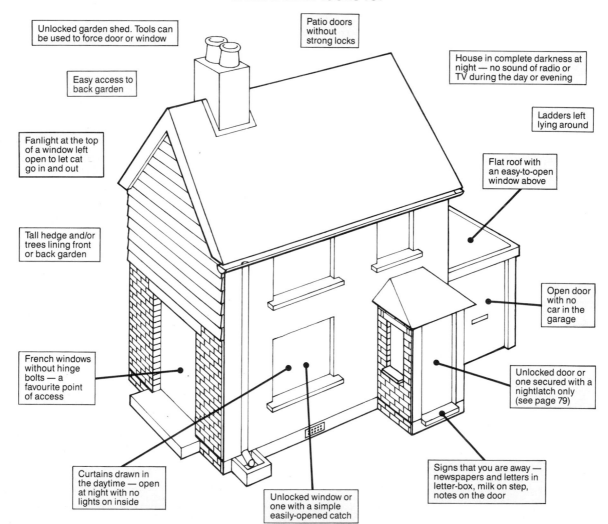

Unlocked garden shed. Tools can be used to force door or window

Patio doors without strong locks

House in complete darkness at night — no sound of radio or TV during the day or evening

Easy access to back garden

Ladders left lying around

Fanlight at the top of a window left open to let cat go in and out

Flat roof with an easy-to-open window above

Tall hedge and/or trees lining front or back garden

Open door with no car in the garage

French windows without hinge bolts — a favourite point of access

Unlocked door or one secured with a nightlatch only (see page 79)

Curtains drawn in the daytime — open at night with no lights on inside

Unlocked window or one with a simple easily-opened catch

Signs that you are away — newspapers and letters in letter-box, milk on step, notes on the door

THE SECURITY PLAN
— the 6 steps to a safe home

1. Put valuables away Keep share certificates, house deeds, precious jewellery etc in a safe deposit box in a bank or security company. If you have to keep large amounts of money at home, consider a wall or floor safe.

2. If you can't, take security measures Don't talk about your valuables, money or forthcoming holidays in a public place. Never place valuables in a room where they can be seen by passers-by. Mark items with special ink which becomes visible under UV light — use your postcode plus house number. Insure valuables adequately — take photographs and keep an inventory.

3. Instal the essential security items There are hundreds of security items on the market — but only a few are essential. Nine out of every 10 entries are through open or inefficiently closed doors or windows. A simple nightlatch on the front door can be opened very easily — you need a mortise deadlock (see page 79). Downstairs windows need key-operated window locks. French windows need hinge bolts and sliding patio doors should have a key-operated security lock at the base.

4. Carry out the essential drill when you are out
If leaving for a short time —
- Lock the external doors and windows — close the garage door
- Switch the radio on. If going out at night switch on at least one light after drawing the curtains of the room. Switch on an outside light if there is one

If going on holiday —
- Cancel the papers, milk and any other regular deliveries
- Keep the curtains open. Lock the external doors and windows — close and lock the garage door and lock the garden shed
- Arrange with a neighbour to keep an eye on the property. This will call for throwing away free newspapers, pushing mail through the letter-box and perhaps cutting the lawn
- Most experts believe that you should not lock drawers nor internal doors when the house is unoccupied

5. Don't ask for trouble Don't do any of the silly things which make the job of a thief easier. The list includes leaving the back door open when watching evening TV, and leaving the key under the mat. Notes to tradesmen pinned to the front door are another open invitation. Don't leave the key for a window lock on the window frame. Change the locks when you move house.

6. If you are cautious, nervous or have valuables, consider the optional extras Fit a door chain on the front door, plus a door viewer if you are especially nervous. The back door will need a deadlock like the front one. Insurance companies will advise you to have key-operated bolts at the top and bottom of all doors which open to the outside.
Fit key-operated locks to upper as well as the downstairs windows (step 3). Double glazing is a great deterrent.
Instal a strong porch light. Fit a light sensor switch in one or two rooms which turns on the light at night and off at dawn. Leave on all the time, not just when you are away. Alternatively you can buy time switches which can be set to turn on the lights and radio at either pre-set or random times. The latest introduction is an outside light with an infra-red sensor which switches on for 2 minutes when you (or an intruder) approaches. A word of warning. Don't try to illuminate your house like a Christmas tree on the nights when you are away — if it doesn't look normal, then an experienced burglar will know you are out.
Burglar alarms are useful — they will frighten off an intruder and warn neighbours of a break-in. Magnetic alarms are the most reliable type, but they are also the most complex and the most expensive. Windows and doors are fitted with magnetic contacts which when opened cause the alarm to ring, and pressure pads are fitted below carpets. Easier to instal are the infra-red and ultrasonic systems, but some of these can be triggered off by draughts. There are still more additional extras — a barking dog can be as good as a burglar alarm, sticky anti-burglar paint can be used on drainpipes and battery-operated personal alarms can be installed by the front door or bedside. An optional extra which will cost you nothing is to obtain advice from your Crime Prevention Officer — ring the police station and he will visit your home.

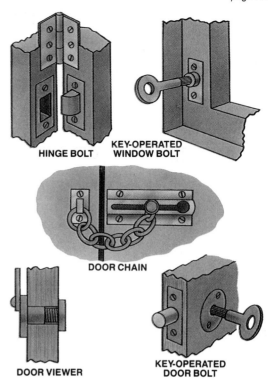

HINGE BOLT **KEY-OPERATED WINDOW BOLT**

DOOR CHAIN

DOOR VIEWER **KEY-OPERATED DOOR BOLT**

The Neighbourhood Watch Scheme

Neighbourhood Watch began in the U.S. and has now taken root in Britain. It is not yet widespread, but already there are indications from some (but not all) groups around the country that its adoption has led to a significant drop in both burglaries and vandalism.
There is nothing new or very clever in the basic concept — Neighbourhood Watch is merely a development of the age-old good neighbour policy, plus some police involvement. There is no well-defined set of rules for starting up a scheme. There are many variations, but the basic principles are generally the same. A police crime officer calls on each house in a street or group of streets to explain the scheme and to enlist support. There are window stickers for the participants, and each member of the scheme takes on the duties of watchfulness without legal liability.
There is no have-a-go or vigilante element. Suspicious actions are reported immediately to the police station, security problems are often discussed and when a member goes on holiday he appoints a key holder. The measure of involvement during periods of absence is agreed by the group — it sometimes involves watering the house plants and feeding the dog!

Burglary the easy way

The most surprising aspect of home security is that many thousands of burglaries do not involve break-ins. A staggering 25% of all home robberies involve a thief who simply enters through an open door or window.
Another method of unforced entry is by the person who calls "from the water board, electricity office, the council to assess the rates" and so on. Never say yes until you have been shown some item of official identification. Read it — if in doubt call his office before allowing entry.
Don't put your name and address on keys, and if possible keep your keys separate from a purse, handbag etc which contains identification information.
The most despicable form of non-forced entry is the false telephone call from the police to say that there has been an accident. The recipient understandably rushes out without closing doors, windows etc and the thief who made the call steps in to an unprotected house. Ring the number back if you have the presence of mind, or ask a neighbour to keep an eye on things as you rush off.

CHAPTER 9
BUYING & SELLING

About 1½ million homes in the U.K. change hands each year. The exchange of contracts is a day of great satisfaction, and moving day is a time of great excitement. For nearly everybody the purchase of a home is the largest financial transaction they will ever make.

There is another side to the picture. For many people house purchase is a period of frustrating anxiety and disappointment. The time taken between the first decision to move and the arrival of the removal van always seems so much longer than expected. The list of woes is a long one — solicitors working at a snail's pace, building societies dragging their feet, surveyors delaying their report, and so on. One of the worst aspects is the discovery that ordinary members of the community can be filled with greed, deceit and thoughtlessness as soon as buying or selling a house is involved!

The setbacks and disappointments at this purchase stage may be upsetting at the time, but they usually only last for a couple of months or so. The long-term problems which sometimes occur are generally much less intense, but can be much more serious. The common one is to find that you have taken on a commitment you simply cannot afford — the answer is to cut your standard of living or to look for something smaller and cheaper. Another possibility is to discover after purchase that there are serious defects in the house which you have to put right.

On average, people change their homes every 8–10 years. The secret of greatly reducing (but not entirely eliminating) the chance of the pitfalls outlined above is to go through a number of clear-cut steps. Never leave out a step and never leave things to chance.

These steps are set out in the next few pages. Note that they apply to England and Wales only — Scotland and Northern Ireland have their own rules. The reason why you need to take care is that the law still does not protect the house purchaser in the same way that the consumer is protected when buying a tin of baked beans. Make a mistake and you are the one who will usually have to suffer, and so in the classic buying situation there are 4 professionals involved. You go to an *Estate Agent* to find the house you want, to a *Building Society* to borrow the extra money you will need, to a *Solicitor* to carry out the conveyancing (transfer of the property from the seller to you) and to a *Surveyor* to make sure that you know what the structural problems are.

This pattern is not fixed, and recent changes in the law mean that a bewilderingly wide range of alternatives is now available. There have always been alternatives to the estate agent (auctions, sales through newspaper advertisements etc) but others have recently joined the house-selling scene — High St. banks, Department stores, solicitors, building societies etc. Until recently the building societies had a near monopoly on lending money for house purchases — now there are several alternative sources of cash. Until 1983 the solicitor did have a monopoly on conveyancing — now it is legal for anyone to do the necessary paperwork. But do take care. Only the role of the professional surveyor remains the same now as it was before the 1980s. The person should be properly qualified and with an older house you leave him (or her) out of the buying process at your peril.

On the subject of perils there are unfortunately several house-buying diseases. Firstly, the **gazump**. This occurs when the seller raises the price between the acceptance of an offer and the exchange of contracts. It is legal, and you have to raise your offer or lose the property. There is no remedy — meet the increase if you can afford it and still want the house, but never accept too quickly or too readily . . . . or you may be gazumped again. Equally distressing is the **contract race**. The seller accepts several offers on the basis that the first one to exchange contracts gets the house. Do be careful before joining the race — you may well be involved in non-recoverable expenses and still lose the house in the end. Unless there are special circumstances, drop out. Finally, the commonest trouble of all is the **broken chain**. All too often the ability to exchange contracts on an agreed date depends on a chain of other sales proceeding without a hitch. A break in the chain means a hold-up, and to proceed with either the sale of your house or the purchase of the new one is a risky venture — you may end up owning 2 houses or none. Unless the hitch is temporary and easily solved, it is usually better to start again.

It looks as if house buying will get easier in the future. More and more new houses are being sold as a package — legal fees, 100% mortgage etc are included in the monthly payment. Also the law changed with regard to building societies in 1987, which means that they are allowed to provide a 'one-stop' service to do everything involved in selling your old house and both finding and financing your new one.

BUYING A HOUSE
STEP 1: The first stage — Work out what you can afford

THE MONEY YOU CAN RAISE

First of all, there are your savings — investments in building societies, national savings, shares etc. In nearly all cases these savings will be far too small to buy a house. There are two main sources of finance for house purchase. **Selling your house** raises the money for at least part of the cost. Go to estate agents and ask for their opinion — take the sum they think the house will fetch, *not* their proposed asking price. Deduct the solicitor's fees you will have to pay on selling (½ – 1% + VAT) and the estate agent's fee (1½ – 3% + VAT). Also deduct the remainder of the mortgage which is outstanding — check if you will be charged for early redemption.

The money you raise by selling your house will probably not be enough. If there is likely to be a deficit you will need a **mortgage** — a loan on which a house is used as security. Shop around — rates and conditions vary (see page 145). Building societies favour their customers — having a savings account will help. The usual mortgage is 2½ – 3 times the annual salary of the breadwinner plus the annual salary of the partner. The usual ceiling is 90 – 95% of the valuation — but you may get 100% on some properties. This mortgage may not be enough. Some loan companies will go up to 3½ times annual salary or 2½ times the earnings of both partners, but you will pay a higher rate. A top-up loan from a bank may be possible.

WHAT YOU WILL HAVE TO SPEND: ONE-OFF EXPENSES

BUILDING SOCIETY VALUATION FEE	The lending house will wish to find out that the house is worth the loan. Note that this survey is for their benefit not yours. Likely cost £30 – 100, depending on house size.
INDEPENDENT SURVEYOR'S FEE	Unless you propose to buy a new house or one under guarantee it is essential to have a structural survey carried out before you buy. Likely cost £100 – 300 depending on age and size of house.
SOLICITOR'S FEE	There is a conveyancing fee — the cost of transferring the property from the seller to you. There is no set scale — much depends on the work required. Likely cost ½ – 1% plus VAT. The same solicitor should be used to arrange the mortgage — total legal costs will then be 1 – 2% of house price (+ VAT).
LAND REGISTRY FEE	In most areas all purchases of property have to be registered with the Land Registry. The fee is not large — about 0.1 – 0.2% of the house price.
STAMP DUTY	Tax payable on the purchase of a house costing more than £30,000. Cost is 1% of the house price — not payable on fixtures and fittings.
SEARCH FEE	Small fee (£12 – 20) paid to the local authority for information on compliance with planning regulations and by-laws.
DEPOSITS	There may be a small holding deposit (about £100) requested when you make an offer. On exchange of contracts you will have to pay 10% of the purchase price — make sure that you have these sums available when required.
HOUSEHUNTING	Do not underestimate the cost of travel, telephoning, time off work etc.
REMOVAL	Depends on many factors — distance, amount to be moved etc. Allow £100 – 200.
REDECORATING & REPAIRS	If you are not a DIY fan and plan to refurbish an old and dilapidated property — you will have to reserve a very large sum. There may be grants available — see page 4.
EXTRA FURNITURE	If the new house is to be larger then you will need more furniture, carpets etc.
INCIDENTALS	There are more than you think — electricity and gas connection charges, mail redirection, Indemnity Policy for higher-than-normal mortgages etc.
RESERVE FUND	Unfortunately things do occasionally go wrong. You may need a bridging loan for a short time to cover the gap between buying the house and selling your old one, or you may be gazumped (see page 142). You should have about 3% of the proposed purchase price in reserve.
TOTAL	£

WHAT YOU WILL HAVE TO SPEND: REGULAR EXPENSES

MORTGAGE REPAYMENT	Find out *exactly* how much you will have to pay each month on the amount you are able to borrow and on the type of mortgage you plan to use (see page 145). You will get full tax relief on the interest payments made on mortgages up to £30,000. By the MIRAS (mortgage interest relief at source) scheme, the interest is paid with basic tax already deducted. This scheme may cover all or only part of the mortgage — discuss with the lender. Lower your sights if these monthly payments are likely to be too high. It is a sobering thought that building societies repossess more than 10,000 properties each year.
RATES, FUEL, WATER, TRAVEL, INSURANCE	These costs will go up if you move to a larger house, to one which is further from your place of work or to a house in a higher rates area.
GROUND RENT	An annual rent on leasehold property — likely cost £50 – 100.
SERVICE CHARGE	The proportion of common services paid for by an apartment owner. Annual service charges vary enormously — most flats are in the £150 – 700 range.
TOTAL	£ per annum

STEP 2: **Start househunting**

You will have started looking in estate agents' windows and reading the homes for sale section in newspapers — but this is only a small part of effective househunting. Begin by trying to decide on the type of property which will make you happy and will serve your needs.

Begin with area. Some people need the activity and facilities of urban life — others prefer the quietness of the country. Only you can decide, but do be careful. It may be that your dream house in the heart of the countryside will be much cheaper than one closer to town and nearer to your place of work. On the other hand you must remember the extra cost of travel and all the problems of the rural environment if you are a townie — friends, shops, theatres, schools etc can be so far away. So pin-point your chosen areas with care and then walk or drive the streets — note traffic, noise, type of people, facilities etc. Will you be happy there?

Next, type of dwelling. House or apartment — it's your choice. An apartment has definite advantages for the elderly and the overworked — no outside maintenance, lower running costs, nearby neighbours, easy to protect etc. But there are drawbacks — all sorts of restrictions, annual service charge, the increased danger of neighbour noise etc.

The house/flat choice is usually easy — the next one to make is the size and facilities required. Obviously Step 1 will modify most of your desires, but do think of your needs before wasting a great deal of time viewing properties. The elderly may need a bungalow, the newly married will need bedrooms for a planned family, the non-keen gardener will need little land and so on. Terraced, semi-detached or detached — try to have a clear idea of the type of house you want plus two quite separate lists — essential requirements and desirable (but not essential) requirements.

Now you are ready to start househunting — use *all* the methods of finding the right house, not just a couple of estate agents.

ESTATE AGENTS
Go to all the estate agents in the chosen area or areas and tell them what you are looking for. Be clear and precise so that they know you mean business. Give a ceiling figure slightly above the one you can afford. Phone regularly. One word of warning — remember that they work solely for the seller and not for you — check all claims carefully.

FOR SALE SIGNS
Knock on the door if the house seems right — a surprisingly high number of successful purchases have been made in this way.

ADVERTISEMENTS
Check local papers, of course, but there are also the national papers, magazines and even notices in shop windows.

AUCTIONS
The place for bargains, if you know what you are doing. A successful bid means a 10% non-returnable deposit, so survey first, not afterwards.

FRIENDS
Do let friends know you are househunting — it is amazing how often somebody knows somebody who wishes to move.

STEP 3: **Spend time inspecting and discussing the property**

This is the stage which most housebuyers handle badly. One or 2 over-excited and over-embarrassed visits are made. We praise features to be polite (which means that the price won't go down) and we start to remodel the rooms out loud (which causes great offence to the owners who happen to be proud of their dwelling). A group of rather pointless questions and an offer is made. It is not surprising that so many repent at leisure after offering in such haste.

First of all, prepare a list of written questions — use the same list for all visits. Typical questions are:

- Reason for selling
- Running costs and rates
- Repair work carried out recently
- Central heating and insulation details
- Fixtures and fittings included in price
- Their house-moving situation — part of a chain (bad) or house already bought and waiting for them (good)
- Existence of other buyers — is the house under offer?
- Age of house — builder's guarantees (if any)
- Number of years left on the lease (if leasehold property)
- Local schools, if applicable

Take three things with you when you call — a friend or relative (to see things you miss and to give a second opinion), a notebook and a tape-measure. Don't worry about embarrassing the sellers but don't be unfeeling. Measure rooms if in doubt — estate agents can be somewhat imaginative. Test doors and windows. Look for rot. Look for damp spots and be suspicious about recently-painted areas. Jump on downstairs floors to test soundness of joists. Look for old-fashioned wiring or plumbing. Listen for neighbour and road noise.

Now look outside. Begin with the roof (missing tiles, poor gutters etc) and work down to the ground (faulty damp-proof course etc). Look for rotten wood and patched-up cracks in the brickwork.

Never make an offer at this stage. If you are happy with the first viewing go back and walk around the area — what about parking, distance to shops, rowdyism at night, traffic noise and so on. See it at night as well as day. Pay a visit with the family — they are going to have to live there.

STEP 4: **Make an offer**

See several houses before making up your mind — don't rush into buying because you are tired of looking at other people's houses. When you have found a house or flat which is really suitable then it's time to make an offer.

The chosen property may be brand-new on an estate. This is often ideal for a first-time buyer — no-deposit schemes exist and all the one-off charges are included in the mortgage. You don't make an offer — the price is fixed.

On other properties you are at the time of haggling. If the property has been on the market for some time, offer 10% less than the asking price. If refused, you can go up and you will have lessened the chance of being gazumped.

If accepted, prepare a written list of everything which is included. It is usual to leave the fixtures — everything attached or rooted. Fittings are usually removed, but you must itemise the halfway house ones — curtain rails, shelves etc. You pay Stamp Duty on the property only and not on fixtures and fittings.

The seller or estate agent may ask for a holding deposit (about £100). Agree to this — it is returnable if the sale falls through, but include a letter with the cheque, stating that 'the offer is subject to contract and survey' and that the money is to be held by the agent 'as stakeholder'. Ask for the house to be taken off the market — they need not accept but it is worth a try. Keep a copy of this (and all other) letters.

STEP 5: **Seek a mortgage (if required) and choose a solicitor**

Now the buying process starts in earnest. The most pressing job is to ensure that no unnecessary delays are occurring in the sale of your existing house and to make a formal mortgage application.

TYPES OF LENDER

BUILDING SOCIETY
Still the major lender for house purchase. Length of mortgage is generally 30 years (25 years for older properties) and there is often a ceiling on the amount which can be advanced. Building societies generally favour people who already have a savings account with them, but it may still be necessary to shop around. Some societies will lend money on short-lease flats, old houses or dilapidated properties whilst others will not.

BANK
The High St. banks have entered the mortgage market in recent years. The method of operation is basically similar to the building society but the ceiling is much higher. If you want a £100,000 + mortgage then the bank and not a building society is generally the place to go to.

LOCAL COUNCIL
Local councils are involved in the mortgage market in 2 ways. Firstly, for people who want to buy the council house they occupy. There are qualifications — 3 years' residence for permission to purchase and 5 years' residence after buying for maximum discount off valuation. Ask your local housing department for details. Secondly, local councils can occasionally provide mortgages for people whose earnings are too low, who are too old or who want to buy a property which is too risky for a building society or bank. Be careful, though — the interest rate is usually higher than from conventional sources.

EMPLOYER
The most satisfactory lender if there is a scheme for mortgages at low interest rates. Check with the personnel department.

MORTGAGE BROKER
If all else fails, go to a mortgage broker. They may be able to help through a finance house, but the rate will be higher than through a building society or bank. Some advertise mortgages of 4 times annual salary, 2½ times joint salaries and so on — but do expect to pay dearly for the privilege. Do not use a mortgage broker who asks for a fee in advance.

INSURANCE COMPANY
Not an active source of first mortgages, but an alternative to a High St. bank when you need a topping-up loan to make up the difference between the mortgage and the amount you require to borrow. Check that the mortgage company will allow you to top-up in this way before you make the arrangements.

TYPES OF MORTGAGE

REPAYMENT MORTGAGE
Part of the monthly payment pays for interest on the residue of the amount borrowed (capital) and the remainder pays off the capital. In the early years little is paid off the capital — after 7 years your debt will have shrunk by only 10%. With this type of mortgage you should take out a protection policy in case of death.

The usual type is the **level repayment mortgage** — you pay the same rate each month (subject to interest rate changes) throughout the life of the mortgage. Banks (but not many building societies) offer an **increasing repayment mortgage** — starts low but monthly payments increase with time. Useful for people who expect to move up the salary scale with time.

ENDOWMENT MORTGAGE
Part of the monthly payment pays for interest on the total amount borrowed (capital) and the remainder pays for the premium on an insurance policy on the capital. The most popular type is the **low-cost endowment mortgage**, and it is not easy to choose between this and a repayment mortgage. As a rule, go for the endowment mortgage if your tax rate is high and interest rates are low. It should provide you with a lump sum at the end and there is no need to have mortgage insurance. On the drawback side you will not be able to absorb mortgage rate rises by increasing the life of the mortgage.

There are other types of endowment mortgage — **(non-profit** and **with-profits)** but these are not very popular.

PERSONAL PENSION PLAN MORTGAGE
This type of mortgage is only available for the self-employed and employed people who are not in a pension scheme. It is quite similar to an endowment mortgage — except that the premium part of the mortgage is paid into a pension plan rather than an endowment policy. It is part of this pension which pays off the loan. All payments to this plan attract tax relief at the top rate paid by the borrower.

Whichever type you choose, and from whoever you decide to borrow, it is necessary to fill out and despatch the application form as soon as possible.

You must also appoint a solicitor at this stage — do try to use one who you know and trust or who has been recommended to you. An overworked one can hold matters up for months. If you are using a building society, it is a good idea to use one from their panel.

STEP 6: **Arrange for a survey**

An essential step unless the house is new and still covered by the NHBC guarantee. Make sure the person you employ is qualified (FRICS, ARICS, FIAS or AIAS) and is able to act quickly. Let him know all your doubts and worries — obtain an estimate before he starts. You can save money and time by asking the building society to instruct their surveyor to carry out a full structural survey at the same time that he is carrying out their valuation report. Many people do not bother with a full structural survey, but the early signs of rot, damp and subsidence call for an experienced eye.

STEP 7: **Confirm or revise your offer**

If there are no snags you should hear from the lender in about a month. It is quite possible that the mortgage offer will be less than the hoped-for figure. Look at your surveyor's report, which you should have either before or at the same time as the mortgage offer. If the surveyor says the house is not worth the asking price, go back to the seller and renegotiate.

It may be, of course, that the seller will not budge — he or she may even raise the price. This is quite legal — see page 142. Revise your calculations for Step 1 — can you still afford to go ahead? Perhaps you can find the extra cash — both building societies and banks claim they have a sympathetic ear. In either case, agree a final price with the vendor or let the thing go. If the price is accepted, fix an approximate completion date which you both agree to work to.

STEP 8: **Sign mortgage offer and instruct solicitor to proceed**

Sign the mortgage offer as soon as you can — make sure you understand what is involved. There may be a time limit given to attend to repairs — there may be a clause withholding part of the money pending such repairs. Boring stuff, but make sure you understand the offer before signing and sending it off.

Now write to your solicitors so that they can start the conveyance. Tell them the address of the property and the name of the seller and estate agent. Let them also have details of your own house which you are going to sell. Provide mortgage details and the planned completion date — enclose the list of fixtures and fittings which you have agreed to purchase. Finally let your solicitors know the name or names of the proposed owner of the house to be bought — it can be **single tenancy, joint tenancy** (in case of death, house goes to surviving partner) or **tenancy-in-common** (in case of death, house goes to person named in the will).

Your solicitors will now carry out a search through the local council to check on the services provided, future developments which might affect the property and whether planning permission was obtained for the building and any extensions. These searches take several weeks. At the same time the solicitors will be studying the draft contract from the seller's solicitors — this will include details of rights of way, legal restrictions on the use of the house, details of services, position of boundaries etc.

No longer need you use a solicitor for conveyancing. You can go to a conveyancing shop, and save money, or you can do it yourself. There are advantages in doing it yourself — you will inspect the property and see features which might call for investigation. A solicitor looks at the papers and not the property, but you really should not try to tackle conveyancing unless you are prepared to study the subject in depth. Make a mistake and you will have nobody to sue but yourself.

STEP 9: **Exchange signed contracts**

Once the details have been agreed by both solicitors, the contracts are drawn up for signature. You sign your copy and hand it with a 10% deposit to your solicitors — that is the point when contracts are exchanged and the deal is legally binding. The seller cannot raise the price or refuse to move and you cannot recover your deposit if you try to withdraw.

The customary period between the exchange of contracts and completion day is 28 days — it can be shorter if agreed by both sides and written into the contract.

STEP 10: **Carry out the necessary steps before completion day**

There remains a lot to do in the 28 days between exchanging contracts and completion day. Insurance must be arranged from the moment contracts are exchanged — the mortgage company will insist on it.

Arrange for removal. DIY moving *is* practical, but only if you have the strength and skill to handle heavy and fragile objects. Obtain quotes from several firms if you plan to use a professional company — make sure the one chosen is a member of the British Association of Removers and take out removal insurance.

Meanwhile your solicitors will have checked that the seller really does own the house and they then send a draft transfer document to the seller's solicitors. There are several other steps, some involving the mortgage company — conveyancing really is a complex business!

Notify all services, from the post office, gas, electricity boards etc to the newsagent and milkman that you will be leaving your home, and at the same time notify your new address to all the necessary services. Ask for meters to be read on completion day. Arrange for time and place of key exchange with the seller.

Finally there is the matter of money. Your solicitors will have given you an account which includes the rest of the money needed for payment of the house. Make sure you have this money available in good time.

STEP 11: **The final stage — Completion day**

Completion takes place when the 2 solicitors meet and money is exchanged for the title deeds. The house is now yours, but the deeds are held by the mortgage company until the loan has been repaid.

Removal can be chaotic if not planned properly. Gas and electric equipment connected to the mains must be disconnected before removal day. Put a 'leave' label on all items to be left — on other pieces of furniture put a numbered label. Draw a plan of the new house showing where each number is to go.

SELLING A HOUSE

Selling a house is much less complicated than buying one, and the detailed account of the buying procedure on the previous pages clarifies most of the stages.

Carry out simple repairs and make sure it is clean and welcoming. However, don't spend a large amount of money to improve the appearance — it is most unlikely that you will recover the cost.

The cheapest plan is, of course, to sell the house yourself. Ask an estate agent to value it for a fee, and then advertise it locally and erect a 'For Sale' sign. The drawbacks are many — you will receive fewer enquiries than if you use an estate agent, and you will have to answer all their technical and financial queries, and have little control over the people who call.

For most (but not all) people it is better to employ an estate agent. If you are in a hurry give it to several — an agent with a sole agency will ask a slightly lower commission (say 1¾% instead of 2½%) but obviously may take longer to find a buyer. Look at the agents' terms *very* carefully. Make sure that you pay nothing if the house is not sold, that you are not responsible for advertising and that commission will only be paid if the buyer was introduced by the agent.

CHAPTER 10

HOME CARE

Most of this book is devoted to the way the home is made, decorated and equipped. Potential dangers and faults are dealt with, and the way to tackle simple repairs is described.

This final chapter deals with everyday upkeep — the cleaning and general maintenance of good order around the home. Oddly, this aspect of being a home expert takes up only a small part of the book, yet absorbs a large part of the day of the person whose job it is to look after the house. The basic reason is that most home care jobs are time-consuming but are both simply described and usually already understood. It is not words but equipment plus energy which are required.

A few people actually enjoy housework, but for the rest it is a chore. The purpose of this chapter is to help to reduce this chore to a minimum whilst maintaining the necessary standards of hygiene, tidiness and cleanliness. Fortunately, the constant scrubbing, polishing and waxing of Mrs Beeton's day are no longer regarded as essential (or indeed desirable) and these days we have both labour-saving materials and cleaning devices. The job is also made easier by the disappearance of the gas lamp and the universal open fire.

But the servants who went with the age of grime have also disappeared, and so housework today is mainly a job which has to be shared among the family.

Reducing the work in housework

- **Learn the best way to do each job.** There is generally a right and wrong way — see pages 150 – 154. You may be wasting time — drying plates, putting on polish each time you dust and so on.

- **Have the right equipment for your needs.** Of course, your range of electrical equipment will depend on the money available, but a waste disposal unit, dishwasher, tumble-drier etc save so much time.

- **Get all the family involved.** If everyone goes to work, the only way to cope is for each member of the family to be responsible for the tidiness of his or her own room plus putting things away after use in the general rooms.

- **Carry a well-equipped cleaning tray with you.** Buy a large-capacity plastic cleaning tray and fill it with the cleaners, polishes and disinfectants you use, together with dusters etc. Take it with you from room to room when doing the housework — so much easier than collecting up bottles and aerosols from a cupboard each time you start the housework. Take a large plastic bag with you to collect papers and other rubbish.

- **Clean up as you go.** An essential requirement if housework is not going to bog you down. Mop up spills immediately, wash or rinse used pots and pans after cooking, and rinse away tide marks in baths and basins straight away instead of the next morning. The house will be tidier and many problems are so much easier to remove when dealt with at once.

- **Have adequate shelf space and storage.** Being able to put everything away makes the house look better and makes routine cleaning much easier. Trying to dust round books, papers, clothes etc is time-consuming.

- **Work out a routine.** The right home care routine for you will depend on many factors — the size of your house, bank balance, family, other commitments, job, age and equipment to mention a few. On page 150 is an example of a standard routine for looking after the home, but it will have to be adapted to your life style. Whatever adaptations you make, remember that you should adopt a routine whatever your circumstances, and this routine *must* be flexible as the unexpected can always be relied upon to occur.

- **Seek professional help, if necessary.** If you have a busy life, or an infirmity or just can't stand housework, a daily help is a good idea . . . if you can afford one. Another type of professional is the specialist cleaner — an excellent idea for carpets and upholstery as the cleaner's skill and equipment will be better than yours. Finally there are organisations which will send in a team to carry out a major spring-clean in each room.

Home care equipment

THE BASIC TOOL KIT

Buy a basic tool kit of essential items. Purchase them individually or as a boxed set, but never look for a 'bargain offer'. These are the tools you will use most often and you should always get the best you can afford. Add to these basic items as your needs and interest grow. Remember that many items can be hired these days, so it is foolish to buy an expensive item (e.g a chainsaw, floor sander or carpet shampooer) if it is to be used very rarely.

Keep tools on racks on the wall — tool-hanging clips on a pegboard are one of the best storage methods. Apply a thin coating of oil on steel surfaces after use and keep all tools well away from children.

ELECTRICAL TOOL KIT
See page 18

HAMMERS

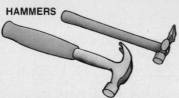

16 oz claw hammer with steel shaft for general woodworking jobs

4 oz pin hammer with wooden shaft for delicate woodworking jobs

SAWS

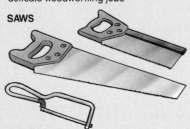

Panel saw (20 – 24 in. long, 10 – 12 points per inch) for general woodworking jobs — see page 110

Tenon saw (10 – 12 in. long, 14 – 16 points) for jointing and small woodworking jobs — see page 110

Junior hacksaw (6 in. blade) for cutting metal and plastic

SCREWDRIVERS

2 slotted-head screwdrivers — one for 6 – 8 gauge screws and the other for 10 – 12 gauge screws. See page 109

1 cross-head screwdriver — use with Phillips or Pozidriv screws

FLEXIBLE TAPE

10 ft steel tape. Look for essential features — return spring, thumb lock and both metric and imperial markings

STEEL RULE

2 ft straight edge for marking and cutting

FOLDING RULE

Boxwood or plastic 3 ft folding ruler — useful in confined spaces

SPIRIT LEVEL

Metal or plastic body about 2 ft long. Buy one with both horizontal and vertical vials set in the body

BRADAWL

Small chisel-like point for starting drill or screw holes. A gimlet has a corkscrew-like tip

COMBINATION SQUARE

Somewhat complex for a basic kit, but extremely useful. Buy one with a 1 ft metal rule, try square and protractor for marking angles on wood, and a spirit level

SURFORM

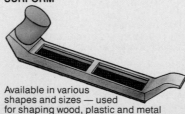

Available in various shapes and sizes — used for shaping wood, plastic and metal

CHISELS

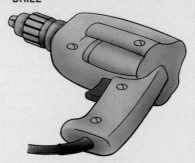

2 chisels — blade widths ¼ in. and ¾ in. Check for plastic handles and slip-on blade covers. See page 110

DRILL

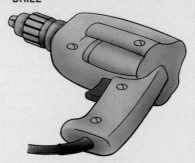

½ in. chuck, 2 speed electric drill plus a range of bits (¹⁄₁₆ – ½ in.) are essential. Buy accessories (sanding disc, circular saw etc) as required. See page 110

BOLSTER CHISEL

2 in. wide blade — used for lifting concrete, plaster and floorboards

ADJUSTABLE SPANNER

Usual type is a crescent spanner adjusted by a screw at the top of the handle

SANDING BLOCK

Block of wood with glasspaper wrapped round for smoothing or keying surfaces

MISCELLANEOUS ITEMS
Oil can, screws, nails and washers, adhesives and fillers, pencil, scissors, plumbline, goggles, rubber gloves, glasspaper, ladder, string, wall plugs, oilstone, putty knife, scraper

THE FIRST-AID & MEDICINE CABINET

The medicine cabinet should be kept well away from children, either on a high shelf or closed with lock and key. Drugs on prescription should be thrown away once the prescribed time for use has expired — do not save them for a future emergency and never administer to someone else. Do not keep packages which have lost their label.

Non-prescription medicines can be bought from your local chemist — the letters BP or BPC after the product name indicate that the name is the basic chemical one and the price is usually much less than the branded variety.

For cuts and wounds

ADHESIVE DRESSING — buy a strip and cut to size for dressing minor wounds

ABSORBENT GAUZE — use for dressing minor wounds before bandaging

COTTON CONFORMING BANDAGE — buy 7 cm and 10 cm widths

TRIANGULAR BANDAGE — 75 cm cotton square, folded for supporting injured joints or limbs

SAFETY PINS

SCISSORS

ANTISEPTIC AQUEOUS CREAM

For splinters

BLUNT-EDGED TWEEZERS — if the splinter cannot be reached, use a sterilised needle

For menstrual cramps

IBUPROFEN TABLETS

For aches and pains, backache and minor sprains

PAIN-RELIEVING TABLETS — choose the one which you find most effective (soluble aspirin, ibuprofen etc)

For coughs and colds

ASPIRIN AND PHOLCODEINE LINCTUS (adults)

PARACETAMOL ELIXIR (children)

For minor indigestion

ANTACID — choose the one which you find most effective (soda mint or proprietary brand)

For constipation

LACTULOSE SOLUTION BP

For insect stings & bites and for itchy rashes of allergic type

HYDROCORTISONE CREAM

For sunburn

CALAMINE LOTION

General Hints

To clean wounds before dressing — use soap and water

To ease pain of burns, scalds and stings — use repeated brief applications of crushed ice in a polythene bag

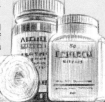

THE CLEANING CUPBOARD

An amazing number of different products are needed to keep the home clean. Make sure that boxes and bottles are closed after use, and put a lock on the door if small children are present.

There is a clear-cut trend these days towards cream cleaners (e.g Jif) and liquid all-purpose cleaners (e.g Flash) and away from the harsh abrasive powders of old. Furniture polishes in aerosol and spray-gun form have taken much of the market away from the traditional tins and screw-topped bottles. Improvements in packaging and ingredients continue to appear — read the instructions carefully and never assume that a new product is designed to be used just like the one you have always employed.

Set out below is the range of cleaning products you could expect to find in a well-stocked cleaning cupboard. Use it as a check list.

- Air freshener
- All-purpose cleaner
- Bath cleaner
- Bicarbonate of soda
- Biological detergent
- Borax
- Carpet cleaner
- Cream cleaner
- De-scaler (hard water areas)
- Dishwasher powder & rinse aid
- Disinfectant
- Dry-cleaning fluid
- Eucalyptus oil
- Fabric conditioner
- Floor polish
- Fly killer
- Furniture polish
- Glycerine
- Hand cleanser
- Household ammonia
- Household bleach
- Hydrogen peroxide
- Lavatory cleaner
- Metal polish
- Methylated spirits
- Rubber gloves
- Scouring pads
- Shoe polishes
- Soap
- Vacuum cleaner bags
- Vanish bar
- Vinegar
- Washing powder
- Washing soda
- Washing-up liquid
- White spirit
- Window cleaner

Brushes

You will need several brushes — a stiff-bristled one for outdoors, a soft hand-held one for use with a dustpan, a lavatory brush, scrubbing brushes and a pot brush for pans and vegetables. If you use the vacuum cleaner attachments you could do without a standard carpet broom and a soft ceiling brush — but most people prefer to use a brush for corners and cobwebs. Wash brushes frequently in soapy water — always store long handled brushes with the head uppermost or hang downwards from a hook.

Dusters

Use plain-surfaced cloths for dusting and fleecy ones for polishing. Dusters must be washed regularly, and all books on home management will advise you to cut up old shirts and flannelette sheets as an economy measure. Disposable cloths (such as J cloths) and paper kitchen towels are definitely not an economy measure, but they are a godsend for dusting, mopping up spills etc for the busy homeowner. If you use a chamois leather for window cleaning, keep it moist at all times in a polythene bag.

Cleaning and caring for things

DAILY TASKS

These are jobs which are performed several times a day or perhaps just once every couple of days, but in each case they must be done very frequently to prevent the home from becoming unhealthy or untidy.

- **TIDY ROOMS** — remove papers, dead flowers, clothing for washing or for hanging up. Straighten towels, cushions, mats etc
- **AIR ROOMS** and make beds
- **WASH** dishes, tide marks in baths and basins, sink and hob surface, and lavatory seat
- **CLEAN UP** crumbs and mishaps (spilt liquid, broken glass etc). Empty ash trays, waste paper bins and kitchen bin
- **MAKE UP** shopping list as items occur to you — have list on kitchen wall
- **FEED & WATER** plants, pets and people as necessary
- **CLEAN OUT** and re-lay fire

WEEKLY/FORTNIGHTLY TASKS

These are the regular routine jobs which are carried out at weekly intervals, although some of the less urgent tasks may be tackled every fortnight when time for housework is limited.

- **DUST & VACUUM** all lived-in rooms
- **CLEAN** floors, mirrors, bath, lavatory, basins and sinks, kitchen fixtures and fittings, table tops and windows
- **POLISH** furniture, brass, copper, silverware
- **CHANGE** towels, bath mats and bed linen
- **ATTEND TO LAUNDRY** — wash, iron, mend, visit dry cleaners
- **DE-GREASE KITCHEN DRAINS** by putting a handful of washing soda into sink plughole and pouring on a kettleful of boiling water
- **STRAIGHTEN FINANCES** — pay bills, check bank statements etc

SEASONAL TASKS

These are jobs which are performed every few months or just once a year, depending on the time available, the urgency of the task and the size of the house. It also must depend upon how house-proud you are.

- **WASH DOWN** all washable surfaces — tiles, paintwork, plastic-coated wallpaper etc. This should include mouldings, picture frames, cupboard fronts
- **WASH OR DRY CLEAN** bedspreads, blankets, quilts — have electric blankets serviced. Also wash or dry clean cushion covers and curtains
- **AIR & TURN** mattresses
- **REMOVE SCALE** around sinks, bath, taps and lavatory
- **DUST** books, blinds, behind heavy objects and on top of cupboards
- **TIDY & CLEAN** the inside of drawers, desks, wardrobes, kitchen cupboards, refrigerator and freezer. Dispose of all unwanted or deteriorated items
- **SHAMPOO** carpets and upholstery
- **SERVICE EQUIPMENT** in order to avoid costly repairs or replacement. Add salt to the dishwasher and defrost the freezer. Clean filters in the washing machine, drier, cooker hood and vacuum cleaner as recommended by the manufacturer. Clean out the toaster. Have large items regularly serviced by a professional
- **SWEEP CHIMNEYS** in rooms which had fires during the winter
- **DUST & VACUUM** spare rooms

THE HOME CARE ROUTINE

The standard routine is to do a number of essential jobs each day, and then once a week clean each room by vacuuming, dusting, washing down tops, mopping floors etc. About once a month one of the rooms is given a more thorough overhaul and then once a year there is a spring-clean for every room in the house — walls are washed down, curtains and upholstery cleaned, kitchen cupboards cleaned inside and out, and so on.

This may not be your routine — there are as many routines as there are housewives! As mentioned on page 147, the routine must fit in with the general job of living, so there can be only suggestions, not rules. Listed opposite are the recommended timings for the basic cleaning jobs — adapt and change to suit your needs.

THE BASIC TECHNIQUES

WASHING UP

Scrape food off plates and soak pans with burnt-on food as soon as you can. The rule is to have a large bowl, a lot of hot water and work from the cleanest items, such as glassware, to the dirtiest, such as the pans, casserole etc. Wipe glassware, silverware and cutlery after washing — leave crockery, pans, bowls etc to dry on a drainer.

WASHING DOWN

Work downwards from ceiling to floor when washing walls or paintwork. Wipe down after washing to avoid streaks.

VACUUMING

All you need are 3 or 4 backward and forward strokes if the machine is properly serviced, the head set at the right height and the bag reasonably empty. Push the cleaner head quite slowly and move steadily across the room.

BRUSHING

The technique is quite different from vacuuming. Use short and quick strokes working from the outer edges to the centre of the room. At this point use a handbrush and dustpan.

DUSTING

Dust after brushing but before vacuuming. Use a dry cloth for wooden surfaces and a damp one for metal. You will need a damp sponge to remove sticky food or beverage rings from glass, wood or other surfaces.

POLISHING

The surface must be thoroughly dry before you start. Add the polish to the cloth and then rub over the surface. Buff with a clean duster. The rules are different for spray-on polishes — follow the instructions.

A-Z GUIDE

ANODISED ALUMINIUM
Trolleys, trays, saucepan lids etc. Remove marks with a damp cloth — polish with a dry one. Do not put in a dishwasher.

BASINS
See BATHS.

BATHS
Remove tide marks with a small amount of washing-up liquid on a cloth. **Porcelain-enamelled** and **vitreous-enamelled** baths should be cleaned with a cream cleaner. Check that it is recommended for vitreous enamel — there will be a V on the label. Never use an abrasive powder cleaner as it can scratch the surface.
Acrylic plastic baths should be wiped down with a mild detergent. Fine scratches can be removed with silver polish and a soft cloth.

In hard-water areas scale and stains build up under and around taps and around plugholes. Buy a proprietary bath-stain remover and follow the instructions exactly.

BLANKETS
Check the care label before washing — if in doubt, use the wool programme on your washing machine. If the machine is too small for the blanket, use the bathtub as in the old days or take it to the laundrette.

Washing is straightforward, but drying can cause problems. In a washing machine the spin should be for a very short time and when the blanket is to be hung out to dry it is essential that it is damp and not wet when put on the line.

BRASS
Utensils: Wash in hot water and detergent. Rinse and dry, then treat with brass or copper polish. If stained, rub with cut lemon sprinkled with salt.
Ornaments: If unlacquered, use brass or copper polish. If lacquered, clean with a soft duster. The lacquer coating breaks down in time, especially if the object is constantly handled. Remove remaining lacquer and the tarnish with acetone. Polish, then respray with transparent lacquer.

BRONZE
Clean with a soft duster. If dirty, wash in hot water and detergent. Rinse and dry. If stained or coated with verdigris, remove as much as you can with a wire brush or knife, then rub surface with paraffin.

CANE
Clean with a soft duster. If dirty, wash with warm salty water — rinse and dry. Do not soak cane or wicker — just wipe down with the solution and leave outdoors to dry.

CARPETS
Regular vacuuming not only makes a carpet look better, it also prolongs its life by removing grit. The usual routine is to vacuum about once a week, but spilt food should be brushed up as soon as possible. Matting should be lifted periodically so that the floor below can be cleaned.

Uneven wear can be a problem. Move furniture about occasionally if you can — place rugs at entry points from outdoors and over the foot zone in front of much-used armchairs. If an area has been crushed by furniture, dampen the patch and then vacuum.

Stains are another problem — the appropriate treatment can be found on pages 126–127. Act quickly — mop up spills with paper towels or rags then squirt affected area with a soda water syphon. Cover grease with talcum powder as soon as possible. The exception to speedy treatment is mud — leave it to dry before scraping or brushing off. With fitted carpets keep a few scraps at laying time — use them for testing the safety of stain removers if one is required at some later date.

At intervals of a few months or a few years (depending on the amount of wear) you will have to shampoo the carpet. There are various DIY systems — dry, wet, aerosol etc. It is a good idea to hire an electrical shampooer for this job, and if the carpet is badly stained you should consider using a professional cleaning company who will come to your home. Always obtain a quote before cleaning starts.

CHINA
See CROCKERY.

CHROME
Clean with a soft duster. If dirty or stained, wash in hot water and detergent. Rinse and dry, then polish with chrome cleaner.

COOKER
Don't let burnt food accumulate on or in the cooker — wipe off spills immediately and brush out the oven after use. Switch off the electricity or gas before you start to clean the cooker. Soak all movable parts (trays, shelves etc) in warm water and a biological detergent — rub stubborn stains with a nylon brush. Rinse and dry thoroughly.

Clean the vitreous enamel body of the cooker with a cream cleaner — use a proprietary oven cleaner for the inside. Never use an abrasive material on the lining of an oven. Wash the oven window with bicarbonate of soda on a damp cloth. Oven cleaning is an unpleasant job — one of the most welcome advances in recent years is the self-cleaning oven.

COPPER
See BRASS.

CROCKERY
Ideally you should wash up immediately after the meal is finished. If this is not possible, rinse and then soak the dishes in cold soapy water. Use a good quality washing-up liquid and warm water — use a brush to remove food from crevices and never use abrasives or scourers on bone china or porcelain. Rinse in clean warm water and leave to dry. With delicate crockery you must avoid sudden changes in temperature which can cause cracking. Stains can be a problem. Remove tea and coffee stains in cups with a hot washing soda solution.

If you have a dishwasher, load after every meal and switch on each evening. Check that the items are dishwasher-proof (see page 45).

CURTAINS
Accumulated dust can destroy your curtains. Vacuum heavy drapes and dust down others, but all curtains need occasional washing or cleaning.

Lined and heavy curtains should be dry cleaned. At the other end of the scale net curtains are easily washed — soak for 15 minutes to loosen the dirt and then wash as recommended on page 44. Dry by hanging along a rod. Other curtains are less easy to wash — remove hooks and take down the hem before you begin.

CUTLERY
Wash cutlery immediately after use — rinse if washing is not possible. The reason is that many foods stain silver plate, and salt affects stainless steel. Keep non-metal handles out of the water if cutlery is left to soak.

Use hot water and washing-up liquid. Rinse and dry — store silver-plated cutlery in a felt-lined box.

FLEXIBLE PLASTIC
Fablon, ConTact etc. Do not use a duster — wipe with a cloth dampened with warm water and a mild detergent. Rinse and leave to dry. Never use an abrasive cleaner.

FLOORS

Sweep or dry-mop the floor regularly — daily if possible. The correct method of cleaning depends on the type of floor, so there can be few general rules. Choose a non-slip product where wax polishing is recommended, and do not use too much water when mopping is recommended. Above all, never build up a thick layer of slippery wax.

Wood: Sweep the floor regularly — daily if possible. Wash only occasionally. If the floor is unsealed it will be necessary to oil or wax polish the surface every 2 months. It is better to apply a sealer which only requires cleaning with a moist mop.

Linoleum: Wipe over with a damp cloth — do not soak the floor with a wet mop. Polish occasionally with a water-based emulsion.

Vinyl: Wipe over with a cloth dampened with mild detergent — do not soak the floor with a wet mop. Remove scratch marks with fine steel wool.

Quarry tiles: Use a detergent solution or a proprietary floor cleaner. Mop sealed floors — scrub unsealed ones. Polish when dry with self-shine tile polish — use very sparingly.

Cork: Wipe over sealed tiles occasionally with a damp cloth — polish with a water-based emulsion. Unsealed tiles should be treated with non-slip wax polish.

FURNITURE

Antique wood: Dust regularly and store properly — keep out of direct sunlight and turn down the central heating to avoid over-dry air. A little furniture cream can be applied occasionally — but the treatment of antique furniture should be left to the experts.

Oiled wood: See page 123. Dust regularly and rub twice a year with a cloth and a little teak or Danish oil. Apply sparingly.

Waxed wood: See page 123. Dust regularly and rub occasionally with wax polish.

Varnished wood: See page 123. Dust regularly and polish occasionally with furniture cream or a silicone-based liquid polish. A range of spray polishes are available.

Painted wood: See PAINTWORK.

Minor Repairs

Removing water and heat rings and spots
Cold liquids cause dark stains on polished surfaces — white stains are usually due to alcohol or hot tea/coffee. Apply metal polish to a soft cloth and rub it over the stain, working along the grain. Polish the area after treatment. Superficial stains will be removed — deeper stains call for stripping off the old surface and applying a new one.

Removing scratches
There is no easy way to remove a deep scratch — stripping and refinishing is the only way. It is often possible, however, to disguise a scratch with a wax crayon or with coloured varnish.

Removing bruises and dents
Shallow dents can be removed by a simple steam treatment in softwood, but the chance of success with hardwood is much less. Spread a damp cloth over the damaged area and run a warm iron over the surface. The damp heat swells the grain and fills the dent.

Removing veneer blisters
Cover affected area with a cloth and run a warm iron over the area.

GLASS

Coffee tables, shelves, etc. Treat in the same way as WINDOWS, using a proprietary window cleaner or a 1 part water/1 part vinegar solution. Remove fine scratches by rubbing the surface with metal polish before washing.

GLASSWARE

Deal with the glassware first when washing up. Use hot soapy water — rinse in warm water and dry immediately to avoid streaking. Never stand or store glasses on their rims — always keep them upright. Standing tumblers inside each other can save space, but they often get stuck. To free them, stand the lower one in hot water and fill the upper one with ice.

Deal with stained decanters and vases by filling with a warm solution of biological detergent — leave overnight. If scale or other film still remains, fill the container with a solution of salt and vinegar in warm water — again leave to stand overnight.

GLOVES

Washable gloves are easily cleaned — put them on and immerse your hands in warm soapy water. Squeeze your hands together, and then repeat the process in clean water to remove the soap. Dry on a towel at room temperature.

Non-washable gloves are more difficult to clean. If dirt is the problem, try an India rubber. If grease spots are the trouble, dust with Fuller's Earth and leave overnight. Brush off the powder — repeat if necessary.

GOLD

Rub with a soft duster. To restore the shine wash in warm water to which a mild detergent and some household ammonia has been added. Rinse, dry and burnish with a soft cloth.

HANDS

Use an all-purpose natural hand cleanser such as Handy. To remove oil, ink, mud, paint etc, place a cherry-sized blob to the palm of one hand and then rub the hands together. Wash off under a running tap.

IRON

The sole plate may become coated with starch, size or burnt fabric. Try scraping with a strip of wood and then rubbing with a nylon scourer. If this fails turn the iron on and when the sole plate is warm to the touch, switch off and rub soap over the affected area. Rub the sole plate on a piece of unwanted cloth. You can buy a proprietary product for this purpose, but it is somewhat unpleasant to use.

IVORY

Unlike antique furniture, ivory should be kept in a sunny spot. Dust regularly — use a paintbrush to clean intricate carvings. Never put in water.

JEWELLERY

You can buy a jewellery kit to polish settings but do be careful when trying to clean stones. Diamonds, Onyx, Topaz, Emeralds, Rubies and many others are cleaned by being dipped into warm soapy water and then brushed gently with a soft brush before drying with a chamois leather. Diamonds are dipped into surgical spirit (or gin!) for their final sparkle. But some precious stones, such as Turquoise and Opal should not be put into water. Simply rub with a chamois leather, but as with all valuable jewellery the best plan is to take it to a professional.

KETTLE

Descaling is necessary at regular intervals in hard-water areas. Cover the element with 1 part vinegar/1 part water and bring to the boil. Leave overnight, empty and rinse. Boil water twice and empty before bringing the kettle into service again.

LAMPSHADES
Plastic and glass can be washed — all other types should be dusted. Plastic lampshades become very dusty — rub with an anti-static cloth before replacing.

LAUNDRY
There is an enormous range of washing aids these days, but there is no common labelling code to tell you which type you are buying. The best plan is to try several brands until you find the one that suits you.

Heavy duty powders are by far the most popular — the soap-based ones (Persil, Fairy Snow etc) are suitable for soft-water regions but in a hard-water area you will require a synthetic detergent — Omo, Surf, Daz and the rest. Some contain enzymes (e.g Ariel) — the so-called 'biological', 'low-temperature' and 'all-temperature' washing powders. These powders are especially useful for removing protein stains such as blood and perspiration, but it seems that some people may develop a rash when handling enzyme-based powders.

Low-foaming products are used in front-loading machines which would not function effectively with lots of suds. The word 'automatic' appears on the label — a few are enzyme-free (e.g Original Persil Automatic) but most are biological — Daz Automatic, Bold 3 etc. Liquids are available — e.g Wisk Automatic.

Light duty products include the liquids, powders and flakes used in hand-hot or cool water — the products used for hand washing. Examples are Stergene, Dreft and Lux.

Fabric conditioners (Lenor, Comfort etc) reduce static and maintain the softness of woollens, brushed fabrics and towelling.

Enzyme-based pre-washers (Bio-tex) are used to remove stains from heavily-soiled articles before washing.

Stiffeners are used to add body to fabrics before ironing. Both powder and spray starches are available.

Sort laundry before washing — if you plan to wash a mixture in one load, you must use the gentlest programme (see page 44). Empty pockets and close zips, brush off dirt and tie up loose ribbons. Treat woollens with care — never wash by machine unless the label recommends it. The standard programme for woollens is to wash by hand and rinse in warm water, and then roll the article in a towel to remove excess moisture. Finally, spread out the garment on a flat surface away from heat and sunlight.

LAVATORY
Clean daily, using a specific lavatory cleaner. Sprinkle inside the pan and after the recommended soaking time clean the inside with a lavatory brush. You can use household bleach as an alternative to a lavatory cleaner, but you should never mix the two together. Wash the seat and outside with warm water and a mild detergent.

LEATHER
Leather furniture is expensive and should be looked after. Dust regularly and occasionally treat with a hide cleaner. Use sparingly, and do not use an ordinary or general-purpose polish. If the leather has become stiff, use saddle soap — if faded, touch up the light spots with leather stain.

MELAMINE
Kitchen unit doors: Wash with warm water and a mild detergent — rinse and dry. Do not rub with a dry duster.
Crockery: Wash by hand, not in a dishwasher.

MIRRORS
Use a proprietary cleaner — the problem with water is that it can damage the silvering behind the glass. Clean with crumpled newspaper and a thin coating of glycerine will prevent the steaming up of bathroom mirrors. Hair lacquer spots are sometimes a problem on bedroom and bathroom mirrors — remove with methylated spirits before cleaning in the normal way.

PAINTWORK
The standard method of cleaning paintwork is to wash with warm water and a little washing-up liquid. Rinse and dry. A few tips — never use washing powder, dust door tops, cupboard tops etc thoroughly before washing and work downwards from ceiling to floor.

Grimy paintwork calls for a different treatment — sugar soap solution and a pail of rinsing water. Rub one patch at a time with a sponge until the dirt is removed — rinse with clean water and dry with a cloth before going on to the next section. Most experts recommend that you should work from ground level upwards, but previously-cleaned patches can be streaked if you follow this advice.

PEWTER
Wash in warm soapy water and dry thoroughly. Burnish with a cabbage leaf.

PLASTIC LAMINATE
Formica, Warerite etc. Wash with warm water and a mild detergent — rinse and dry. Do not rub with a dry duster.

POLYETHYLENE
Wash with warm water and a mild detergent. Keep polyethylene articles away from naked flames.

POTS & PANS
Soak immediately after use and then clean with a pan scourer and hot soapy water. Burnt-on food can be removed by soaking overnight in a biological detergent. Apart from these general rules there are specific instructions for the different materials.

Aluminium: Avoid harsh abrasives and allow pans, bakeware etc to cool before washing. Black stains can be removed by boiling dilute vinegar or an acid food (e.g rhubarb) in the pan. Always dry aluminium cookware immediately after washing.

Vitreous enamel: Avoid harsh abrasive cleaners and abrasive pan scourers — use a cream cleaner approved for enamel. Remove stains with dilute household bleach.

Cast iron: Frying pans should only be washed if they cannot be cleaned by the recommended method — a small amount of oil rubbed in with kitchen paper. If washed, dry immediately and thoroughly.

Stainless steel: Avoid harsh abrasive cleaners and abrasive pan scourers. Dry immediately after washing — polish occasionally with lemon juice or a proprietary stainless steel cleaner.

Non-stick surfaces: Follow the maker's instructions — avoid harsh abrasive powders and abrasive pan scourers.

Tinware: After baking wash and wipe the cake tins and place in the still-warm oven to dry thoroughly.

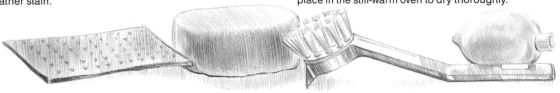

PVC
See VINYL.

SHOES
Wash off surface dirt before polishing — allow to dry. Shoes must be polished regularly to feed and protect the leather as well as to improve the appearance. Once it was a matter of brushing a good quality wax polish into the surface (especially the welt) and then brushing the surface with a polishing brush before buffing the surface with a soft cloth. Nowadays there are all sorts of products — creams, aerosols, self-shining liquids, sponge-headed applicators and so on. Be guided by the assistant — follow the instructions. Scuffed shoes will need a renovating polish — tight shoes call for a leather-expanding product. Rub patent leather shoes occasionally with a little petroleum jelly.

SILVER
Silver and silver-plated articles should be polished regularly to prevent the development of tarnish. Many silver cleaners are available — the impregnated wadding type is the most popular. Tarnish is a problem on intricately-modelled pieces — use a silver-cleaning dip and follow the instructions exactly. After polishing rub with a soft duster — silver-cleaning cloths are available which delay tarnish formation. A recent introduction is Silver Solution which silver-plates articles when rubbed over the surface.

SINKS
Wash regularly with hot water and washing-up liquid. Never use harsh abrasives to remove stains — clean stainless steel sinks with a specific sink cleaner and use a cream cleaner on vitreous enamel ones.

STAINLESS STEEL
Despite the name, stainless steel can be stained or pitted by a number of agents — salt, acidic foods, bleach, some detergents etc. Always wipe stainless steel immediately after washing — even when taken from the dishwasher. Wipe with lemon juice or a cut lemon to brighten the surface. For specific instructions see CUTLERY, POTS & PANS and SINKS.

STEEL
Iron and steel pans, knives etc should be washed in hot water and detergent — remove deposits with an abrasive powder or steel wool pad. Rinse and dry immediately and thoroughly.

STONE
Never wash stone with soapy water — the residual scum will be hard to remove. Wipe or scrub with washing soda in hot water — rinse with plain water.

SUEDE
Despite what others do, never use a wire brush. Suede coats, jackets and shoes should be brushed with a rubber brush. Treat grubby spots with oatmeal — leave for a couple of hours and then remove with a soft brush. Treat occasionally with suede dressing (shoes) or suede cleaner (clothing).

TILES
Wipe with warm water and washing-up liquid. Alternatively use a spray or aerosol window cleaner. Clean grouting with a brush and dilute household bleach. Rinse and dry.

UPHOLSTERY
Remove cushions from sofas and armchairs before thoroughly brushing or vacuuming. Pay special attention to the edges and crevices — old crumbs can attract mice. Reverse cushions when replacing them to ensure even wear.

Stains should be dealt with promptly — see pages 126–127. Cleaning is necessary once or twice a year — consult the care leaflet which came with the furniture. Most fabrics can be treated with dry-foam upholstery shampoo but some cannot. These fabrics (velvet, tapestry, silk, wool) should be left to a professional cleaner. Dry clean or wash loose covers — if washed, replace on chairs whilst still damp. Vinyl and other plastic should be wiped with a soft cloth and a mild detergent. You can use a cream cleaner or spray polish recommended for plastics, but never use abrasives, solvents or wax polish.

VENETIAN BLINDS
Dust regularly — wear an old pair of cotton gloves and run your hand along the slats.

VINYL
Wash with warm water and a mild detergent. Mop up spilled liquids immediately — remove stains with a cream cleaner. Do not use dry-cleaning fluid.

WALL COVERINGS
Gently dust or vacuum wallpaper to prevent griminess. If the paper has dirty patches, rub the affected areas with stale white bread.

Washable wallpapers should be cleaned with a sponge dampened with water and a little washing-up liquid. Avoid over-wetting the surface — work up and down, not side to side.

Vinyls are much more resistant to water — they can be lightly scrubbed to remove marks and grease.

Fabrics need gentle handling. Use a long-handled soft brush or a vacuum fitted with a brush attachment. Do not use liquid cleaners.

WINDOWS
The traditional method of washing windows is to use a bucket of warm water and a couple of wash leathers (chamois leather, synthetic chamois leather or lint-free cloth). Wash with one, wrung out so that it is damp and not wet, working from the edges to the middle. The other cloth should be almost dry — wipe over the washed surface.

Wash windows on dull, frost-free days. If the windows are very dirty add a little washing-up liquid to the water. Change the water frequently.

It is much quicker but more expensive to wash windows with a spray-on or aerosol window cleaner — a solution of 1 part water/1 part vinegar is a cheap substitute. Simply spray on a fine film and then wipe off with a clean cloth. For sparkling glass, finish off with crumpled newspaper.

CHAPTER II

INDEX

A great deal of care has been taken to ensure that the information in this book is as accurate as possible, but the Publishers cannot be held responsible for any errors or omissions that may be found in the text or may occur at a future date as a result of changes in rules, laws or equipment.

Acknowledgements

As the author of The Home Expert I wish to express my thanks to the team which helped me. Included here are John Woodbridge for his design skills and his leadership of the production group, Gill Jackson for her remarkable organisational, secretarial and proofing skills, and Pauline Dobbs for her painstaking research. In addition, I am grateful for the paintings produced by Deborah Achilleos, and the checking of proofs by Gerard McEvilly, Maurice Gardner, Angelina Gibbs and Constance Barry.

Grateful acknowledgement is also made for the help, artwork or photographs received from Aga-Rayburn, Heather Angell, Ariston Domestic Appliances Ltd, Armitage Shanks Ltd, BBC Ceefax, Berry Magicoal Ltd, Blomberg, Bosch, Brabantia (U.K.) Ltd, Breville, British Gas plc, Carleton Photographic, Carron Stainless Products Ltd, T.I. Creda Ltd, Dimplex Heating Ltd, Michael Dunne/EWA, Electrolux Domestic Appliances Ltd, ESWA Ltd, EWA, Federation of Heathrow Anti-Noise Groups, Garden Studio, Joan Hessayon, Hoover Plc, Hotpoint, Hurseal (Sales) Ltd, Husqvarna Ltd, Rodney Hyatt/EWA, Ideal-Standard Ltd, Kelvinator, Leisure-Glynwed Consumer & Building Products Ltd, Miele Co Ltd, Morphy Richards, Moulinex Ltd, Michael Nicholson/EWA, Jacqueline Norris, Philips Home Appliances, Picturepoint-London, Spike Powell/EWA, Rentokil, Yvon Still, Sunbeam, Kim Taylor/Bruce Coleman Ltd, Thorn EMI Domestic Appliances Ltd, Timber Research & Development Association, Valor Heating Ltd, Wonderfire and Zanussi.

In addition I am grateful for the information received from Aaronson Bros Plc, Association of British Insurers, Beecham Proprietaries, Black & Decker Ltd, Bondaglass-Voss, Bostik Ltd, BBC Engineering Dept, BCMA, BEAB, British Flat Roofing Council, British Gas, British Pest Control Association, BSI, British Telecom, Broxbourne Borough Council, Building Research Establishment, Colgate-Palmolive Ltd, CORGI, Cussons (U.K.) Ltd, DPPA, Drycleaning Information Bureau, Energy Efficiency Office, Flat Roofing Contractors' Advisory Board, Formica, Glass & Glazing Federation, Glass Manufacturers Federation, Harrods Ltd, HM Inspectors of Taxes Hertford, Home Laundering Consultative Council, Hunter Building Products, Institute of Metals, John Lewis Partnership Brent Cross, Dr John Llewelyn, Nicholas Kiwi, HM Land Registry, Lever Bros Ltd, London Electricity Board, Microwave Association, NBF, NHBC, National TV Licence Records Office, NICEIC, Noise Abatement Society, Osborne & Little, Perstorp Warerite Ltd, Pilkington Glass Ltd, Port Sunlight Heritage Centre, pbi Information Dept, Post Office, Prestel British Telecom, Procter & Gamble Ltd, RIBA, Royal Institution of Chartered Surveyors, Rustins Ltd, SHAC, Shell U.K. Oil, Solid Fuel Advisory Service, Thorn EMI Lighting, Water Research Centre, Western Cork Ltd, Weston Hyde Products Plc, Cutlery & Allied Trades Research Association, Bernard Hellawell and Copper Development Association.